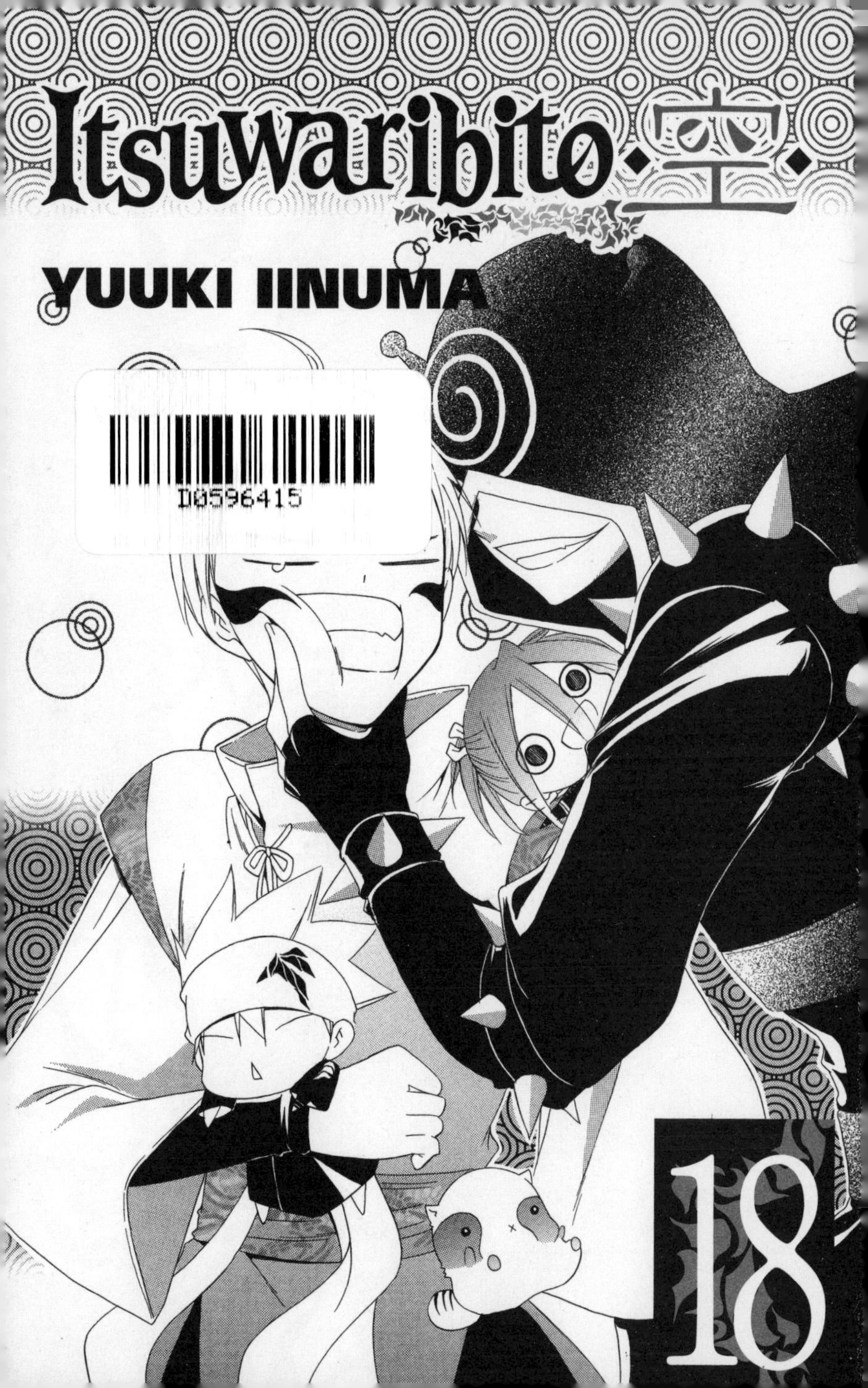
Itsuwaribito 空
YUUKI IINUMA
18

Contents

Chapter 168 Assassins 3

Chapter 169 The Assassins' Objective 21

Chapter 170 Neya vs. Rama 39

Chapter 171 Herd Behavior 57

Chapter 172 Private Army 75

Chapter 173 Another Doctor 93

Chapter 174 The Reason You Lose 113

Chapter 175 The Coming Battle 131

Chapter 176 Kin's Objective 149

Chapter 177 What Kin Seeks 167

Chapter 168 Assassins

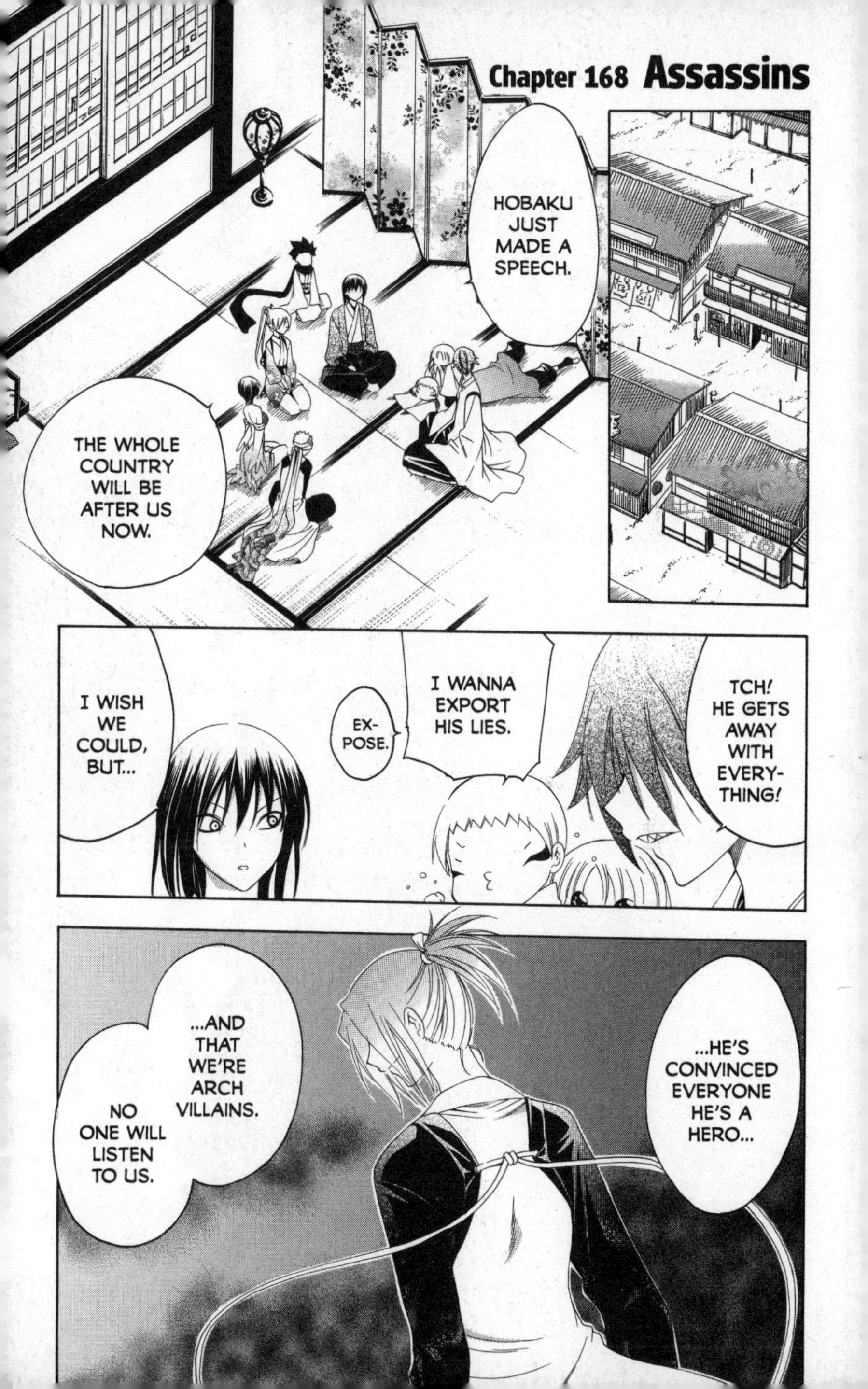
HOBAKU JUST MADE A SPEECH.
THE WHOLE COUNTRY WILL BE AFTER US NOW.
TCH! HE GETS AWAY WITH EVERYTHING!
I WANNA EXPORT HIS LIES.
EXPOSE.
I WISH WE COULD, BUT...
...HE'S CONVINCED EVERYONE HE'S A HERO...
...AND THAT WE'RE ARCH VILLAINS.
NO ONE WILL LISTEN TO US.

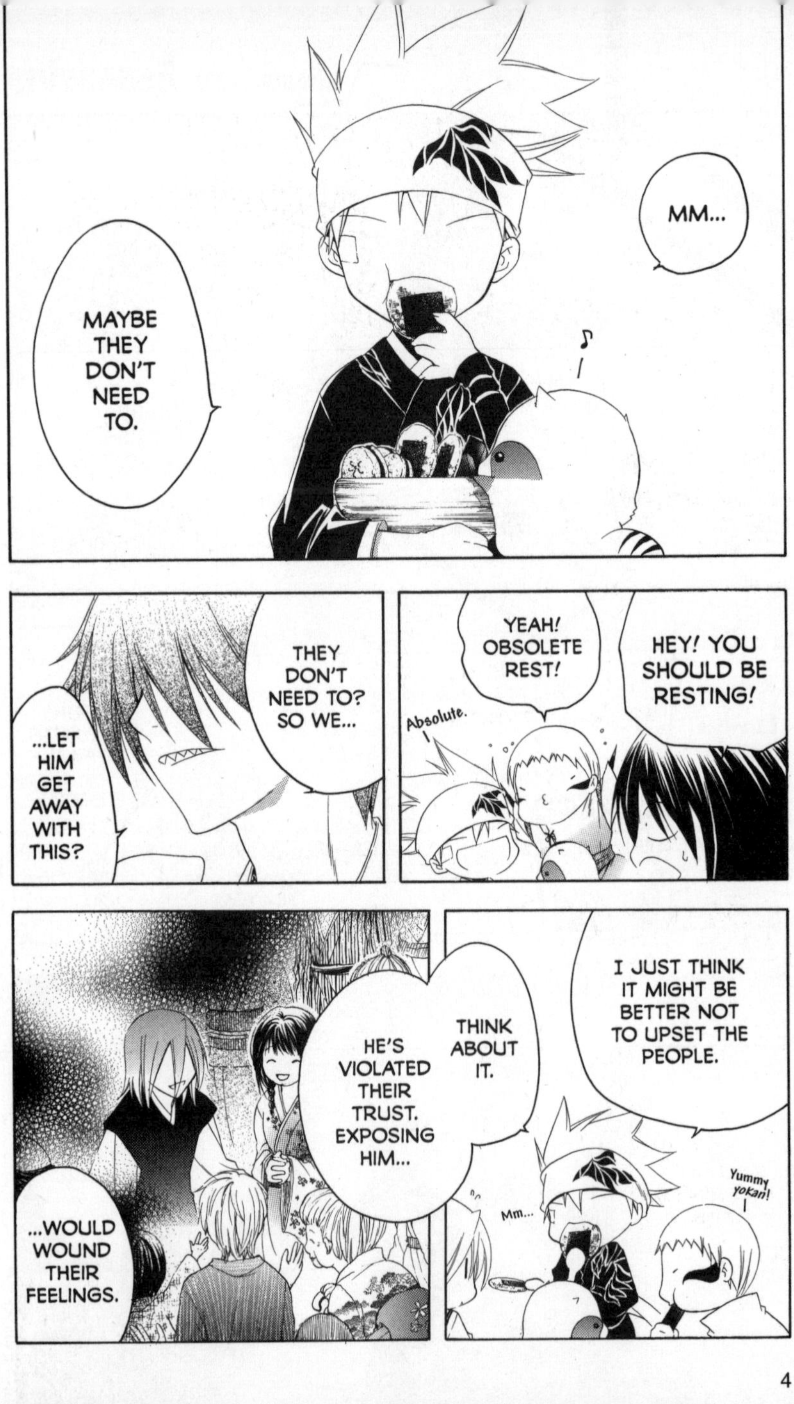
MM...
MAYBE THEY DON'T NEED TO.
HEY! YOU SHOULD BE RESTING!
YEAH! OBSOLETE REST!
Absolute.
THEY DON'T NEED TO? SO WE...
...LET HIM GET AWAY WITH THIS?
I JUST THINK IT MIGHT BE BETTER NOT TO UPSET THE PEOPLE.
Yummy yokan!
Mm...
THINK ABOUT IT.
HE'S VIOLATED THEIR TRUST. EXPOSING HIM...
...WOULD WOUND THEIR FEELINGS.

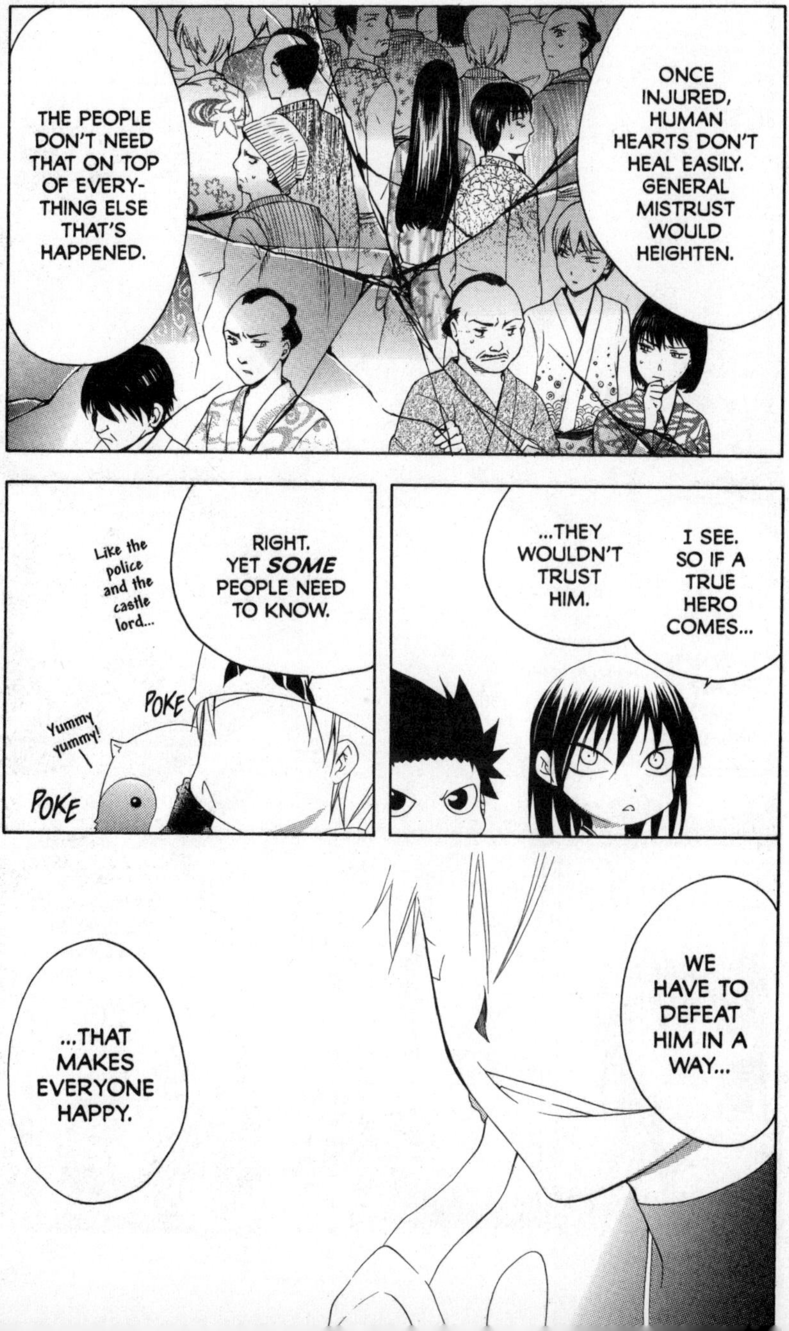
ONCE INJURED, HUMAN HEARTS DON'T HEAL EASILY. GENERAL MISTRUST WOULD HEIGHTEN.
THE PEOPLE DON'T NEED THAT ON TOP OF EVERY-THING ELSE THAT'S HAPPENED.
I SEE. SO IF A TRUE HERO COMES...
...THEY WOULDN'T TRUST HIM.
RIGHT. YET *SOME* PEOPLE NEED TO KNOW.
Like the police and the castle lord...
POKE
Yummy yummy!
POKE
WE HAVE TO DEFEAT HIM IN A WAY...
...THAT MAKES EVERYONE HAPPY.

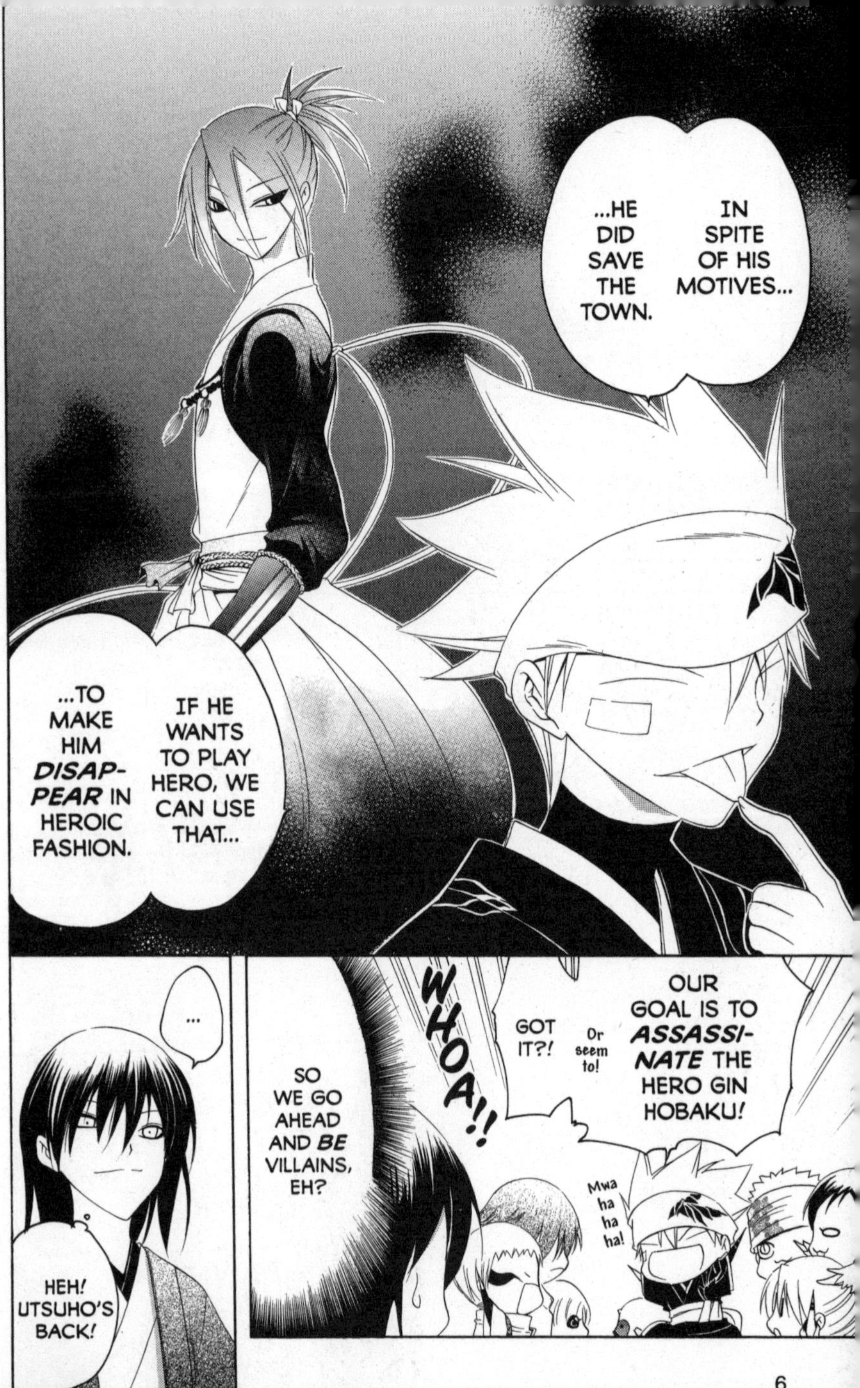
IN SPITE OF HIS MOTIVES...
...HE DID SAVE THE TOWN.
IF HE WANTS TO PLAY HERO, WE CAN USE THAT...
...TO MAKE HIM DISAPPEAR IN HEROIC FASHION.
OUR GOAL IS TO ASSASSINATE THE HERO GIN HOBAKU!
Or seem to!
GOT IT?!
WHOA!!
Mwa ha ha ha!
SO WE GO AHEAD AND BE VILLAINS, EH?
...
HEH! UTSUHO'S BACK!

Chapter 168
Assassins

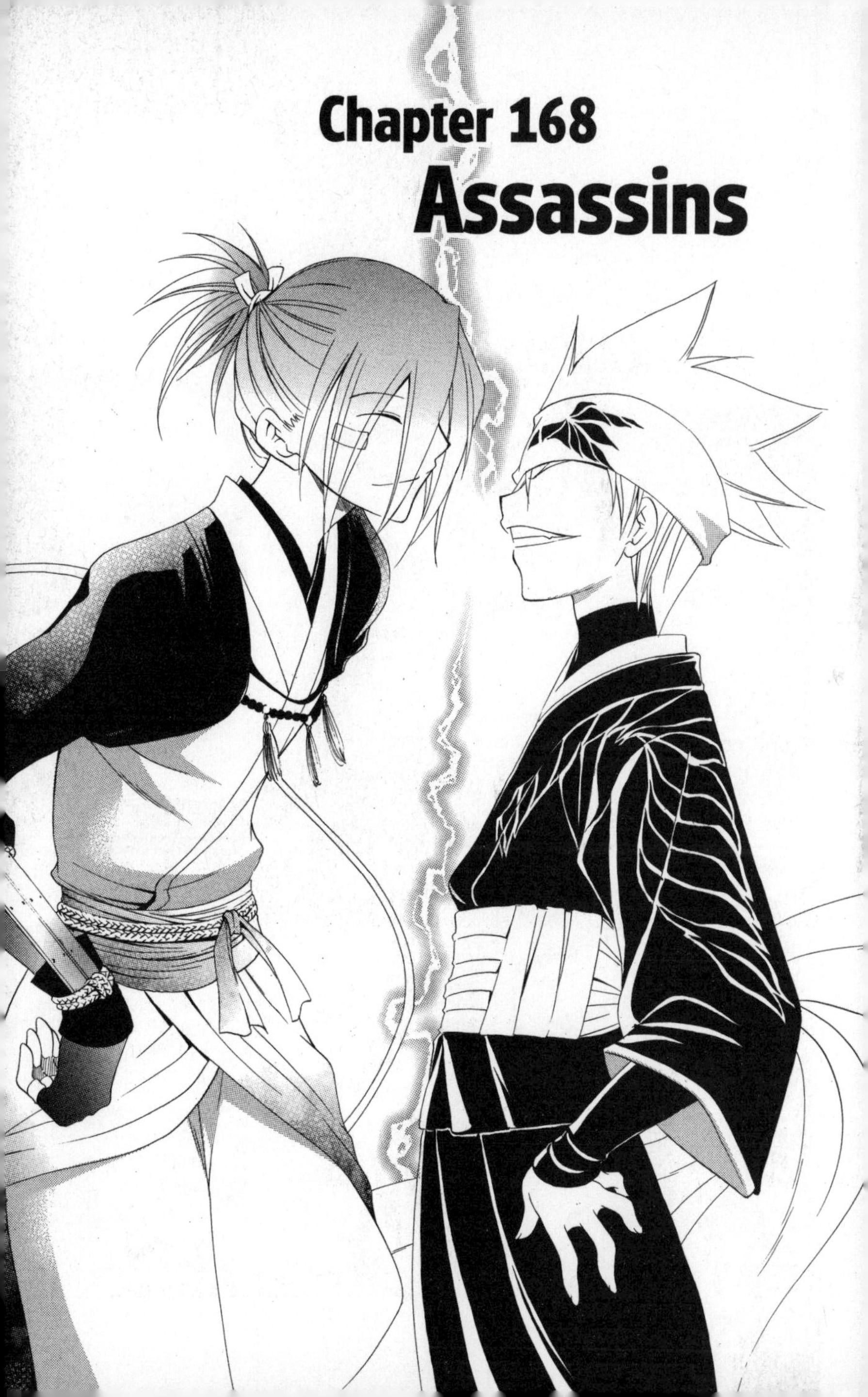

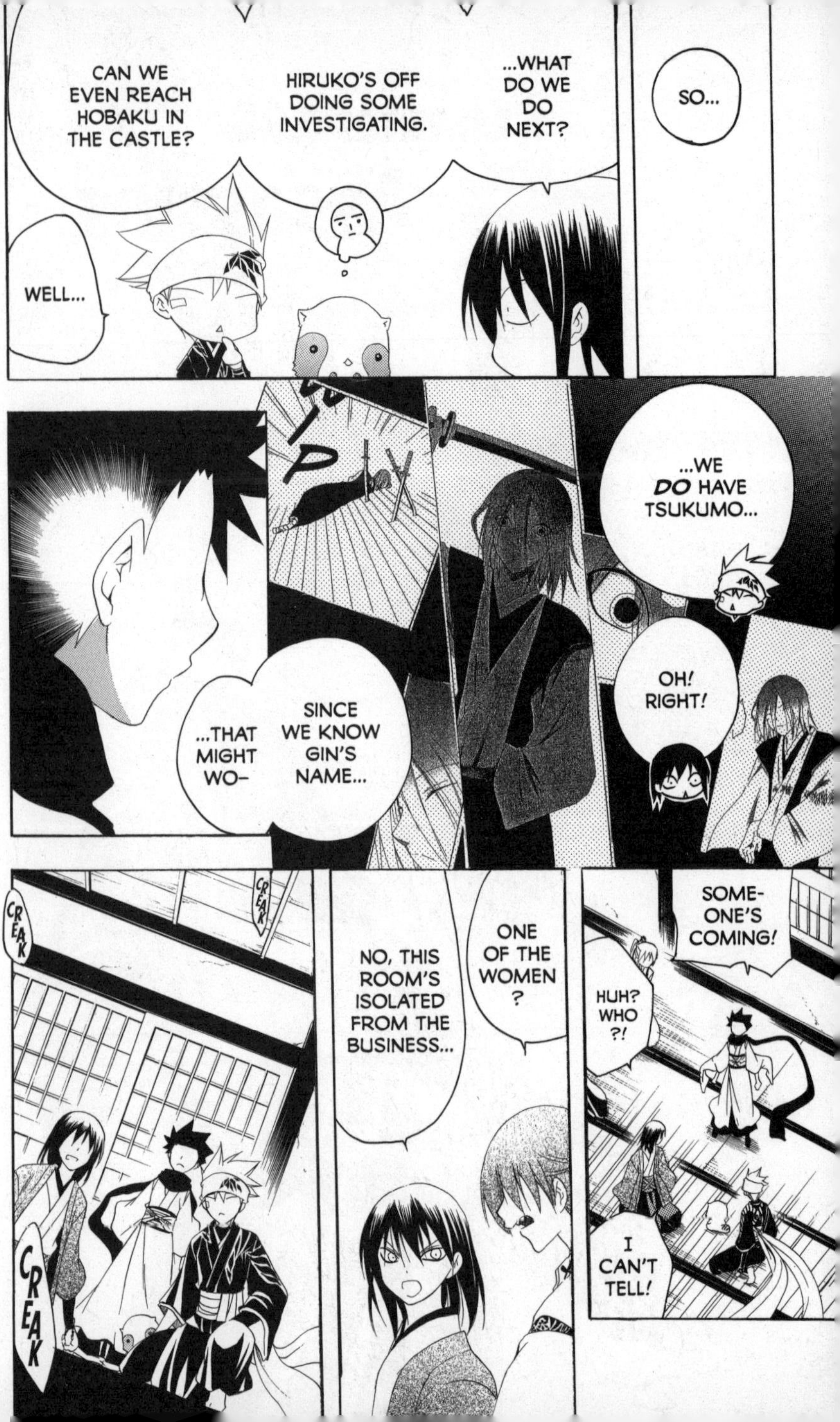
SO...
...WHAT DO WE DO NEXT?
HIRUKO'S OFF DOING SOME INVESTIGATING.
CAN WE EVEN REACH HOBAKU IN THE CASTLE?
WELL...
...WE *DO* HAVE TSUKUMO...
OH! RIGHT!
SINCE WE KNOW GIN'S NAME...
...THAT MIGHT WO-
SOME-ONE'S COMING!
HUH? WHO?!
I CAN'T TELL!
ONE OF THE WOMEN?
NO, THIS ROOM'S ISOLATED FROM THE BUSINESS...
CREAK
CREAK
CREAK
CREAK

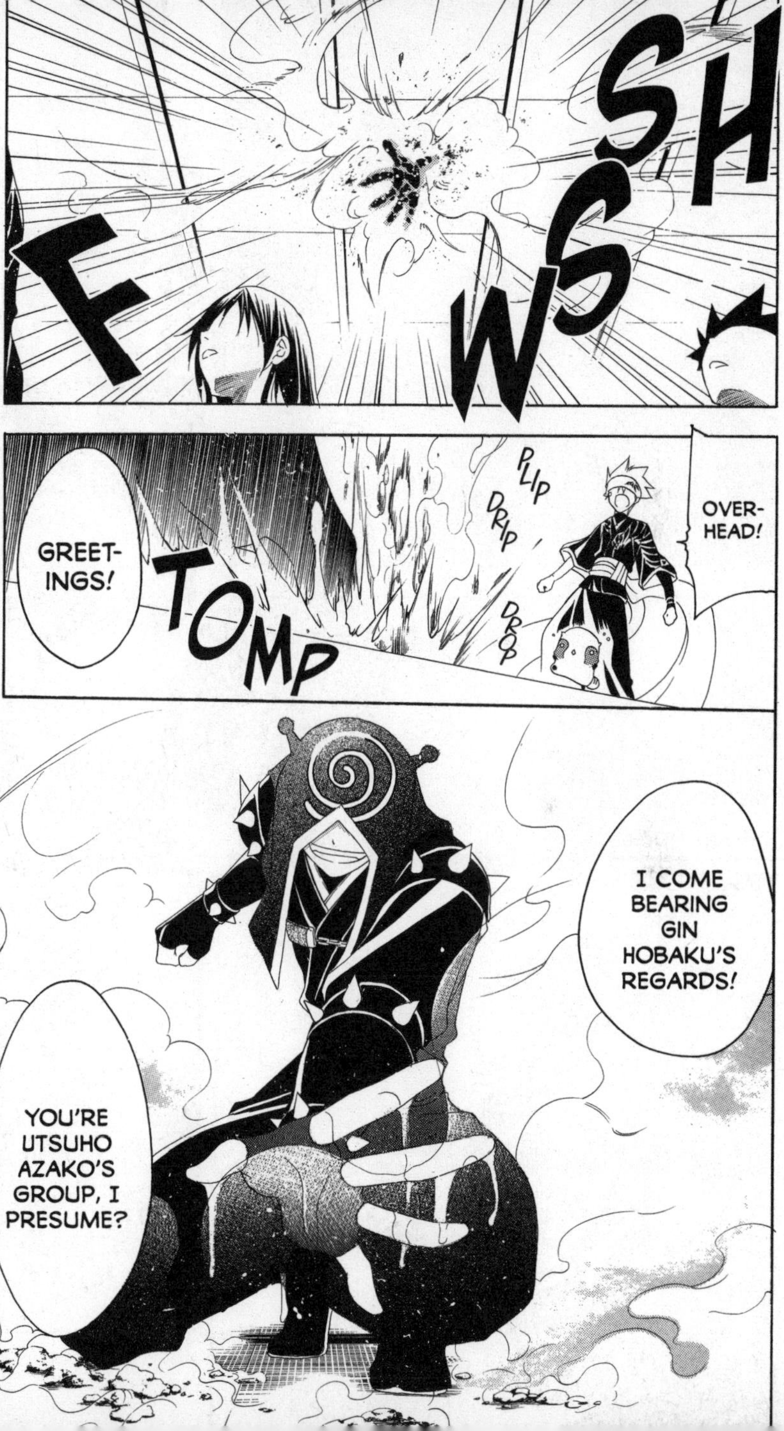

SH
SH
S
W
F
OVER-HEAD!
PLIP
DRIP
DROP
TOMP
GREET-INGS!
I COME BEARING GIN HOBAKU'S REGARDS!
YOU'RE UTSUHO AZAKO'S GROUP, I PRESUME?

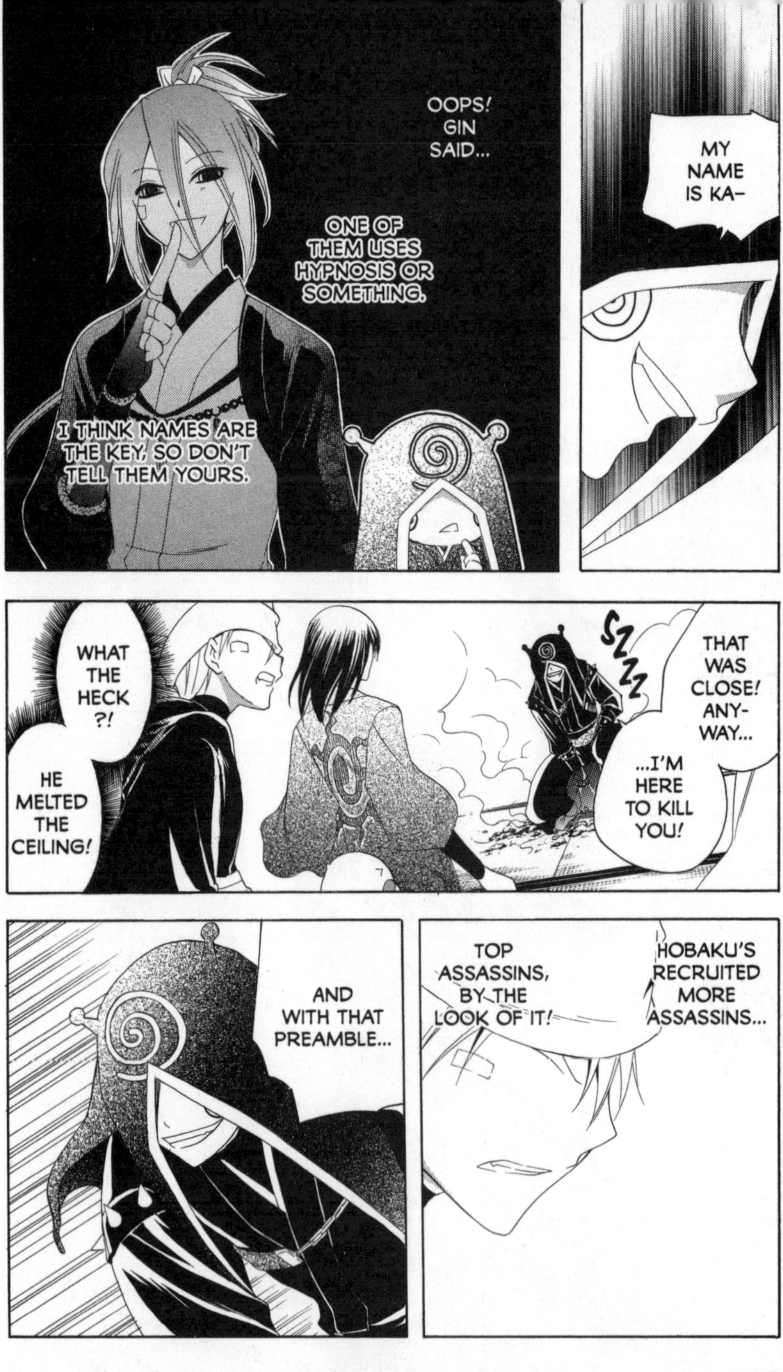
MY NAME IS KA-
OOPS! GIN SAID...
ONE OF THEM USES HYPNOSIS OR SOMETHING.
I THINK NAMES ARE THE KEY, SO DON'T TELL THEM YOURS.
SZZZ
THAT WAS CLOSE! ANY-WAY...
...I'M HERE TO KILL YOU!
WHAT THE HECK ?!
HE MELTED THE CEILING!
HOBAKU'S RECRUITED MORE ASSASSINS...
TOP ASSASSINS, BY THE LOOK OF IT!
AND WITH THAT PREAMBLE...

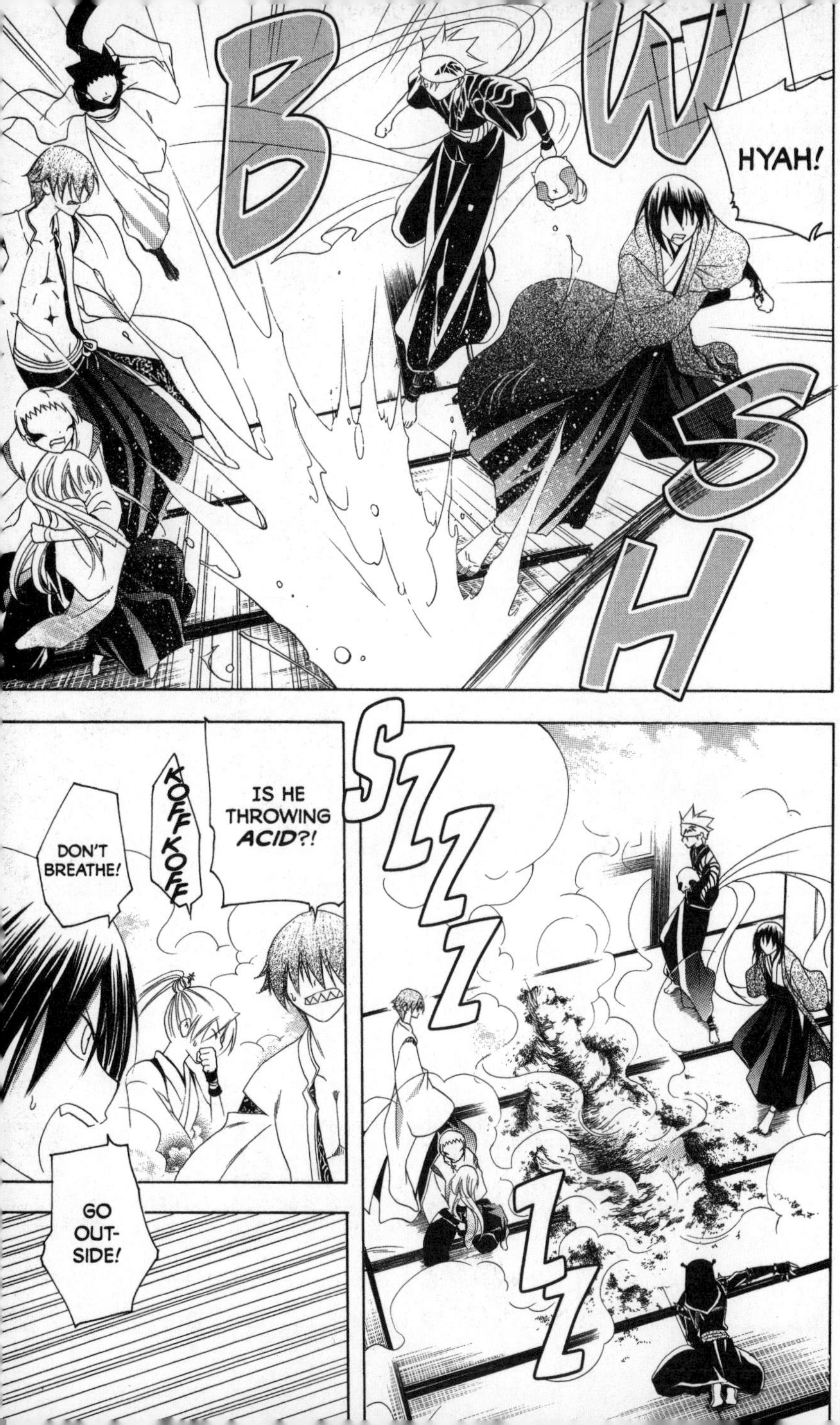

BWSH
HYAH!
SIZZZZ
IS HE THROWING *ACID*?!
KOFF KOFF
DON'T BREATHE!
GO OUT-SIDE!

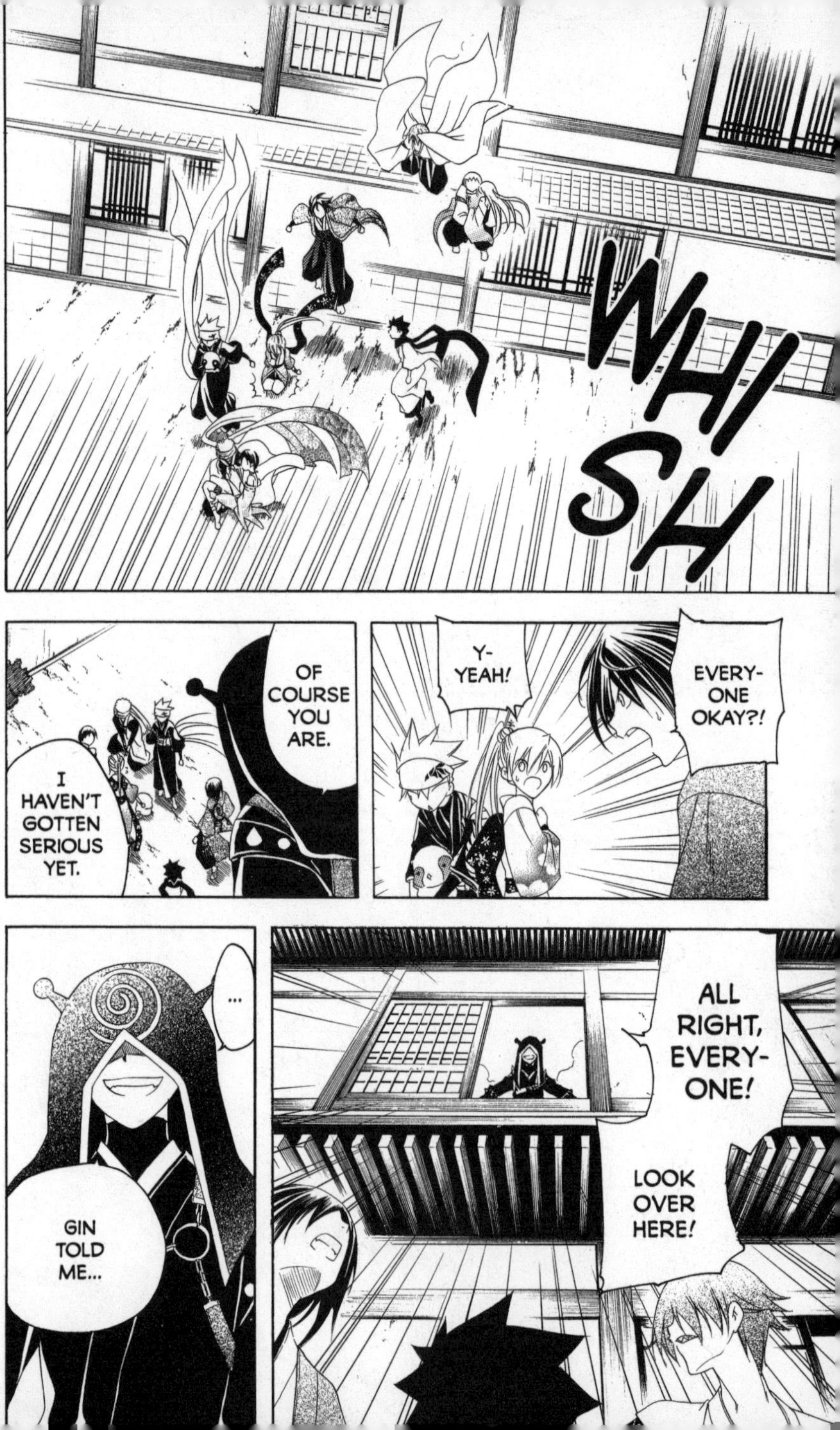
WHISH
EVERY-ONE OKAY?!
Y-YEAH!
OF COURSE YOU ARE.
I HAVEN'T GOTTEN SERIOUS YET.
ALL RIGHT, EVERY-ONE!
LOOK OVER HERE!
...
GIN TOLD ME...

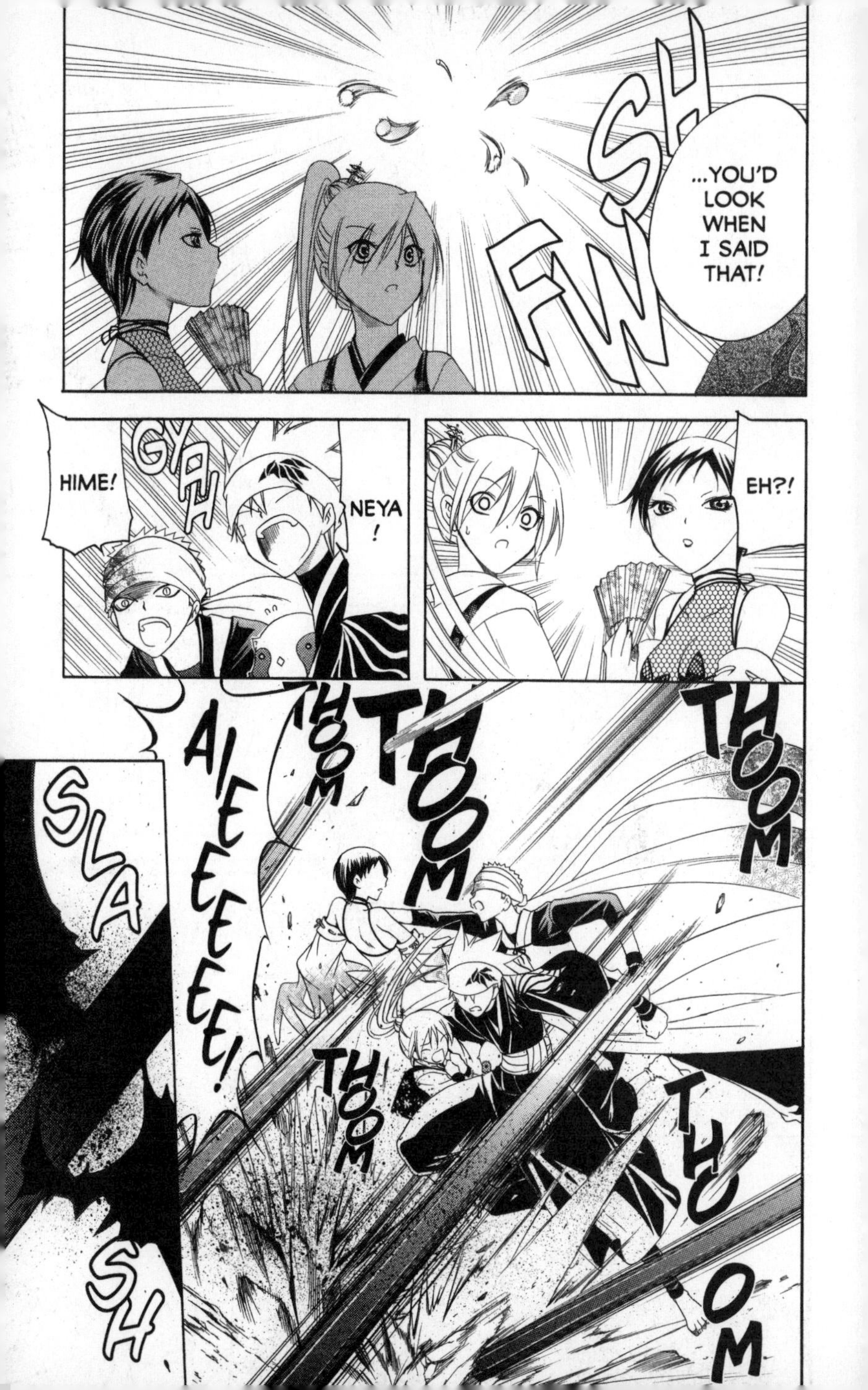
FWSH
...YOU'D LOOK WHEN I SAID THAT!
EH?!
NEYA!
GYAH
HIME!
THOOM
THOOM
THOOM
AIEEEEEEE!
SLASH
THOOM
THOOM

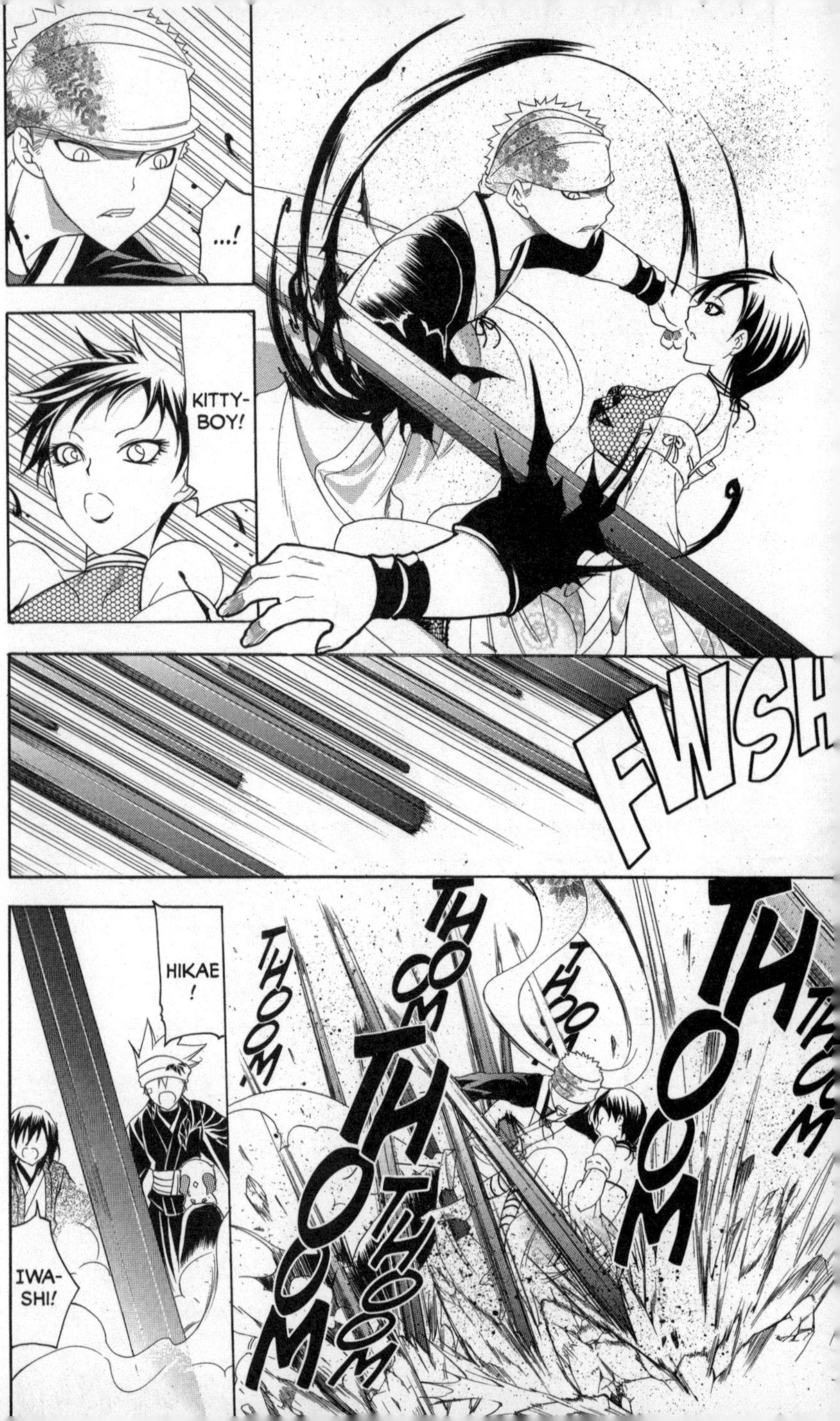
...!
KITTY-BOY!
FWSH
THOOM
THOOM
THOOM
THOOM
THOOOM
THOOM
THOOM
HIKAE!
IWA-SHI!

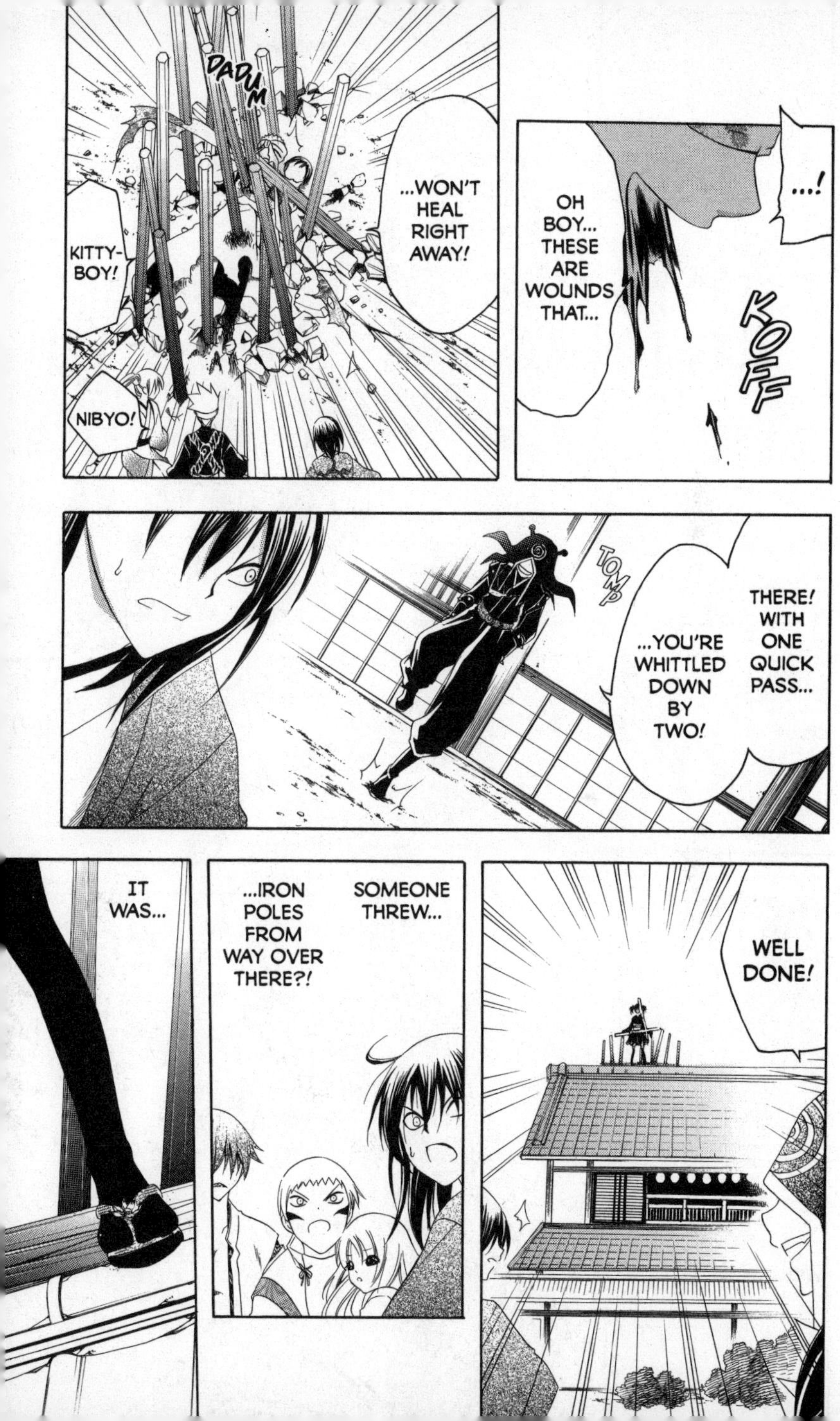
...!
KOFF
OH BOY... THESE ARE WOUNDS THAT...
...WON'T HEAL RIGHT AWAY!
DADUM
KITTY-BOY!
NIBYO!
THERE! WITH ONE QUICK PASS...
...YOU'RE WHITTLED DOWN BY TWO!
TOMP
WELL DONE!
SOMEONE THREW...
...IRON POLES FROM WAY OVER THERE?!
IT WAS...

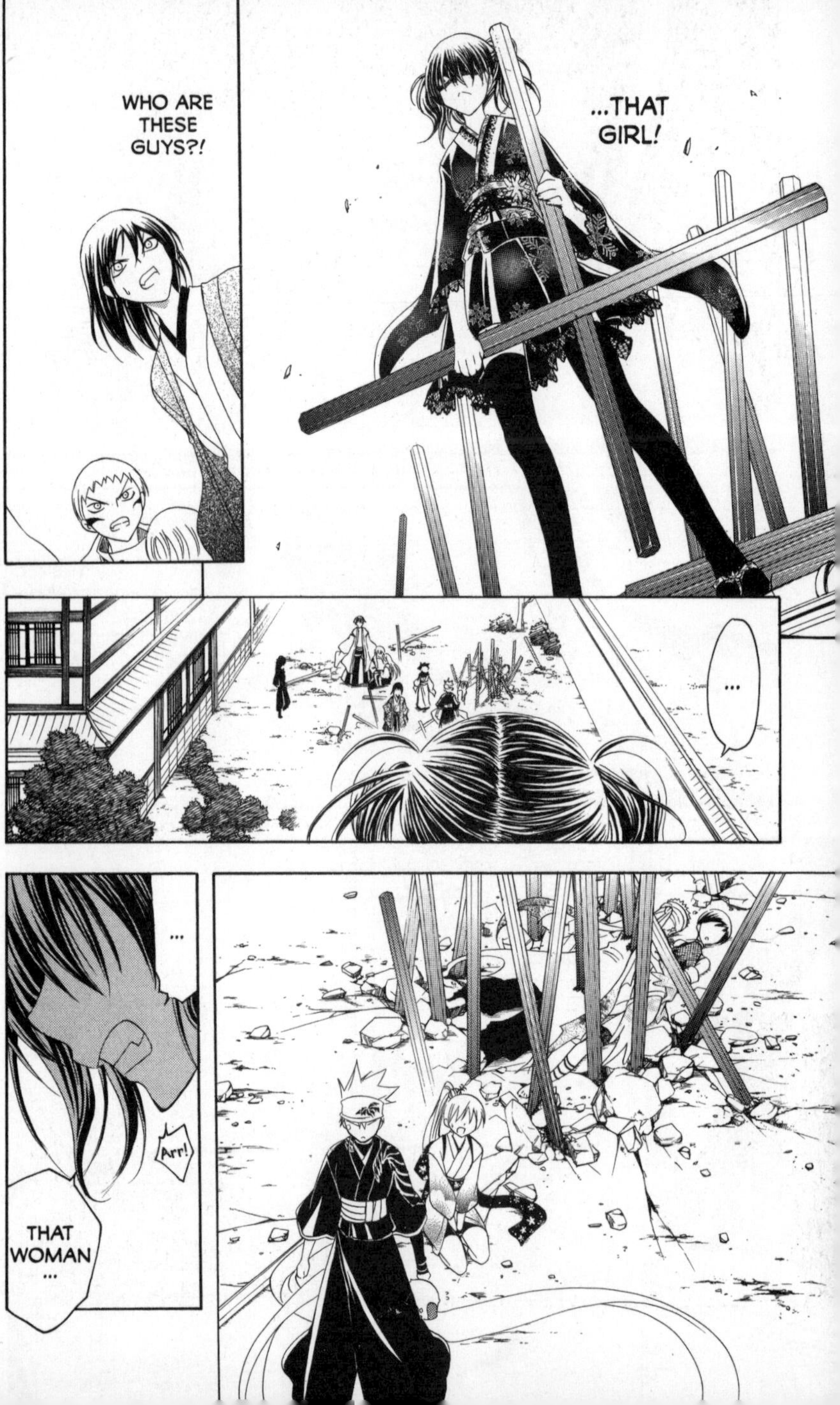
...THAT GIRL!
WHO ARE THESE GUYS?!
...
...
Arr!
THAT WOMAN ...

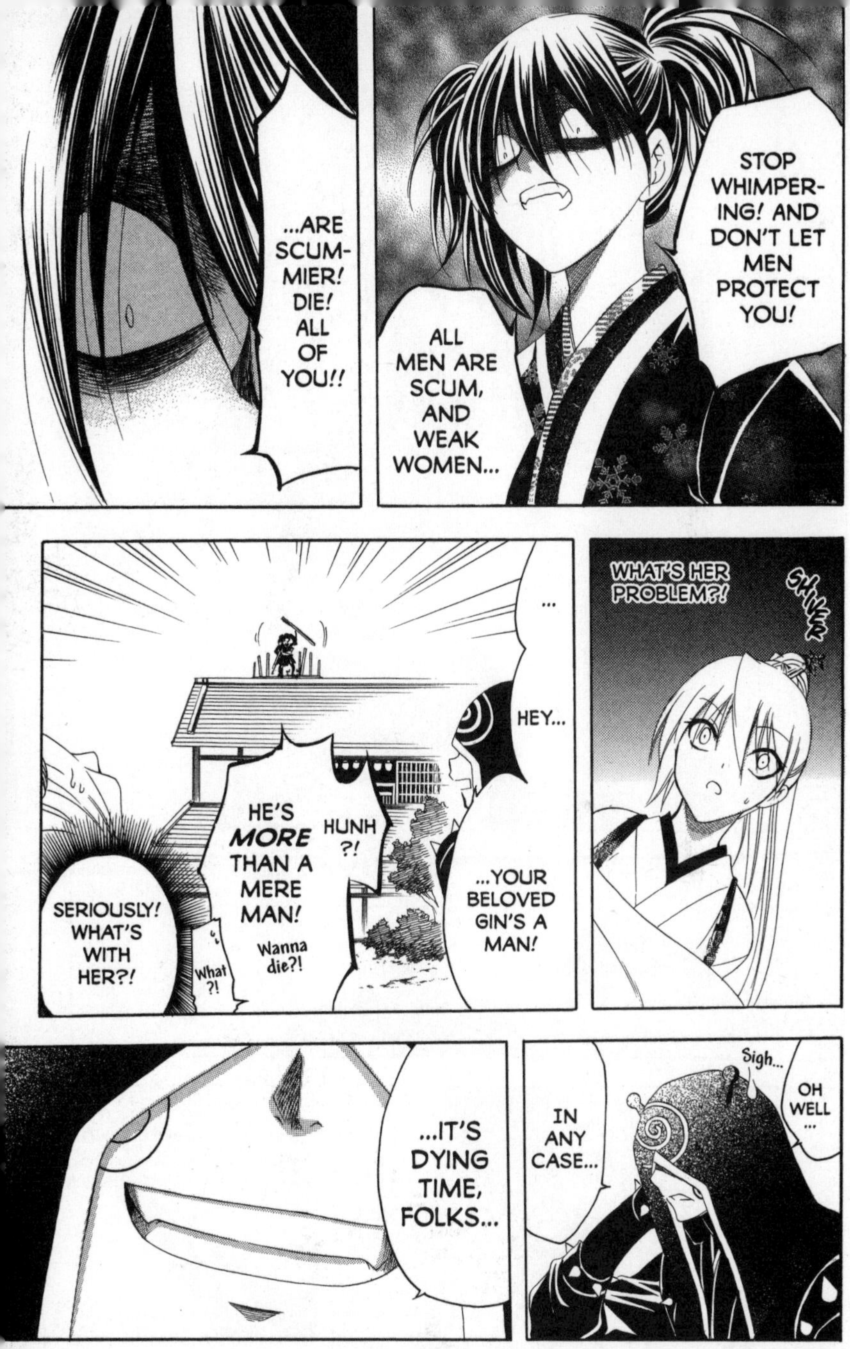
STOP WHIMPERING! AND DON'T LET MEN PROTECT YOU!
ALL MEN ARE SCUM, AND WEAK WOMEN...
...ARE SCUMMIER! DIE! ALL OF YOU!!
WHAT'S HER PROBLEM?!
SHIVER
...
HEY...
...YOUR BELOVED GIN'S A MAN!
HUNH?!
HE'S *MORE* THAN A MERE MAN!
Wanna die?!
What?!
SERIOUSLY! WHAT'S WITH HER?!
Sigh...
OH WELL...
IN ANY CASE...
...IT'S DYING TIME, FOLKS...

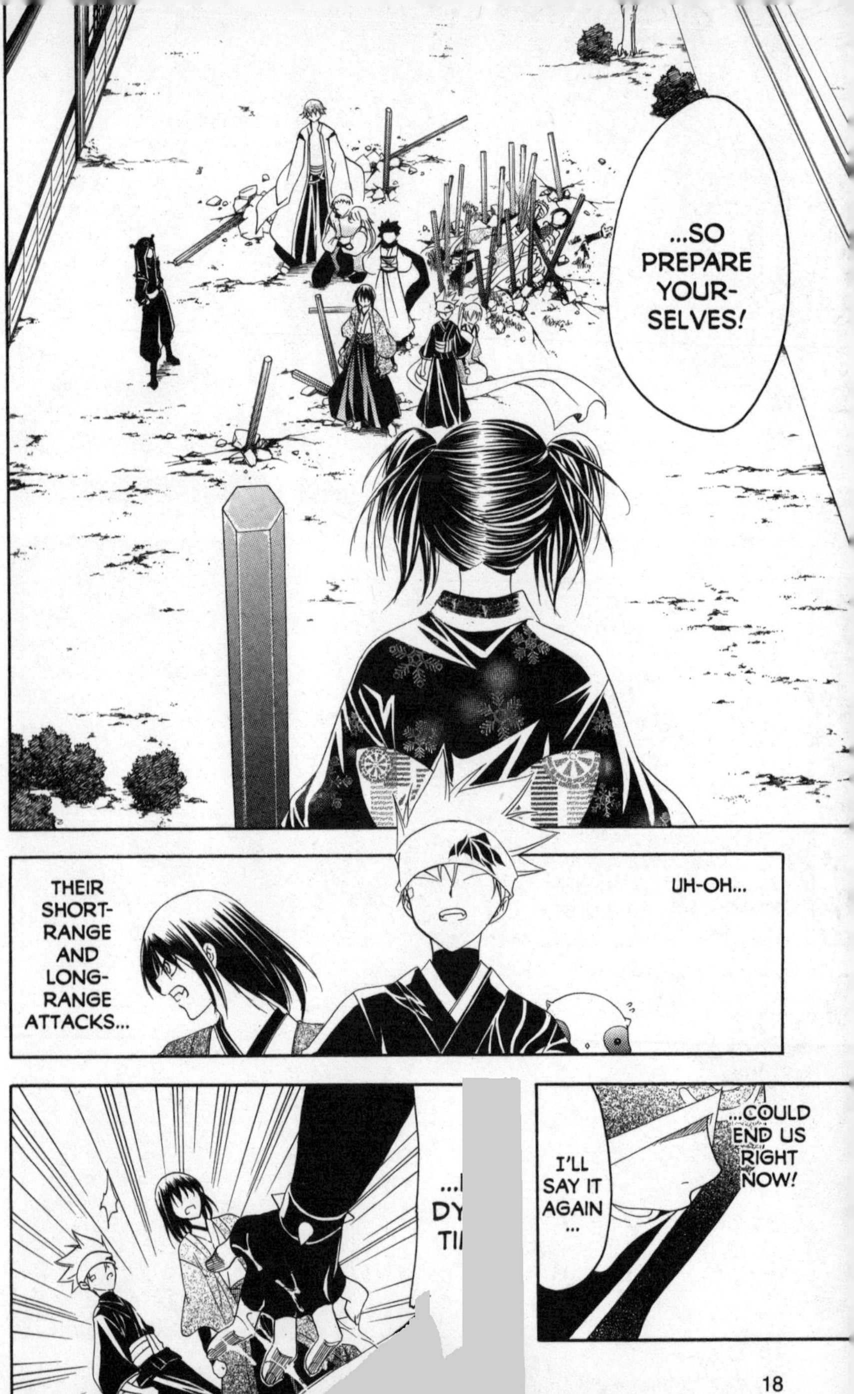
...SO PREPARE YOUR-SELVES!
UH-OH...
THEIR SHORT-RANGE AND LONG-RANGE ATTACKS...
...COULD END US RIGHT NOW!
I'LL SAY IT AGAIN...

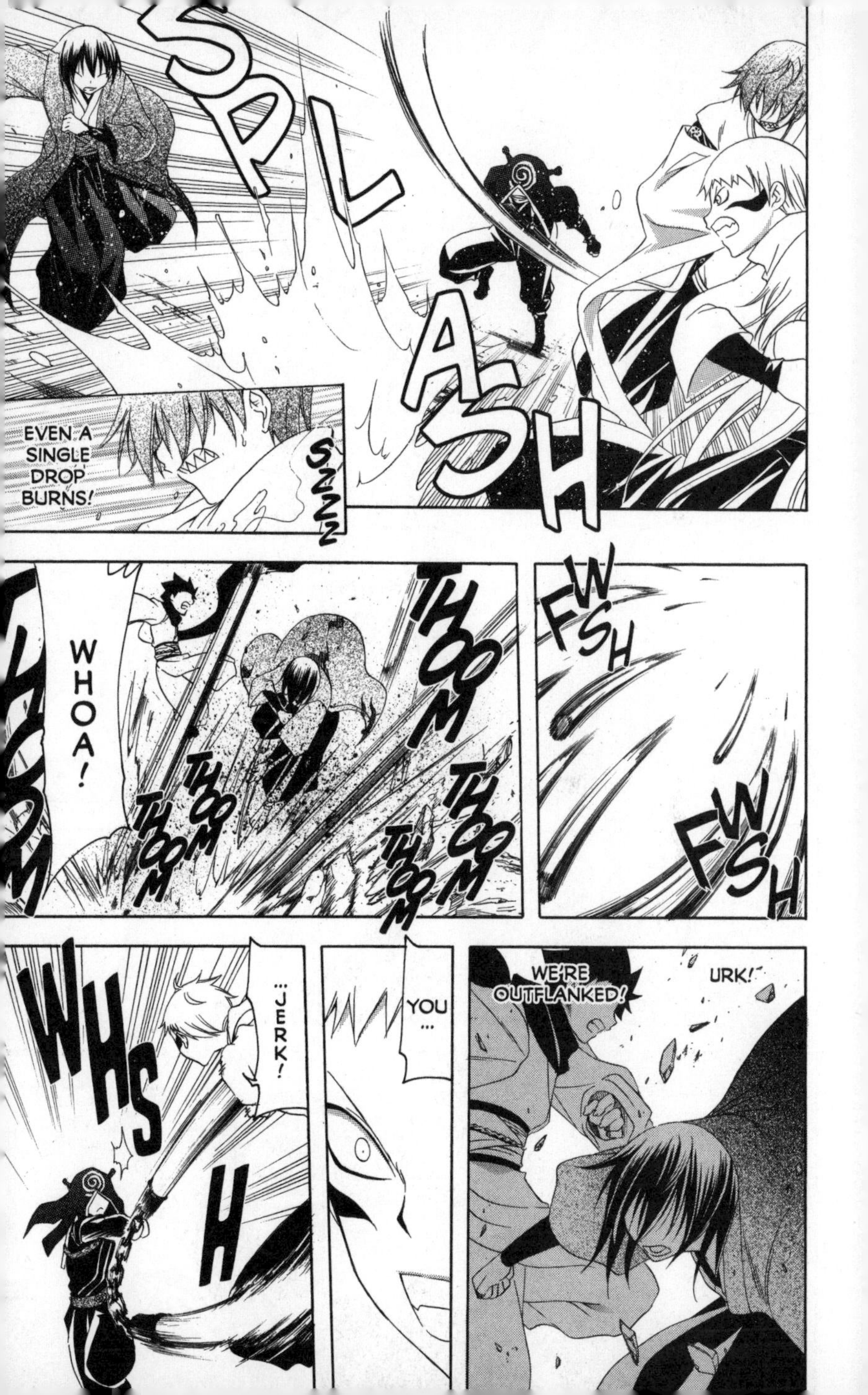
SPLASH
EVEN A SINGLE DROP BURNS!
SZZZ
FWSH
FWSH
THOOM
THOOM
WHOA!
THOOM
THOOM
THOOM
THOOM
URK!
WE'RE OUTFLANKED!
YOU...
...JERK!
WHSH

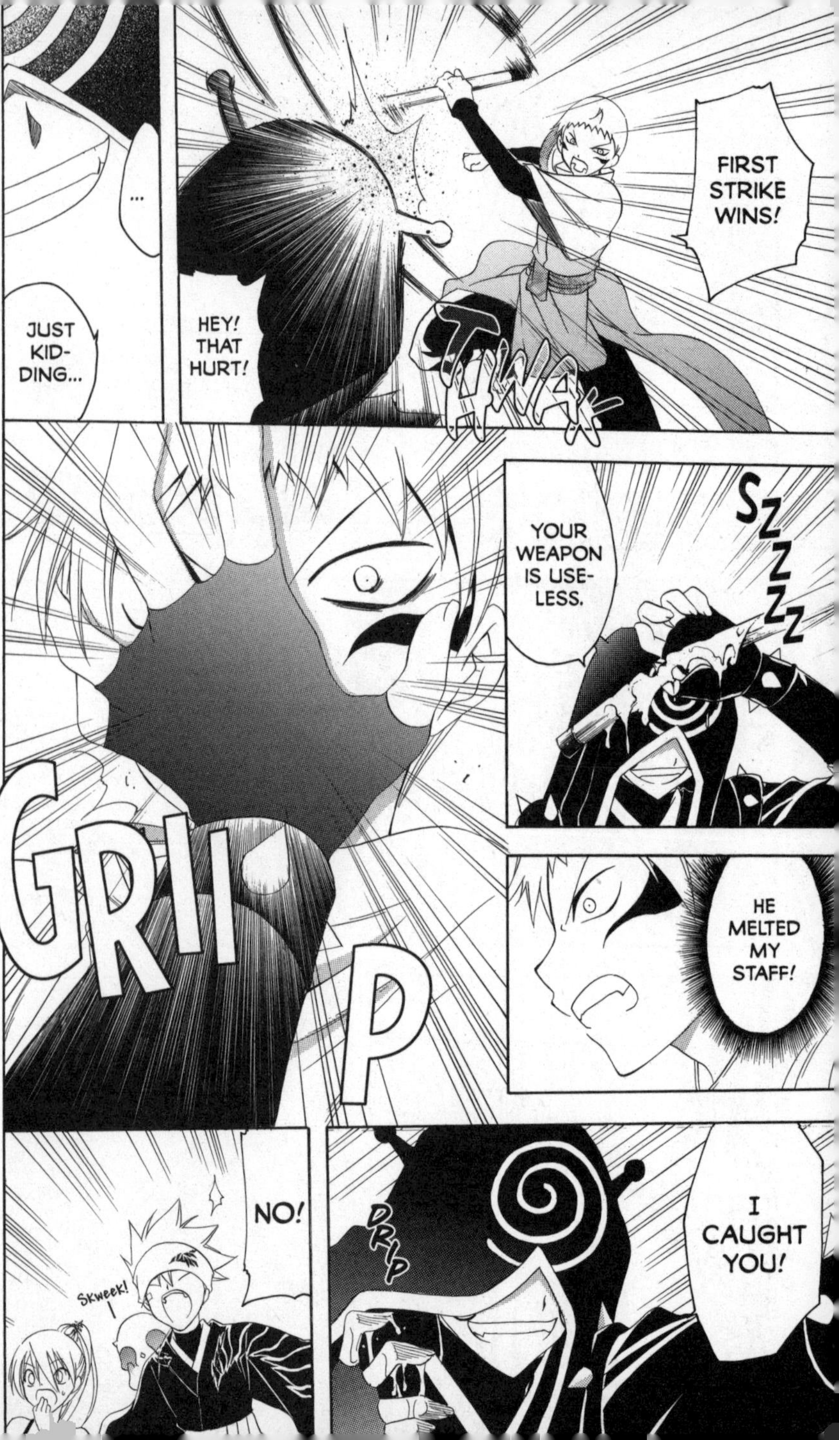

FIRST STRIKE WINS!
THWAK
HEY! THAT HURT!
...
JUST KID-DING...
YOUR WEAPON IS USE-LESS.
SZZZZ
HE MELTED MY STAFF!
GRIIP
I CAUGHT YOU!
DRIP
NO!
Skweek!

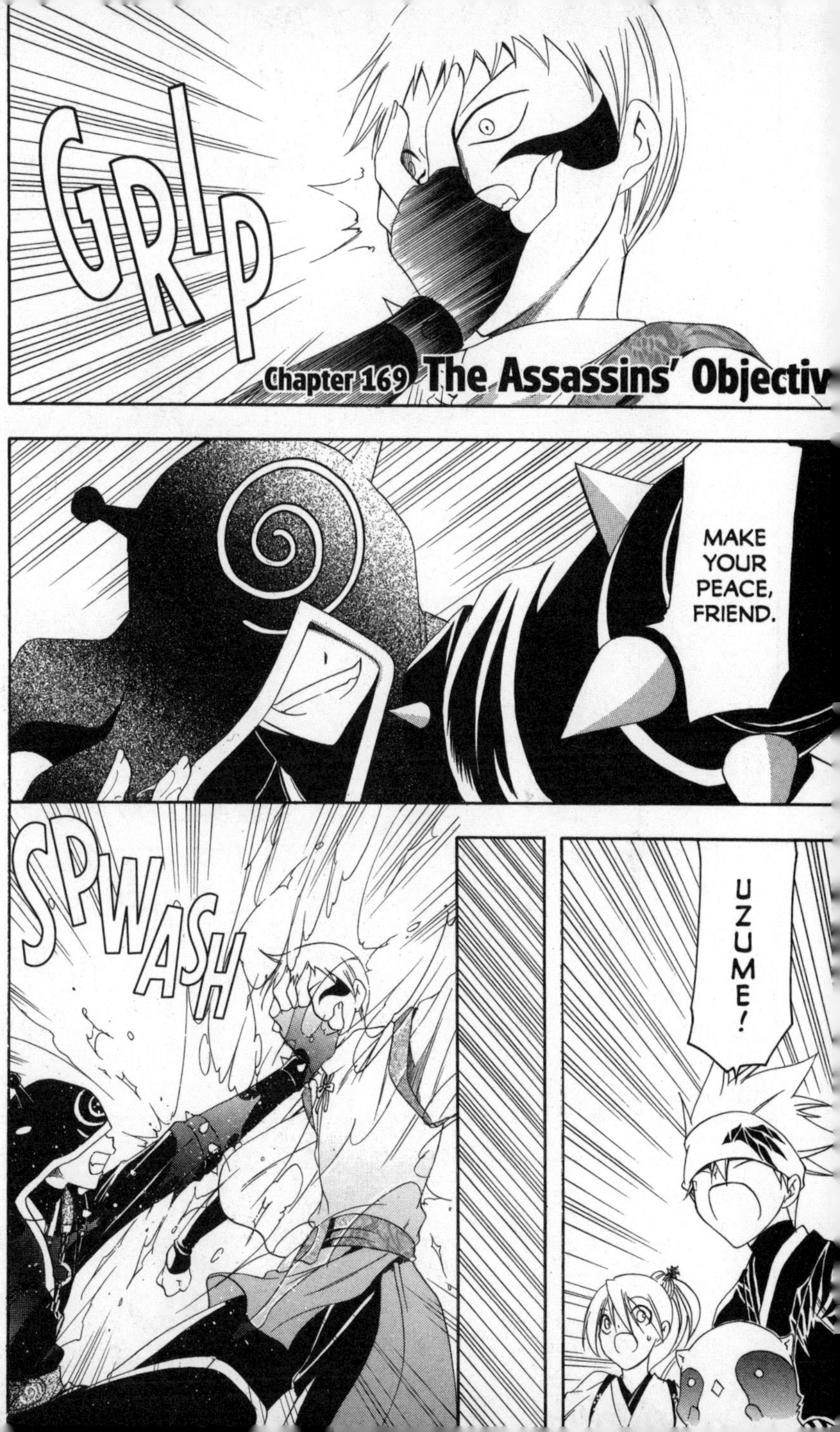
GRIP
Chapter 169 The Assassins' Objectiv
MAKE YOUR PEACE, FRIEND.
UZUME!
SPWASH

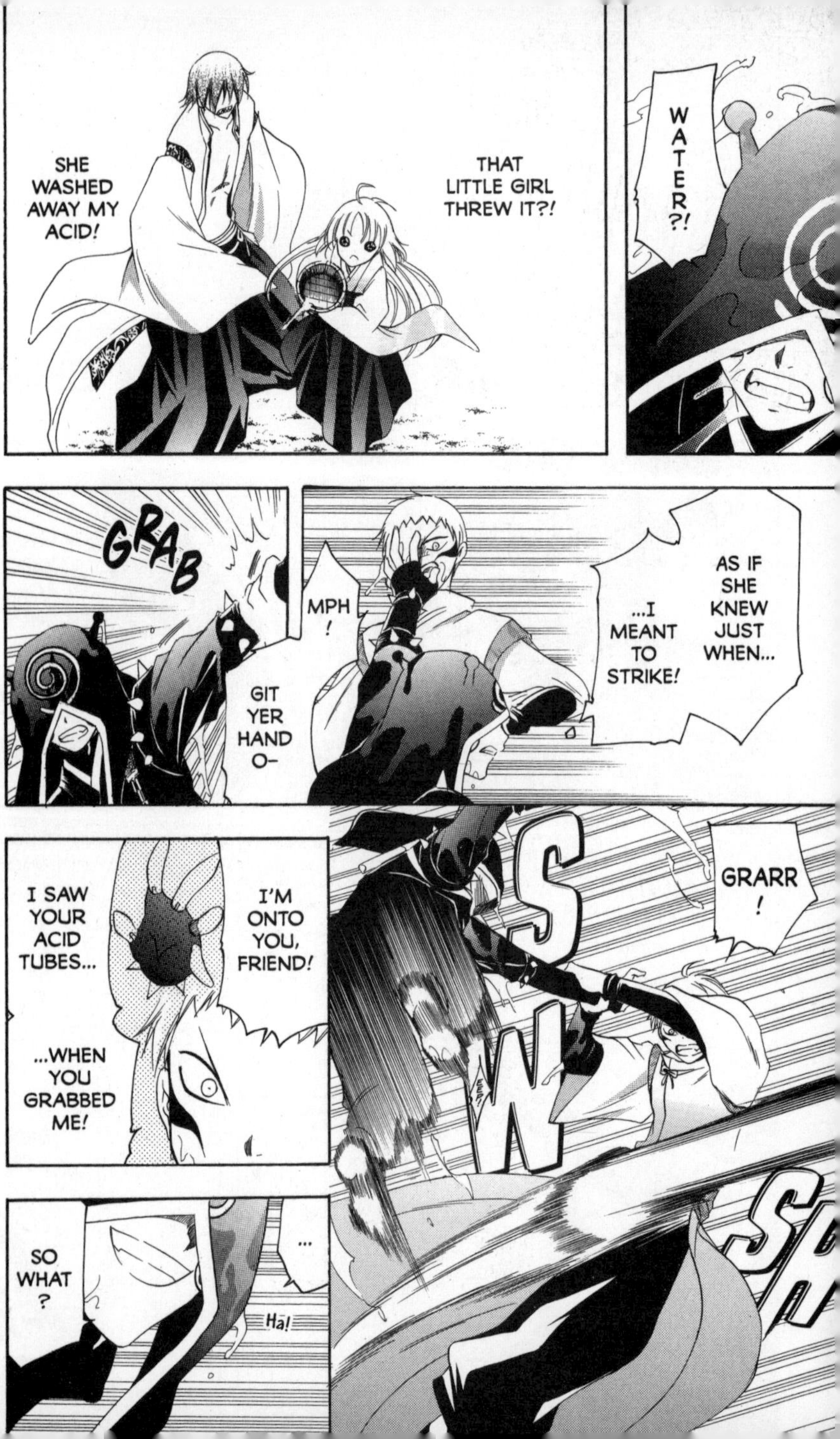
WATER?!
THAT LITTLE GIRL THREW IT?!
SHE WASHED AWAY MY ACID!
AS IF SHE KNEW JUST WHEN...
...I MEANT TO STRIKE!
MPH!
GRAB
GIT YER HAND O-
GRARR!
I'M ONTO YOU, FRIEND!
I SAW YOUR ACID TUBES...
...WHEN YOU GRABBED ME!
...
SO WHAT?
Ha!

Chapter 169
The Assassins' Objective

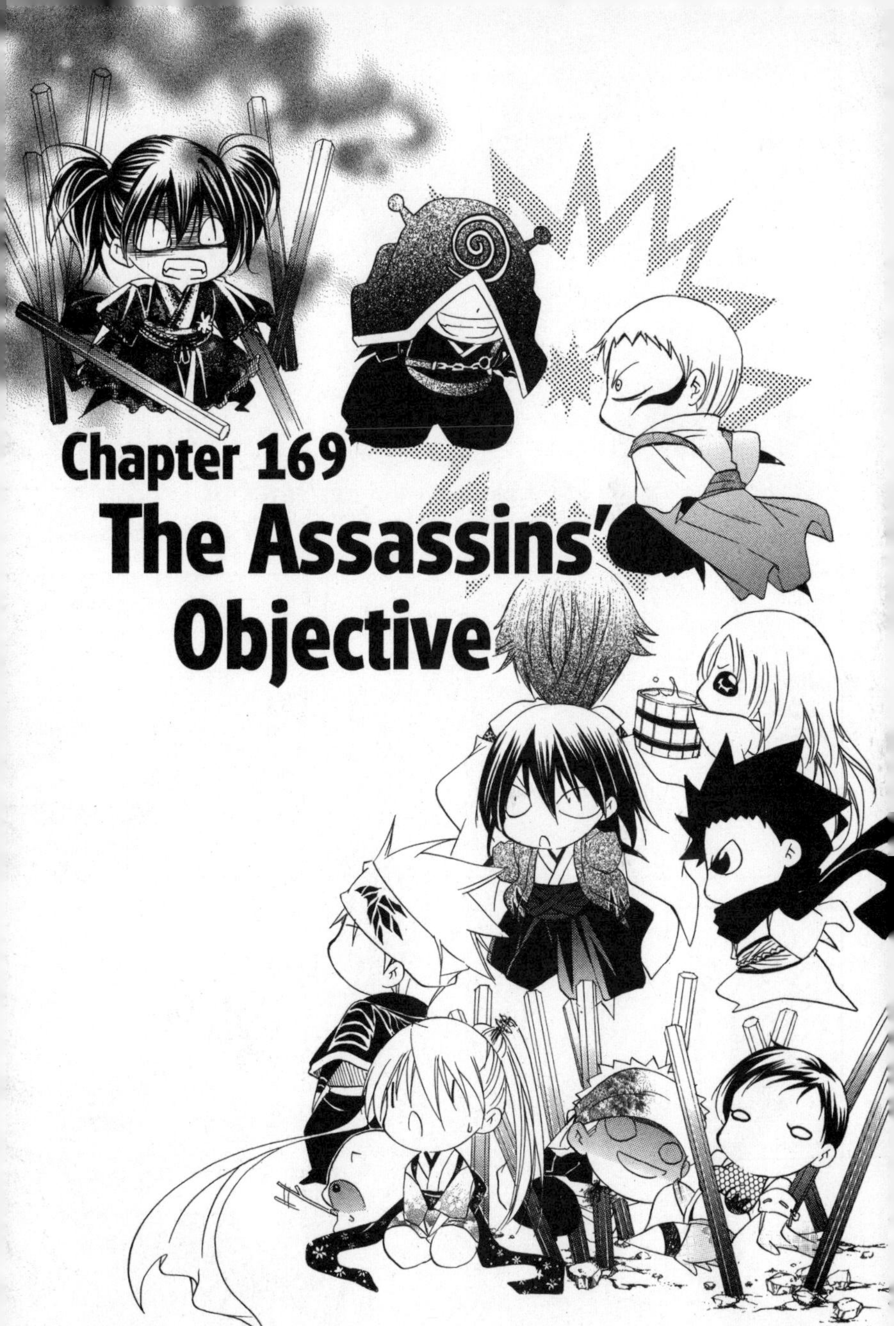

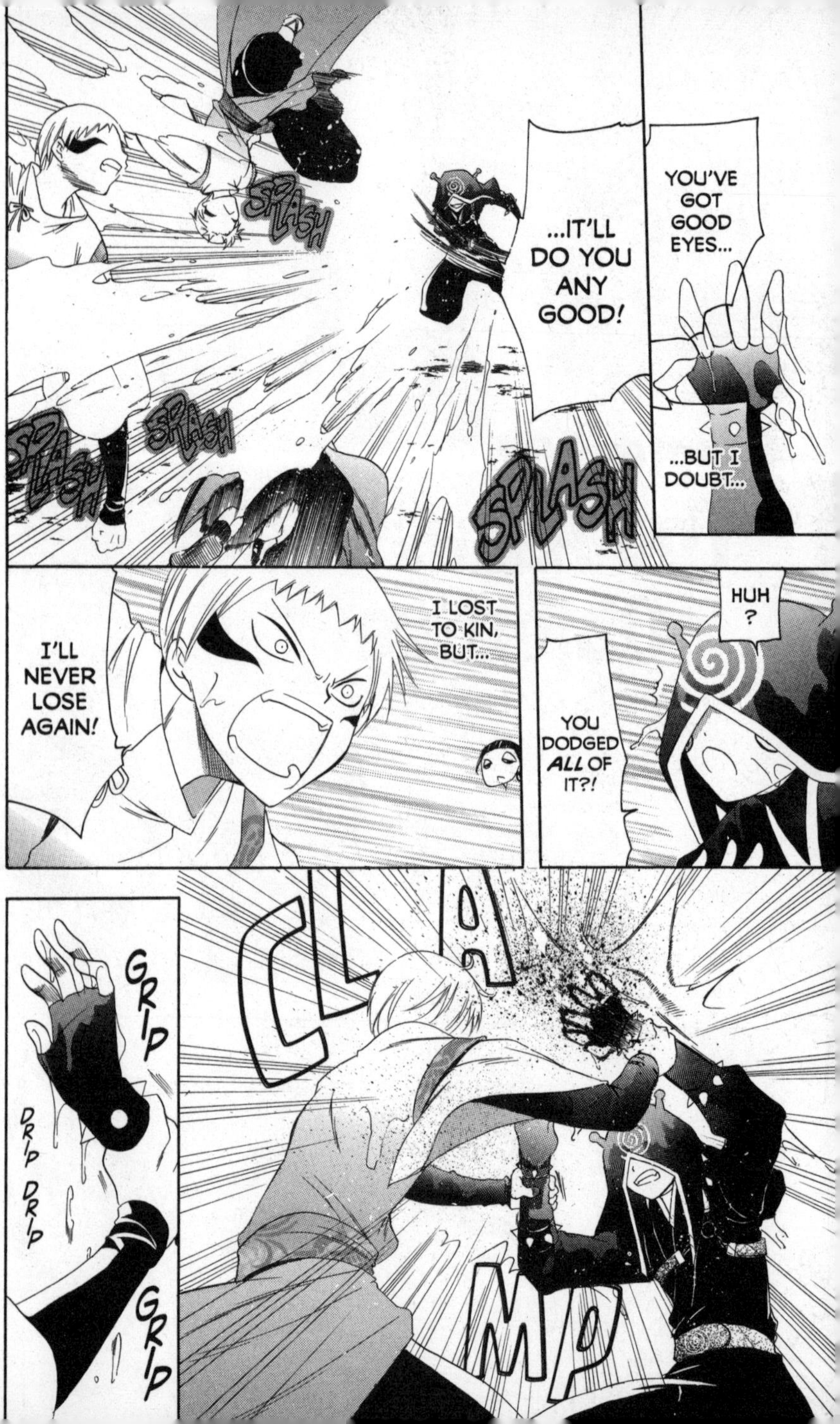
YOU'VE GOT GOOD EYES...
...BUT I DOUBT...
...IT'LL DO YOU ANY GOOD!
SPLASH
SPLASH
SPLASH
SPLASH
HUH ?
YOU DODGED *ALL* OF IT?!
I LOST TO KIN, BUT...
I'LL NEVER LOSE AGAIN!
CLAMP
GRIP
DRIP DRIP
GRIP

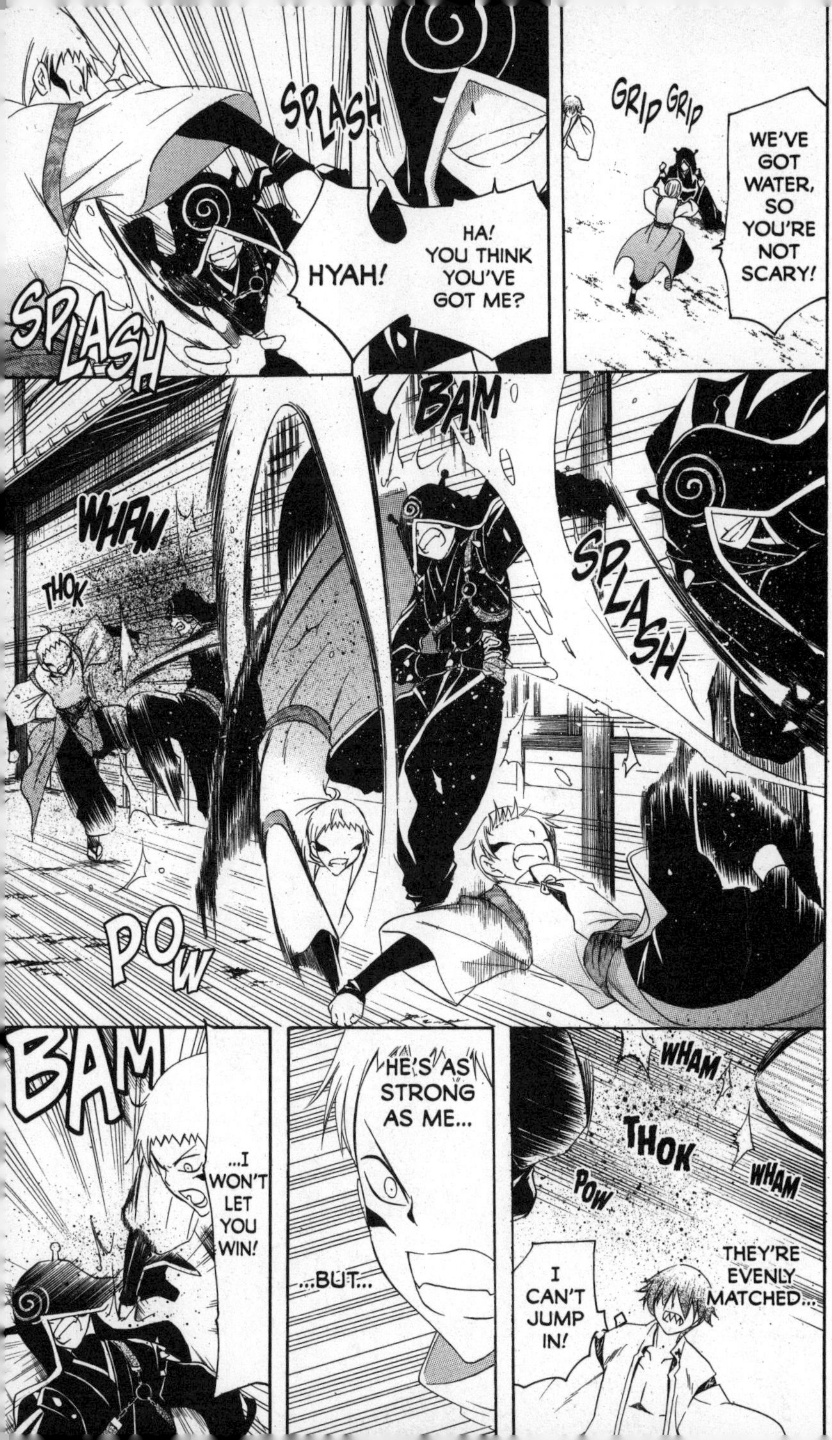
GRIP GRIP
WE'VE GOT WATER, SO YOU'RE NOT SCARY!
SPLASH
HA! YOU THINK YOU'VE GOT ME?
HYAH!
SPLASH
BAM
SPLASH
WHAM
THOK
POW
WHAM
THOK
WHAM
POW
THEY'RE EVENLY MATCHED...
I CAN'T JUMP IN!
HE'S AS STRONG AS ME...
...BUT...
BAM
...I WON'T LET YOU WIN!

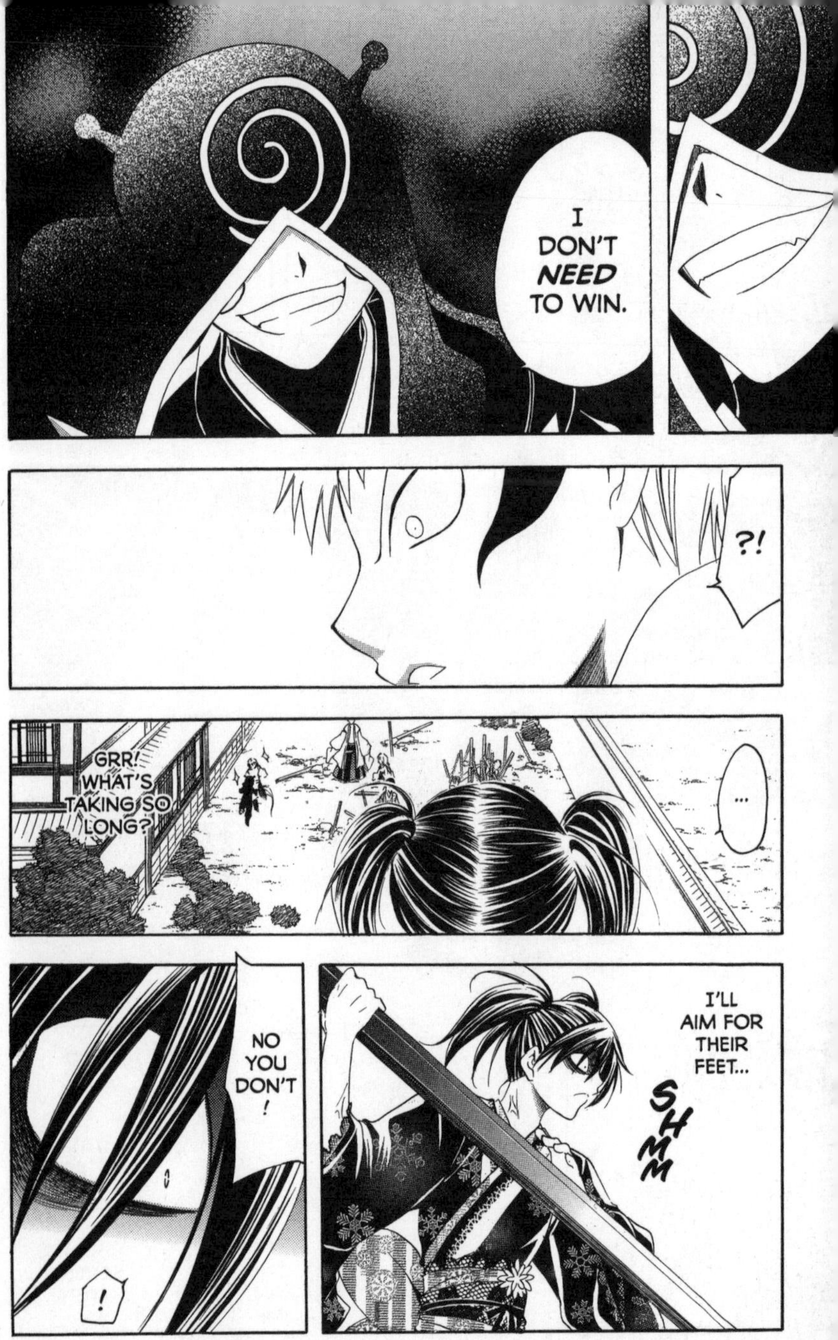
I DON'T NEED TO WIN.
?!
...
GRR! WHAT'S TAKING SO LONG?
I'LL AIM FOR THEIR FEET...
SHMM
NO YOU DON'T!
!

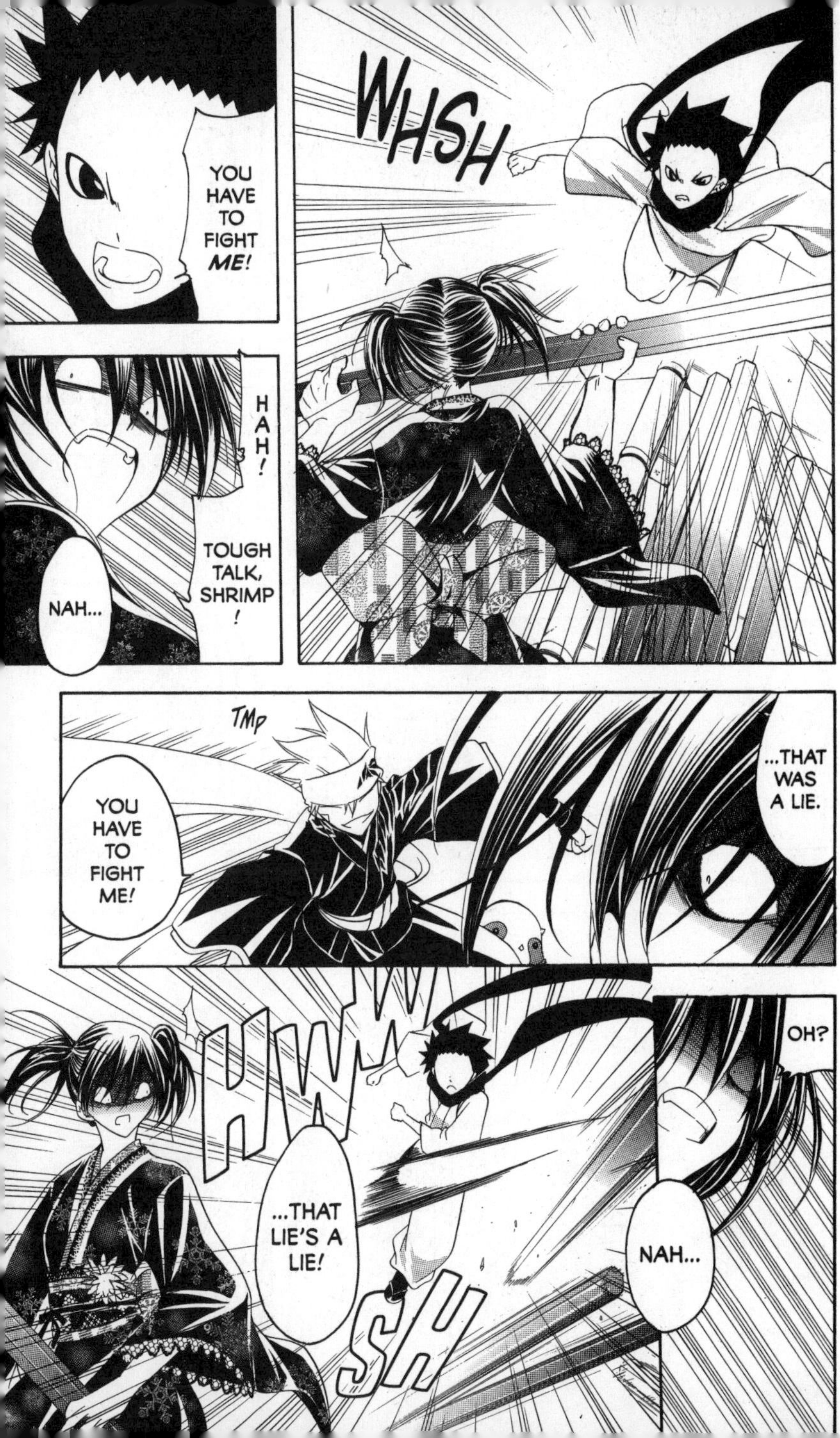
WHSH
YOU HAVE TO FIGHT ME!
HAH!
TOUGH TALK, SHRIMP!
NAH...
...THAT WAS A LIE.
TMP
YOU HAVE TO FIGHT ME!
OH?
NAH...
HWW
...THAT LIE'S A LIE!
SH

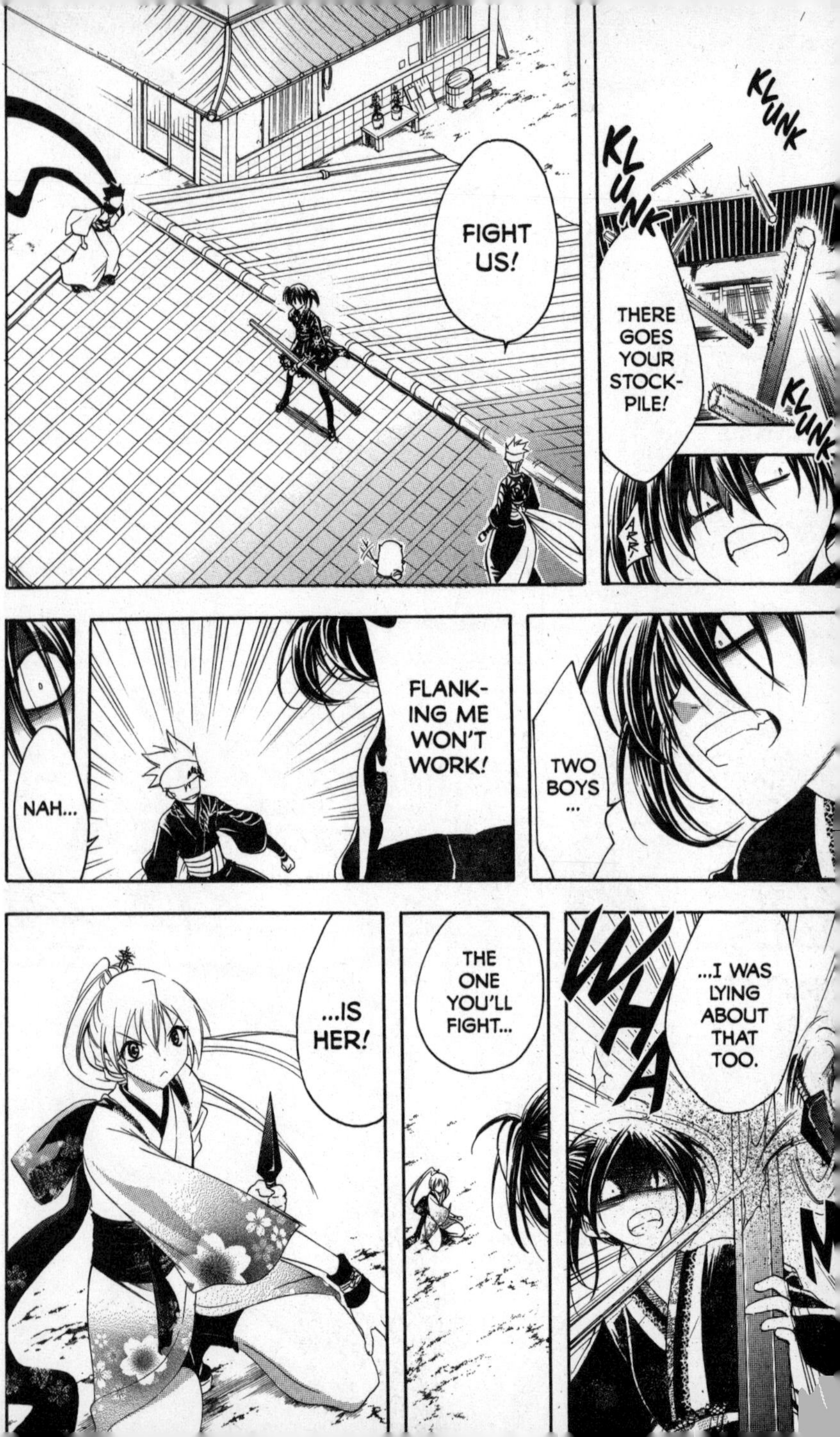
KLUNK
KLUNK
THERE GOES YOUR STOCKPILE!
KLUNK
ARK!
FIGHT US!
TWO BOYS...
FLANKING ME WON'T WORK!
NAH...
WHA
...I WAS LYING ABOUT THAT TOO.
THE ONE YOU'LL FIGHT...
...IS HER!

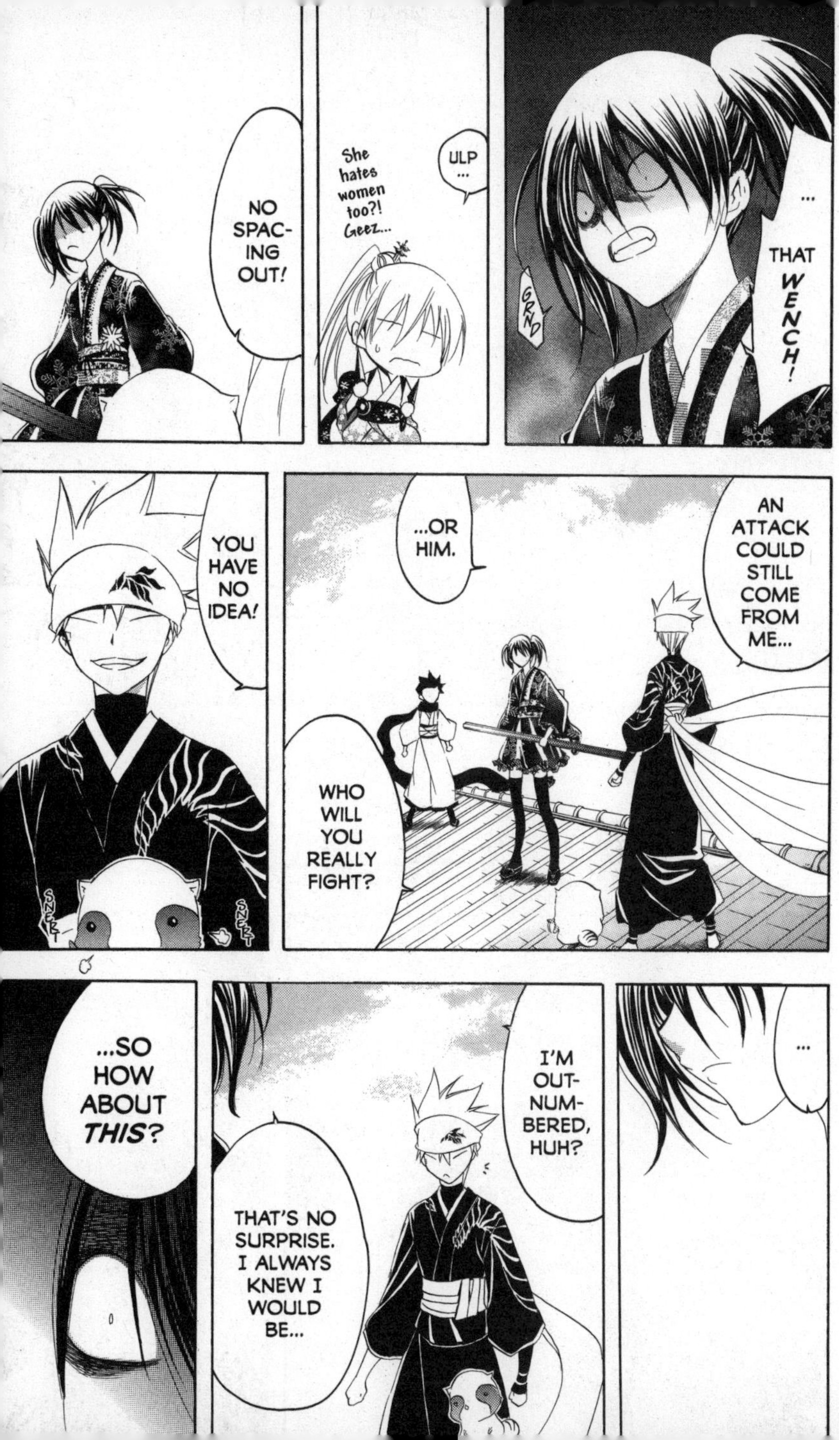
...
THAT WENCH!
GRND
ULP ...
She hates women too?! Geez...
NO SPACING OUT!
AN ATTACK COULD STILL COME FROM ME...
...OR HIM.
WHO WILL YOU REALLY FIGHT?
YOU HAVE NO IDEA!
SNERT
SNERT
...
I'M OUTNUMBERED, HUH?
THAT'S NO SURPRISE. I ALWAYS KNEW I WOULD BE...
...SO HOW ABOUT *THIS*?

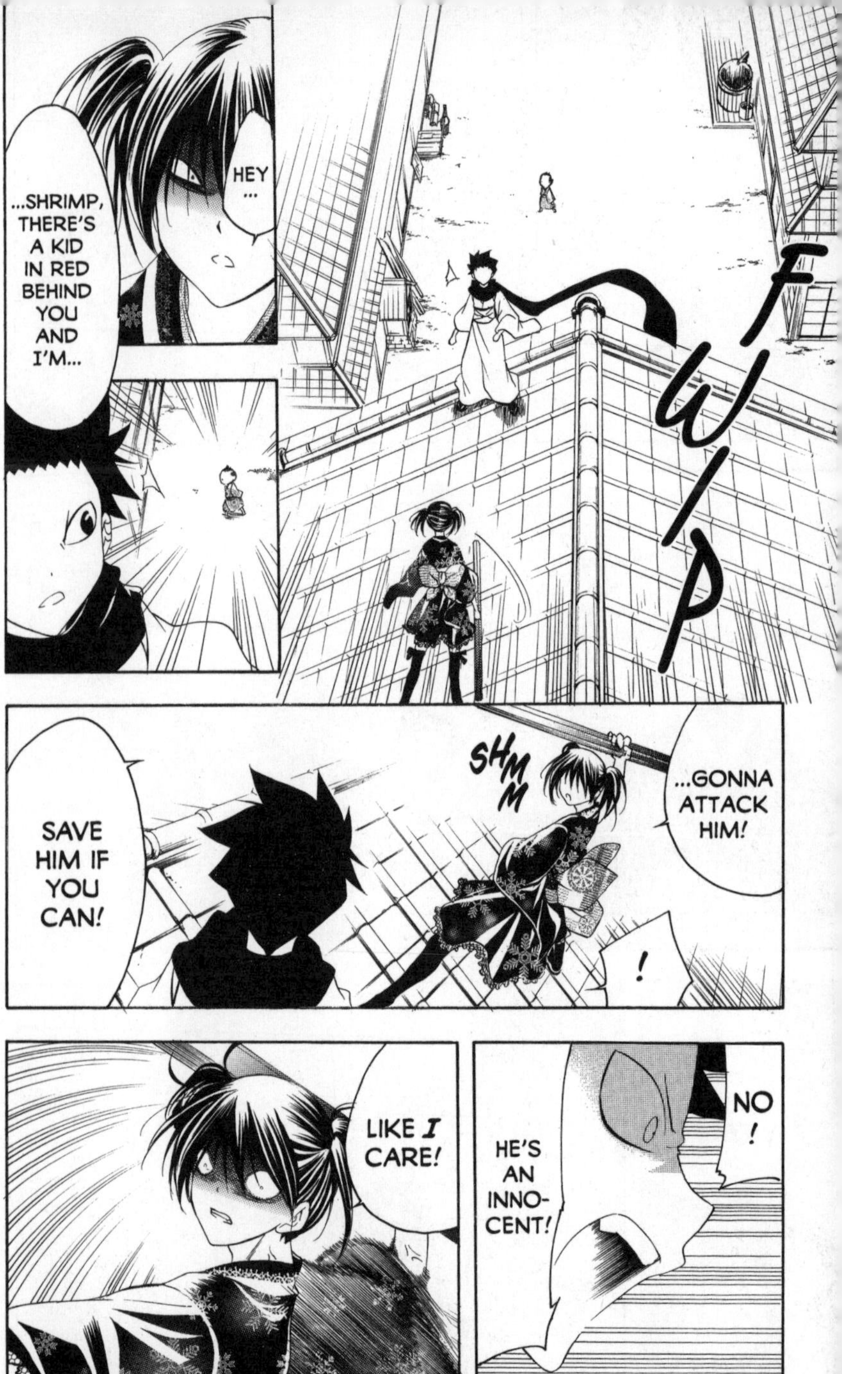
FWIP
HEY...
...SHRIMP, THERE'S A KID IN RED BEHIND YOU AND I'M...
...GONNA ATTACK HIM!
SHMMM
!
SAVE HIM IF YOU CAN!
NO!
HE'S AN INNO-CENT!
LIKE *I* CARE!

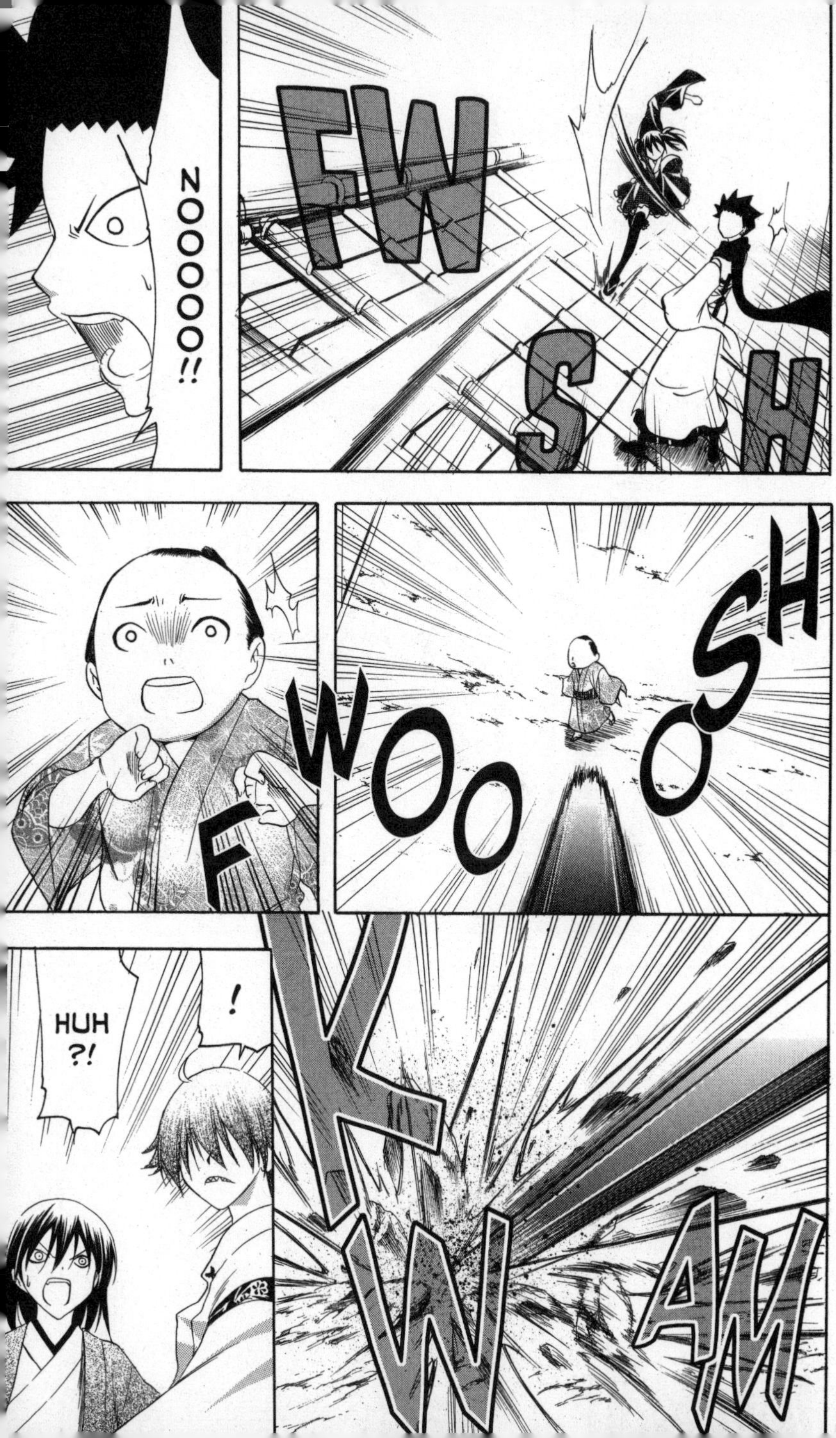
FWSH
NOOOOOO!!
FWOOOSH
HUH ?!
!
KWAM

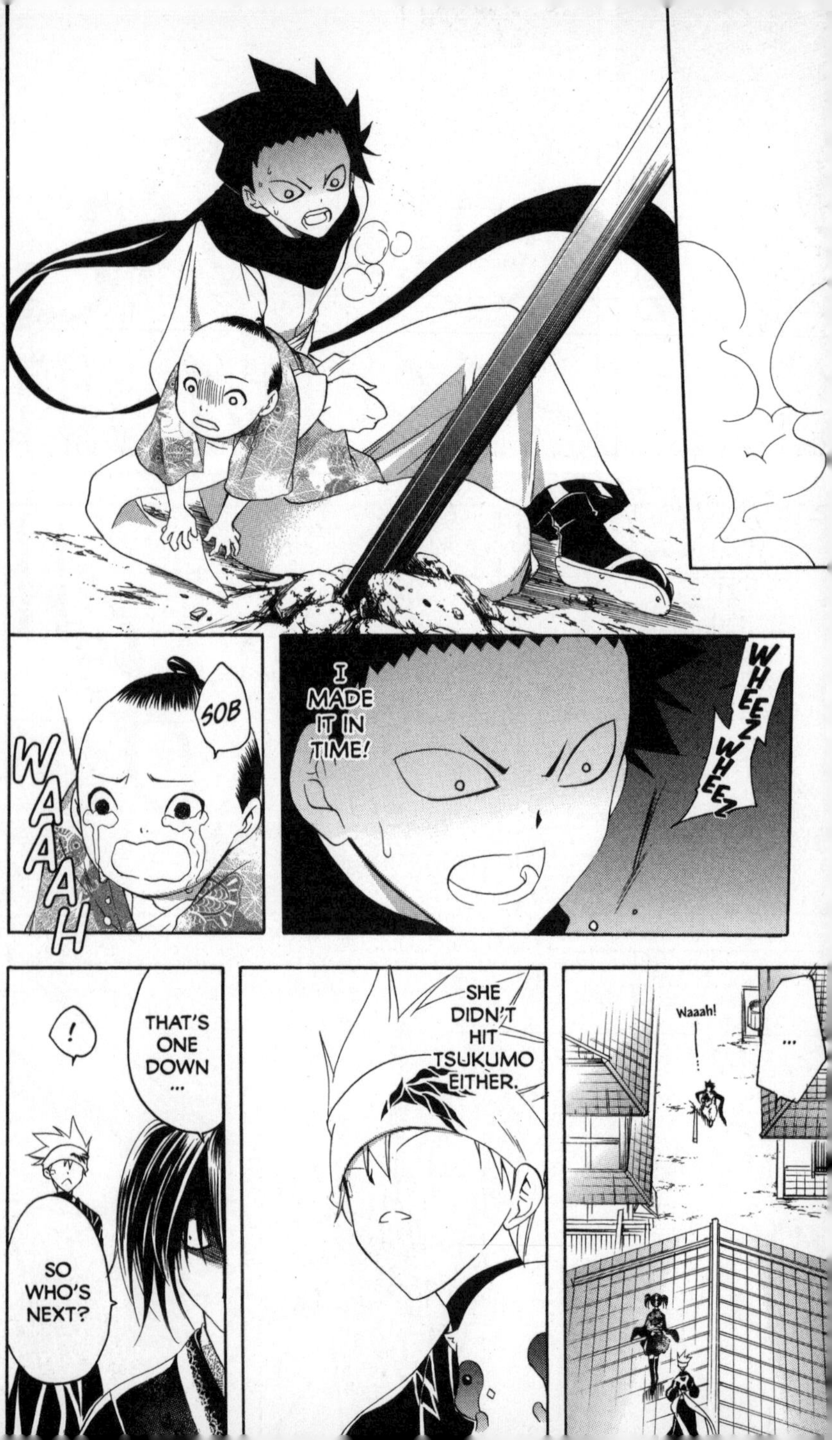
WHEEZ WHEEZ
I MADE IT IN TIME!
SOB
WAAAAH
Waaah!
...
SHE DIDN'T HIT TSUKUMO EITHER.
!
THAT'S ONE DOWN...
SO WHO'S NEXT?

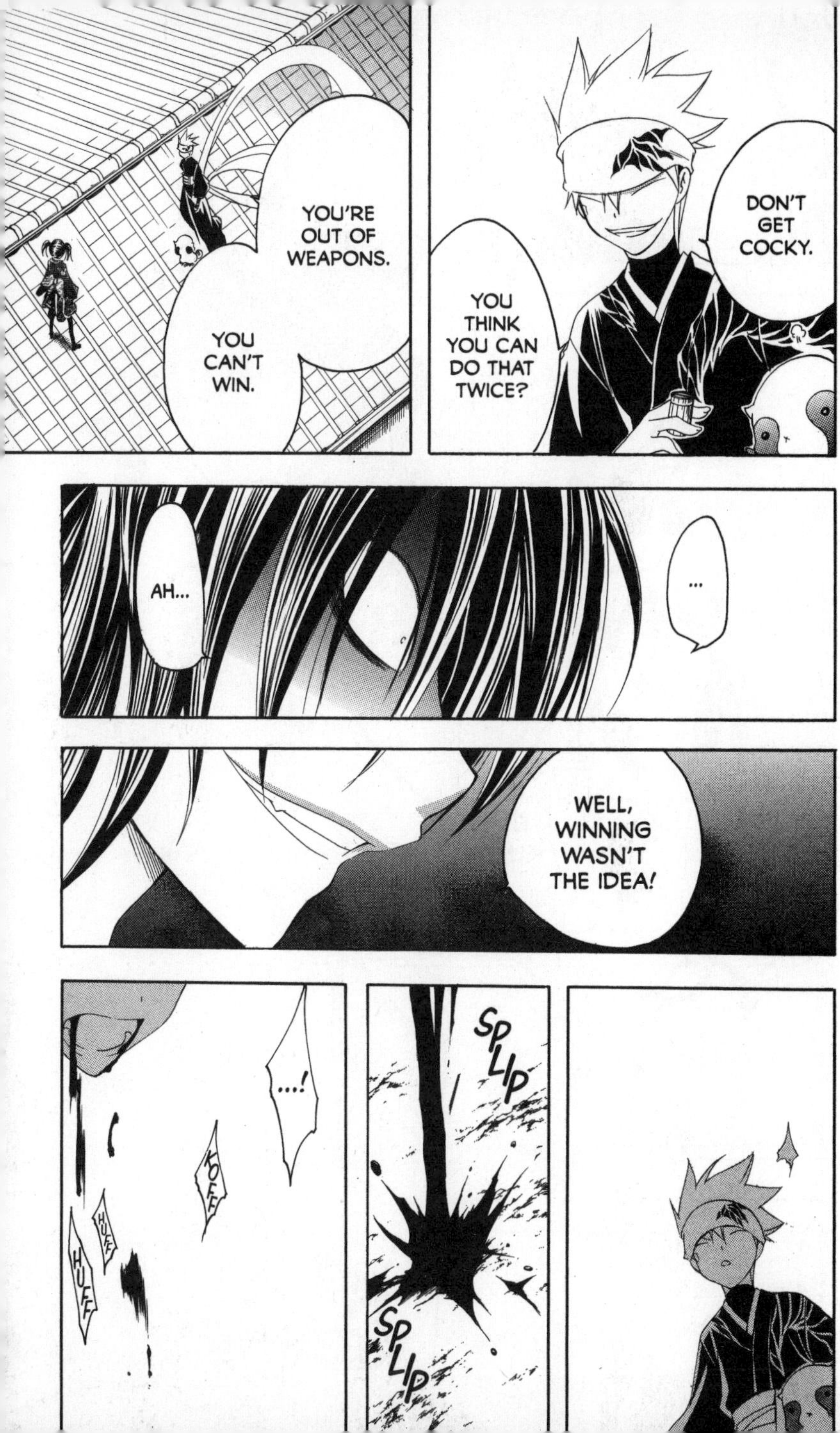
DON'T GET COCKY.
YOU THINK YOU CAN DO THAT TWICE?
YOU'RE OUT OF WEAPONS.
YOU CAN'T WIN.
...
AH...
WELL, WINNING WASN'T THE IDEA!
SPLIP
SPLIP
...!
KOFF
HUFF
HUFF

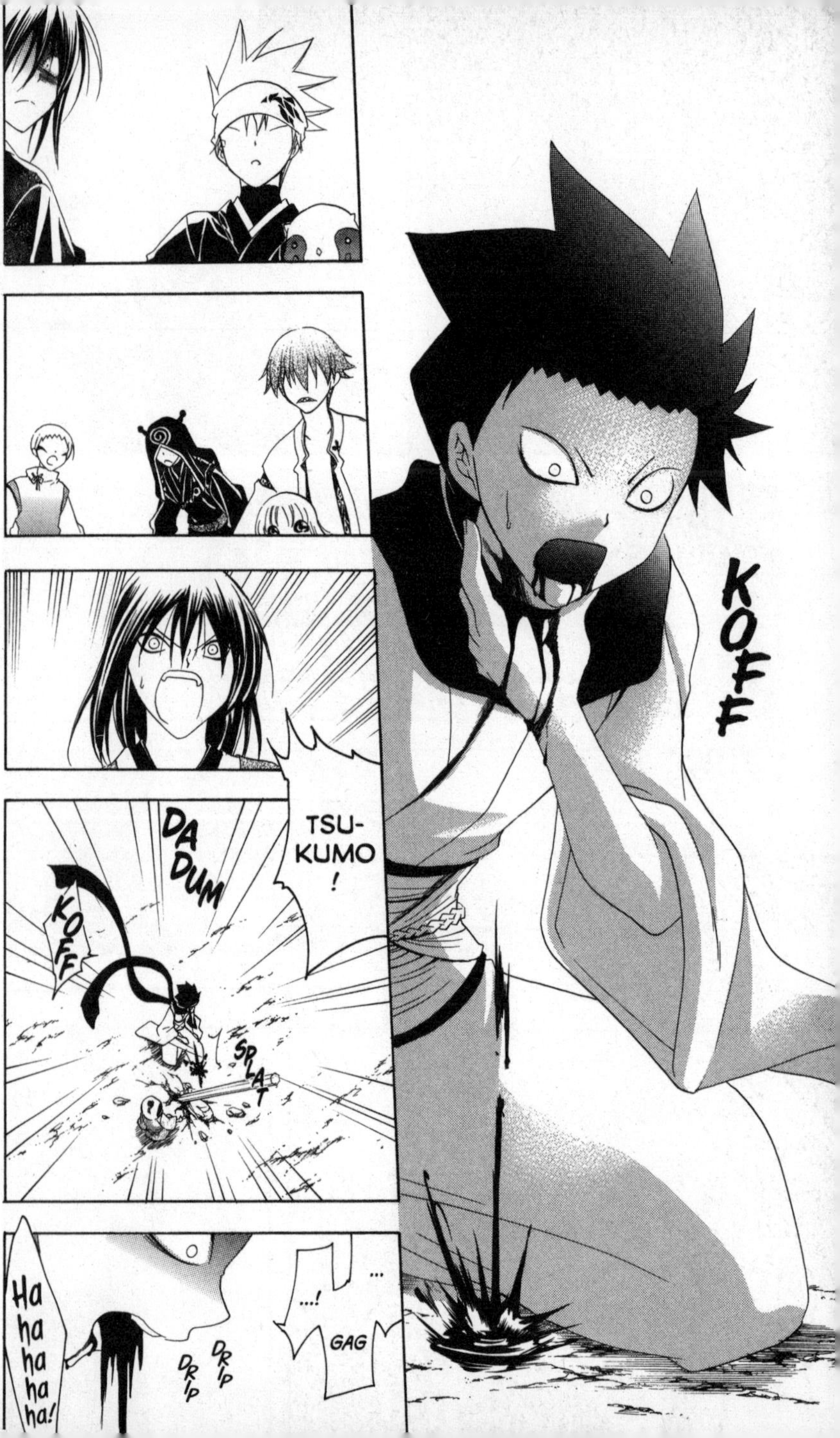
KOFF
TSU-KUMO!
DA DUM
KOFF
SPLAT
...
...!
GAG
DRIP DRIP
Ha ha ha ha ha!

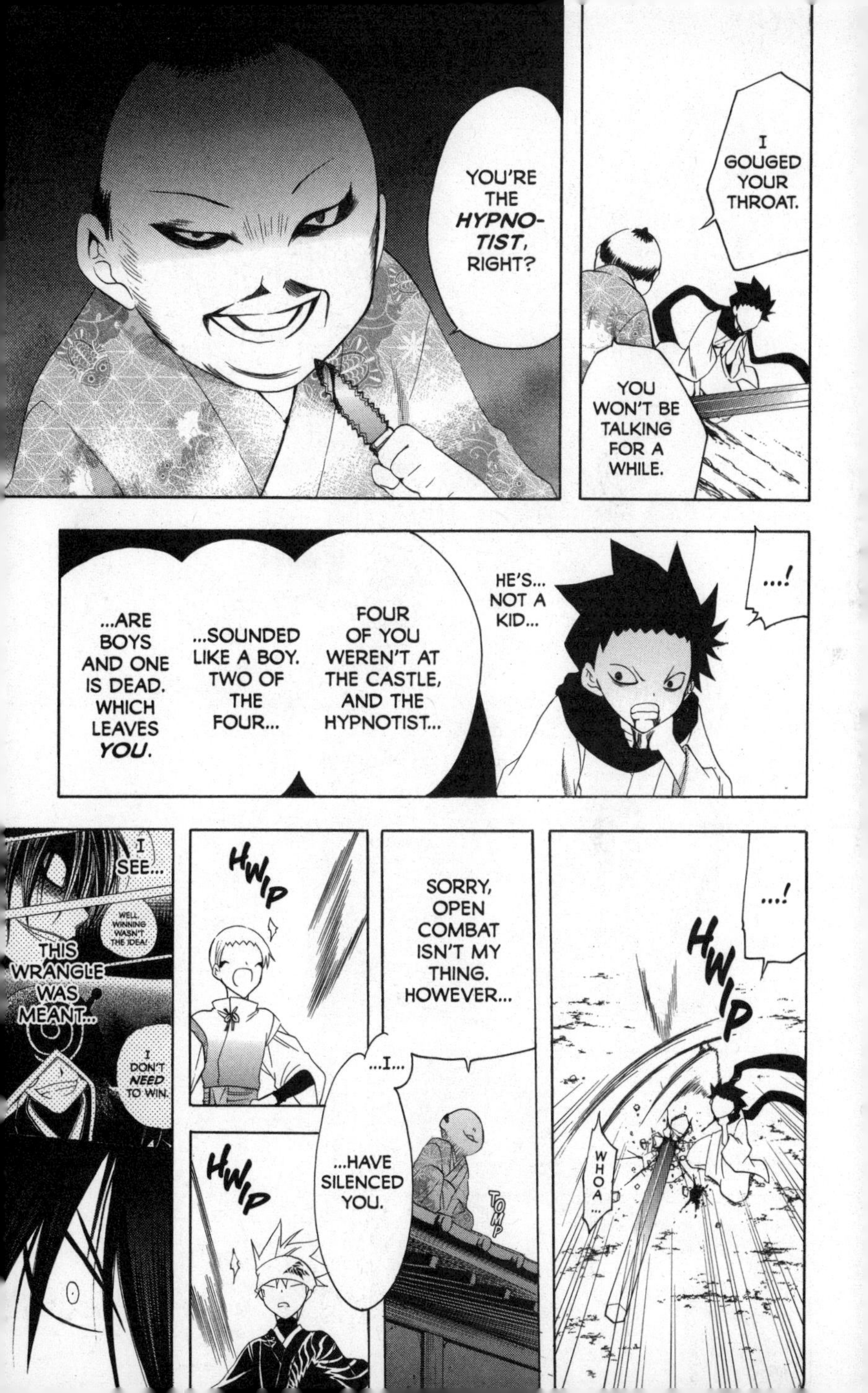
I GOUGED YOUR THROAT.
YOU WON'T BE TALKING FOR A WHILE.
YOU'RE THE *HYPNOTIST*, RIGHT?
...!
HE'S... NOT A KID...
FOUR OF YOU WEREN'T AT THE CASTLE, AND THE HYPNOTIST...
...SOUNDED LIKE A BOY. TWO OF THE FOUR...
...ARE BOYS AND ONE IS DEAD. WHICH LEAVES *YOU*.
...!
HWIP
WHOA...
SORRY, OPEN COMBAT ISN'T MY THING. HOWEVER...
HWIP
...I...
...HAVE SILENCED YOU.
TOMP
HWIP
I SEE...
WELL, WINNING WASN'T THE IDEA!
THIS WRANGLE WAS MEANT...
I DON'T *NEED* TO WIN.

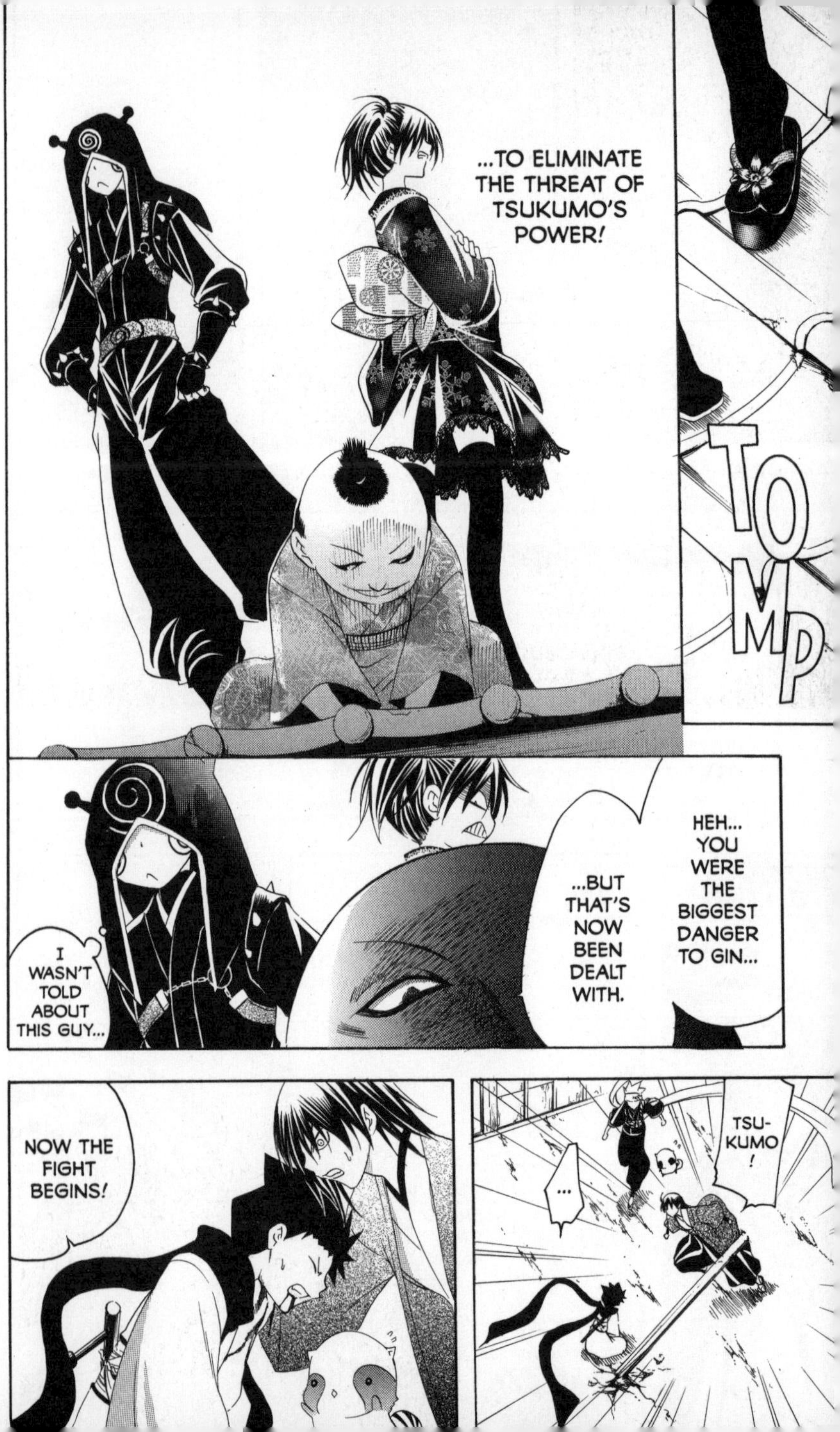
TOMP
...TO ELIMINATE THE THREAT OF TSUKUMO'S POWER!
HEH... YOU WERE THE BIGGEST DANGER TO GIN...
...BUT THAT'S NOW BEEN DEALT WITH.
I WASN'T TOLD ABOUT THIS GUY...
TSU-KUMO!
...
NOW THE FIGHT BEGINS!

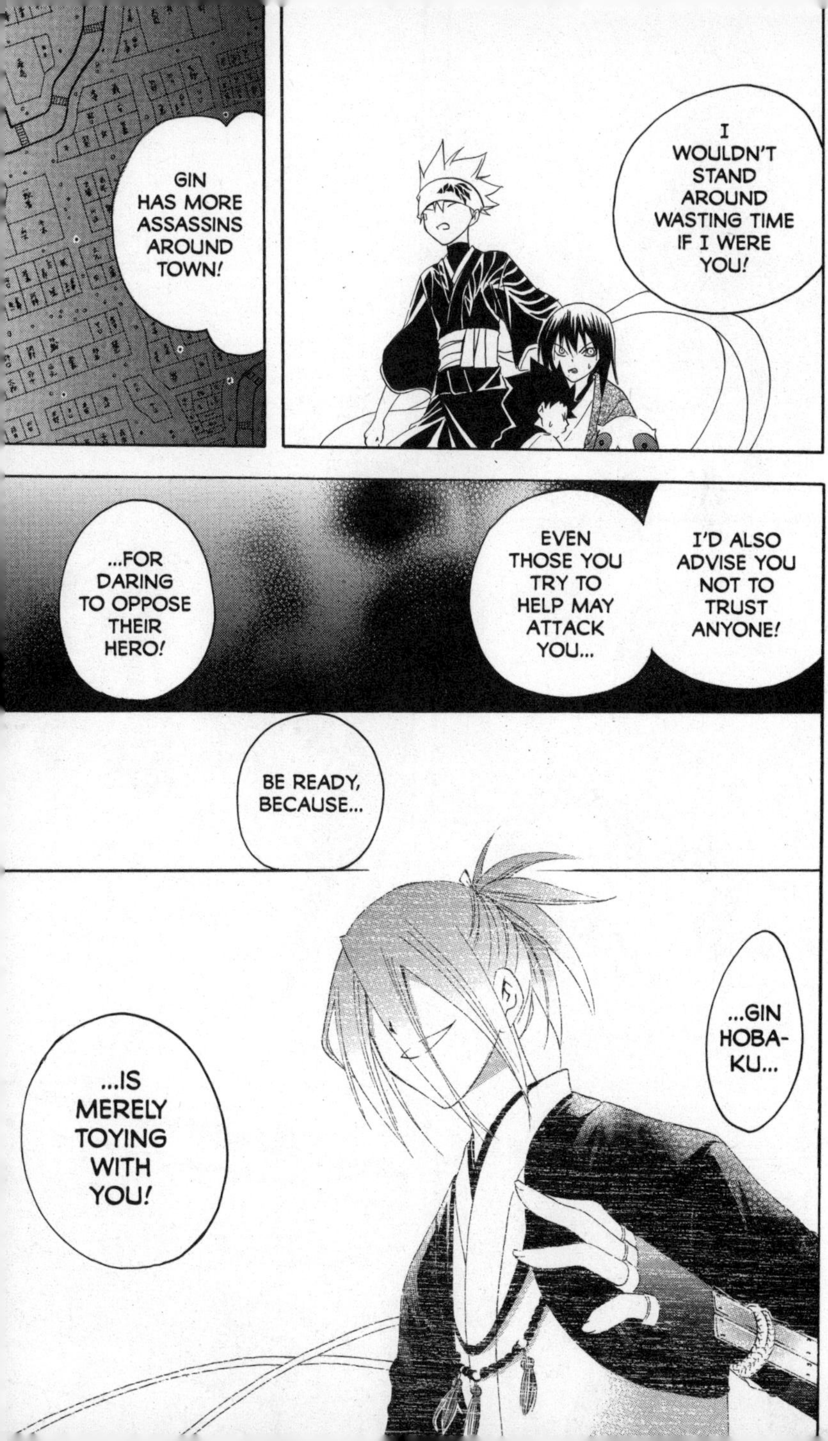
I WOULDN'T STAND AROUND WASTING TIME IF I WERE YOU!
GIN HAS MORE ASSASSINS AROUND TOWN!
I'D ALSO ADVISE YOU NOT TO TRUST ANYONE!
EVEN THOSE YOU TRY TO HELP MAY ATTACK YOU...
...FOR DARING TO OPPOSE THEIR HERO!
BE READY, BECAUSE...
...GIN HOBA-KU...
...IS MERELY TOYING WITH YOU!

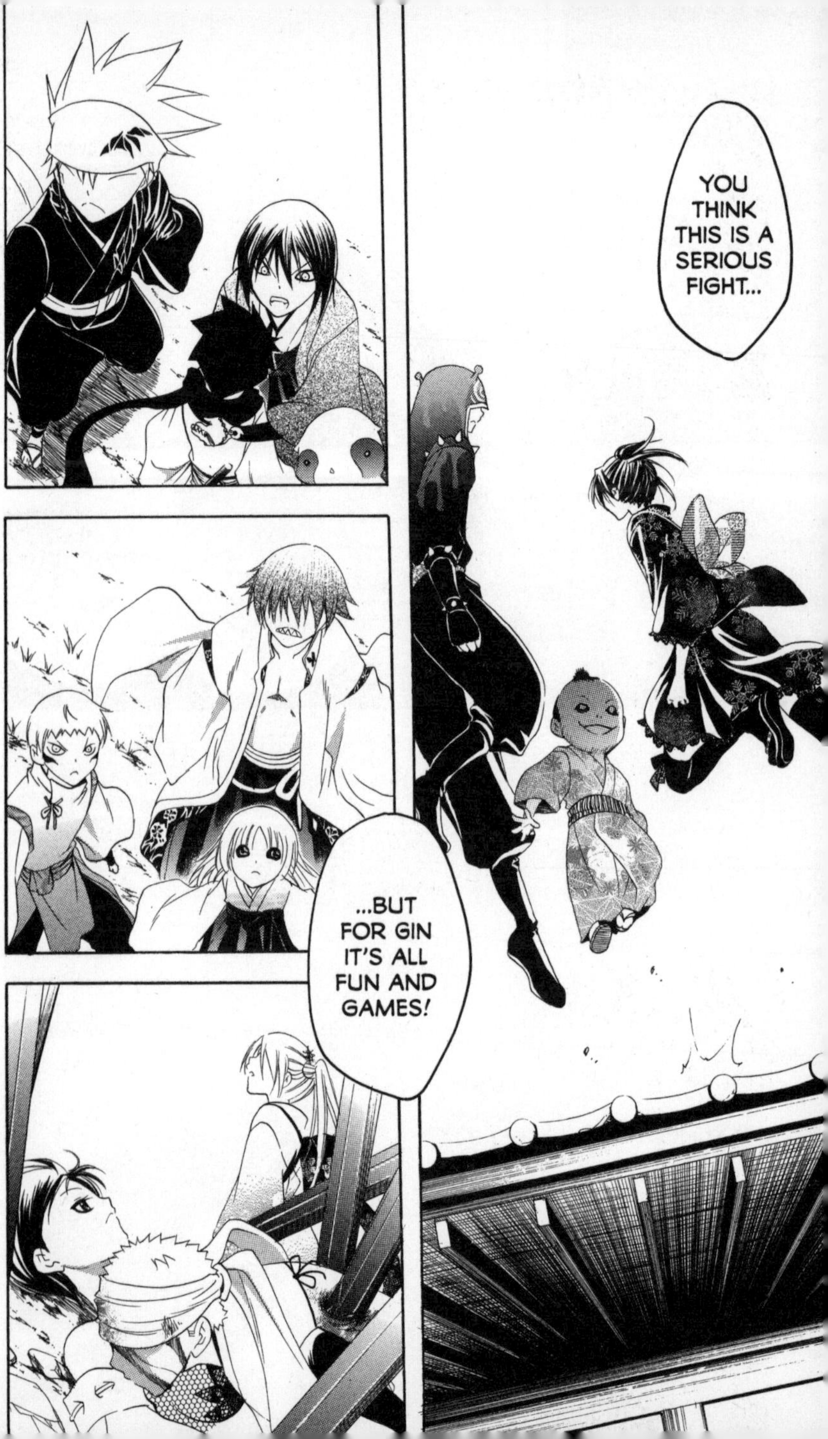
YOU THINK THIS IS A SERIOUS FIGHT...
...BUT FOR GIN IT'S ALL FUN AND GAMES!

Chapter 170 Neya vs. Rama

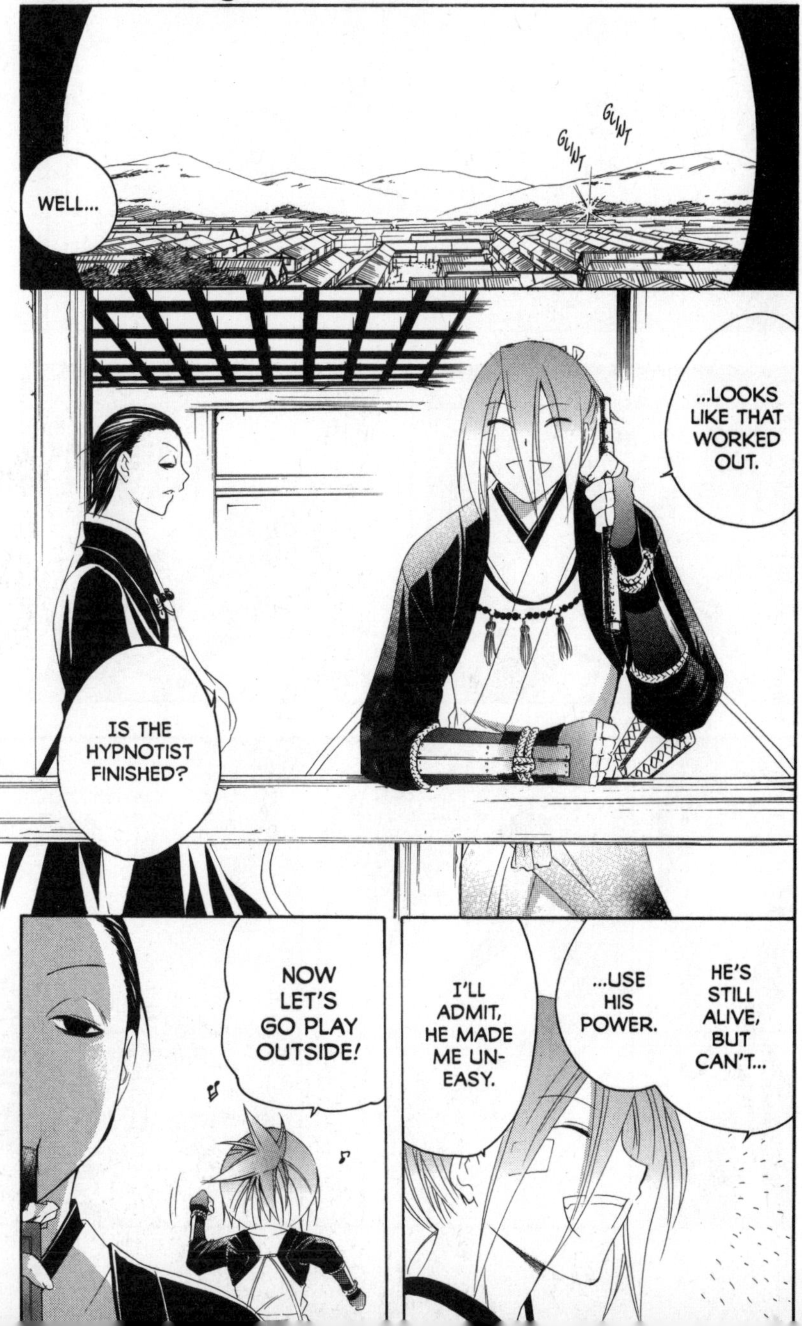
GLINT
GLINT
WELL...
...LOOKS LIKE THAT WORKED OUT.
IS THE HYPNOTIST FINISHED?
HE'S STILL ALIVE, BUT CAN'T...
...USE HIS POWER.
I'LL ADMIT, HE MADE ME UN-EASY.
NOW LET'S GO PLAY OUTSIDE!

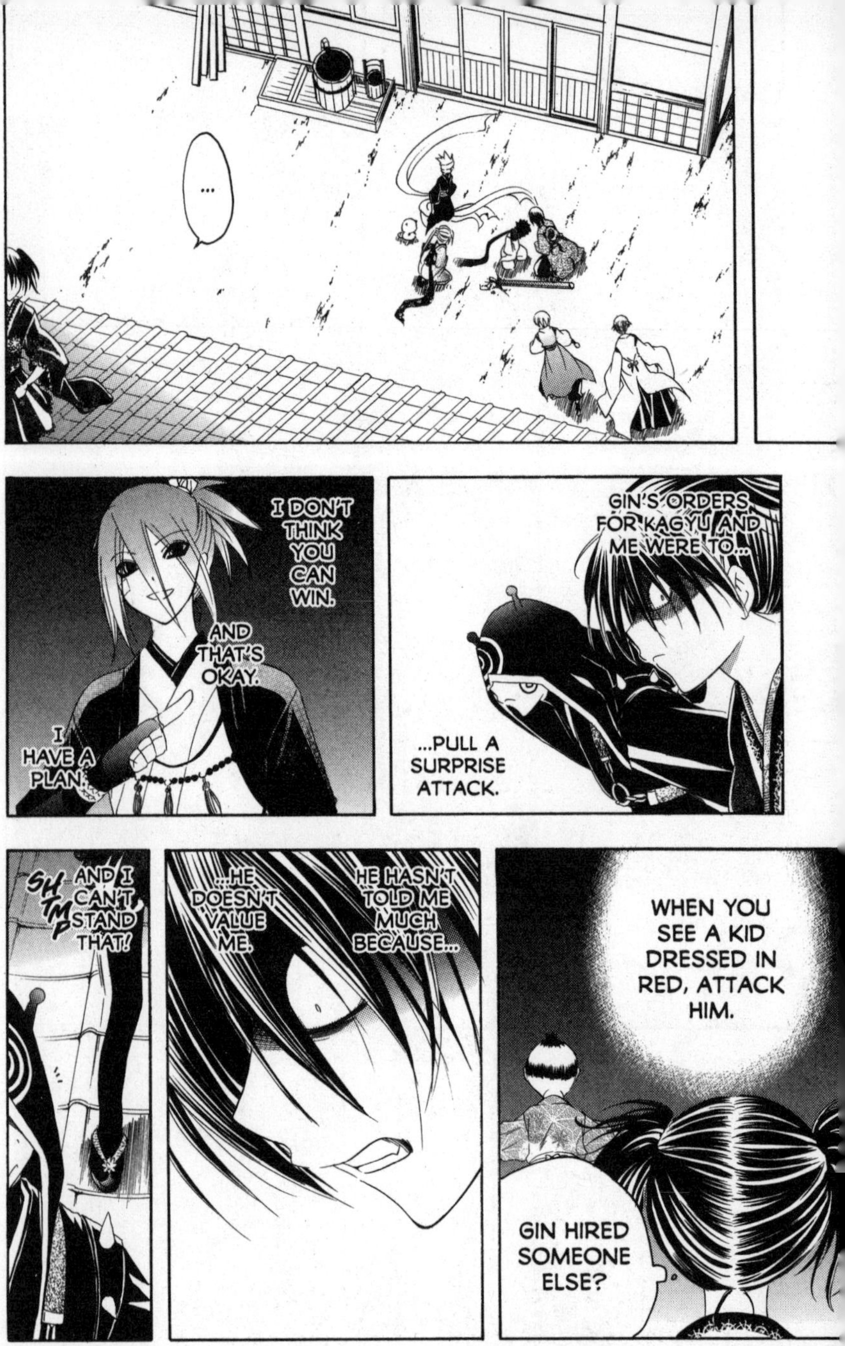
...
GIN'S ORDERS FOR KAGYU AND ME WERE TO...
...PULL A SURPRISE ATTACK.
I DON'T THINK YOU CAN WIN.
AND THAT'S OKAY.
I HAVE A PLAN.
WHEN YOU SEE A KID DRESSED IN RED, ATTACK HIM.
GIN HIRED SOMEONE ELSE?
HE HASN'T TOLD ME MUCH BECAUSE...
...HE DOESN'T VALUE ME.
AND I CAN'T STAND THAT!
SHTMP

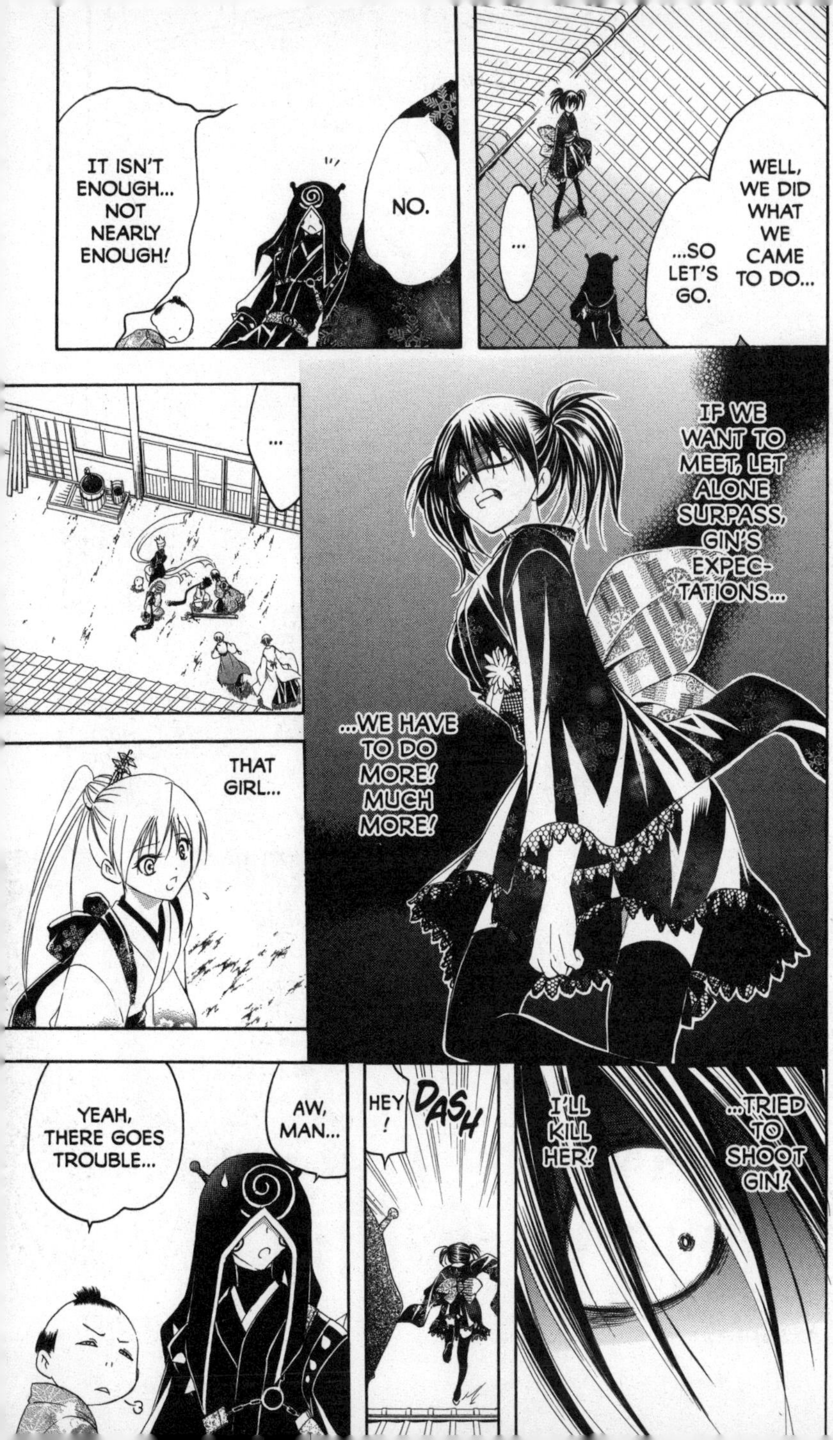
WELL, WE DID WHAT WE CAME TO DO...
...SO LET'S GO.
...
NO.
IT ISN'T ENOUGH... NOT NEARLY ENOUGH!
IF WE WANT TO MEET, LET ALONE SURPASS, GIN'S EXPECTATIONS...
...WE HAVE TO DO MORE! MUCH MORE!
...
THAT GIRL...
...TRIED TO SHOOT GIN!
I'LL KILL HER!
DASH
HEY!
AW, MAN...
YEAH, THERE GOES TROUBLE...

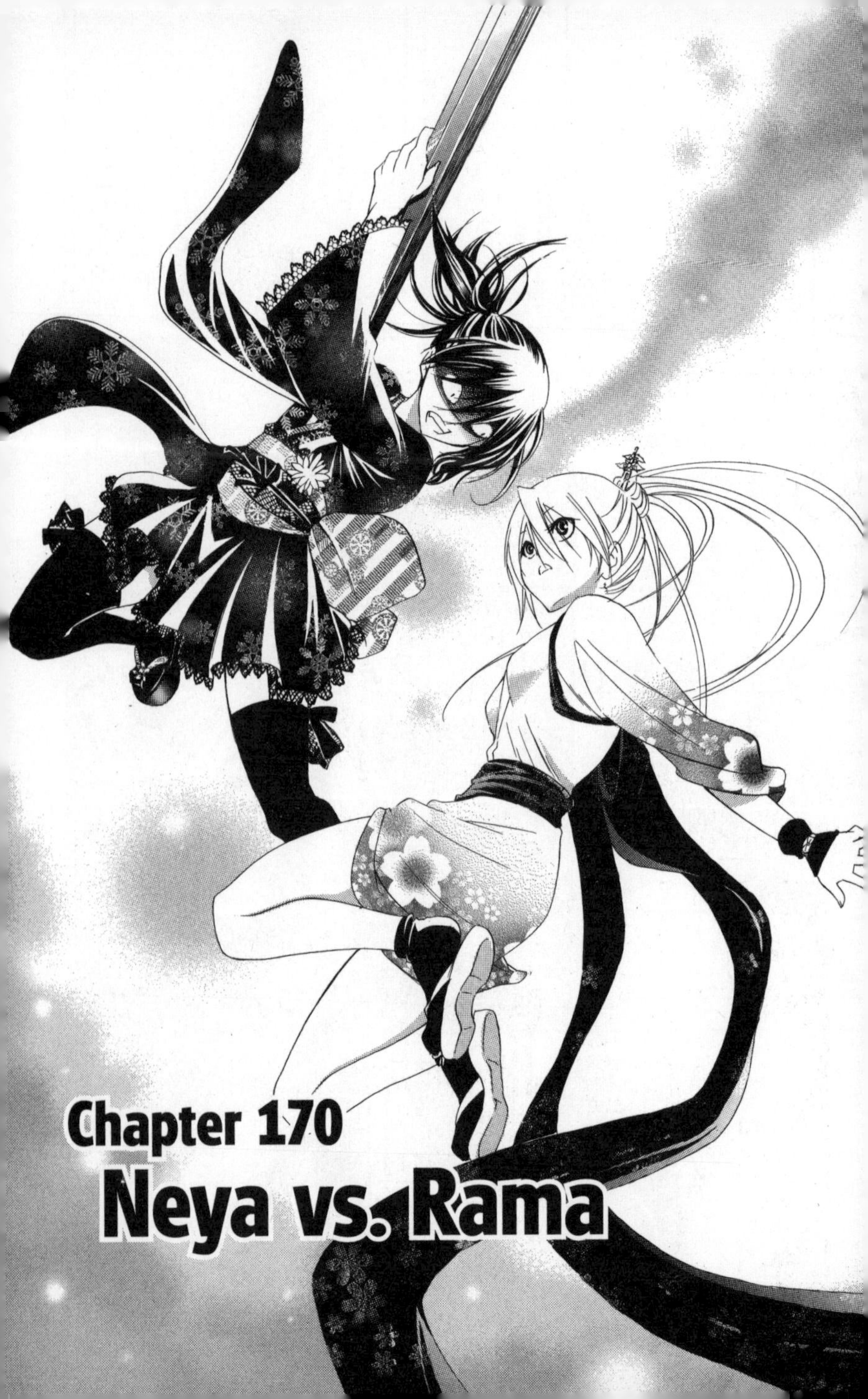
Chapter 170
Neya vs. Rama

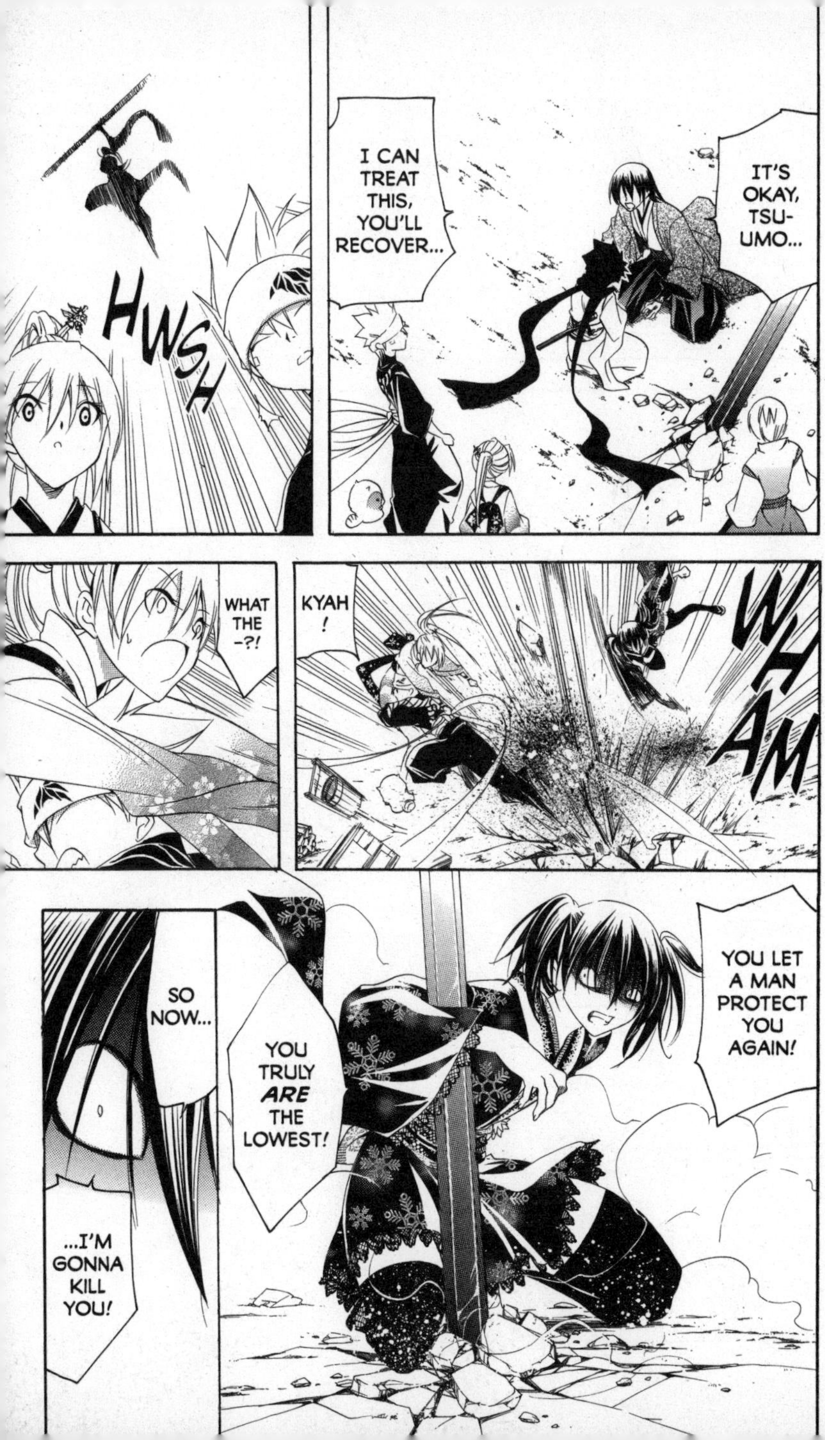
IT'S OKAY, TSU-UMO...
I CAN TREAT THIS, YOU'LL RECOVER...
HWSH
WHAM
KYAH!
WHAT THE -?!
YOU LET A MAN PROTECT YOU AGAIN!
YOU TRULY ***ARE*** THE LOWEST!
SO NOW...
...I'M GONNA KILL YOU!

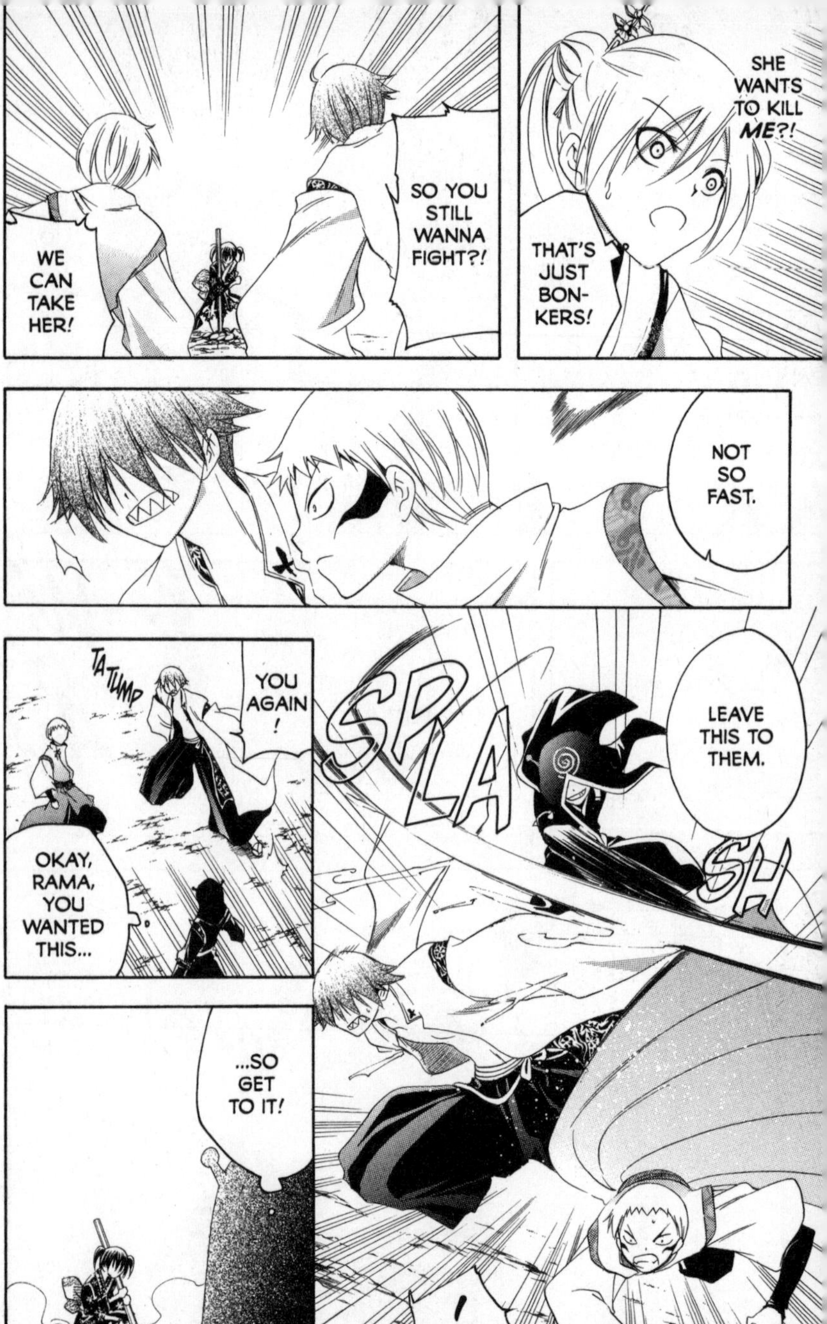
SHE WANTS TO KILL *ME*?!
THAT'S JUST BON-KERS!
SO YOU STILL WANNA FIGHT?!
WE CAN TAKE HER!
NOT SO FAST.
LEAVE THIS TO THEM.
SPLA
SH
!
YOU AGAIN!
TA-TUMP
OKAY, RAMA, YOU WANTED THIS...
...SO GET TO IT!

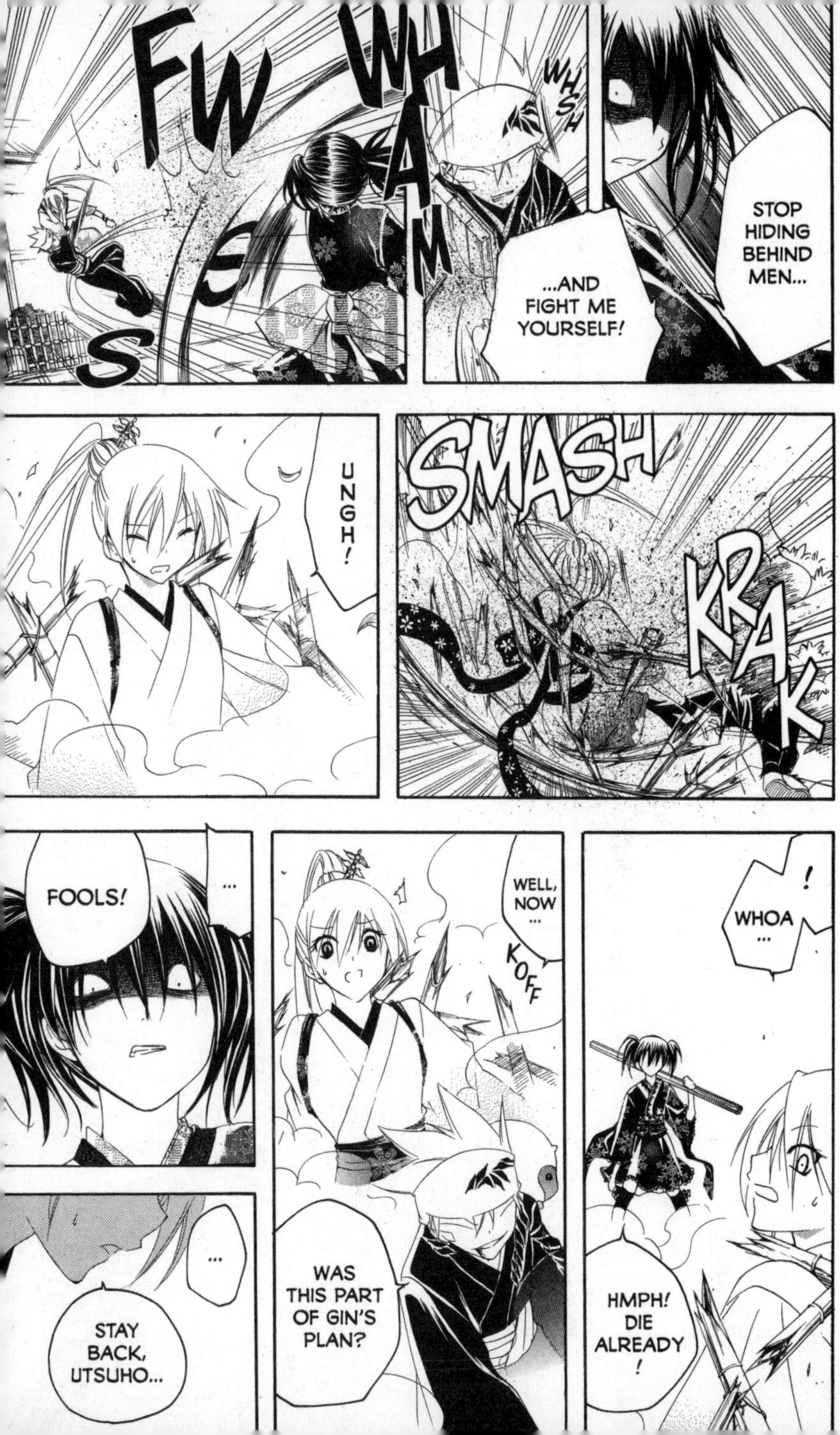
STOP HIDING BEHIND MEN...
...AND FIGHT ME YOURSELF!
WHSH
WHAM
FW
SSS
SMASH
KRAK
UNGH!
!
WHOA...
HMPH! DIE ALREADY!
WELL, NOW...
KOFF
WAS THIS PART OF GIN'S PLAN?
...
FOOLS!
...
STAY BACK, UTSUHO...

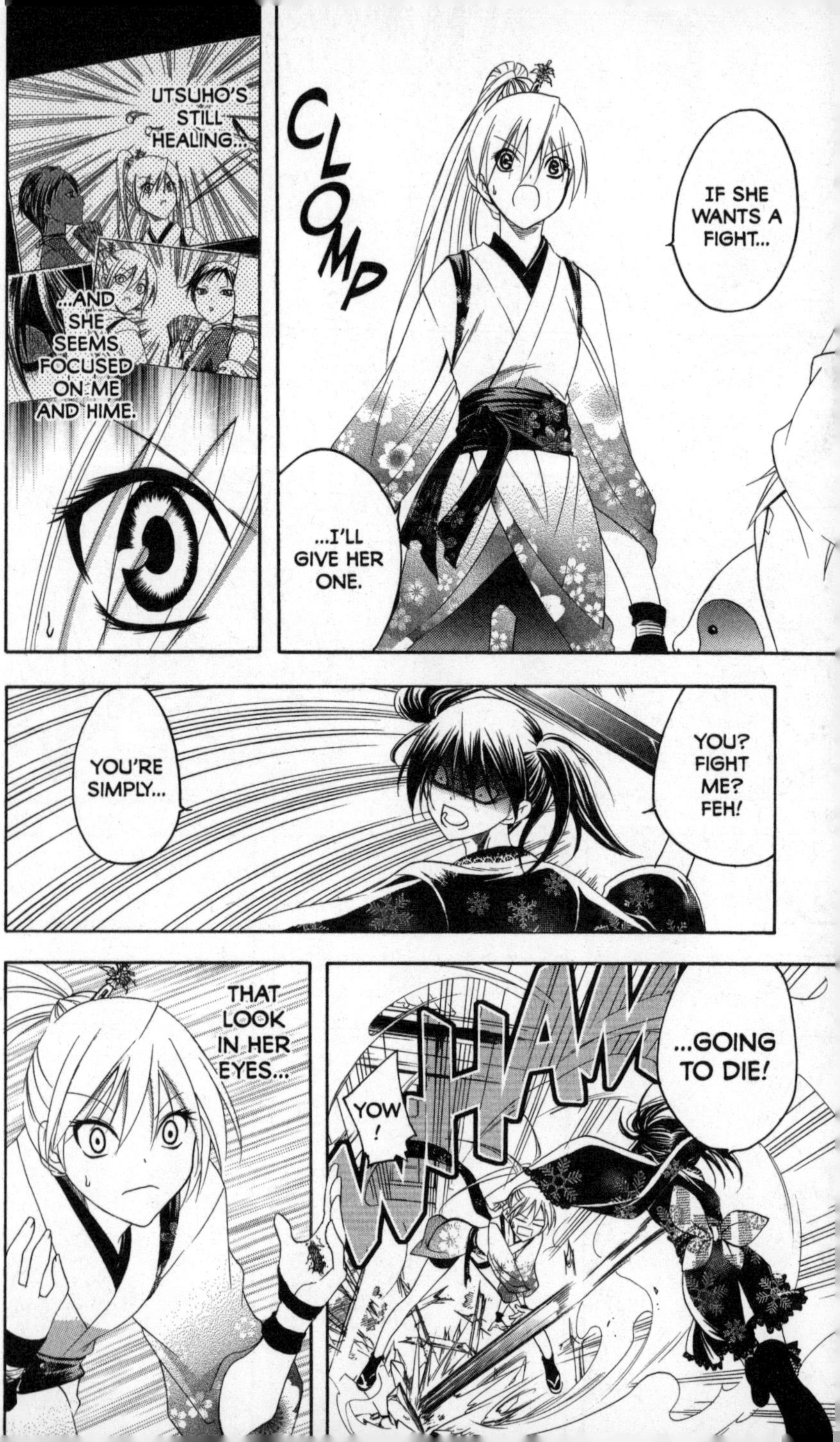
IF SHE WANTS A FIGHT...
CLOMP
...I'LL GIVE HER ONE.
UTSUHO'S STILL HEALING...
...AND SHE SEEMS FOCUSED ON ME AND HIME.
YOU? FIGHT ME? FEH!
YOU'RE SIMPLY...
...GOING TO DIE!
WHAM
YOW!
THAT LOOK IN HER EYES...

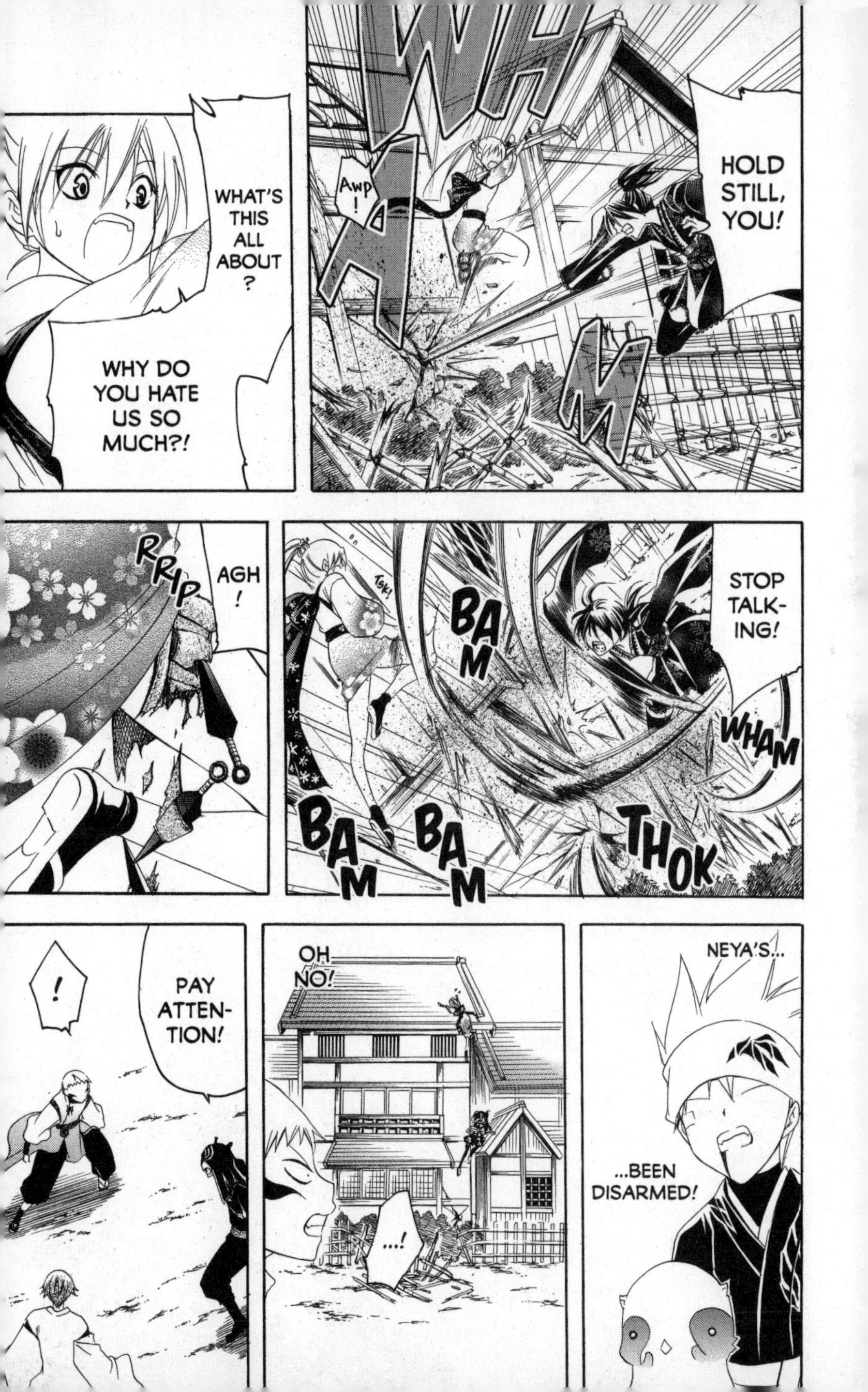
HOLD STILL, YOU!
WHAM
Awp!
WHAT'S THIS ALL ABOUT?
WHY DO YOU HATE US SO MUCH?!
STOP TALKING!
TSK!
BAM
WHAM
THOK
BAM
BAM
AGH!
RRIP
NEYA'S...
...BEEN DISARMED!
OH NO!
....!
PAY ATTENTION!
!

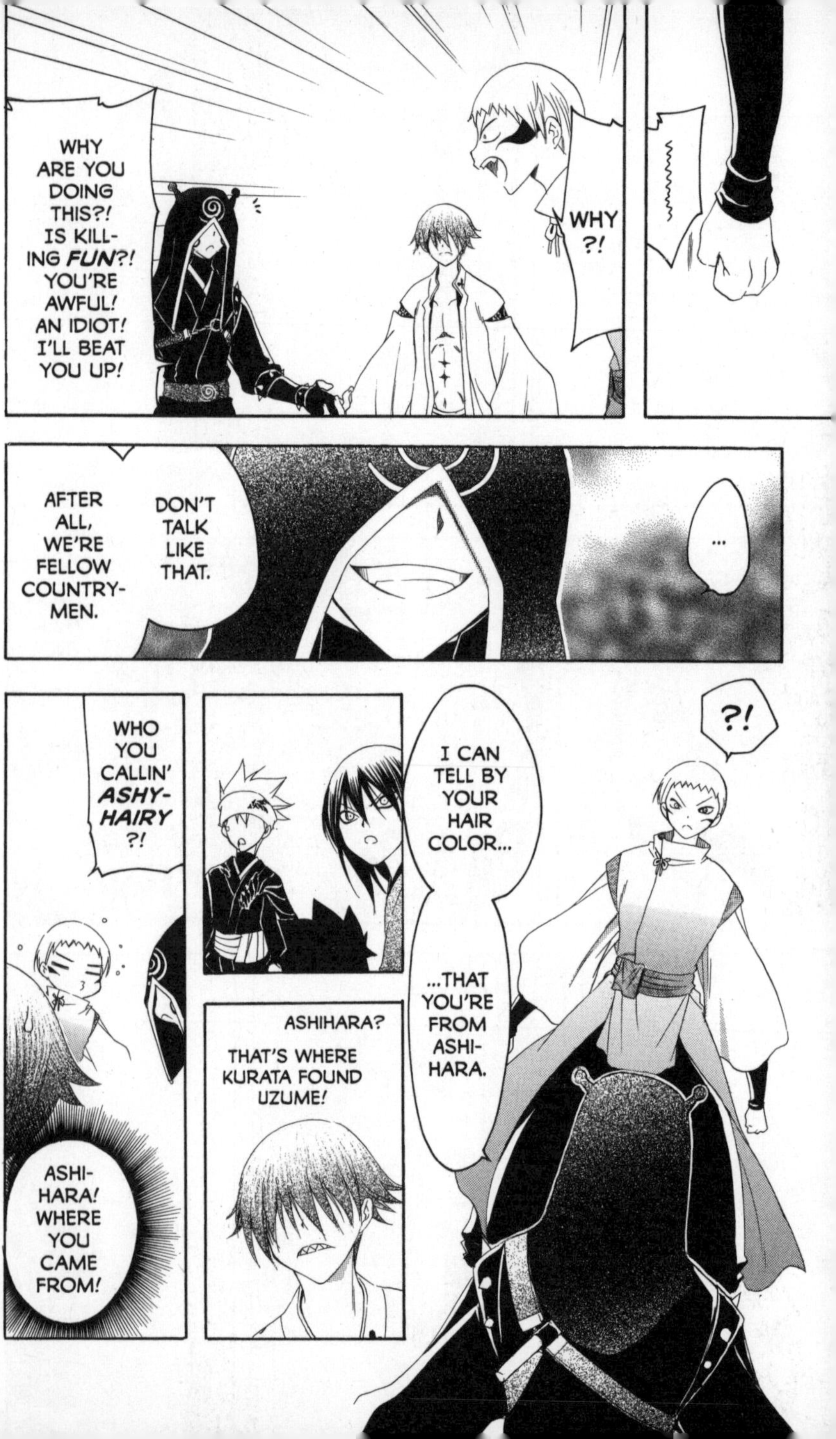
WHY ?!
WHY ARE YOU DOING THIS?! IS KILLING FUN?! YOU'RE AWFUL! AN IDIOT! I'LL BEAT YOU UP!
...
DON'T TALK LIKE THAT.
AFTER ALL, WE'RE FELLOW COUNTRYMEN.
?!
I CAN TELL BY YOUR HAIR COLOR...
...THAT YOU'RE FROM ASHIHARA.
ASHIHARA?
THAT'S WHERE KURATA FOUND UZUME!
WHO YOU CALLIN' ASHY-HAIRY?!
ASHIHARA! WHERE YOU CAME FROM!

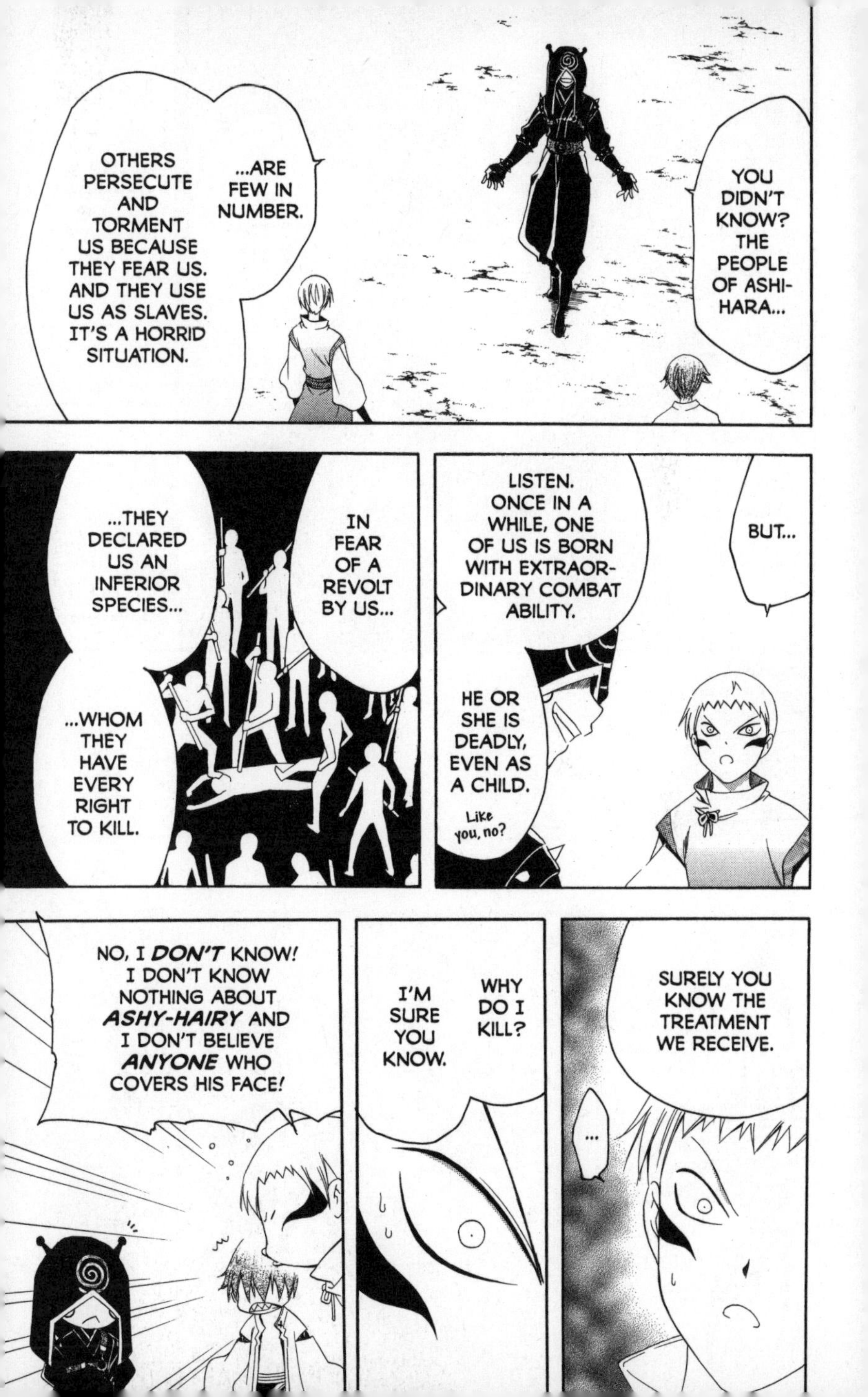
YOU DIDN'T KNOW? THE PEOPLE OF ASHI-HARA...
...ARE FEW IN NUMBER.
OTHERS PERSECUTE AND TORMENT US BECAUSE THEY FEAR US. AND THEY USE US AS SLAVES. IT'S A HORRID SITUATION.
BUT...
LISTEN. ONCE IN A WHILE, ONE OF US IS BORN WITH EXTRAOR-DINARY COMBAT ABILITY.
HE OR SHE IS DEADLY, EVEN AS A CHILD.
Like you, no?
IN FEAR OF A REVOLT BY US...
...THEY DECLARED US AN INFERIOR SPECIES...
...WHOM THEY HAVE EVERY RIGHT TO KILL.
SURELY YOU KNOW THE TREATMENT WE RECEIVE.
...
WHY DO I KILL?
I'M SURE YOU KNOW.
NO, I *DON'T* KNOW! I DON'T KNOW NOTHING ABOUT *ASHY-HAIRY* AND I DON'T BELIEVE *ANYONE* WHO COVERS HIS FACE!

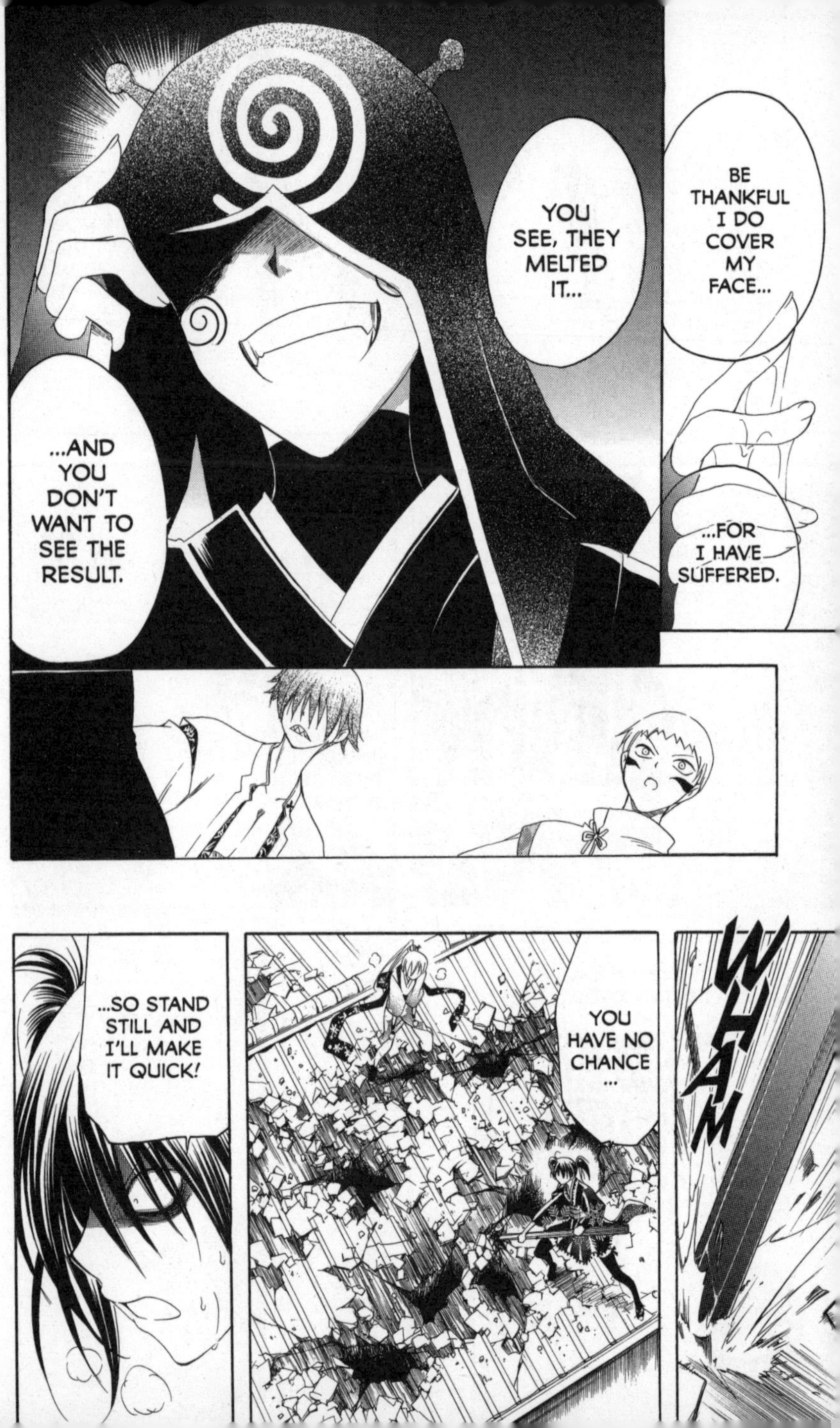
BE THANKFUL I DO COVER MY FACE...
...FOR I HAVE SUFFERED.
YOU SEE, THEY MELTED IT...
...AND YOU DON'T WANT TO SEE THE RESULT.
WHAM
YOU HAVE NO CHANCE ...
...SO STAND STILL AND I'LL MAKE IT QUICK!

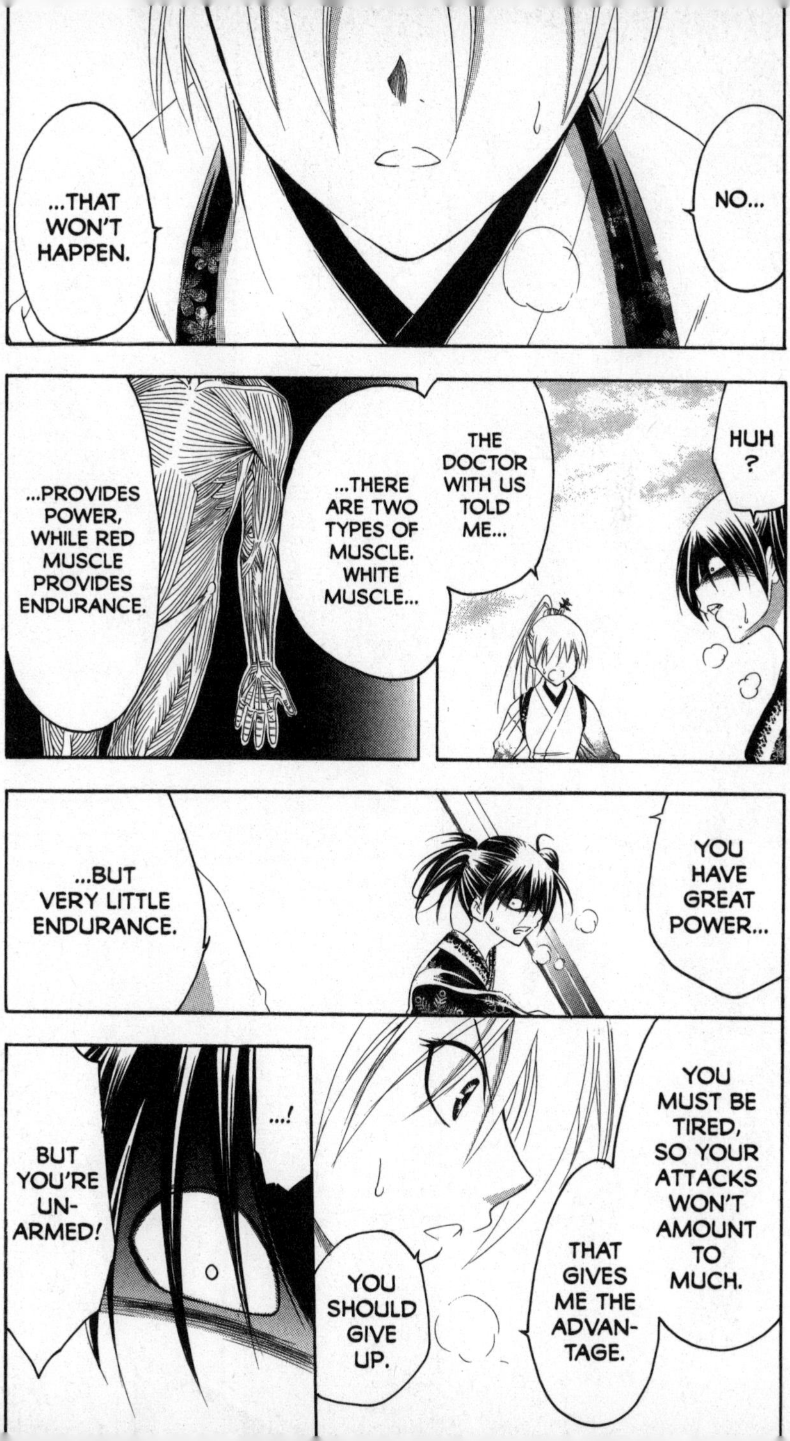
NO...
...THAT WON'T HAPPEN.
HUH?
THE DOCTOR WITH US TOLD ME...
...THERE ARE TWO TYPES OF MUSCLE. WHITE MUSCLE...
...PROVIDES POWER, WHILE RED MUSCLE PROVIDES ENDURANCE.
YOU HAVE GREAT POWER...
...BUT VERY LITTLE ENDURANCE.
YOU MUST BE TIRED, SO YOUR ATTACKS WON'T AMOUNT TO MUCH.
THAT GIVES ME THE ADVAN-TAGE.
YOU SHOULD GIVE UP.
...!
BUT YOU'RE UN-ARMED!

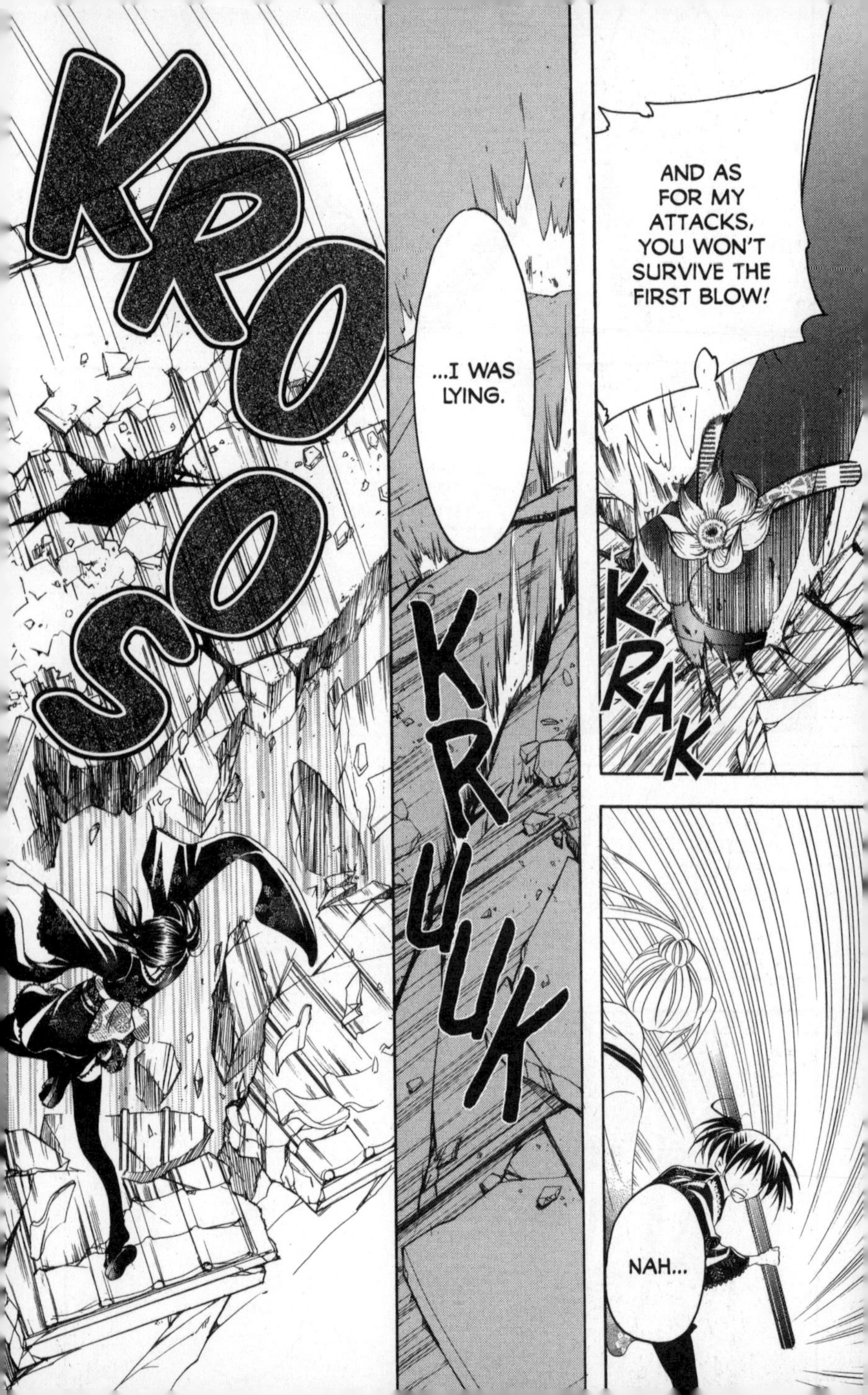
AND AS FOR MY ATTACKS, YOU WON'T SURVIVE THE FIRST BLOW!
KRAK
NAH...
...I WAS LYING.
KRRUUK
KROOS

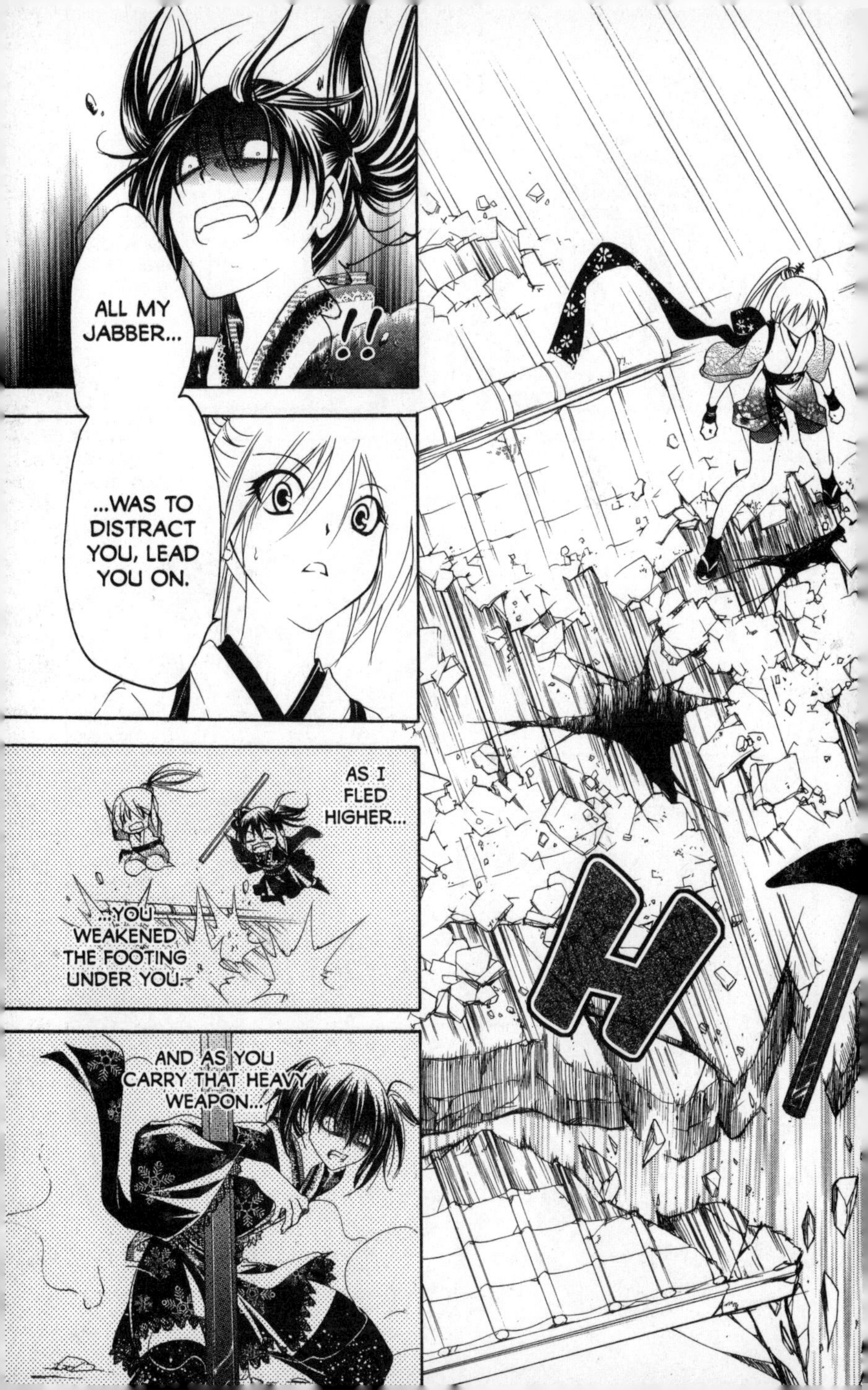
H
ALL MY JABBER...
!!
...WAS TO DISTRACT YOU, LEAD YOU ON.
AS I FLED HIGHER...
...YOU WEAKENED THE FOOTING UNDER YOU.
AND AS YOU CARRY THAT HEAVY WEAPON...

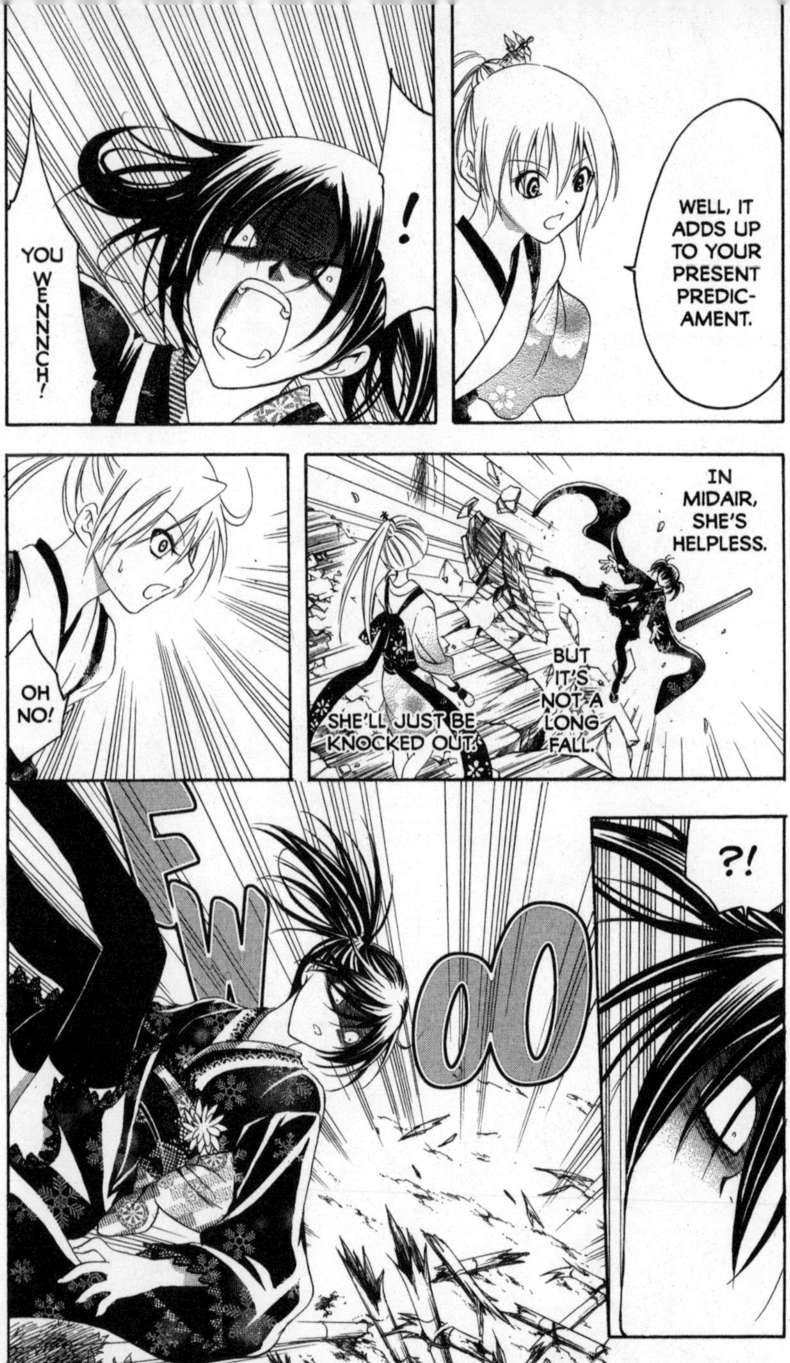
WELL, IT ADDS UP TO YOUR PRESENT PREDIC-AMENT.
!
YOU WENNNCH!
IN MIDAIR, SHE'S HELPLESS.
BUT IT'S NOT A LONG FALL.
SHE'LL JUST BE KNOCKED OUT.
OH NO!
?!
FWOOO

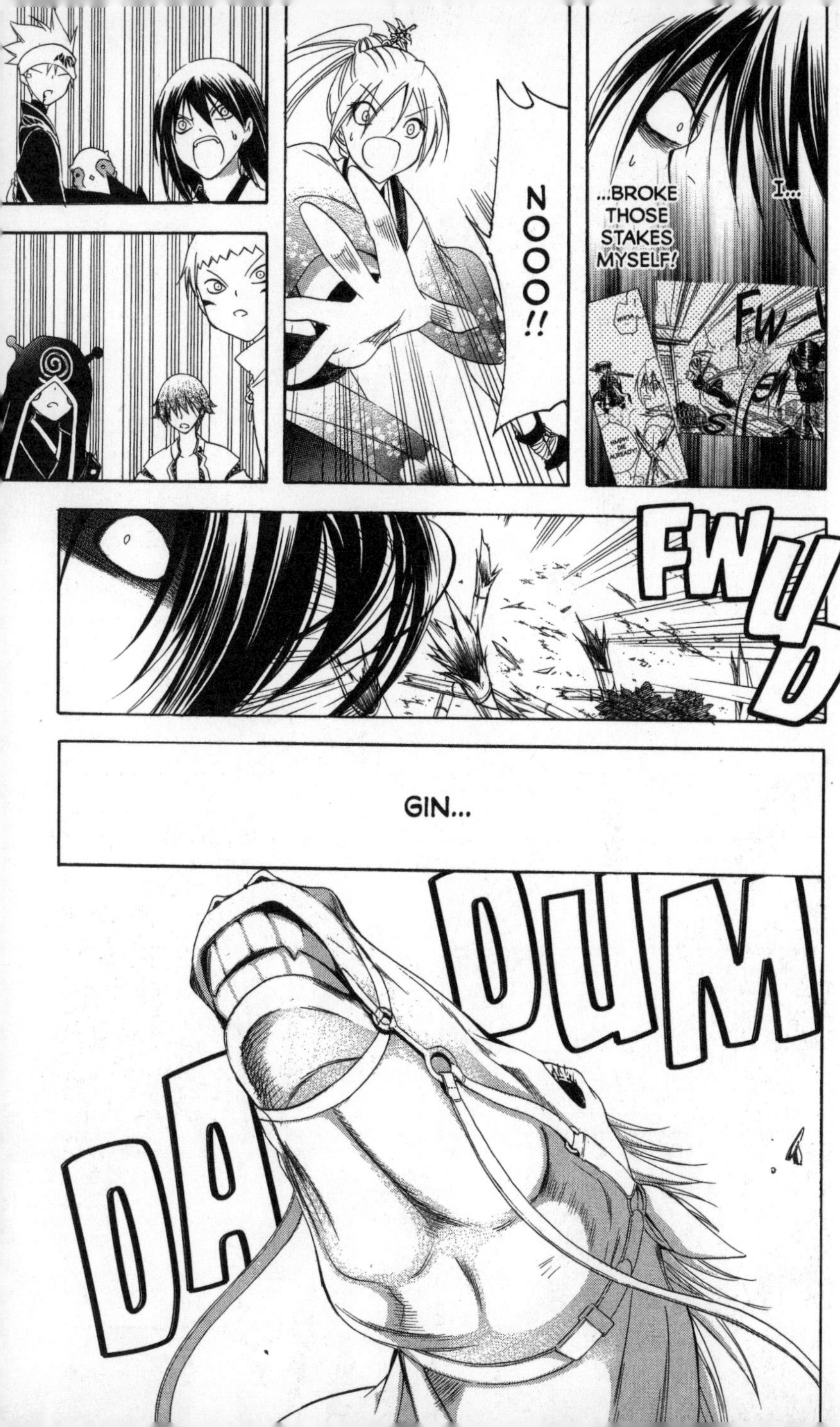
I...
...BROKE THOSE STAKES MYSELF!
FW
NOOOO!!
FWUD
GIN...
DA
DUM

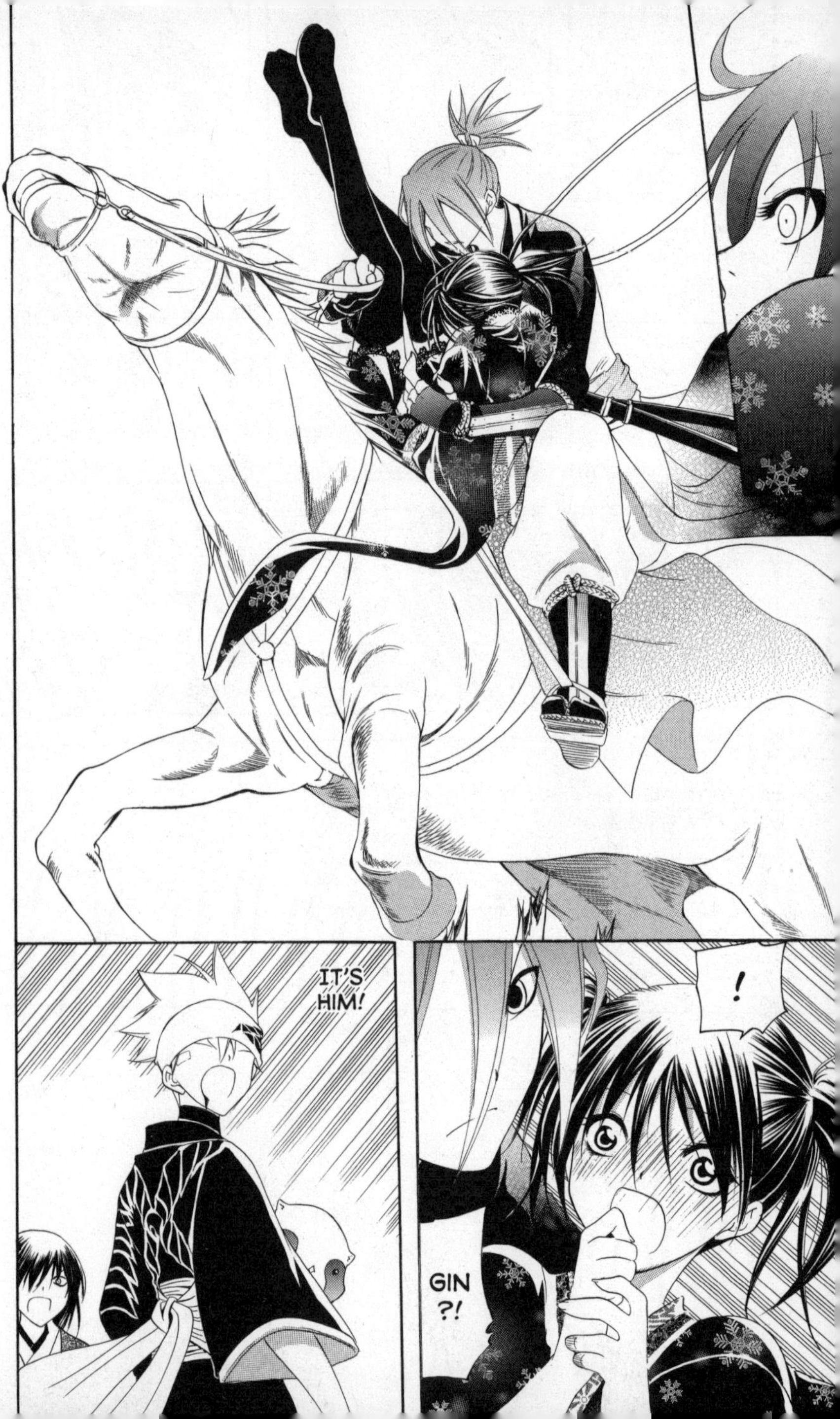
!
GIN ?!
IT'S HIM!

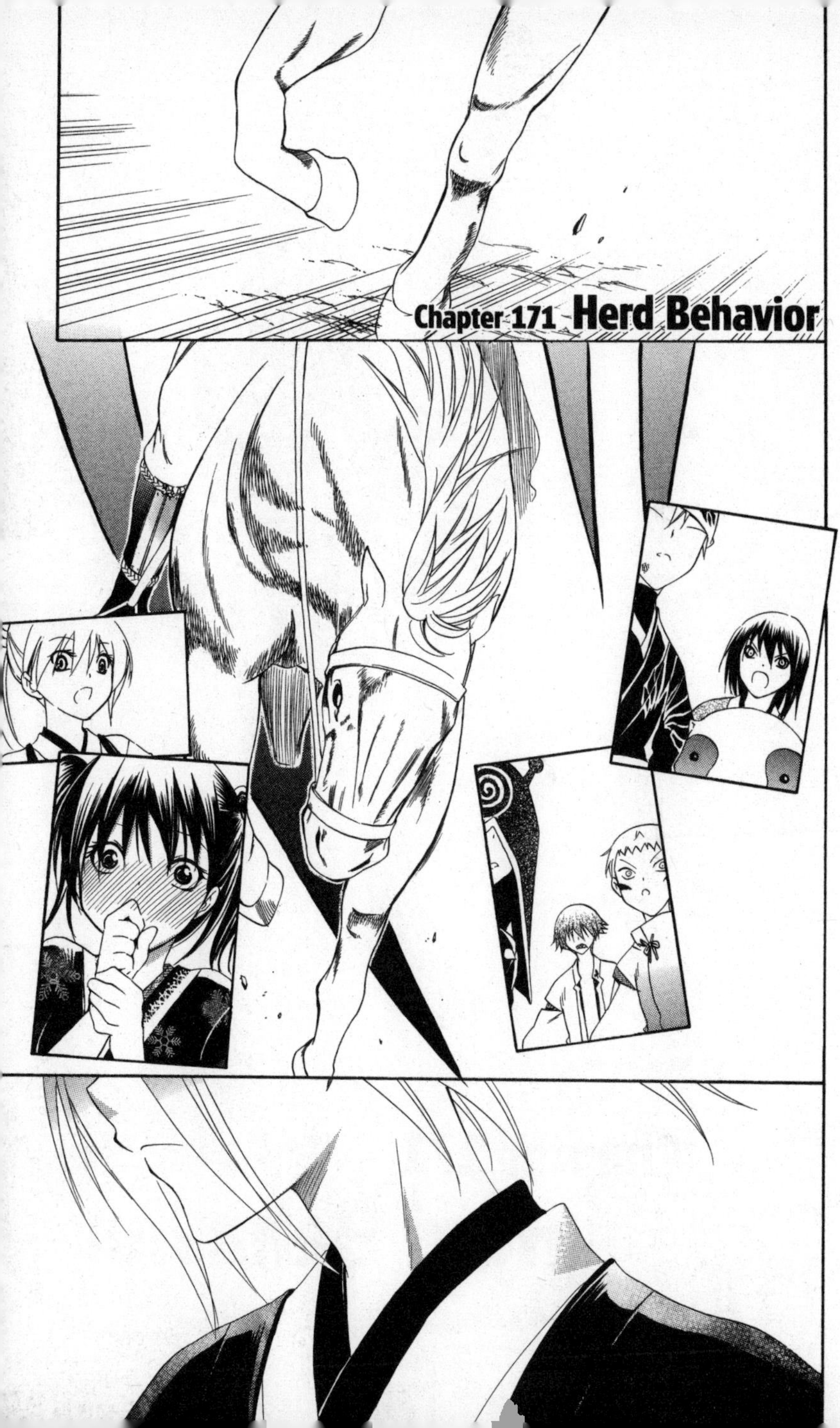
Chapter 171 Herd Behavior

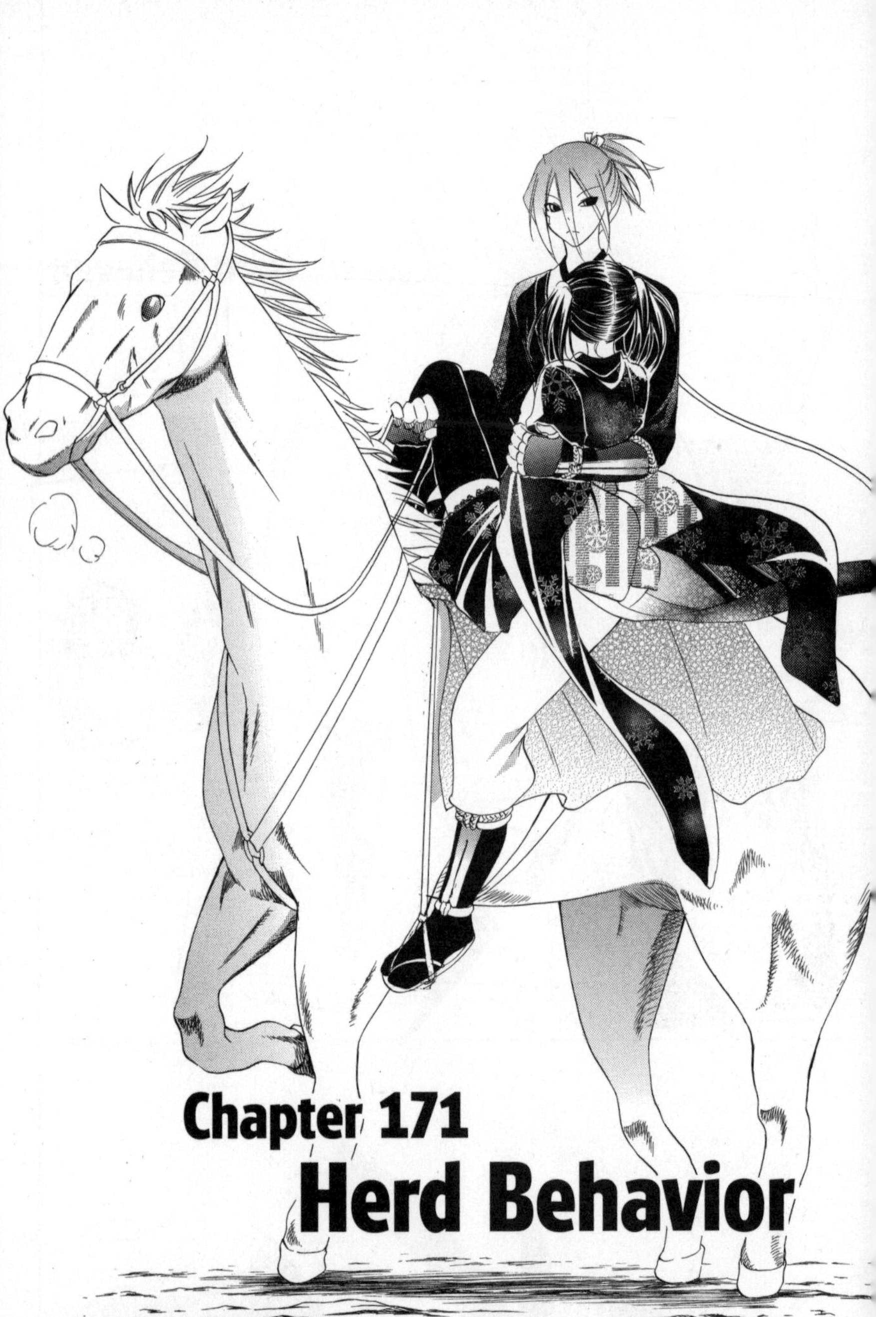
Chapter 171
Herd Behavior

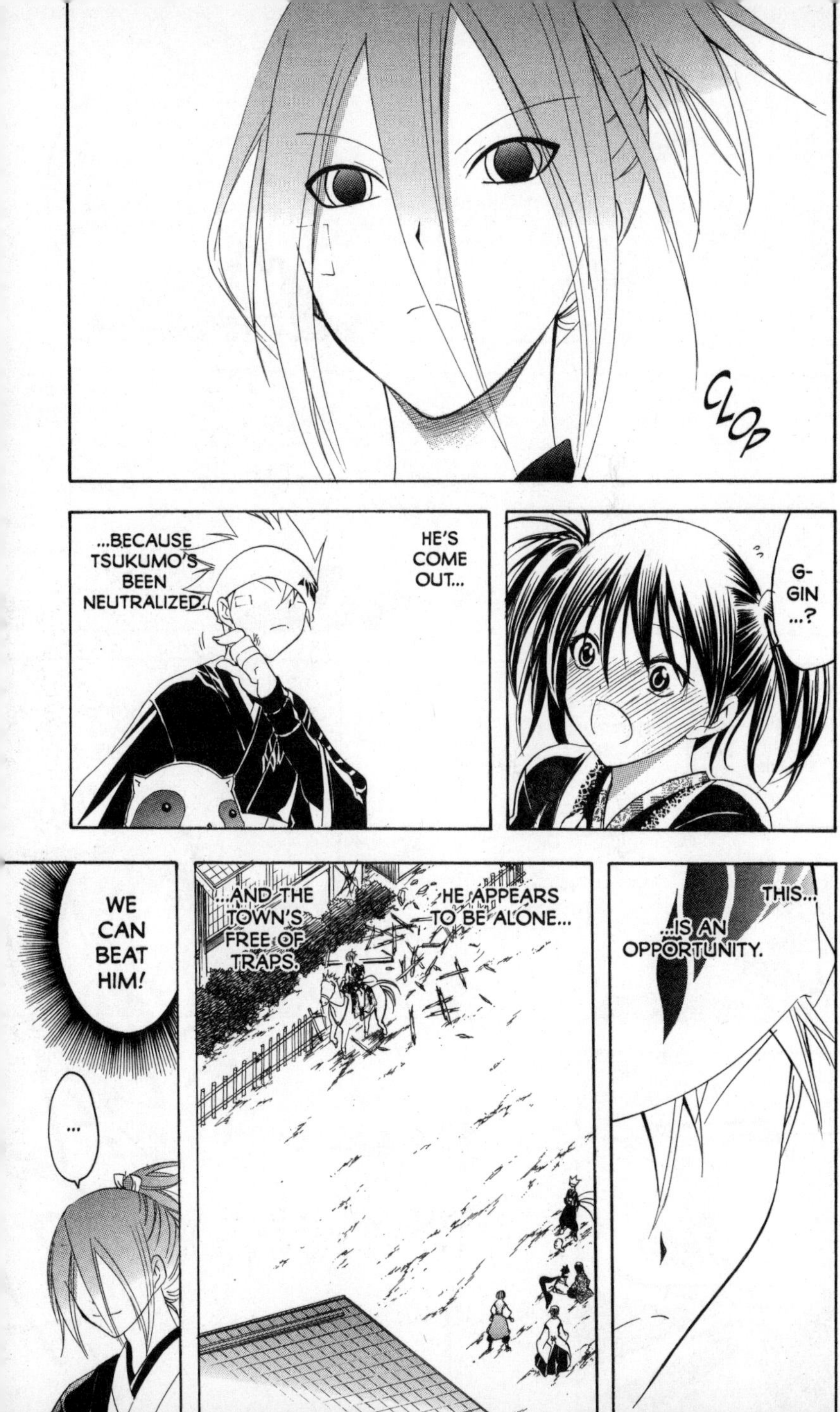
CLOP
G-GIN ...?
HE'S COME OUT...
...BECAUSE TSUKUMO'S BEEN NEUTRALIZED.
THIS...
...IS AN OPPORTUNITY.
HE APPEARS TO BE ALONE...
...AND THE TOWN'S FREE OF TRAPS.
WE CAN BEAT HIM!
...

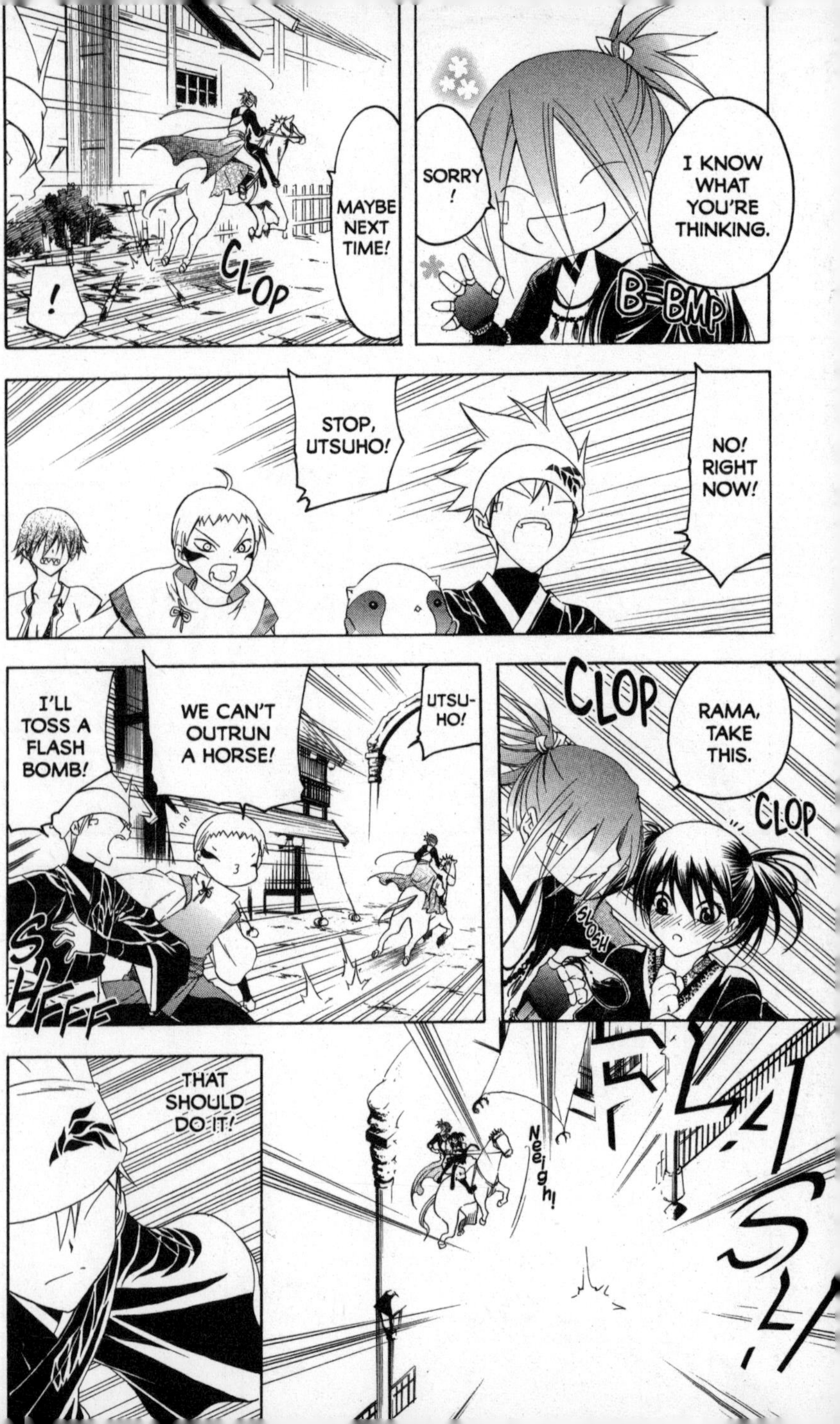
I KNOW WHAT YOU'RE THINKING.
SORRY!
B-BMP
MAYBE NEXT TIME!
CLOP
!
NO! RIGHT NOW!
STOP, UTSUHO!
CLOP
RAMA, TAKE THIS.
CLOP
SLOSH
UTSU-HO!
WE CAN'T OUTRUN A HORSE!
I'LL TOSS A FLASH BOMB!
SHFFF
Neeigh!
THAT SHOULD DO IT!

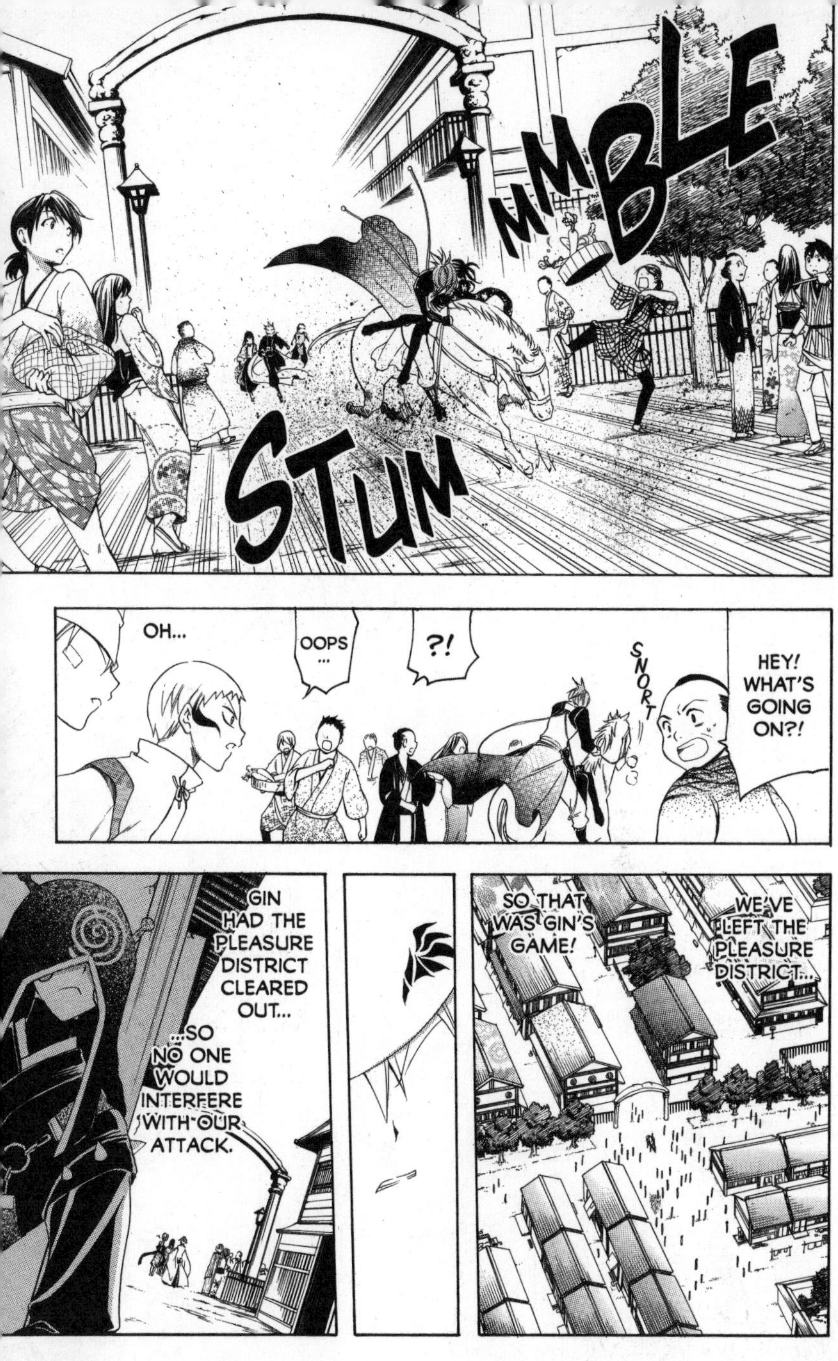
STUM
MMBLE
HEY! WHAT'S GOING ON?!
SNORT
?!
OOPS...
OH...
WE'VE LEFT THE PLEASURE DISTRICT...
SO THAT WAS GIN'S GAME!
GIN HAD THE PLEASURE DISTRICT CLEARED OUT...
...SO NO ONE WOULD INTERFERE WITH OUR ATTACK.

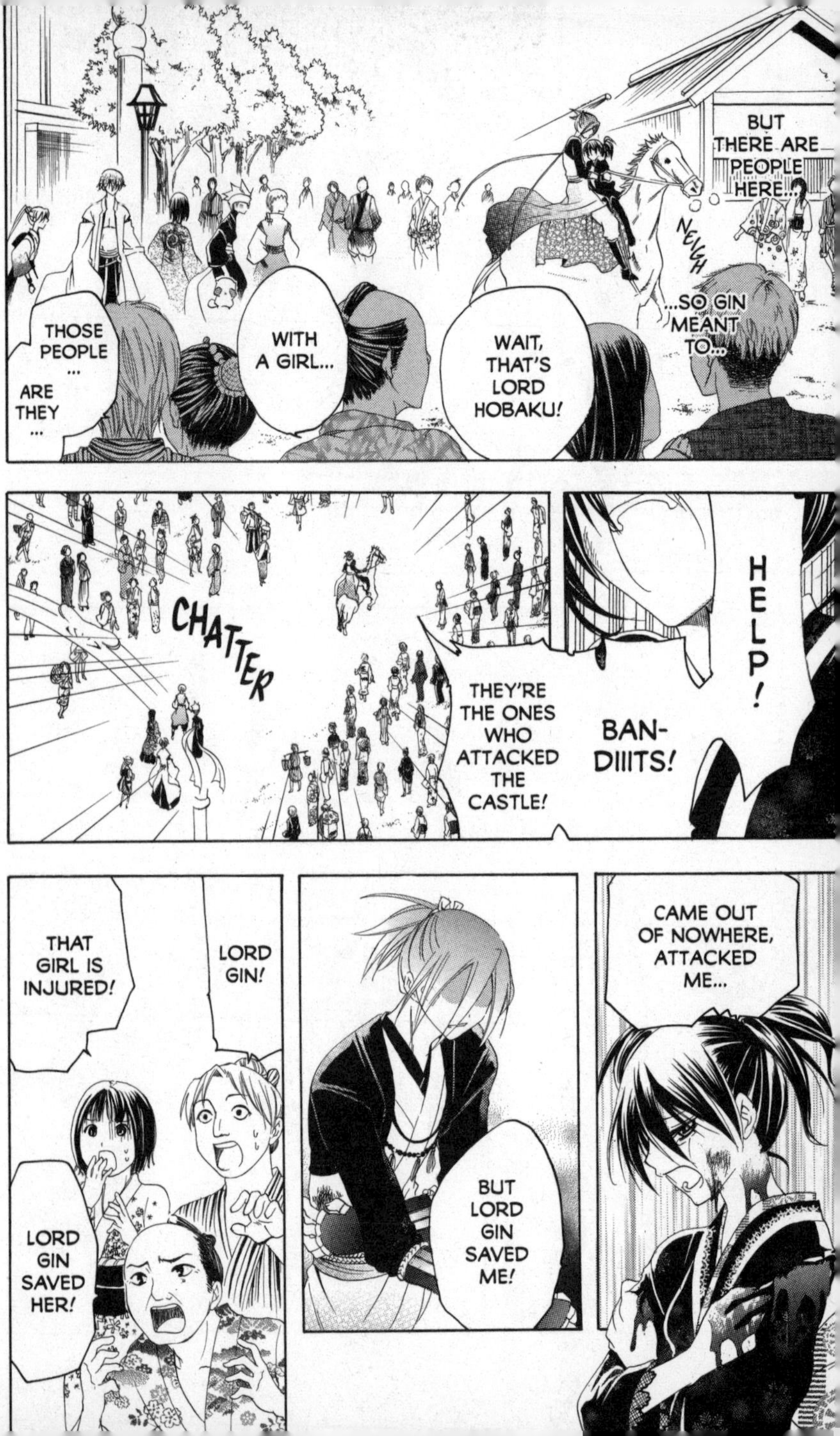
BUT THERE ARE PEOPLE HERE...
NEIGH
...SO GIN MEANT TO...
WAIT, THAT'S LORD HOBAKU!
WITH A GIRL...
THOSE PEOPLE ... ARE THEY ...
HELP!
BAN-DIIITS!
THEY'RE THE ONES WHO ATTACKED THE CASTLE!
CHATTER
CAME OUT OF NOWHERE, ATTACKED ME...
BUT LORD GIN SAVED ME!
LORD GIN!
THAT GIRL IS INJURED!
LORD GIN SAVED HER!

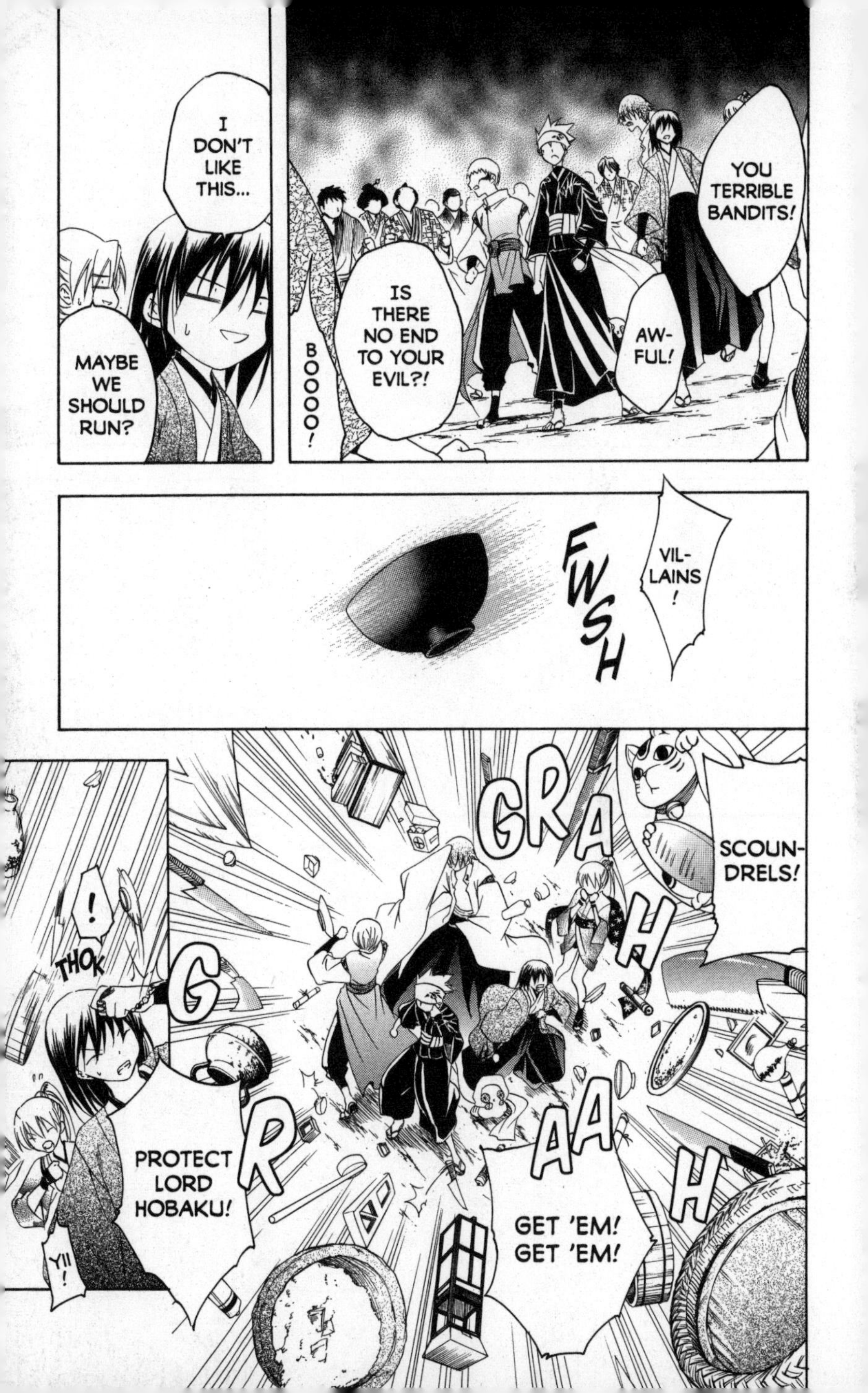

YOU TERRIBLE BANDITS!
AW-FUL!
IS THERE NO END TO YOUR EVIL?!
BOOOOO!
I DON'T LIKE THIS...
MAYBE WE SHOULD RUN?
VIL-LAINS!
FWSH
SCOUN-DRELS!
GRAH
GET 'EM! GET 'EM!
GRAAH
!
THOK
PROTECT LORD HOBAKU!
YII!

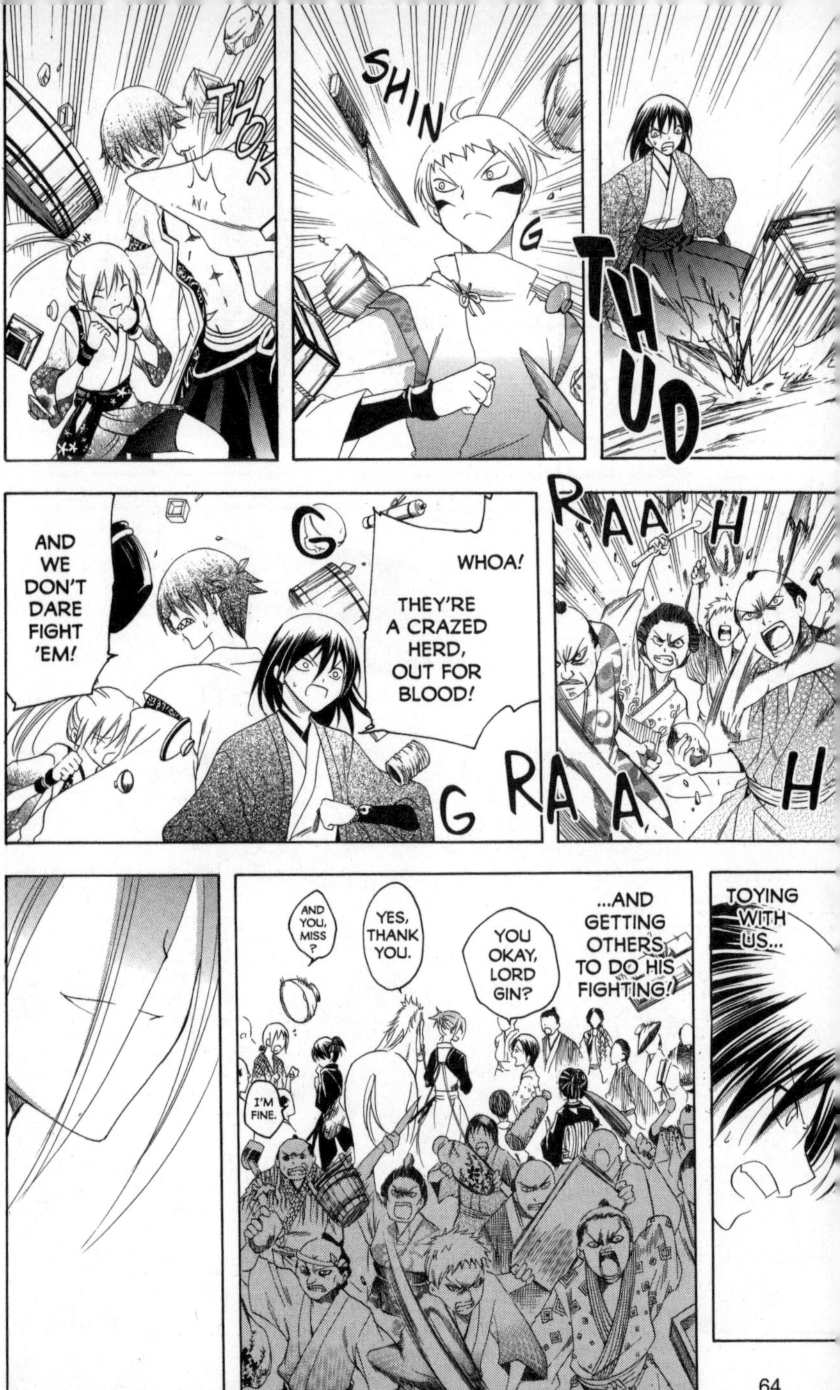
THUD
SHING
THOK
RAAAH
GRAAAH
WHOA!
THEY'RE A CRAZED HERD, OUT FOR BLOOD!
AND WE DON'T DARE FIGHT 'EM!
GG
TOYING WITH US...
...AND GETTING OTHERS TO DO HIS FIGHTING!
YOU OKAY, LORD GIN?
YES, THANK YOU.
AND YOU, MISS?
I'M FINE.

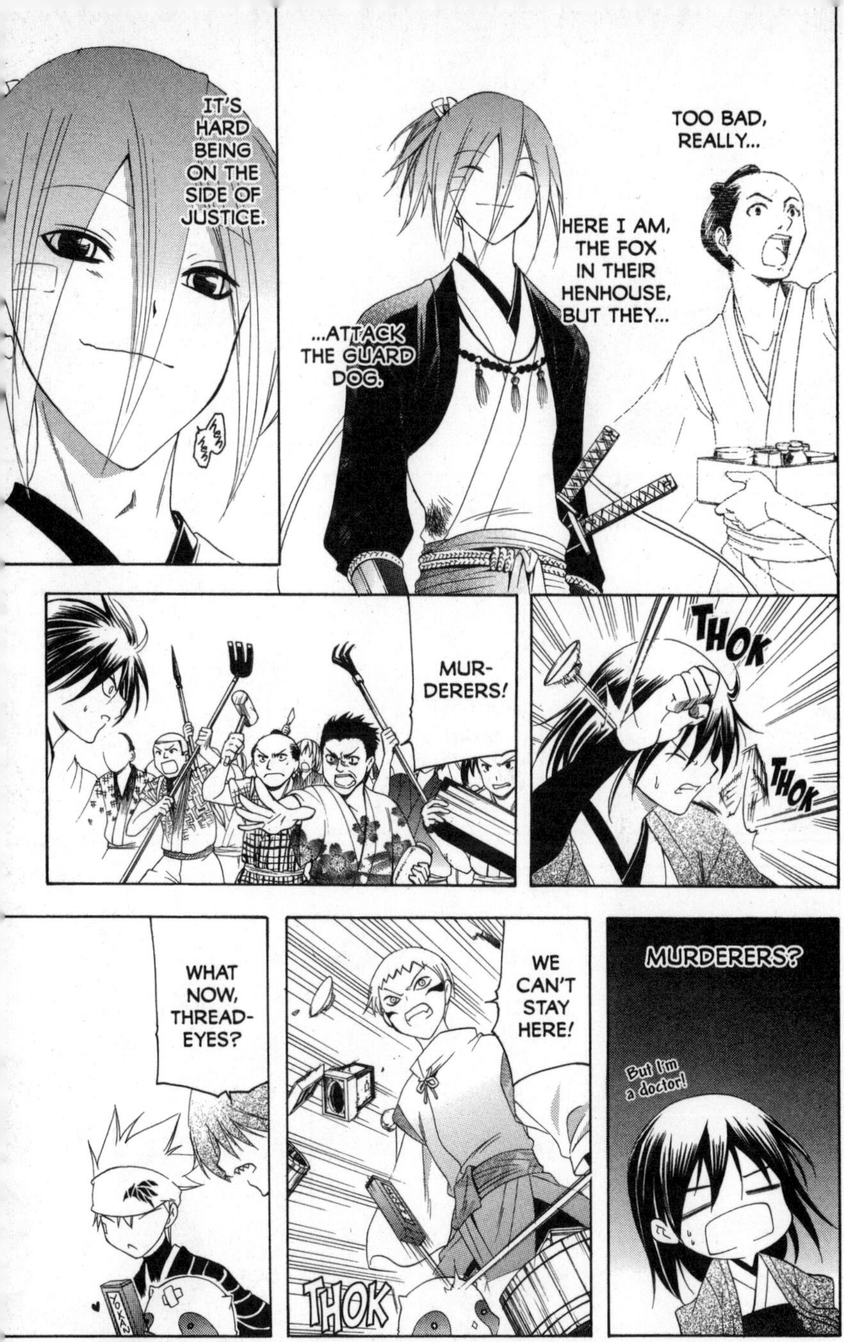
TOO BAD, REALLY...
HERE I AM, THE FOX IN THEIR HENHOUSE, BUT THEY...
...ATTACK THE GUARD DOG.
IT'S HARD BEING ON THE SIDE OF JUSTICE.
heh heh
THOK
THOK
MURDERERS!
MURDERERS?
But I'm a doctor!
WE CAN'T STAY HERE!
THOK
WHAT NOW, THREAD-EYES?
YOKAN

See what Pochi catch!

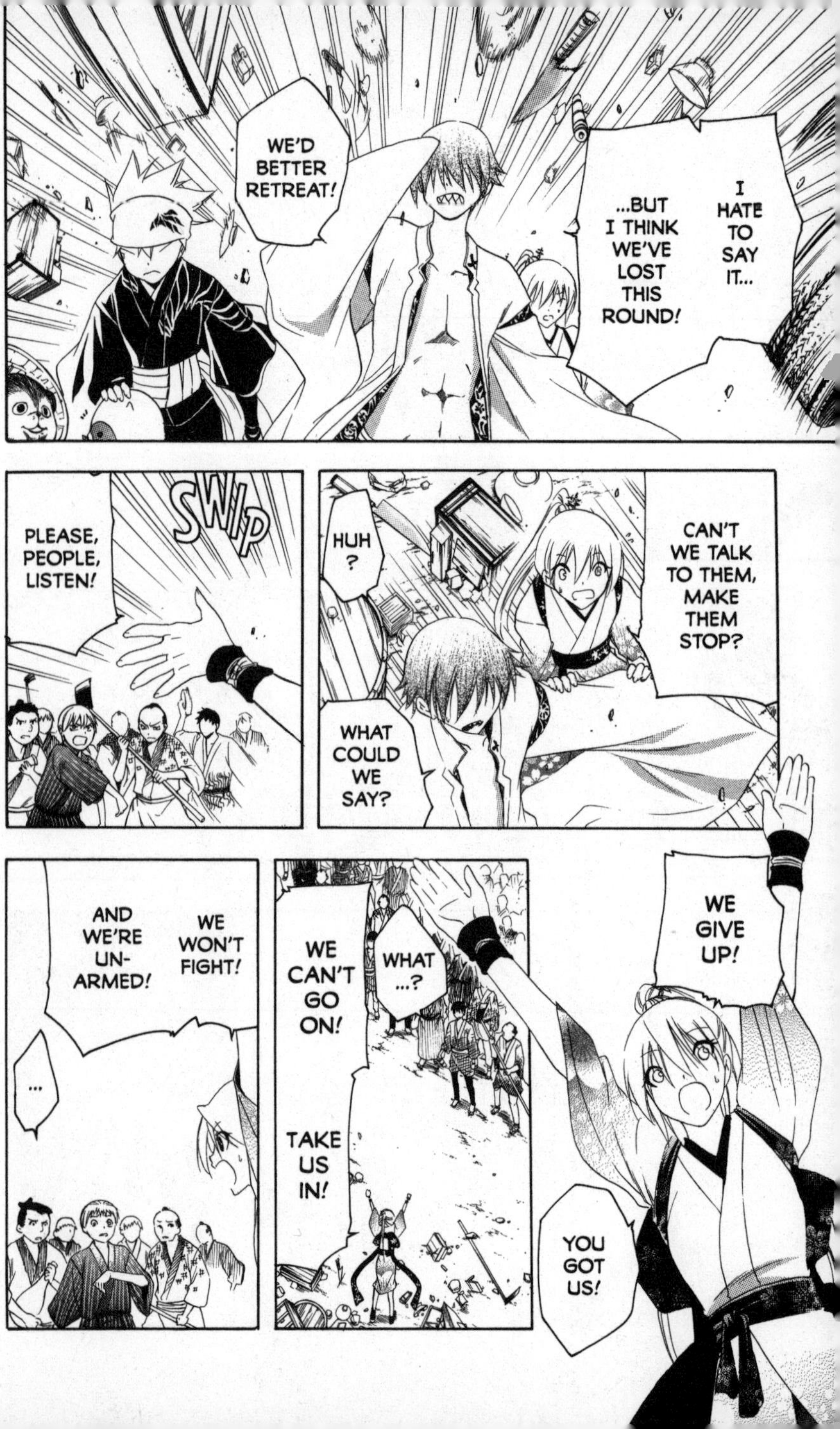
I HATE TO SAY IT...
...BUT I THINK WE'VE LOST THIS ROUND!
WE'D BETTER RETREAT!
CAN'T WE TALK TO THEM, MAKE THEM STOP?
HUH?
WHAT COULD WE SAY?
SWIP
PLEASE, PEOPLE, LISTEN!
WE GIVE UP!
YOU GOT US!
WHAT ...?
WE CAN'T GO ON!
TAKE US IN!
WE WON'T FIGHT!
AND WE'RE UN-ARMED!
...

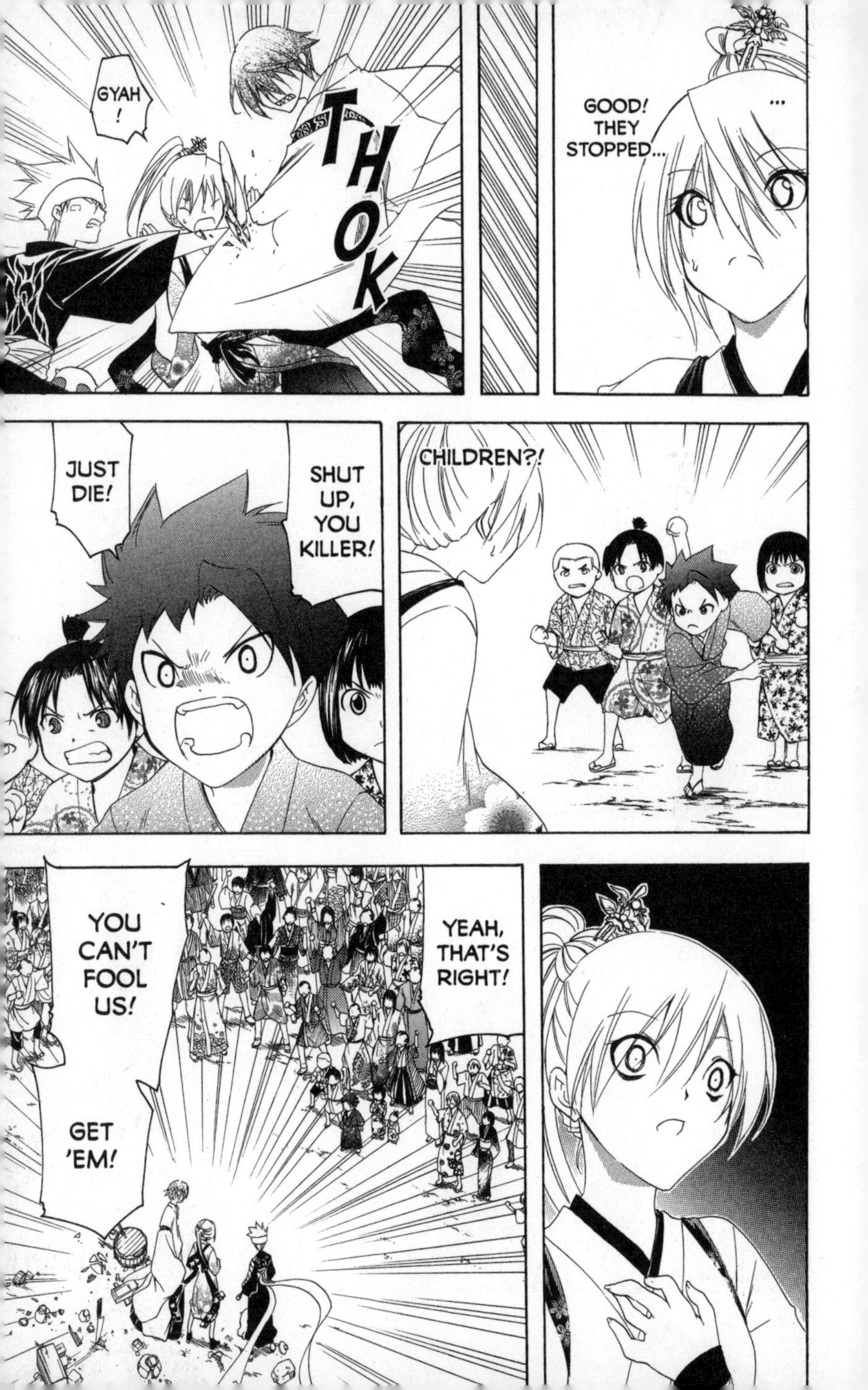
...
GOOD! THEY STOPPED...
THOK
GYAH!
CHILDREN?!
SHUT UP, YOU KILLER!
JUST DIE!
YEAH, THAT'S RIGHT!
YOU CAN'T FOOL US!
GET 'EM!

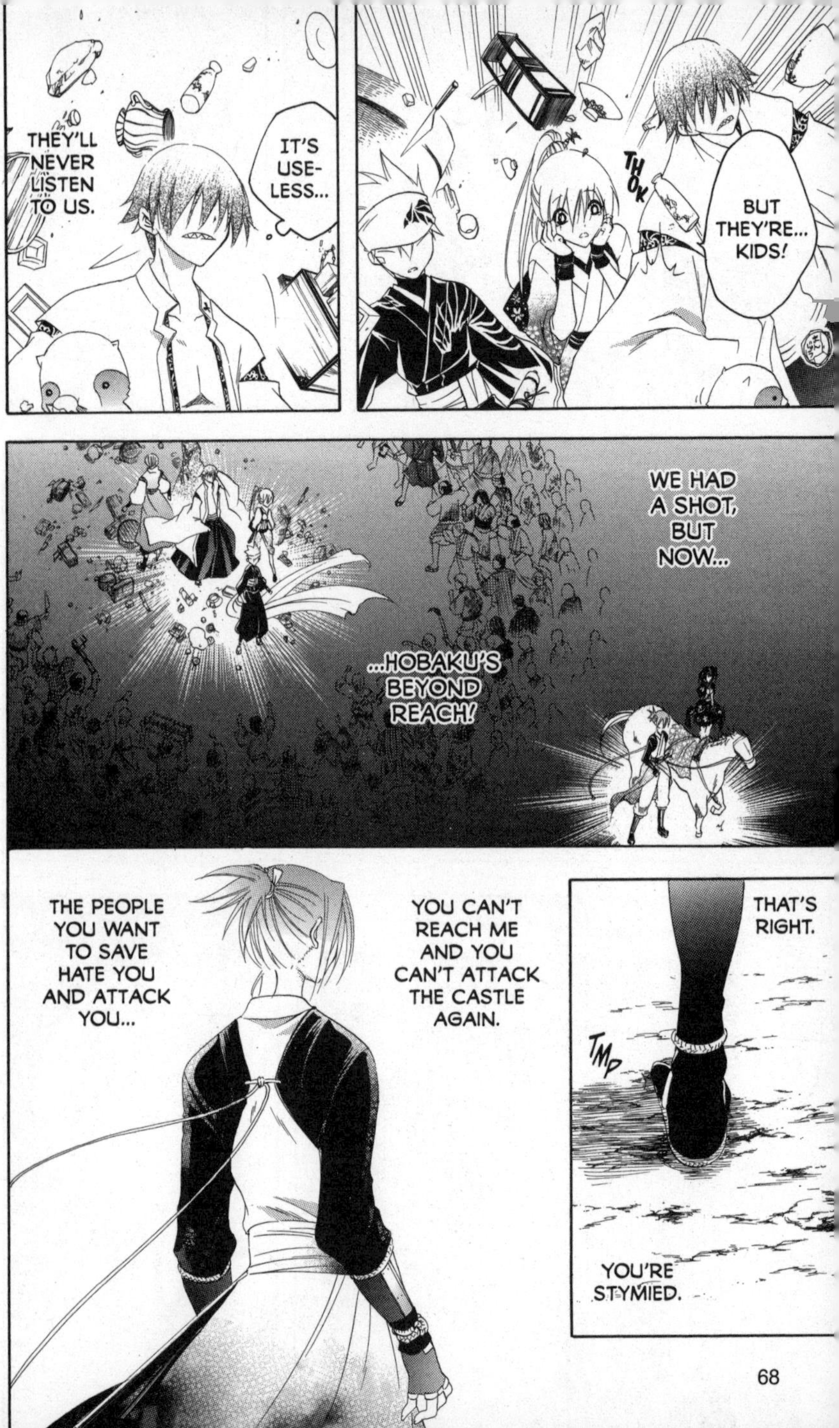
THOK
BUT THEY'RE... KIDS!
IT'S USELESS...
THEY'LL NEVER LISTEN TO US.
WE HAD A SHOT, BUT NOW...
...HOBAKU'S BEYOND REACH!
THAT'S RIGHT.
TMP
YOU'RE STYMIED.
YOU CAN'T REACH ME AND YOU CAN'T ATTACK THE CASTLE AGAIN.
THE PEOPLE YOU WANT TO SAVE HATE YOU AND ATTACK YOU...

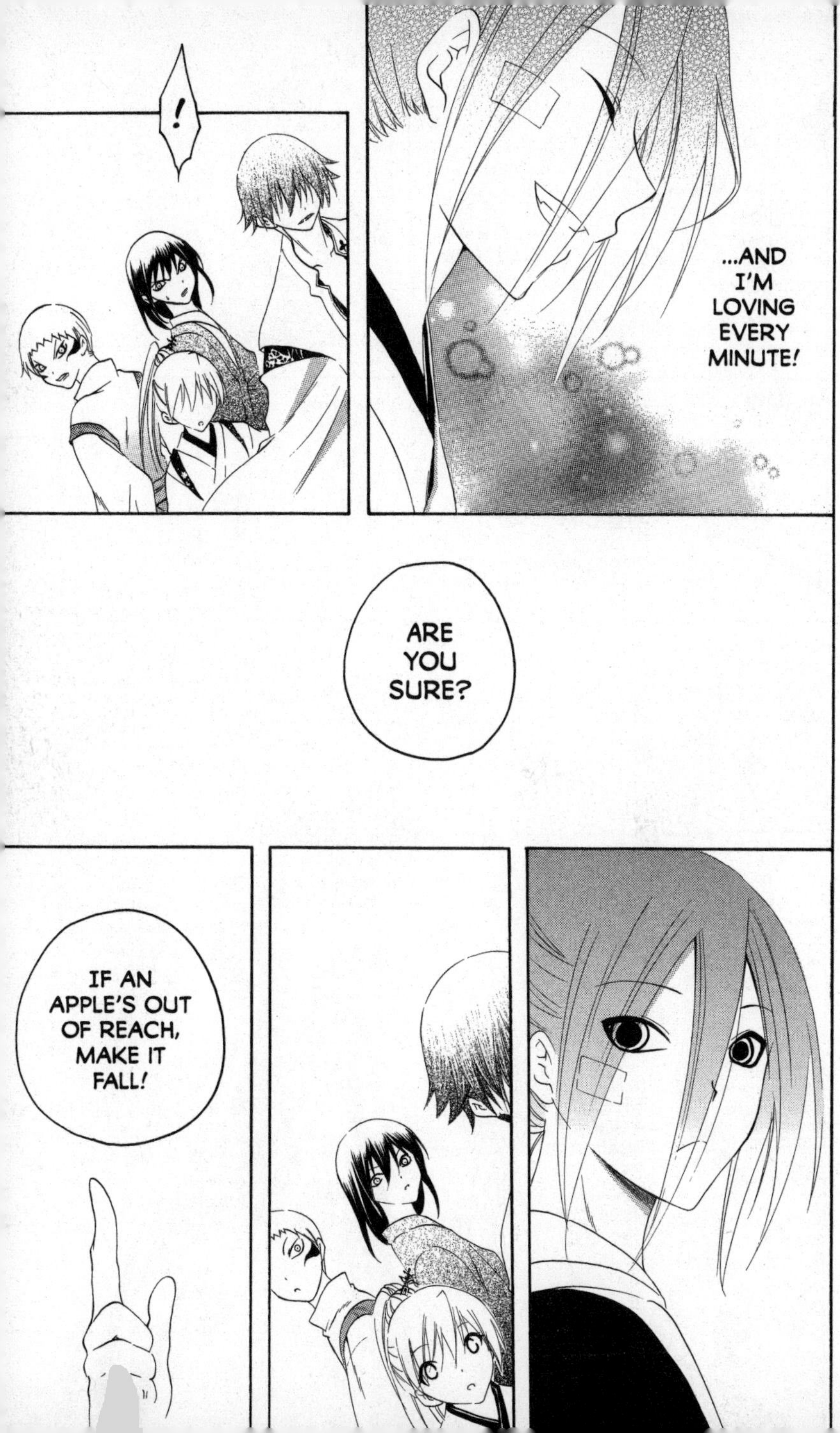
...AND I'M LOVING EVERY MINUTE!
!
ARE YOU SURE?
IF AN APPLE'S OUT OF REACH, MAKE IT FALL!

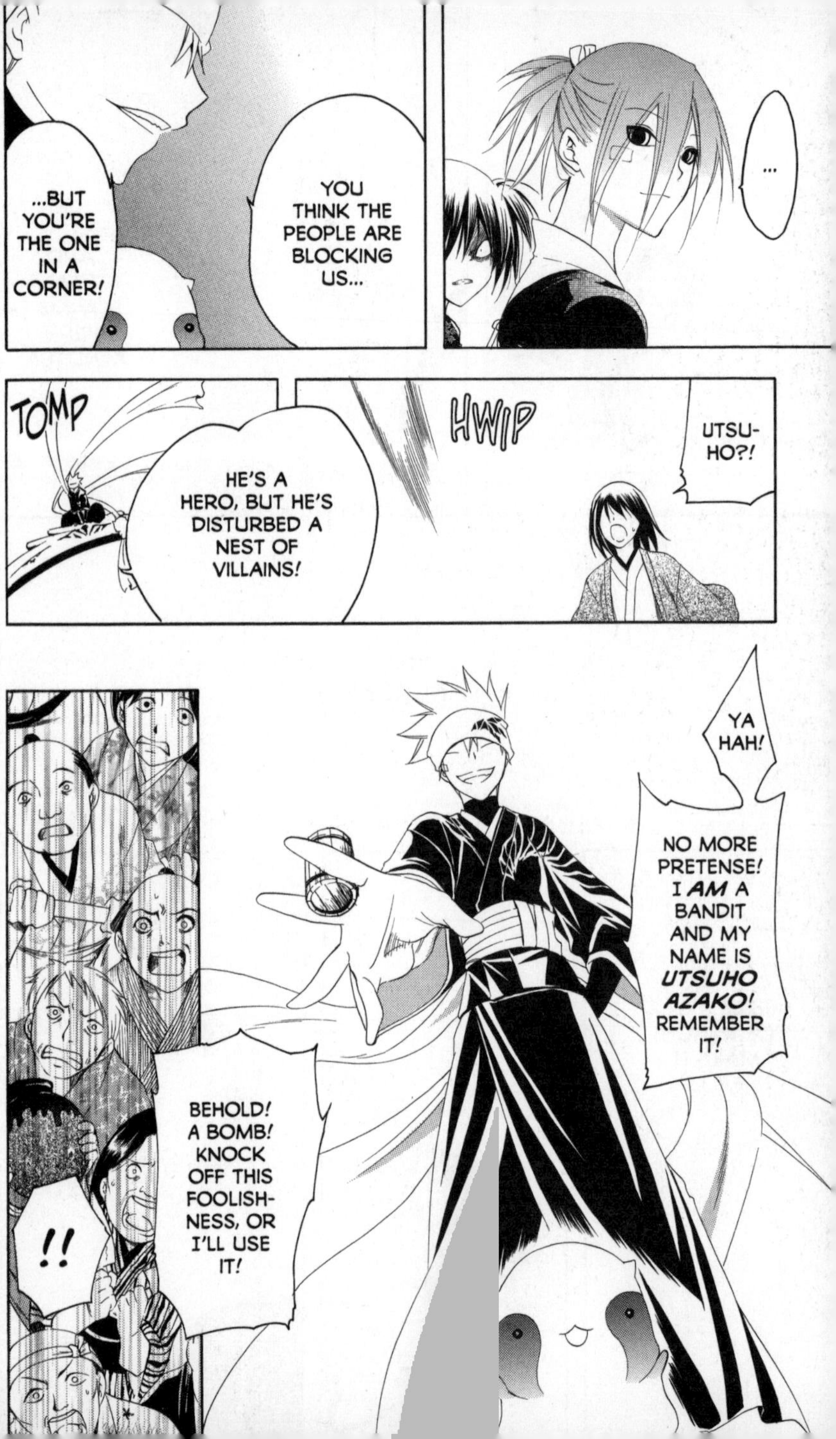
...
YOU THINK THE PEOPLE ARE BLOCKING US...
...BUT YOU'RE THE ONE IN A CORNER!
UTSU-HO?!
HWIP
HE'S A HERO, BUT HE'S DISTURBED A NEST OF VILLAINS!
TOMP
YA HAH!
NO MORE PRETENSE! I ***AM*** A BANDIT AND MY NAME IS ***UTSUHO AZAKO***! REMEMBER IT!
BEHOLD! A BOMB! KNOCK OFF THIS FOOLISHNESS, OR I'LL USE IT!
!!

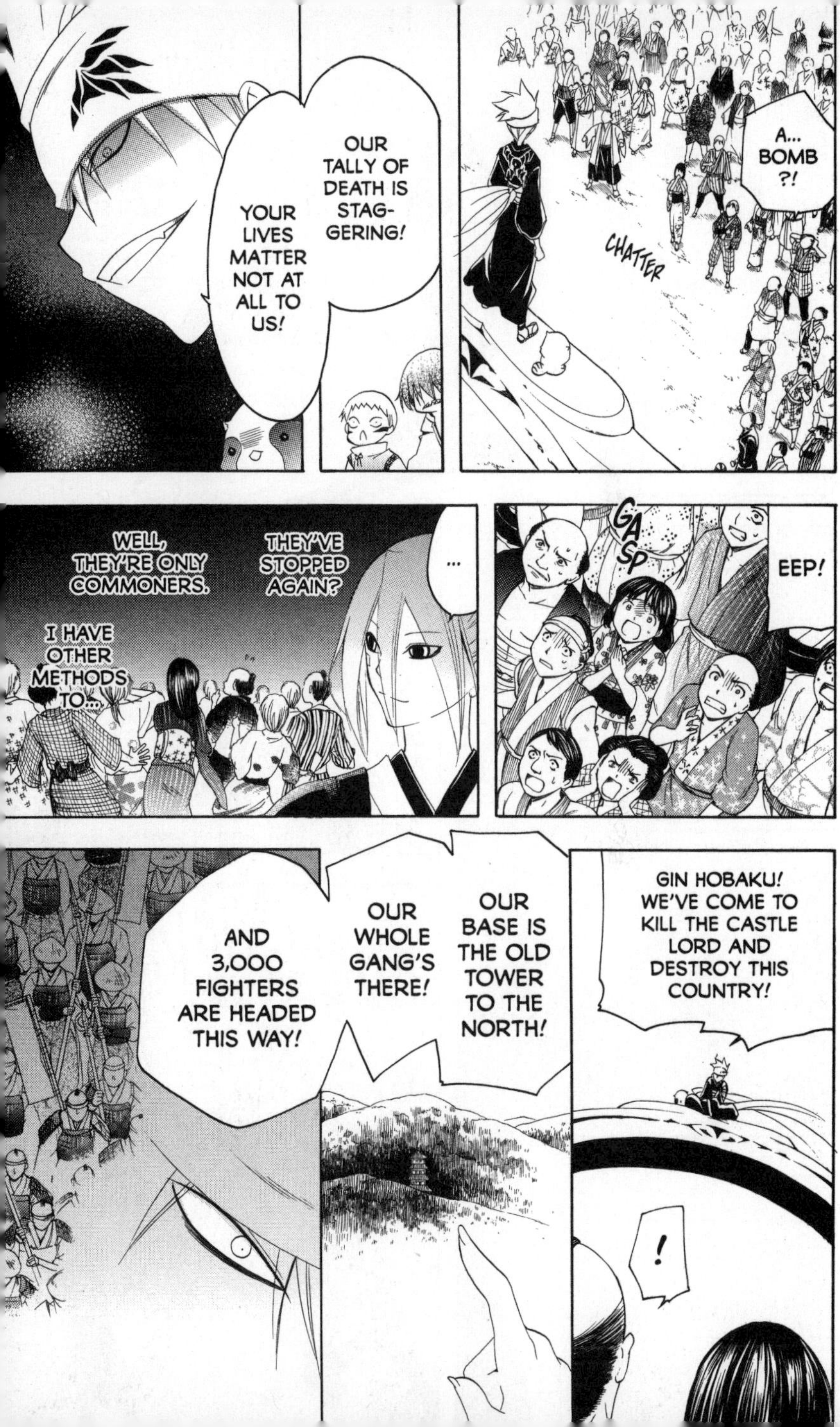
A... BOMB ?!
CHATTER
OUR TALLY OF DEATH IS STAGGERING!
YOUR LIVES MATTER NOT AT ALL TO US!
GASP
EEP!
...
THEY'VE STOPPED AGAIN?
WELL, THEY'RE ONLY COMMONERS.
I HAVE OTHER METHODS TO...
GIN HOBAKU! WE'VE COME TO KILL THE CASTLE LORD AND DESTROY THIS COUNTRY!
!
OUR BASE IS THE OLD TOWER TO THE NORTH!
OUR WHOLE GANG'S THERE!
AND 3,000 FIGHTERS ARE HEADED THIS WAY!

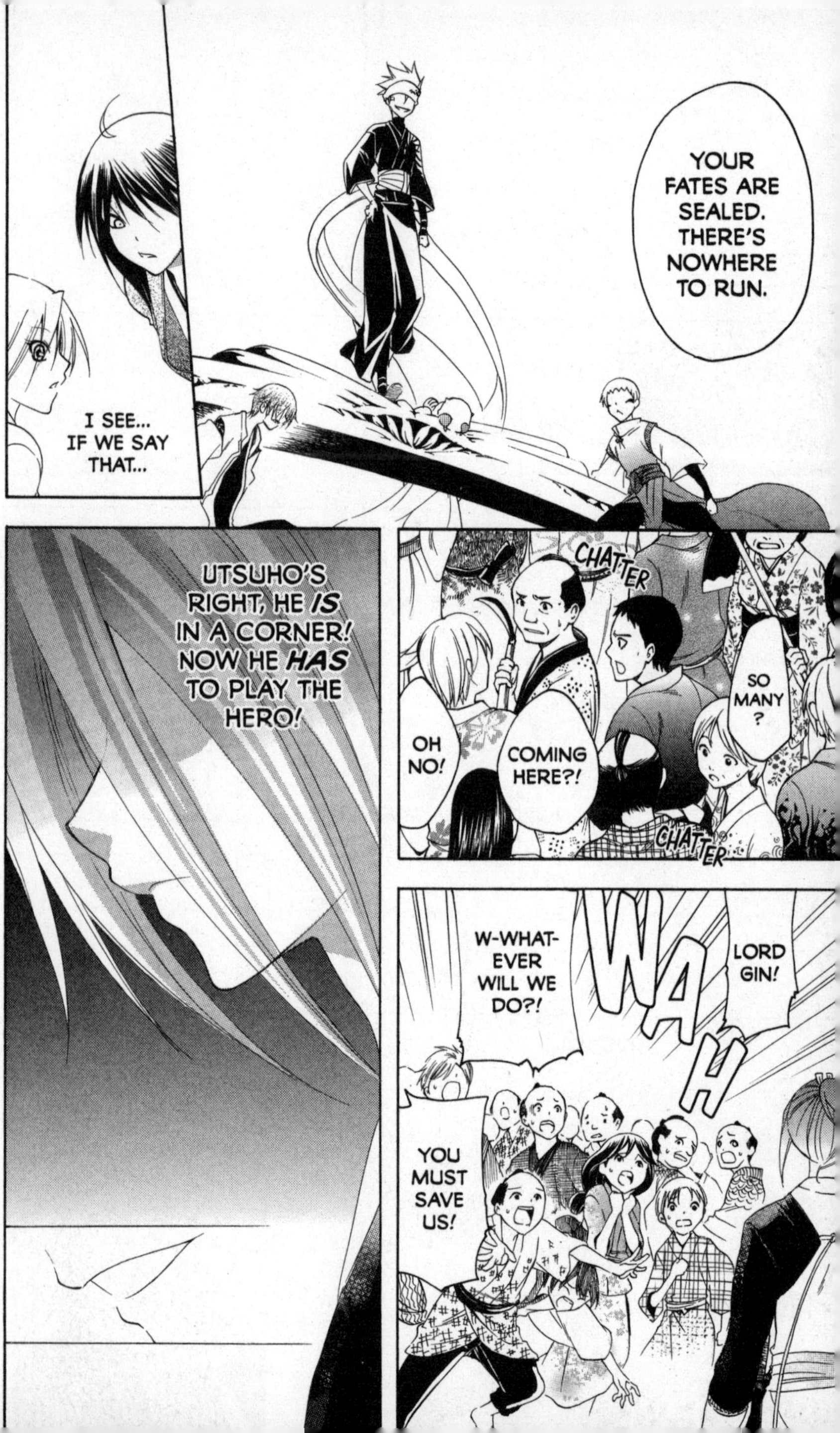
YOUR FATES ARE SEALED. THERE'S NOWHERE TO RUN.
I SEE... IF WE SAY THAT...
CHATTER
SO MANY?
COMING HERE?!
OH NO!
CHATTER
LORD GIN!
WAH
W-WHAT-EVER WILL WE DO?!
YOU MUST SAVE US!
UTSUHO'S RIGHT, HE *IS* IN A CORNER! NOW HE ***HAS*** TO PLAY THE HERO!

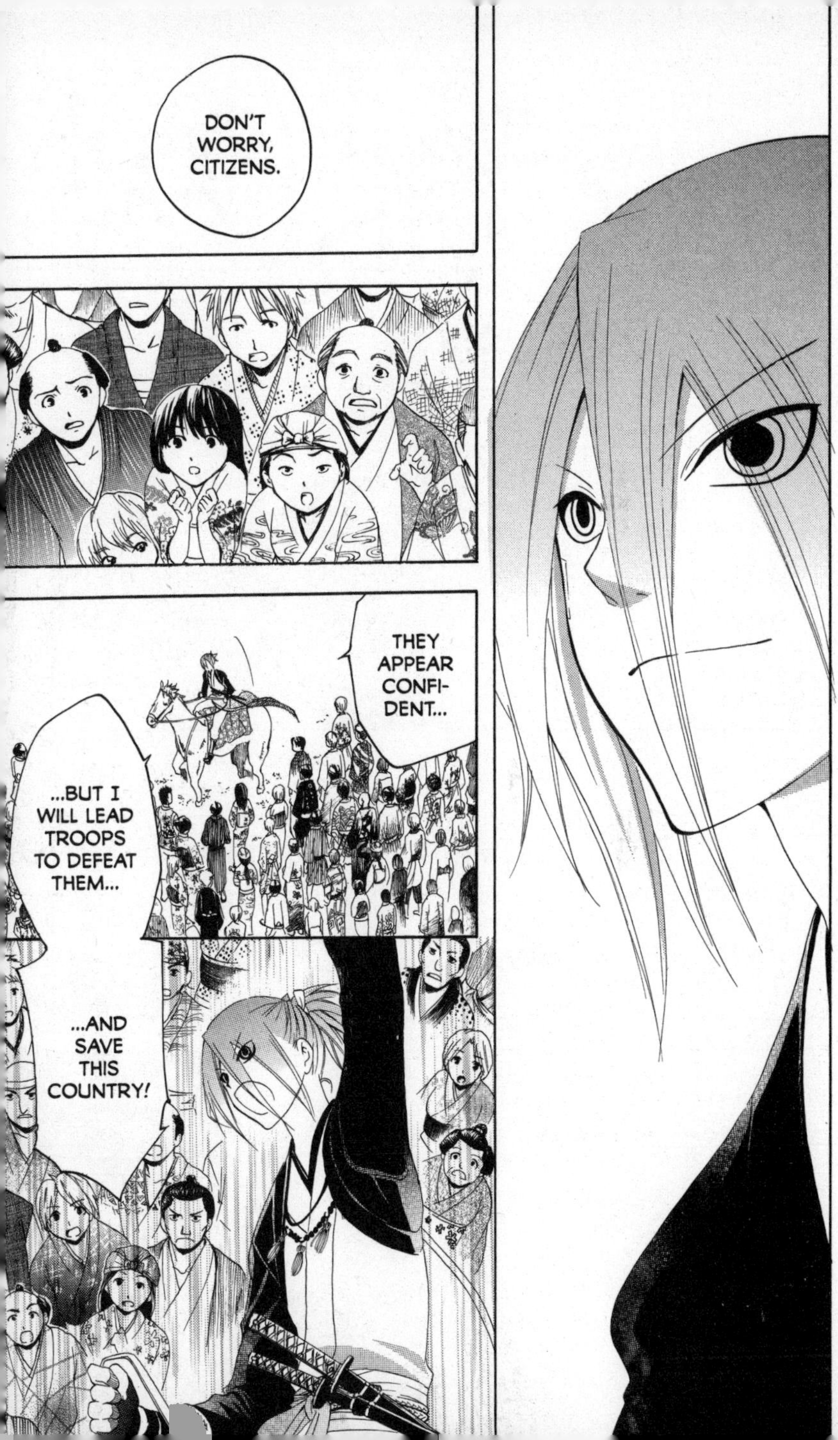
DON'T WORRY, CITIZENS.
THEY APPEAR CONFI-DENT...
...BUT I WILL LEAD TROOPS TO DEFEAT THEM...
...AND SAVE THIS COUNTRY!

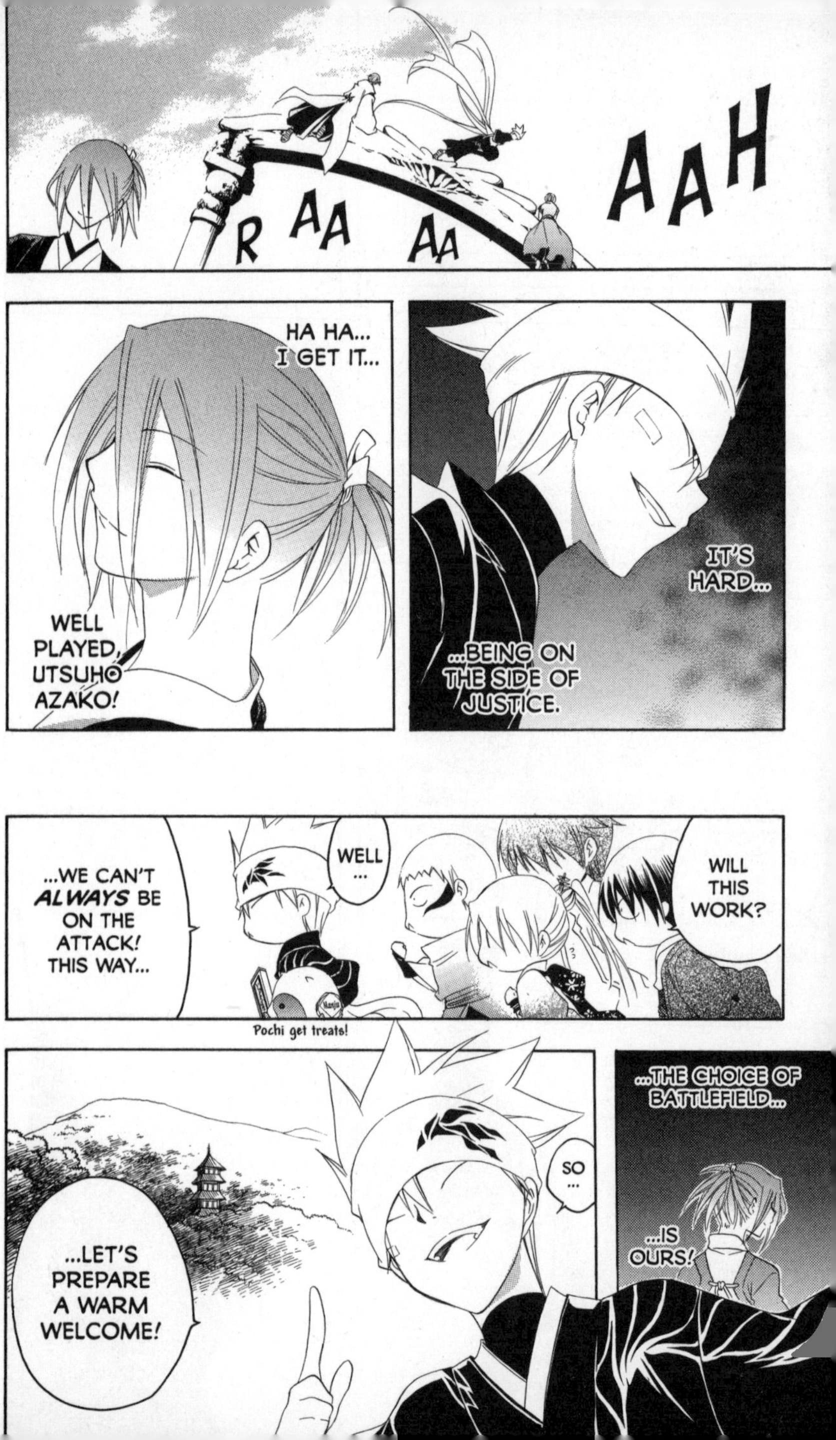
RAAAAAAH
IT'S HARD...
...BEING ON THE SIDE OF JUSTICE.
HA HA... I GET IT...
WELL PLAYED, UTSUHO AZAKO!
WILL THIS WORK?
WELL ...
...WE CAN'T *ALWAYS* BE ON THE ATTACK! THIS WAY...
Nanju
Pochi get treats!
...THE CHOICE OF BATTLEFIELD...
...IS OURS!
SO ...
...LET'S PREPARE A WARM WELCOME!

Chapter 172 Private Army

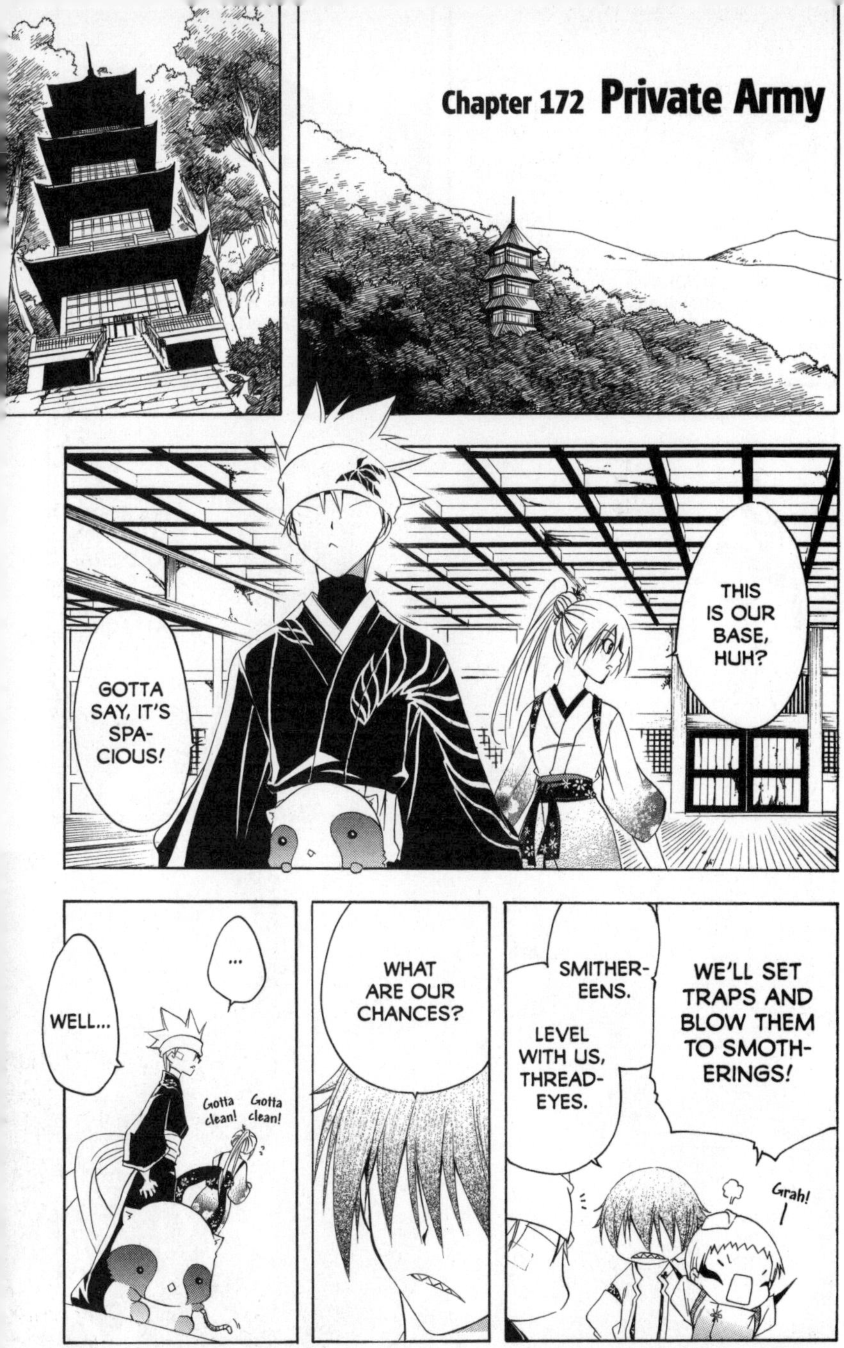

THIS IS OUR BASE, HUH?
GOTTA SAY, IT'S SPA-CIOUS!
WE'LL SET TRAPS AND BLOW THEM TO SMOTH-ERINGS!
SMITHER-EENS.
LEVEL WITH US, THREAD-EYES.
Grah!
WHAT ARE OUR CHANCES?
...
WELL...
Gotta clean!
Gotta clean!

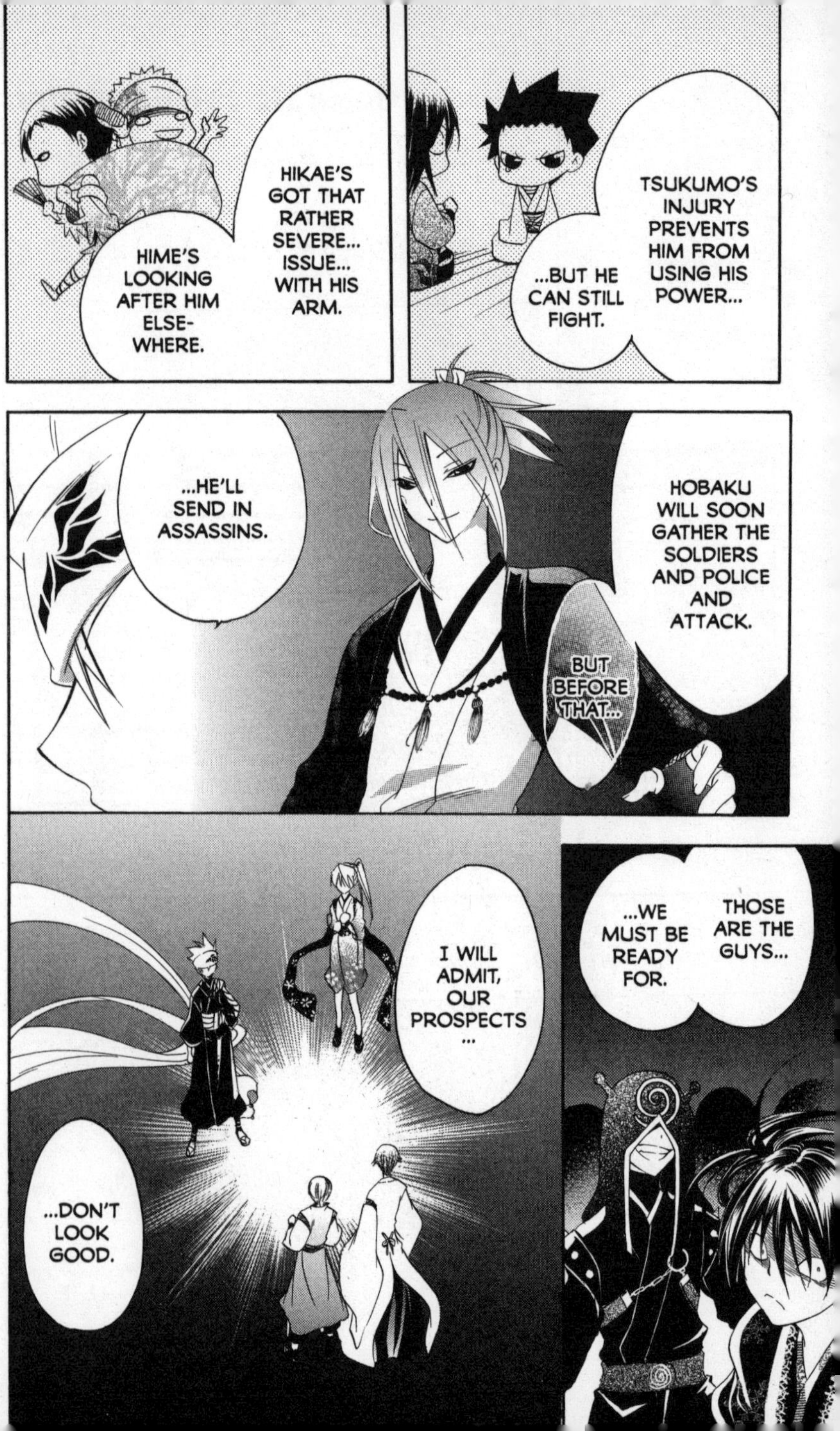
TSUKUMO'S INJURY PREVENTS HIM FROM USING HIS POWER...
...BUT HE CAN STILL FIGHT.
HIKAE'S GOT THAT RATHER SEVERE... ISSUE... WITH HIS ARM.
HIME'S LOOKING AFTER HIM ELSE-WHERE.
HOBAKU WILL SOON GATHER THE SOLDIERS AND POLICE AND ATTACK.
BUT BEFORE THAT...
...HE'LL SEND IN ASSASSINS.
THOSE ARE THE GUYS...
...WE MUST BE READY FOR.
I WILL ADMIT, OUR PROSPECTS ...
...DON'T LOOK GOOD.

Chapter 172
Private Army

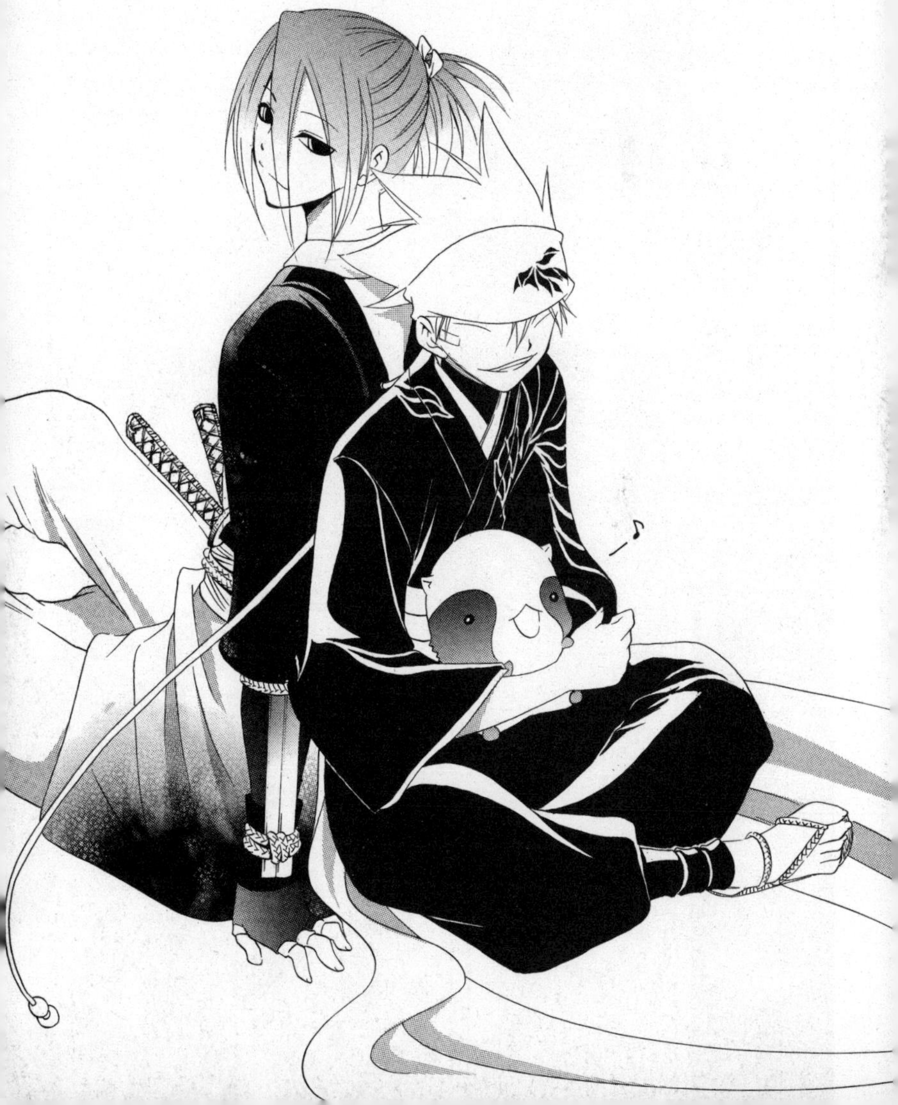

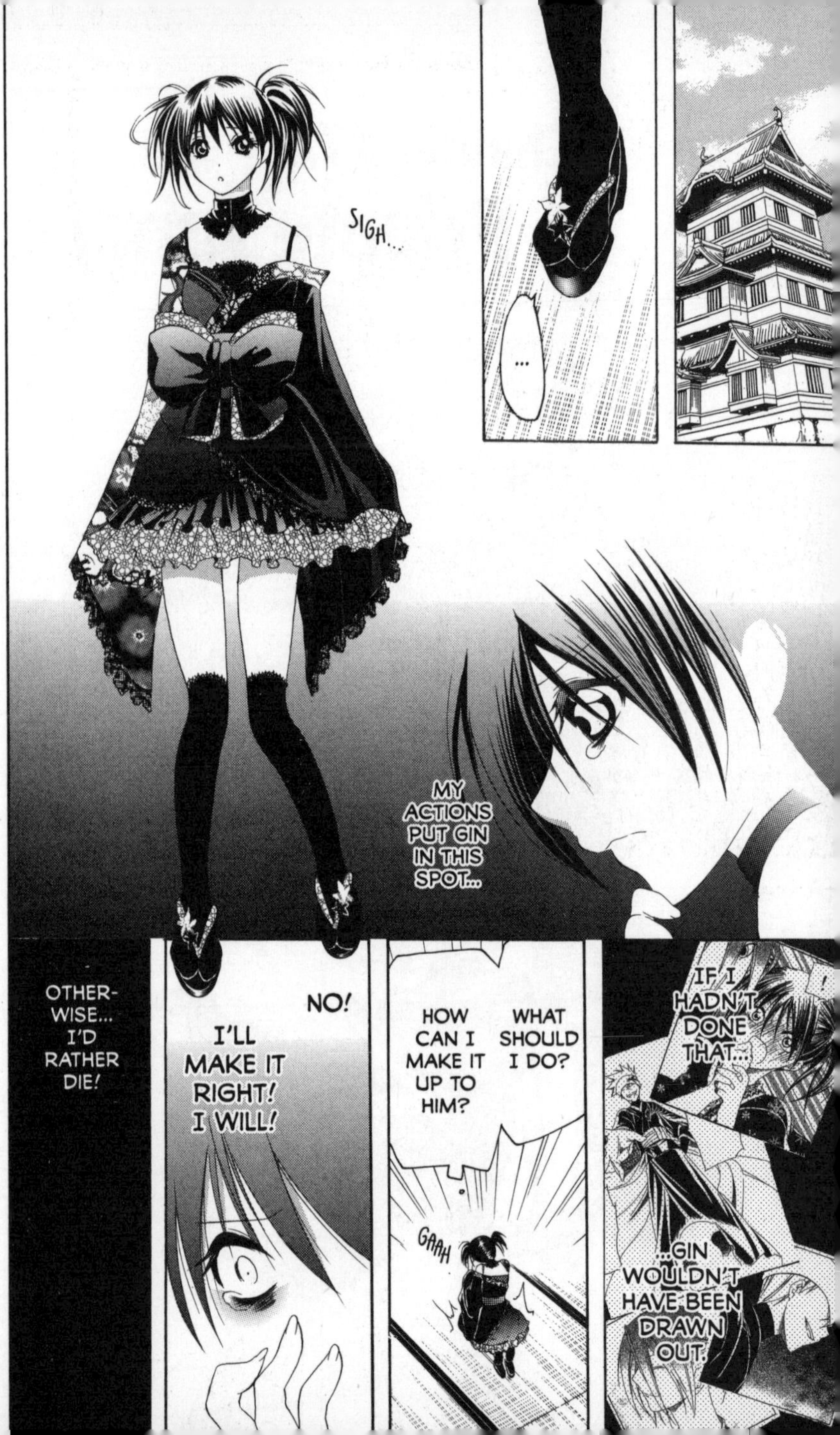
...
MY ACTIONS PUT GIN IN THIS SPOT...
SIGH...
IF I HADN'T DONE THAT...
!
...GIN WOULDN'T HAVE BEEN DRAWN OUT.
WHAT SHOULD I DO?
HOW CAN I MAKE IT UP TO HIM?
GAAH
NO!
I'LL MAKE IT RIGHT! I WILL!
OTHER-WISE... I'D RATHER DIE!

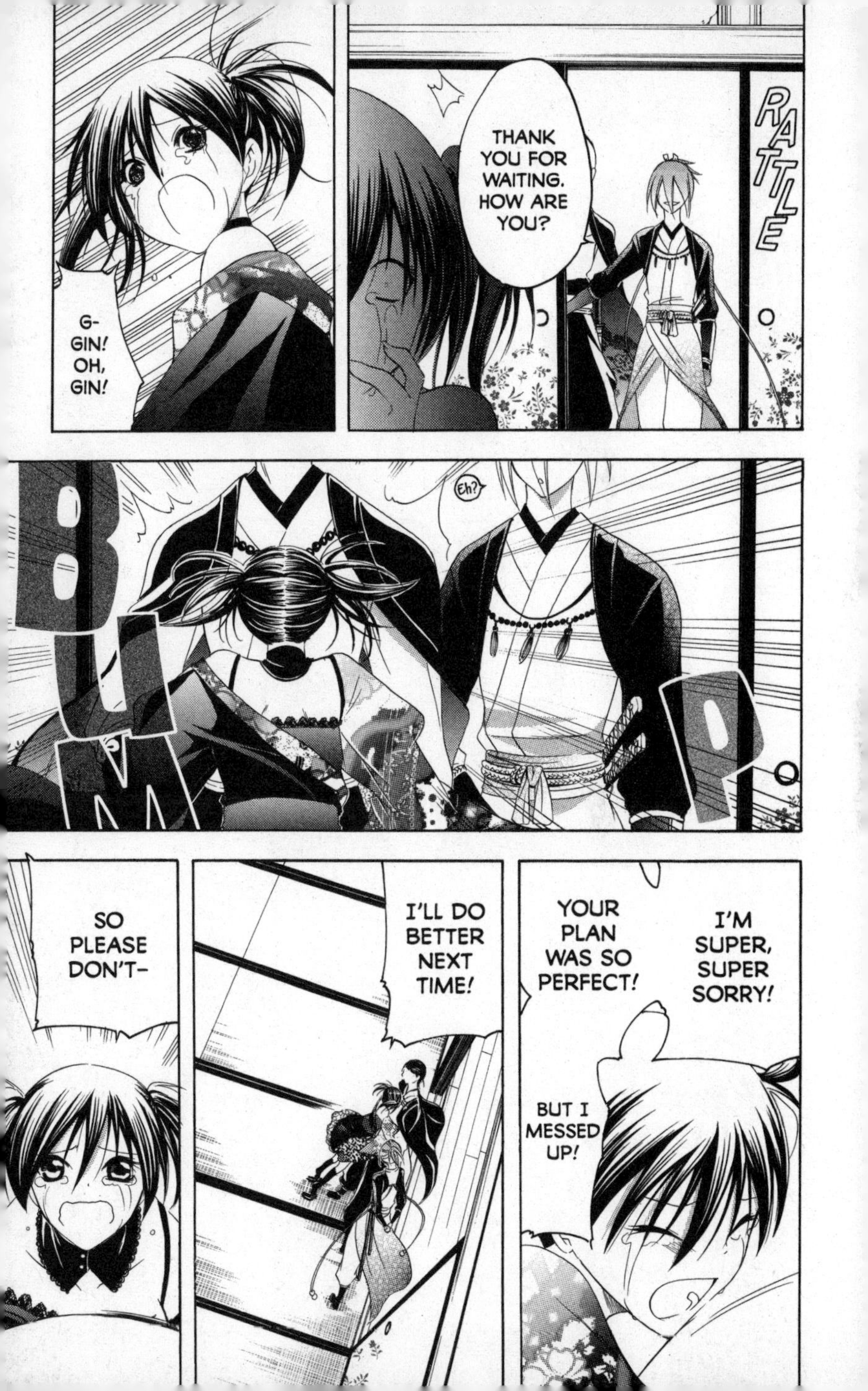
RATTLE
THANK YOU FOR WAITING. HOW ARE YOU?
G-GIN! OH, GIN!
Eh?
BUMP
I'M SUPER, SUPER SORRY!
YOUR PLAN WAS SO PERFECT!
BUT I MESSED UP!
I'LL DO BETTER NEXT TIME!
SO PLEASE DON'T-

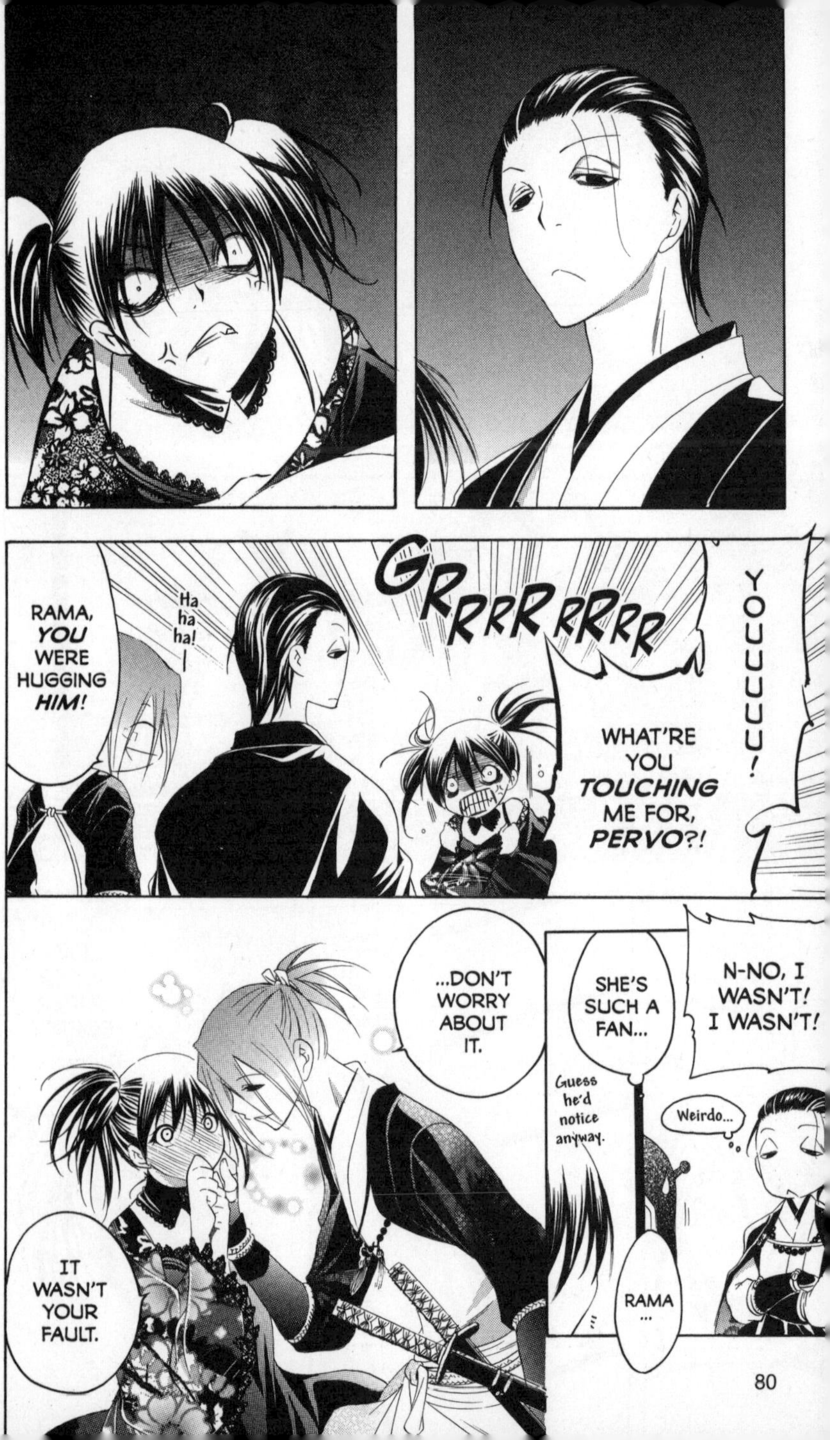
YOUUUUU!
GRRRRRRRR
WHAT'RE YOU *TOUCHING* ME FOR, *PERVO*?!
Ha ha ha!
RAMA, *YOU* WERE HUGGING *HIM*!
N-NO, I WASN'T! I WASN'T!
Weirdo...
SHE'S SUCH A FAN...
Guess he'd notice anyway.
RAMA ...
...DON'T WORRY ABOUT IT.
IT WASN'T YOUR FAULT.

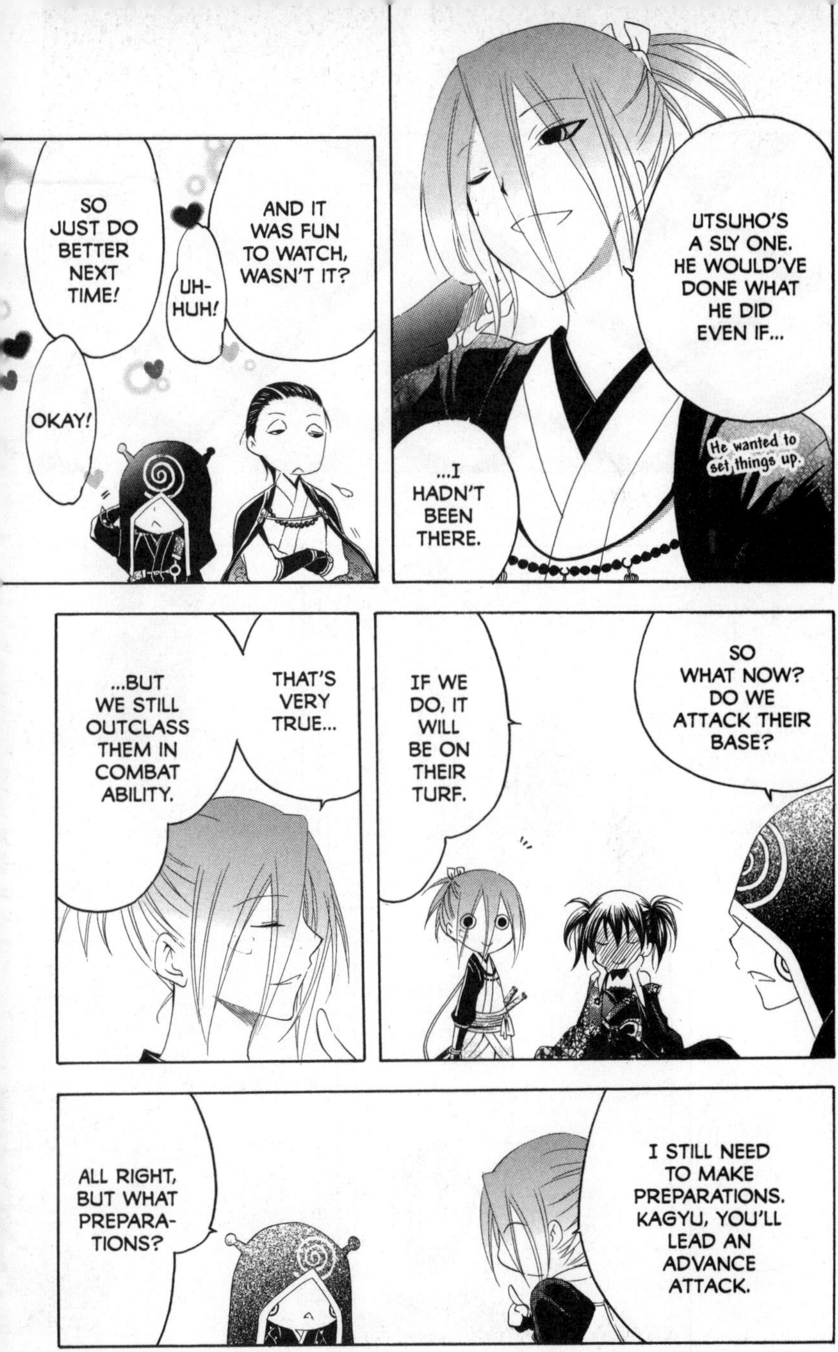
UTSUHO'S A SLY ONE. HE WOULD'VE DONE WHAT HE DID EVEN IF...
He wanted to set things up.
...I HADN'T BEEN THERE.
AND IT WAS FUN TO WATCH, WASN'T IT?
UH-HUH!
SO JUST DO BETTER NEXT TIME!
OKAY!
SO WHAT NOW? DO WE ATTACK THEIR BASE?
IF WE DO, IT WILL BE ON THEIR TURF.
THAT'S VERY TRUE...
...BUT WE STILL OUTCLASS THEM IN COMBAT ABILITY.
I STILL NEED TO MAKE PREPARATIONS. KAGYU, YOU'LL LEAD AN ADVANCE ATTACK.
ALL RIGHT, BUT WHAT PREPARA-TIONS?

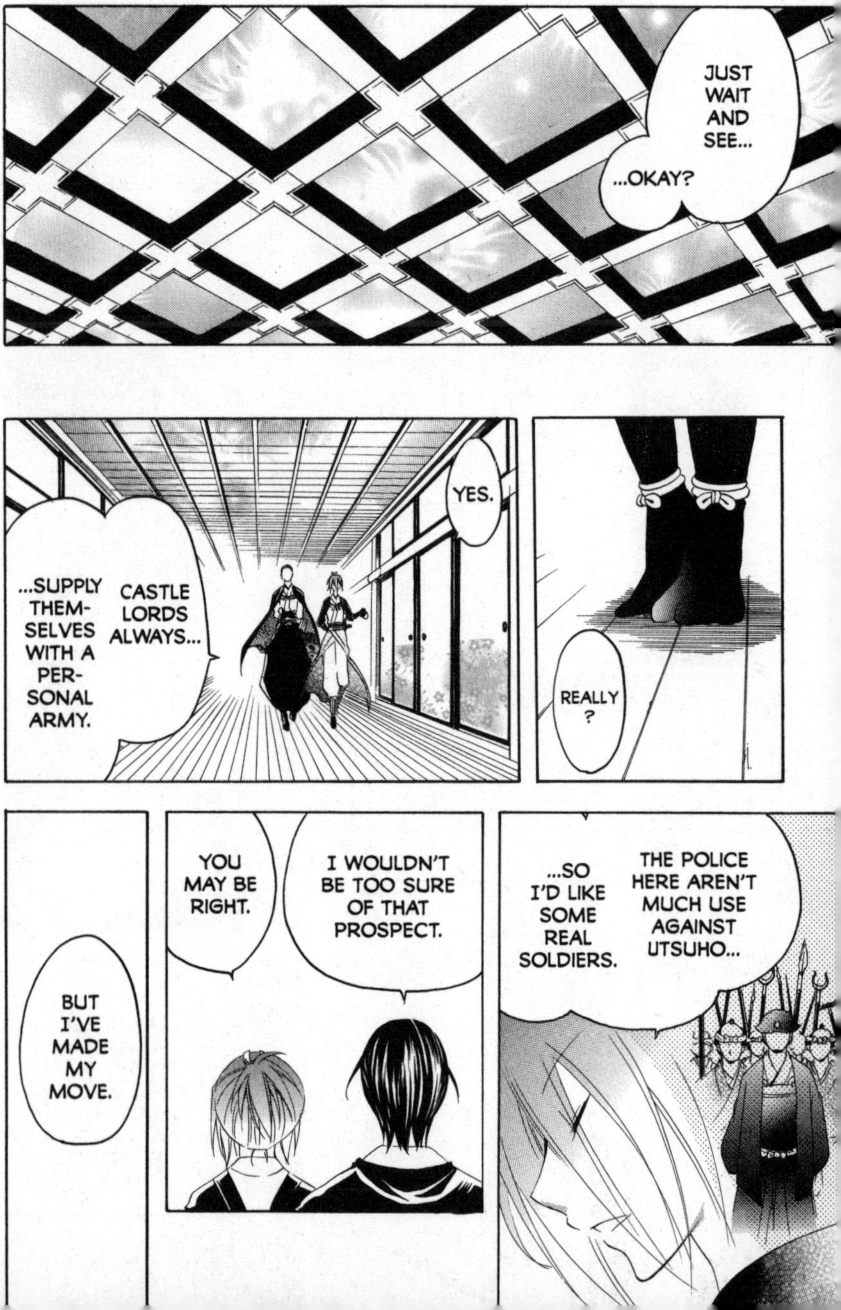
JUST WAIT AND SEE...
...OKAY?
REALLY?
YES.
CASTLE LORDS ALWAYS...
...SUPPLY THEMSELVES WITH A PERSONAL ARMY.
THE POLICE HERE AREN'T MUCH USE AGAINST UTSUHO...
...SO I'D LIKE SOME REAL SOLDIERS.
I WOULDN'T BE TOO SURE OF THAT PROSPECT.
YOU MAY BE RIGHT.
BUT I'VE MADE MY MOVE.

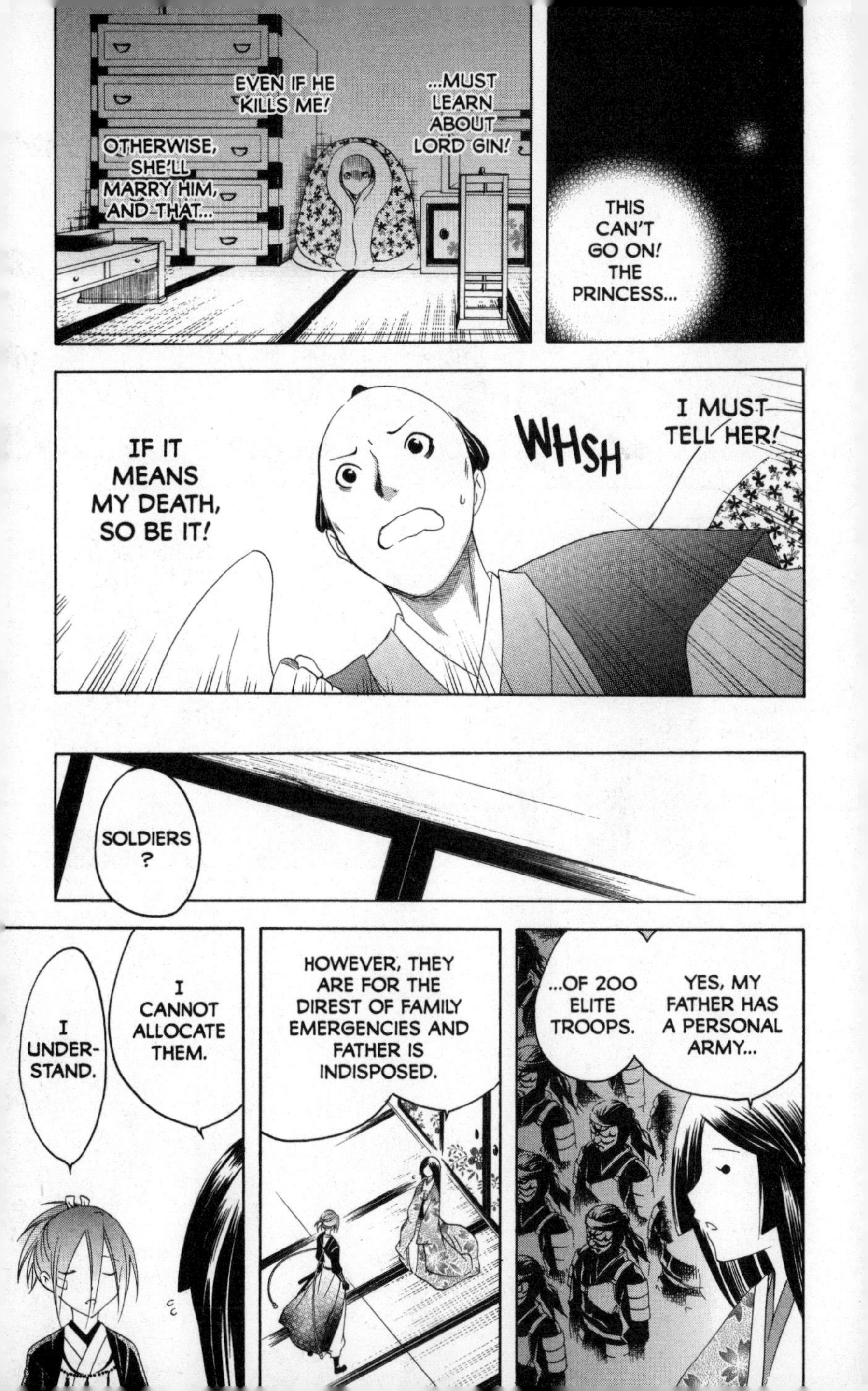
THIS CAN'T GO ON! THE PRINCESS...
...MUST LEARN ABOUT LORD GIN!
EVEN IF HE KILLS ME!
OTHERWISE, SHE'LL MARRY HIM, AND THAT...
I MUST TELL HER!
WHSH
IF IT MEANS MY DEATH, SO BE IT!
SOLDIERS?
YES, MY FATHER HAS A PERSONAL ARMY...
...OF 200 ELITE TROOPS.
HOWEVER, THEY ARE FOR THE DIREST OF FAMILY EMERGENCIES AND FATHER IS INDISPOSED.
I CANNOT ALLOCATE THEM.
I UNDERSTAND.

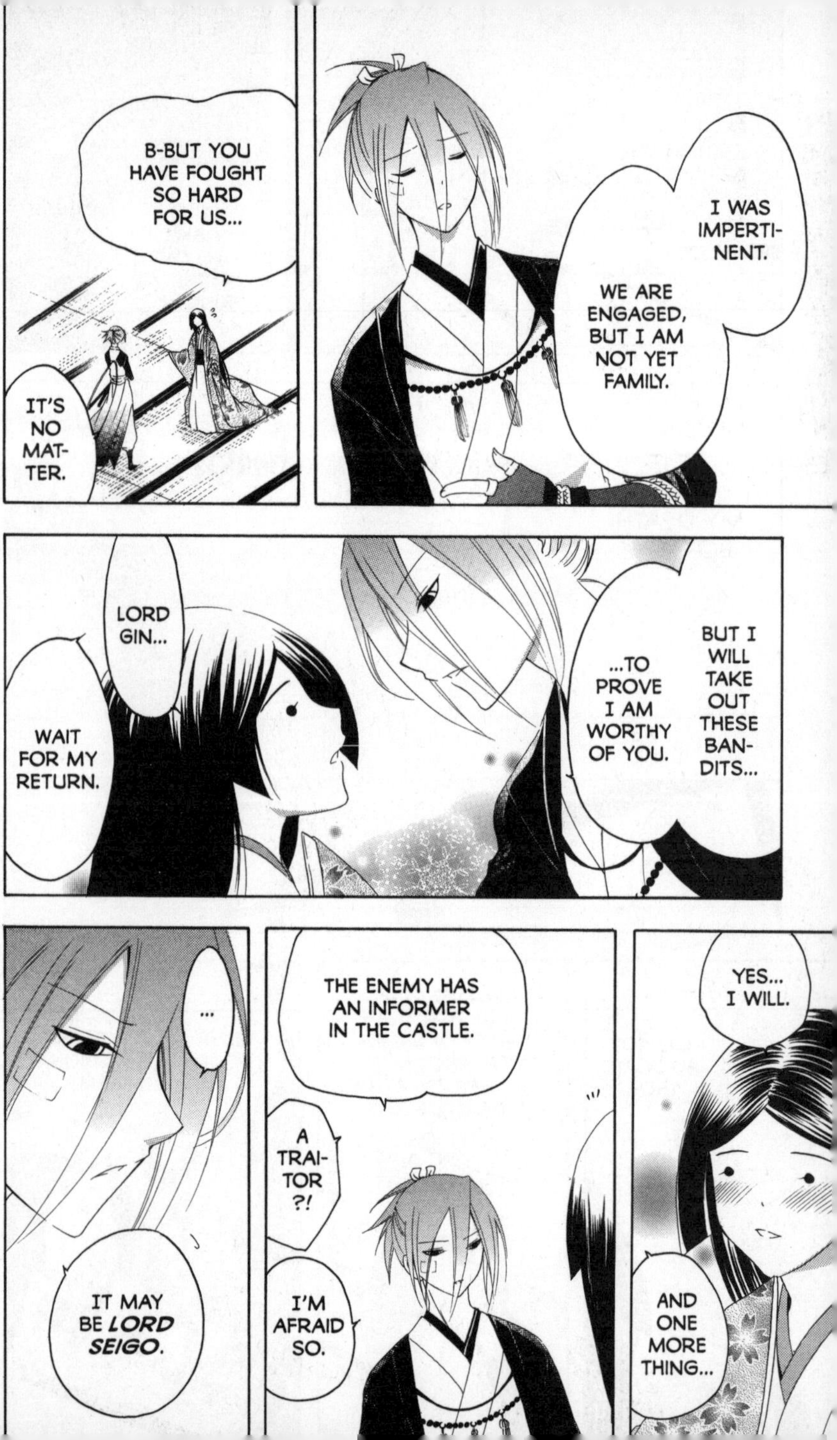

I WAS IMPERTI-NENT.
WE ARE ENGAGED, BUT I AM NOT YET FAMILY.
B-BUT YOU HAVE FOUGHT SO HARD FOR US...
IT'S NO MAT-TER.
BUT I WILL TAKE OUT THESE BAN-DITS...
...TO PROVE I AM WORTHY OF YOU.
LORD GIN...
WAIT FOR MY RETURN.
YES... I WILL.
AND ONE MORE THING...
THE ENEMY HAS AN INFORMER IN THE CASTLE.
A TRAI-TOR?!
I'M AFRAID SO.
...
IT MAY BE *LORD SEIGO*.

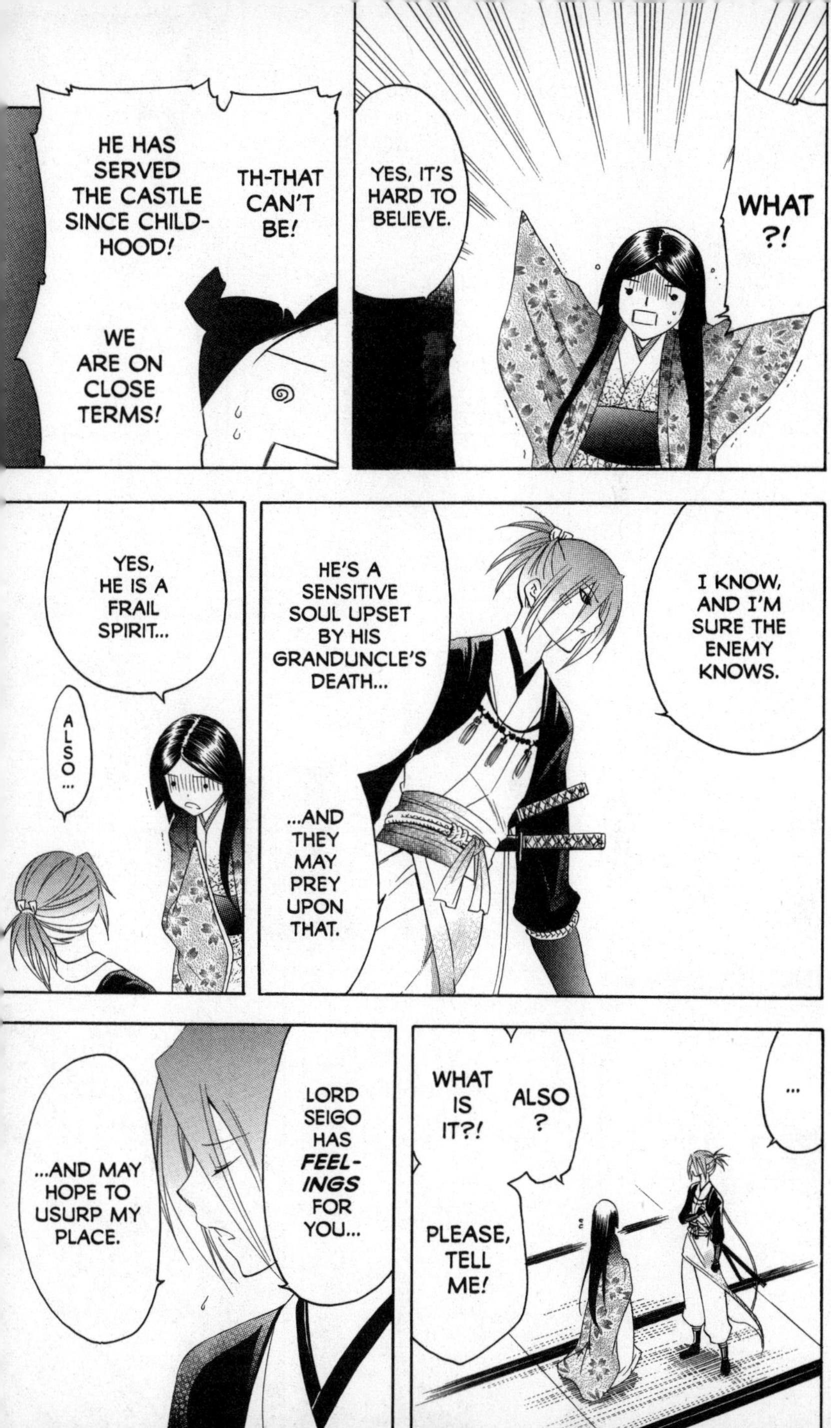
WHAT ?!
YES, IT'S HARD TO BELIEVE.
TH-THAT CAN'T BE!
HE HAS SERVED THE CASTLE SINCE CHILD-HOOD!
WE ARE ON CLOSE TERMS!
I KNOW, AND I'M SURE THE ENEMY KNOWS.
HE'S A SENSITIVE SOUL UPSET BY HIS GRANDUNCLE'S DEATH...
...AND THEY MAY PREY UPON THAT.
YES, HE IS A FRAIL SPIRIT...
ALSO...
...
ALSO ?
WHAT IS IT?!
PLEASE, TELL ME!
LORD SEIGO HAS FEEL-INGS FOR YOU...
...AND MAY HOPE TO USURP MY PLACE.

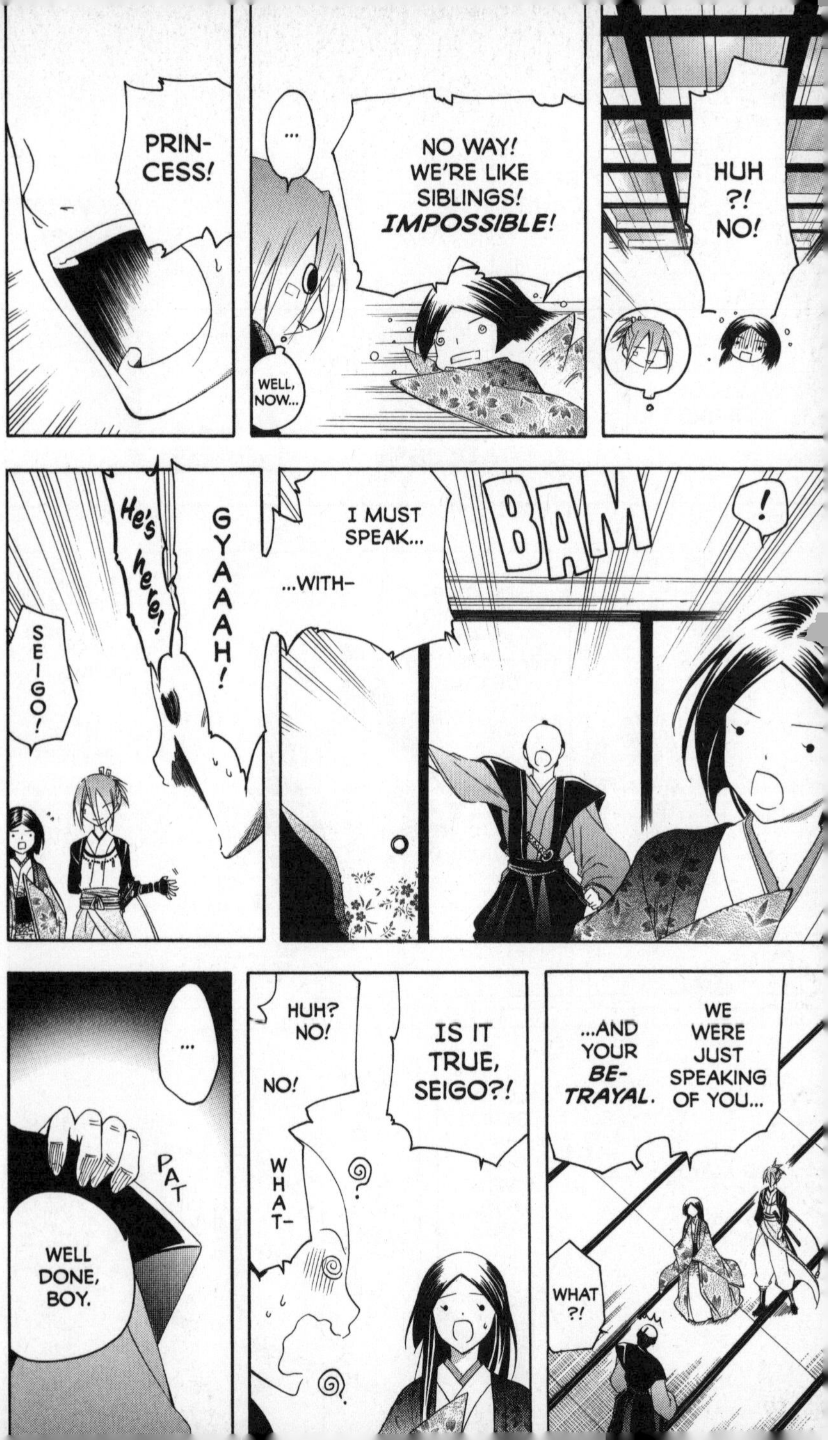
HUH ?! NO!
NO WAY! WE'RE LIKE SIBLINGS! *IMPOSSIBLE*!
...
WELL, NOW...
PRIN-CESS!
BAM
!
I MUST SPEAK...
...WITH-
GYAAAAH!
He's here!
SEIGO!
WE WERE JUST SPEAKING OF YOU...
...AND YOUR *BE-TRAYAL*.
WHAT ?!
IS IT TRUE, SEIGO?!
HUH? NO!
NO!
WHAT-
...
PAT
WELL DONE, BOY.

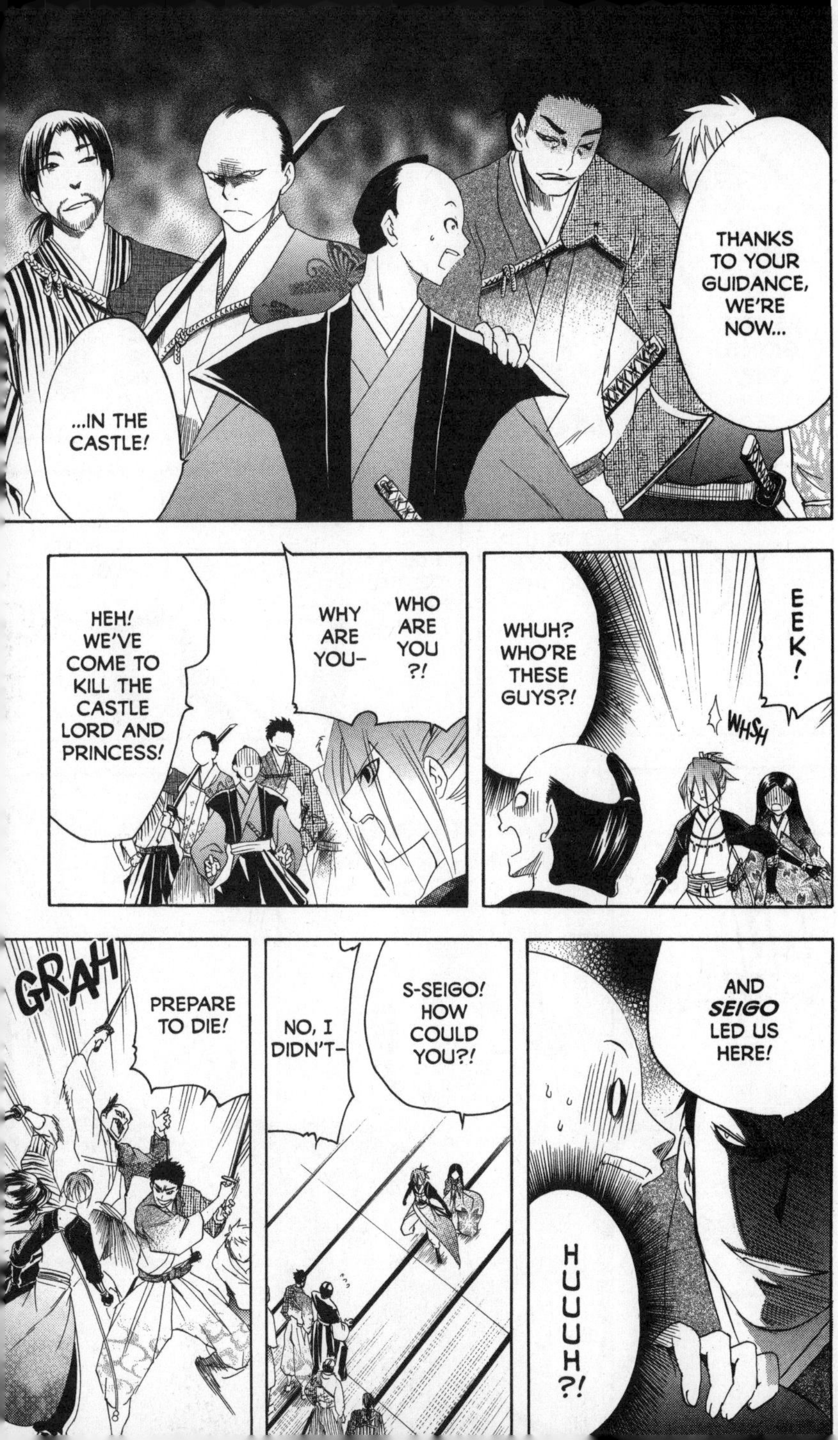
THANKS TO YOUR GUIDANCE, WE'RE NOW...
...IN THE CASTLE!
EEK!
WHSH
WHUH? WHO'RE THESE GUYS?!
WHO ARE YOU ?!
WHY ARE YOU-
HEH! WE'VE COME TO KILL THE CASTLE LORD AND PRINCESS!
AND *SEIGO* LED US HERE!
HUUUH?!
S-SEIGO! HOW COULD YOU?!
NO, I DIDN'T-
GRAH
PREPARE TO DIE!

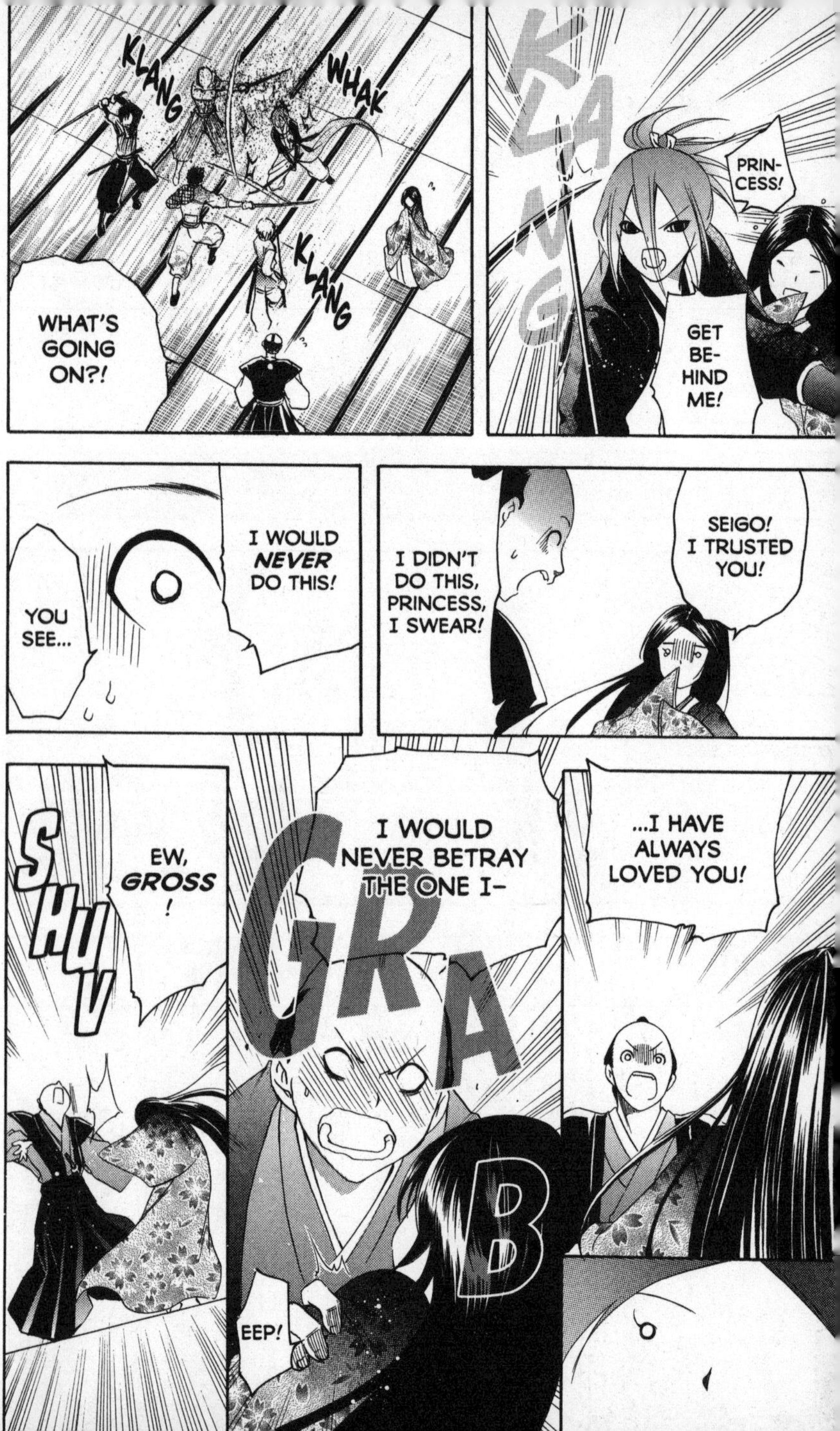
KLANG
PRIN-CESS!
GET BE-HIND ME!
KLANG
WHAK
KLANG
WHAT'S GOING ON?!
SEIGO! I TRUSTED YOU!
I DIDN'T DO THIS, PRINCESS, I SWEAR!
I WOULD *NEVER* DO THIS!
YOU SEE...
...I HAVE ALWAYS LOVED YOU!
I WOULD NEVER BETRAY THE ONE I–
GRAB
EEP!
EW, *GROSS*!
SHUV

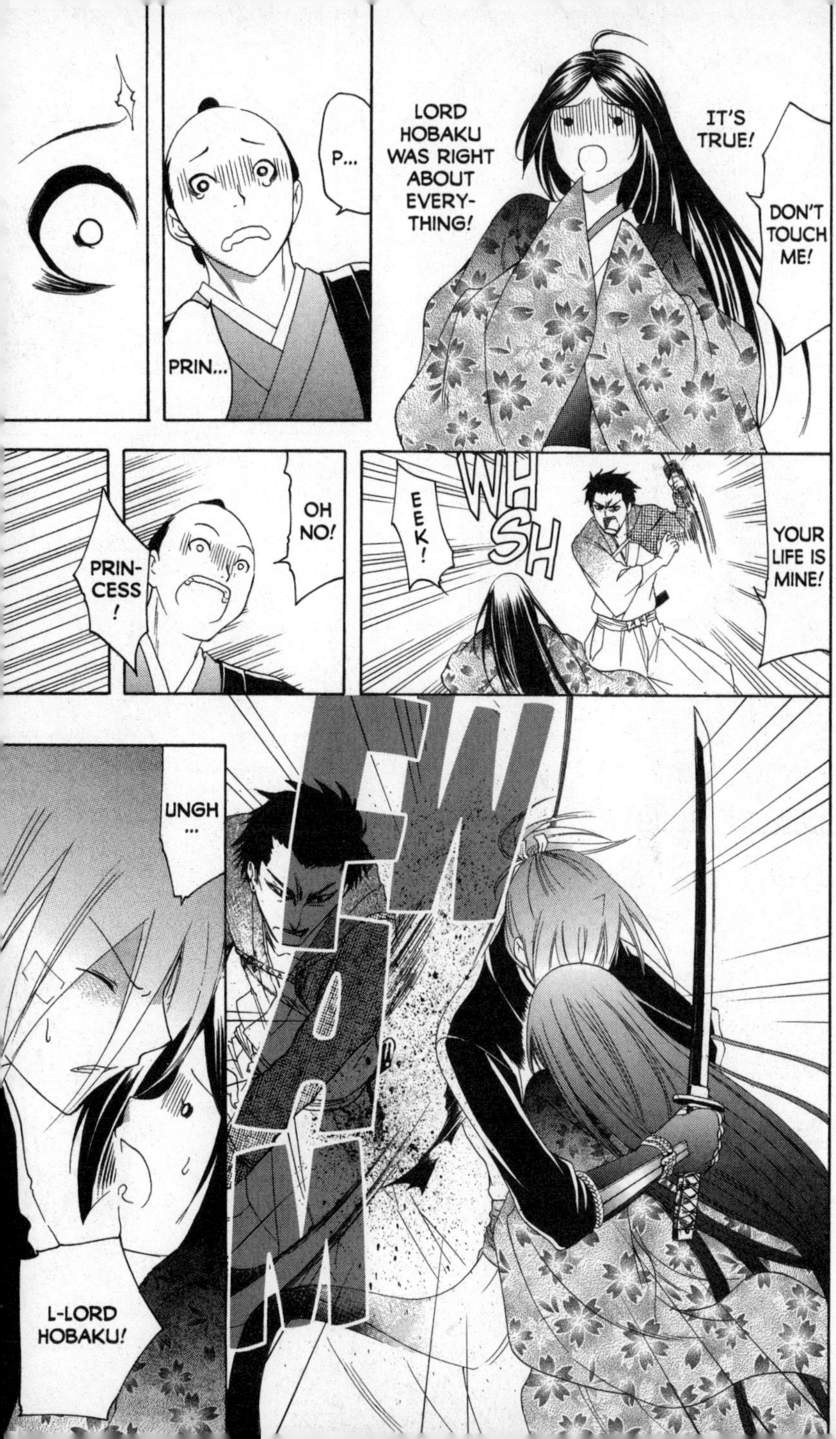
IT'S TRUE!
DON'T TOUCH ME!
LORD HOBAKU WAS RIGHT ABOUT EVERYTHING!
P...
PRIN...
YOUR LIFE IS MINE!
WHSH
EEK!
OH NO!
PRINCESS!
UNGH...
L-LORD HOBAKU!

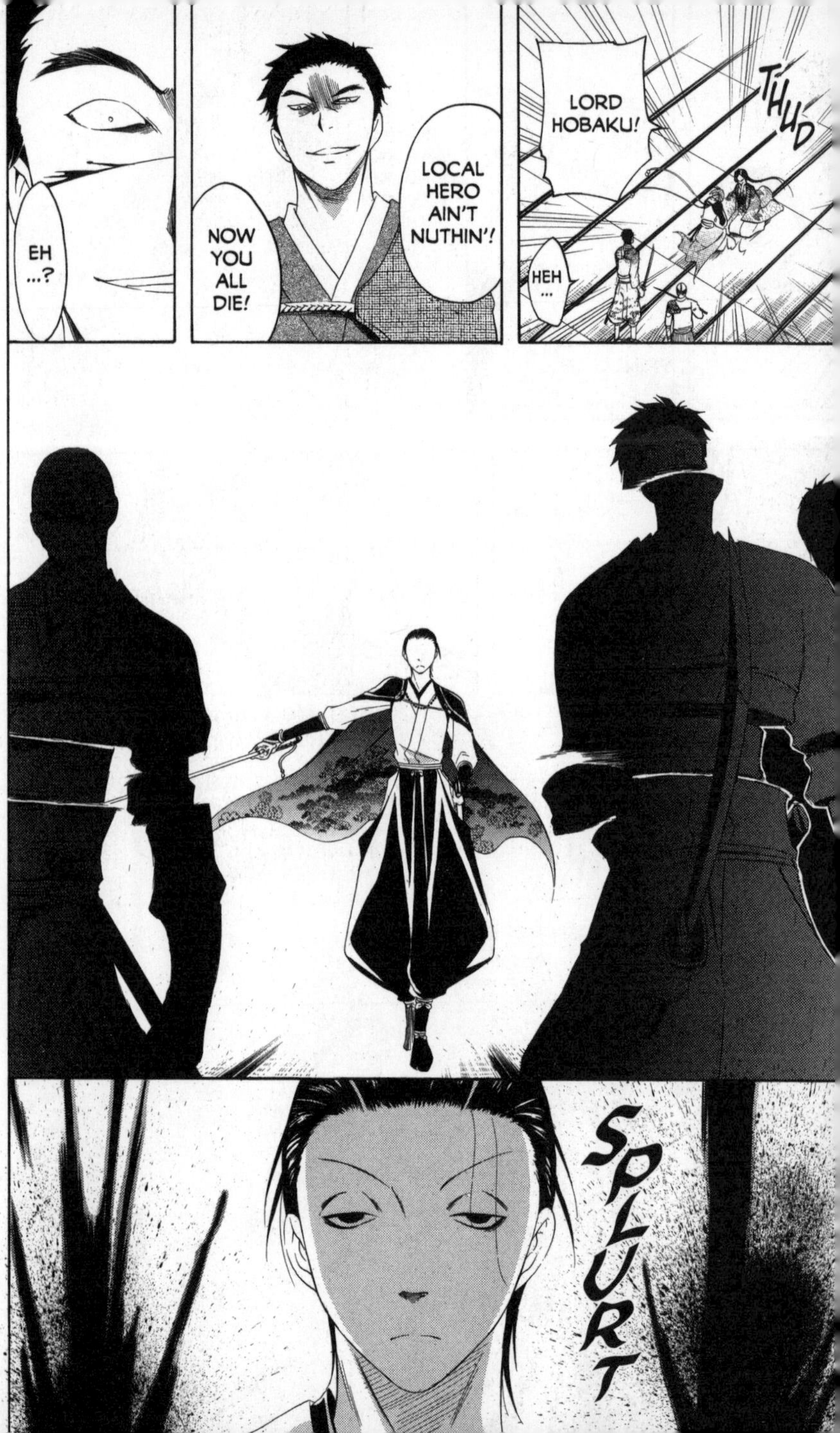
LORD HOBAKU!
THUD
HEH ...
LOCAL HERO AIN'T NUTHIN'!
NOW YOU ALL DIE!
EH ...?
SPLURT

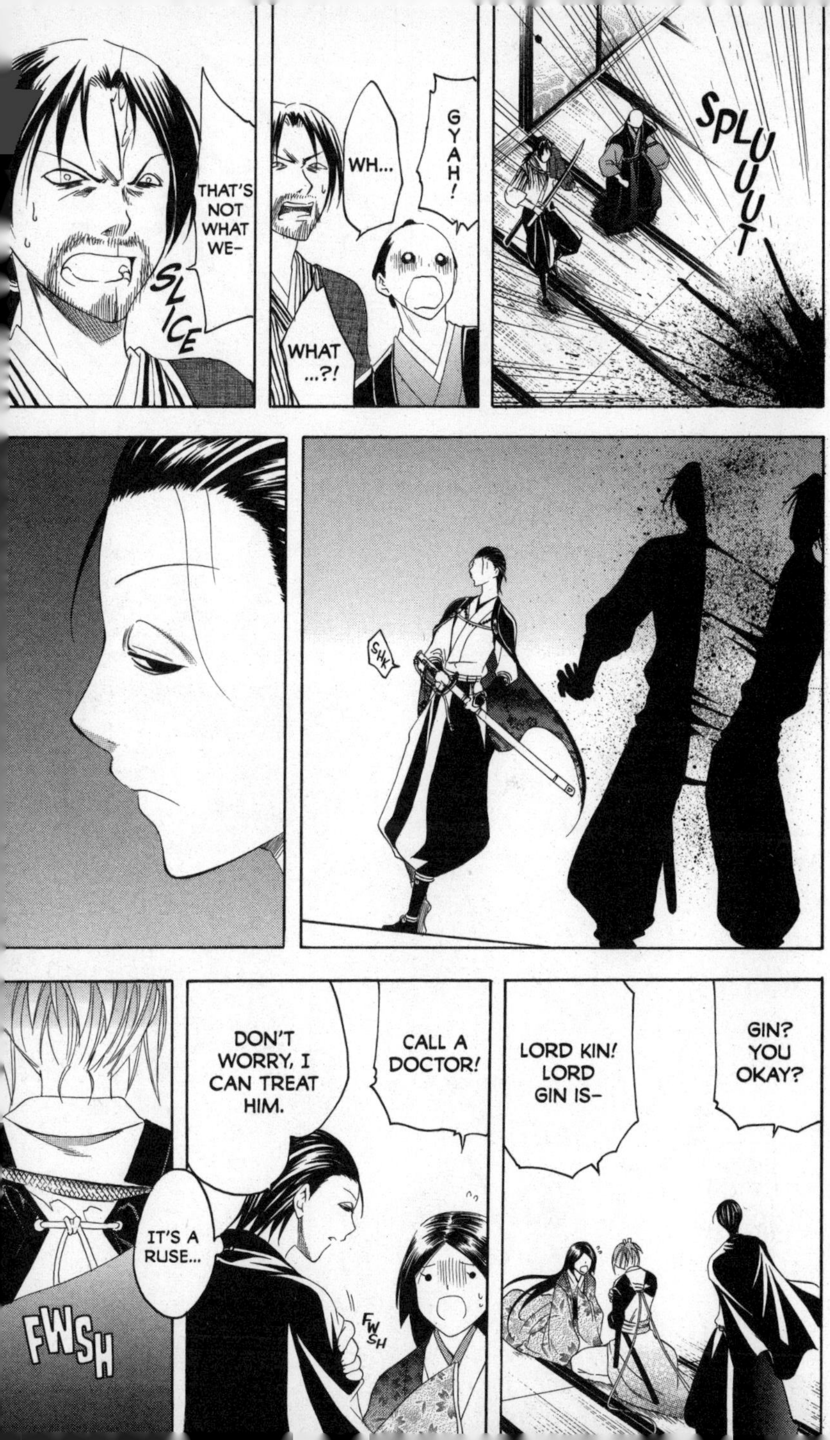
SPLUUUUT
GYAH!
WH...
WHAT ...?!
THAT'S NOT WHAT WE-
SLICE
SHK
GIN? YOU OKAY?
LORD KIN! LORD GIN IS-
CALL A DOCTOR!
DON'T WORRY, I CAN TREAT HIM.
FWSH
IT'S A RUSE...
FWSH

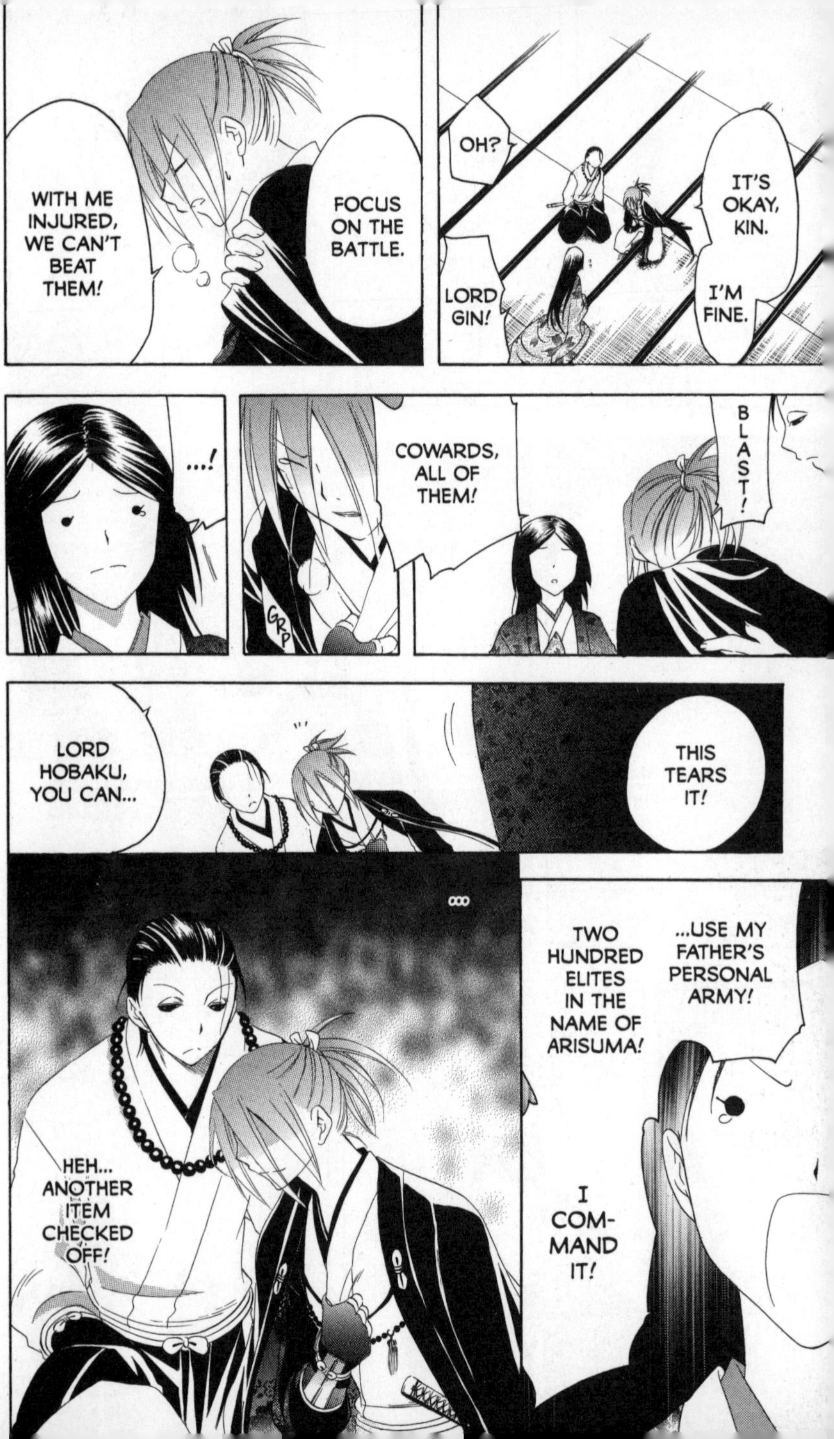
IT'S OKAY, KIN.
I'M FINE.
OH?
LORD GIN!
FOCUS ON THE BATTLE.
WITH ME INJURED, WE CAN'T BEAT THEM!
BLAST!
COWARDS, ALL OF THEM!
GRP
...!
THIS TEARS IT!
LORD HOBAKU, YOU CAN...
...USE MY FATHER'S PERSONAL ARMY!
TWO HUNDRED ELITES IN THE NAME OF ARISUMA!
I COMMAND IT!
HEH... ANOTHER ITEM CHECKED OFF!

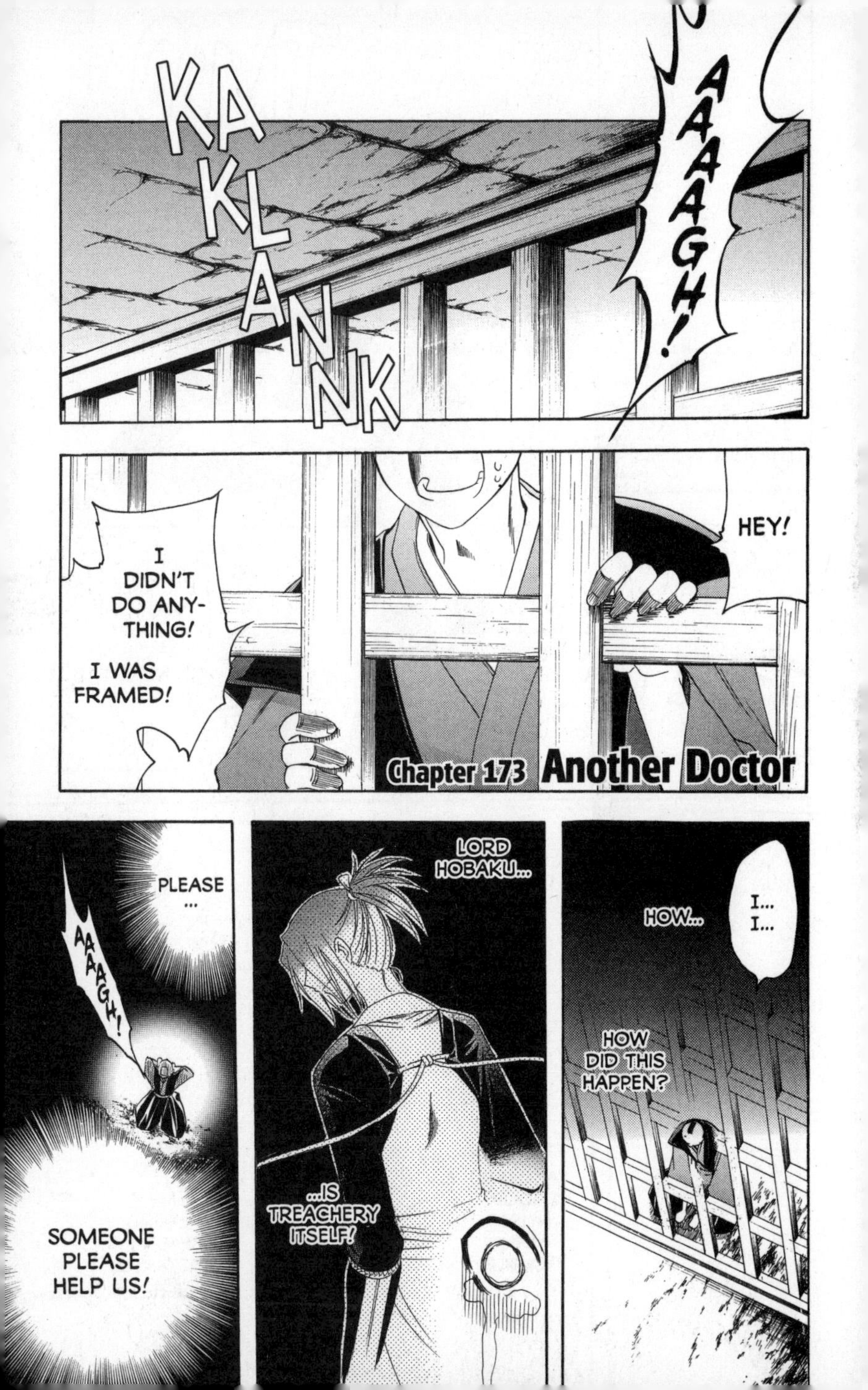
AAAAAGH!
KAKLANNK
HEY!
I DIDN'T DO ANY-THING!
I WAS FRAMED!
Chapter 173 Another Doctor
I... I...
HOW...
HOW DID THIS HAPPEN?
LORD HOBAKU...
...IS TREACHERY ITSELF!
PLEASE ...
AAAAGH!
SOMEONE PLEASE HELP US!

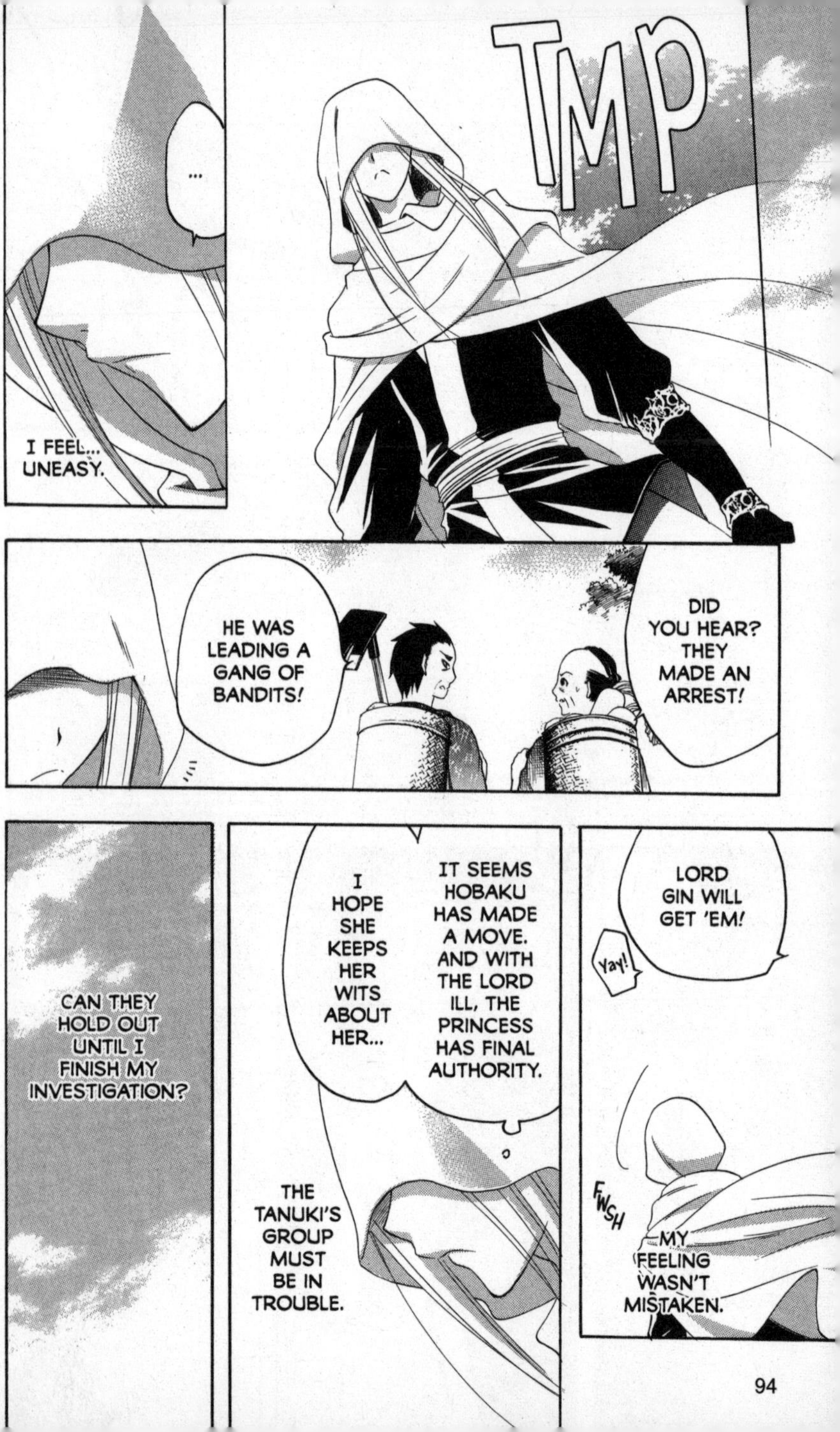
TMP
...
I FEEL... UNEASY.
DID YOU HEAR? THEY MADE AN ARREST!
HE WAS LEADING A GANG OF BANDITS!
LORD GIN WILL GET 'EM!
Yay!
FWSH
MY FEELING WASN'T MISTAKEN.
IT SEEMS HOBAKU HAS MADE A MOVE. AND WITH THE LORD ILL, THE PRINCESS HAS FINAL AUTHORITY.
I HOPE SHE KEEPS HER WITS ABOUT HER...
THE TANUKI'S GROUP MUST BE IN TROUBLE.
CAN THEY HOLD OUT UNTIL I FINISH MY INVESTIGATION?

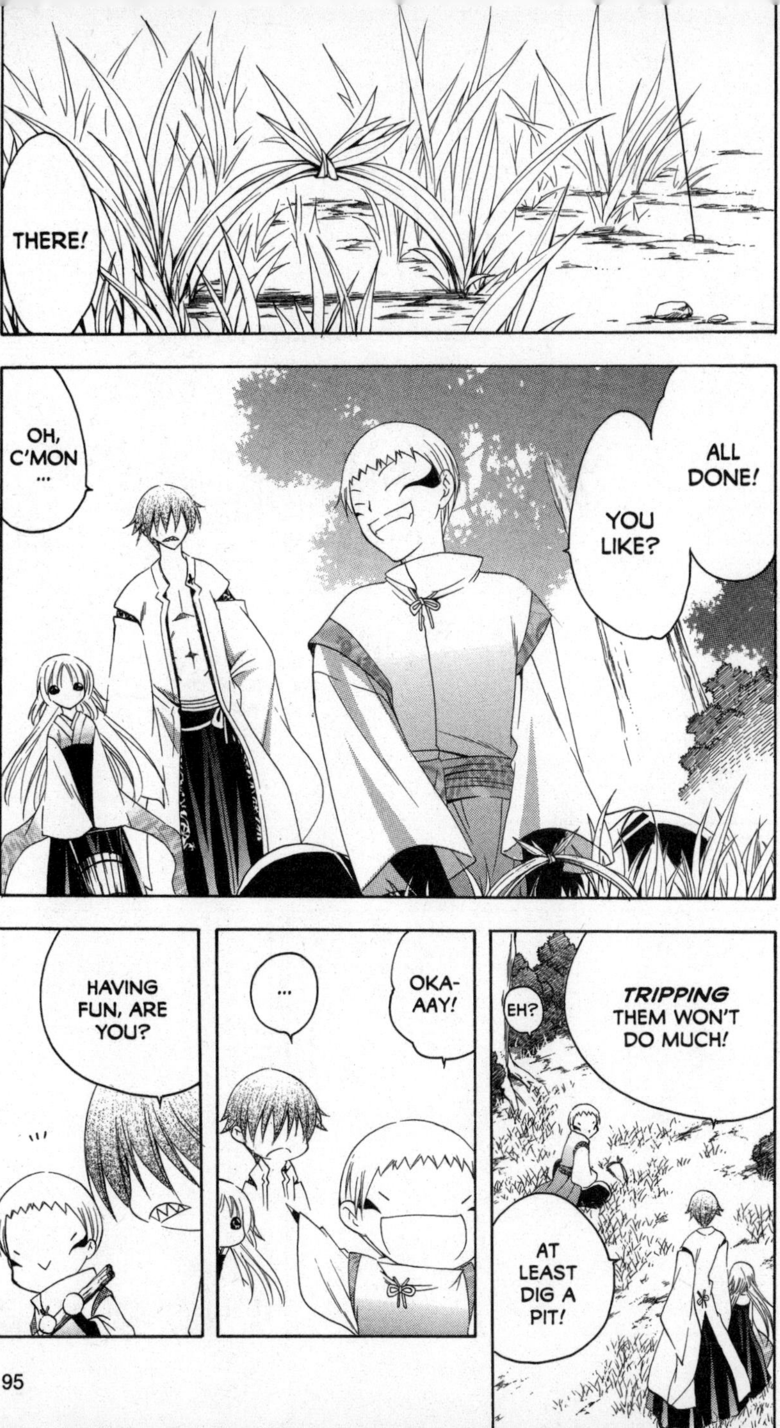
THERE!
ALL DONE!
YOU LIKE?
OH, C'MON ...
TRIPPING THEM WON'T DO MUCH!
EH?
AT LEAST DIG A PIT!
OKA-AAY!
...
HAVING FUN, ARE YOU?

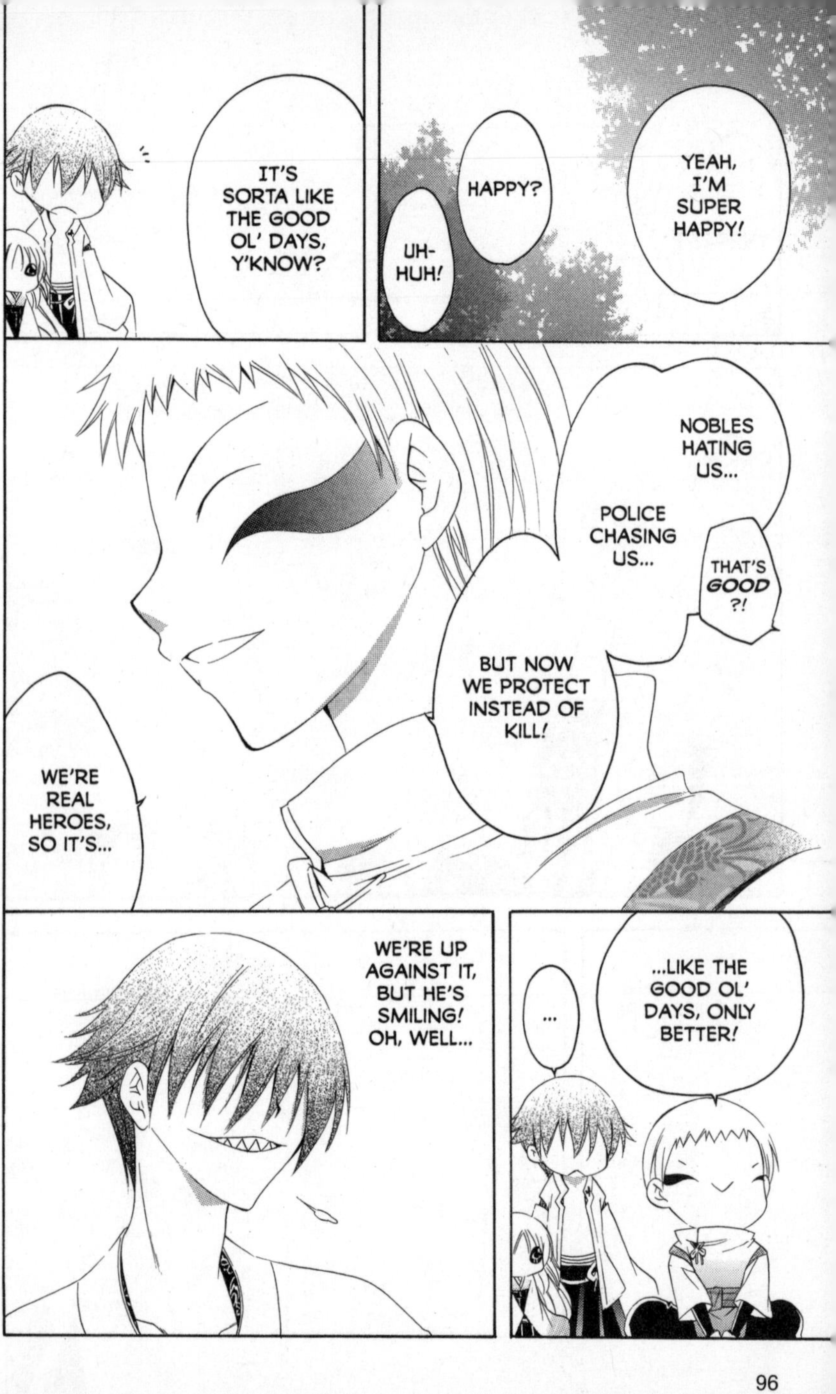
YEAH, I'M SUPER HAPPY!
HAPPY?
UH-HUH!
IT'S SORTA LIKE THE GOOD OL' DAYS, Y'KNOW?
NOBLES HATING US...
POLICE CHASING US...
THAT'S *GOOD* ?!
BUT NOW WE PROTECT INSTEAD OF KILL!
WE'RE REAL HEROES, SO IT'S...
...LIKE THE GOOD OL' DAYS, ONLY BETTER!
...
WE'RE UP AGAINST IT, BUT HE'S SMILING! OH, WELL...

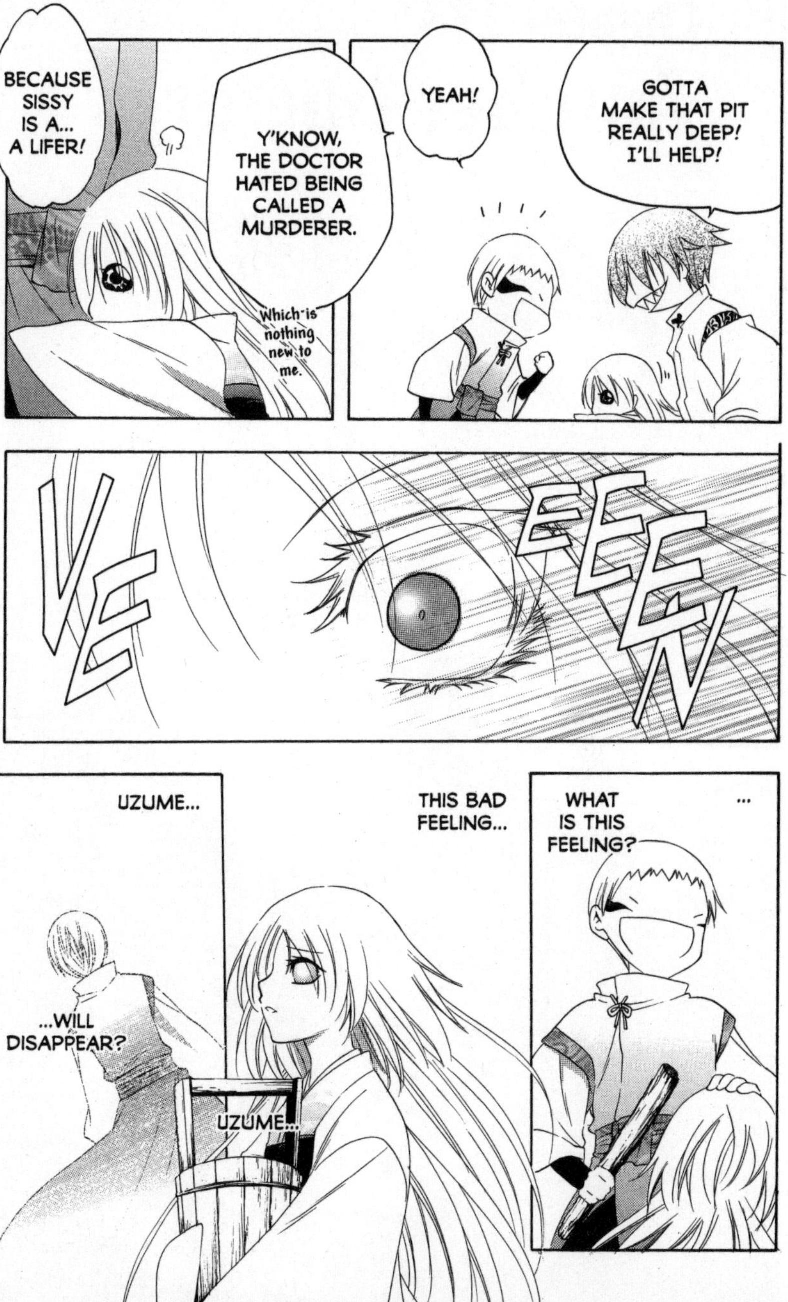
GOTTA MAKE THAT PIT REALLY DEEP! I'LL HELP!
YEAH!
Y'KNOW, THE DOCTOR HATED BEING CALLED A MURDERER.
Which is nothing new to me.
BECAUSE SISSY IS A... A LIFER!
VEEEEEN
...
WHAT IS THIS FEELING?
THIS BAD FEELING...
UZUME...
...WILL DISAPPEAR?
UZUME...

Chapter 173
Another Doctor

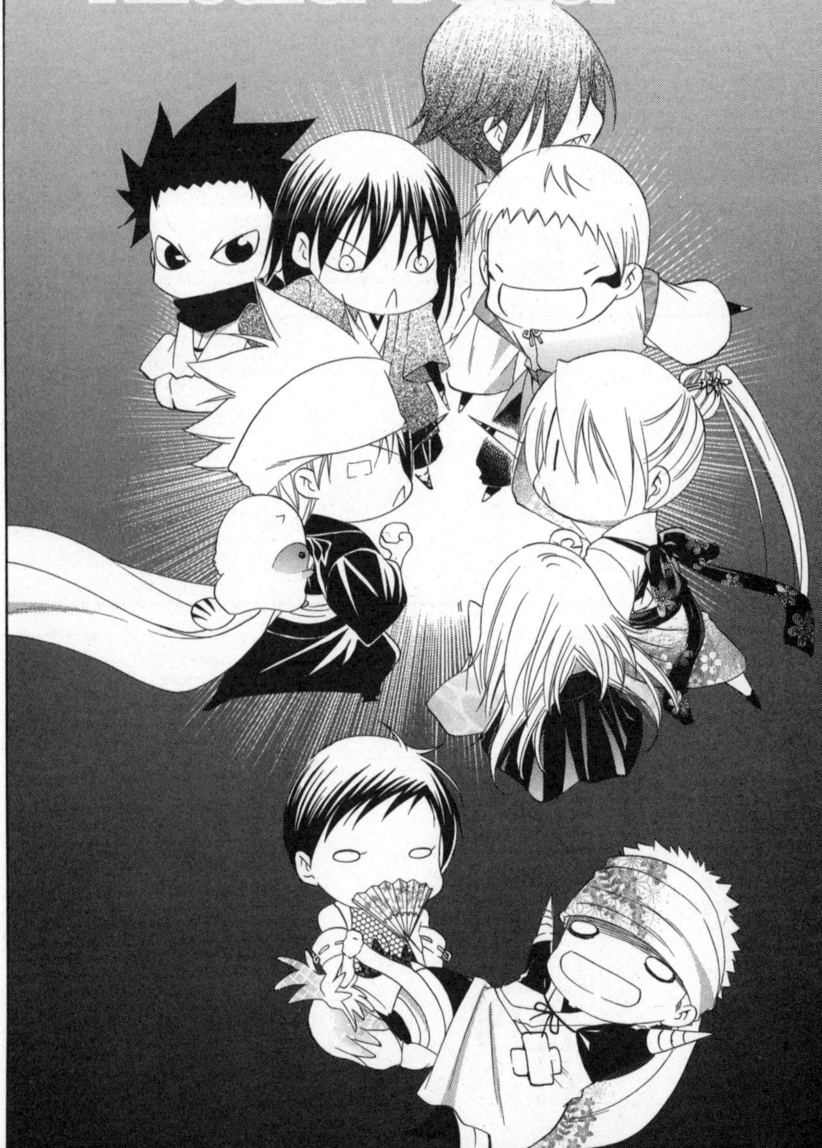

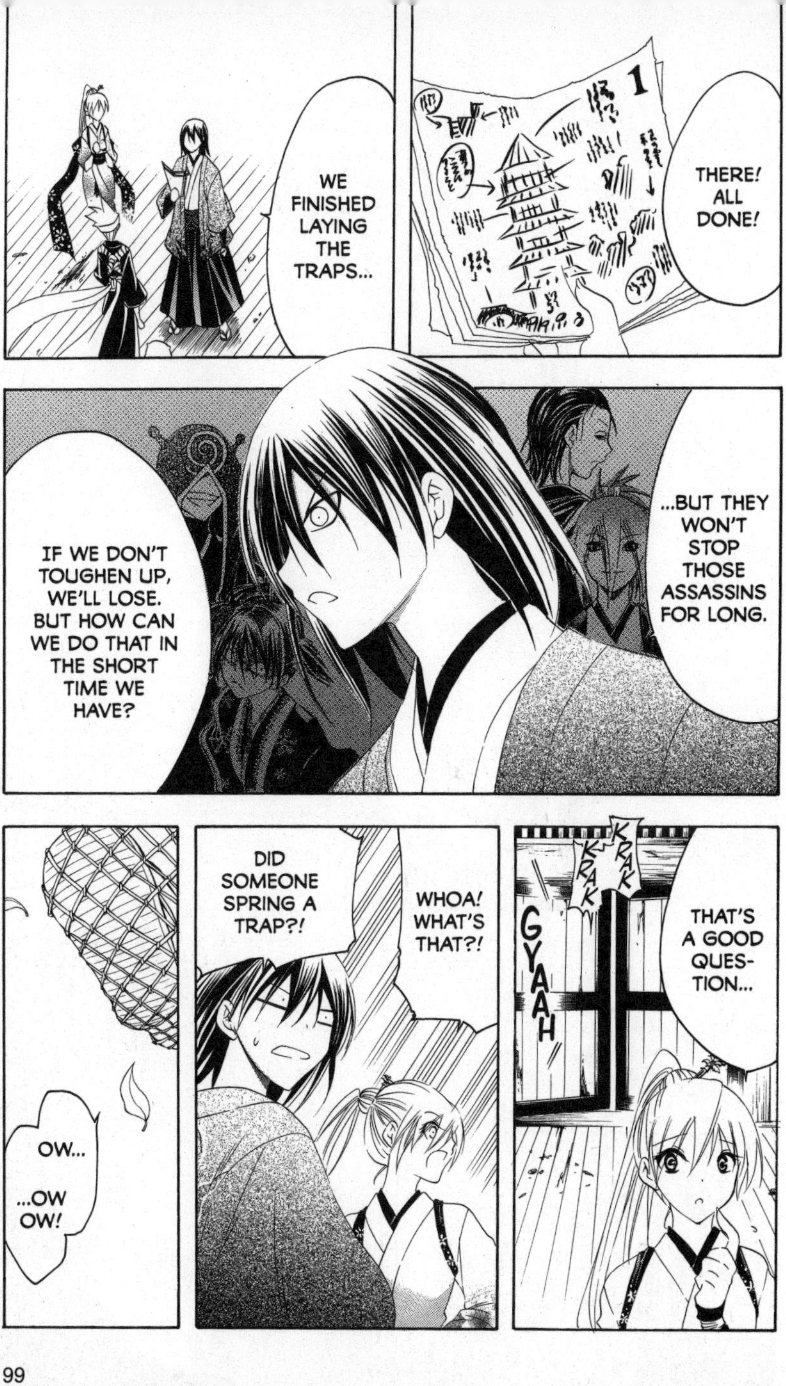
THERE! ALL DONE!
WE FINISHED LAYING THE TRAPS...
...BUT THEY WON'T STOP THOSE ASSASSINS FOR LONG.
IF WE DON'T TOUGHEN UP, WE'LL LOSE. BUT HOW CAN WE DO THAT IN THE SHORT TIME WE HAVE?
THAT'S A GOOD QUES-TION...
KRAK
KRAK
GYAAH
WHOA! WHAT'S THAT?!
DID SOMEONE SPRING A TRAP?!
OW...
...OW OW!

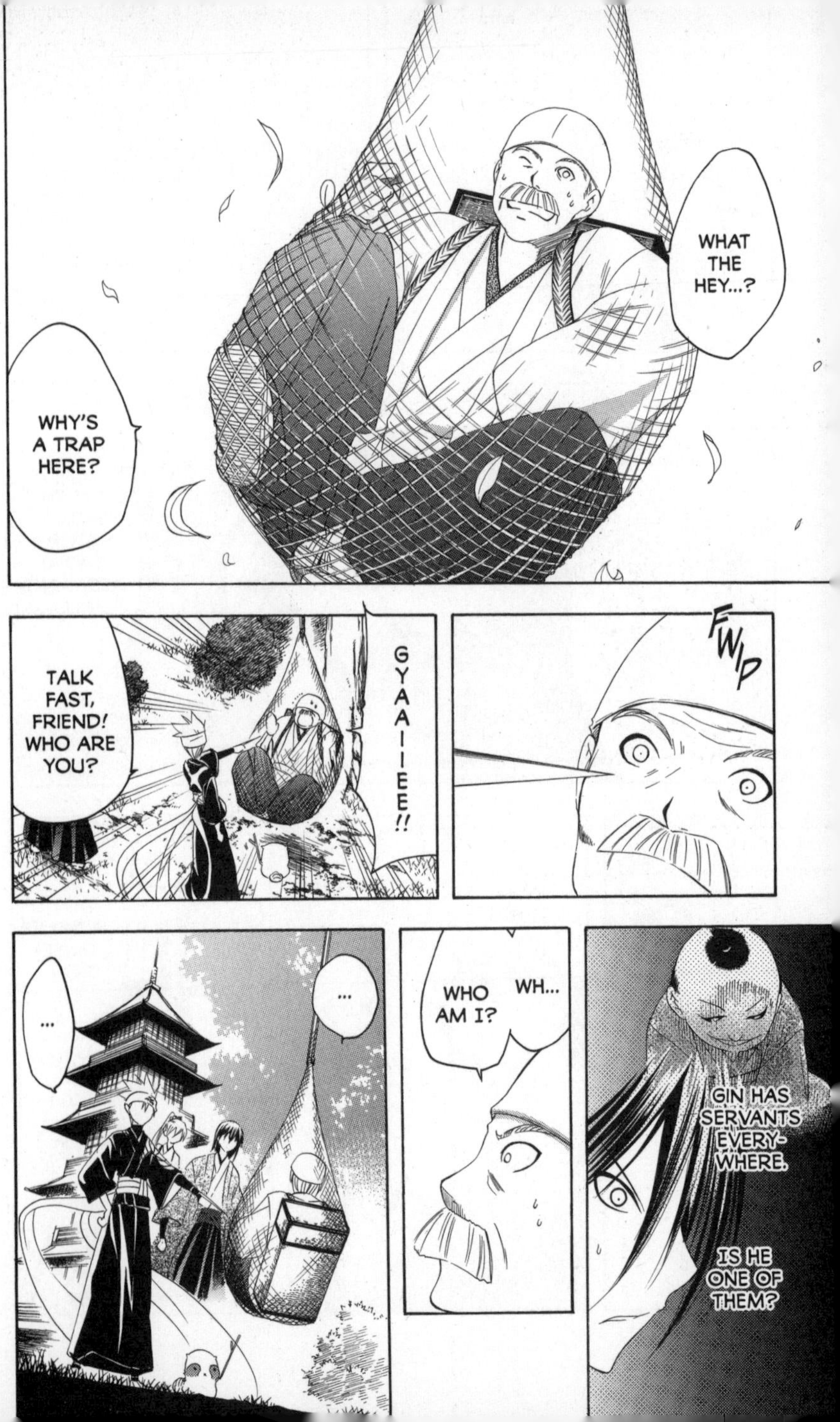
WHAT THE HEY...?
WHY'S A TRAP HERE?
FWIP
GYAAIIEE!!
TALK FAST, FRIEND! WHO ARE YOU?
GIN HAS SERVANTS EVERY-WHERE.
IS HE ONE OF THEM?
WH...
WHO AM I?
...
...

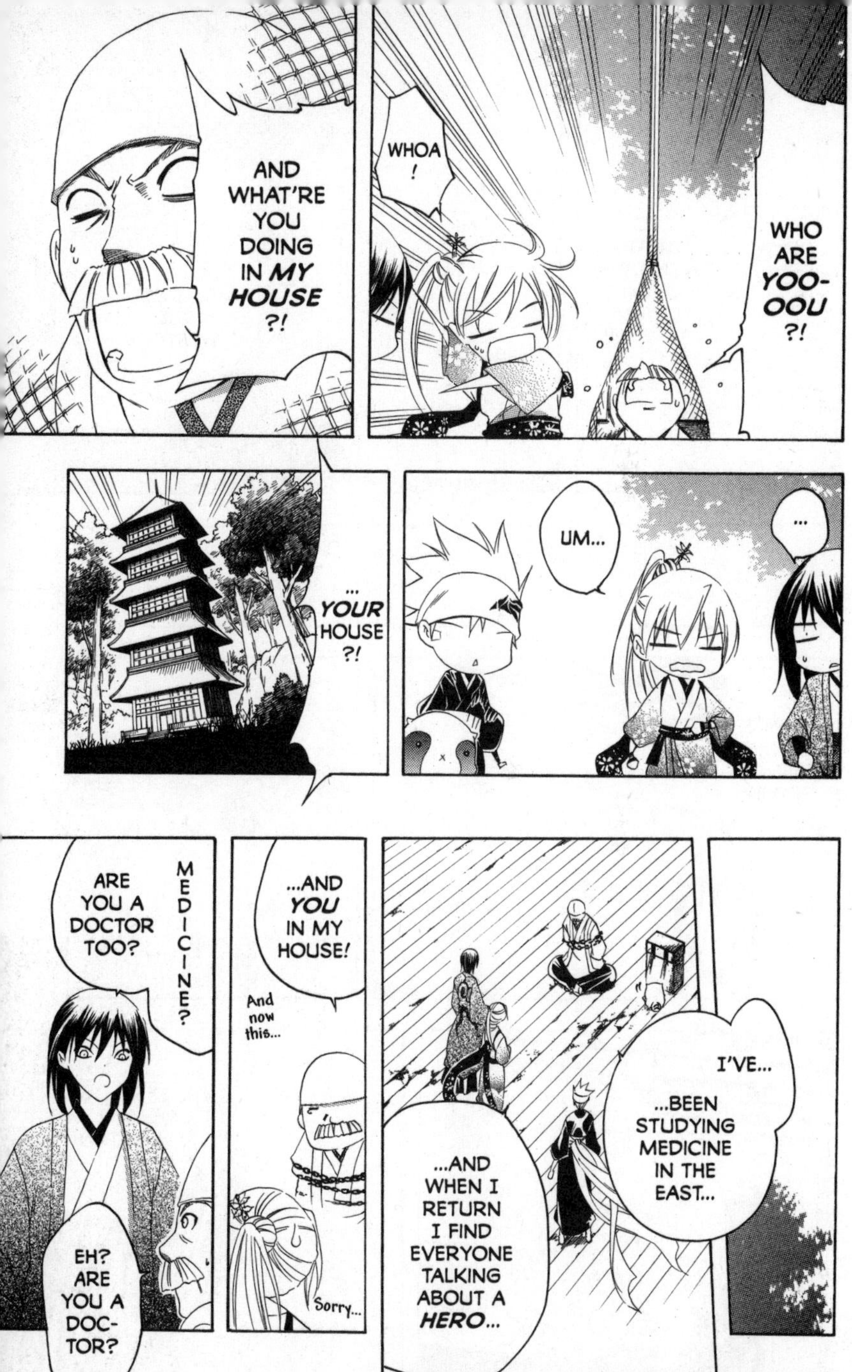
WHO ARE YOO-OOU?!
WHOA!
AND WHAT'RE YOU DOING IN *MY HOUSE*?!
...
UM...
...*YOUR* HOUSE?!
I'VE...
...BEEN STUDYING MEDICINE IN THE EAST...
...AND WHEN I RETURN I FIND EVERYONE TALKING ABOUT A *HERO*...
...AND *YOU* IN MY HOUSE!
And now this...
Sorry...
MEDICINE?
ARE YOU A DOCTOR TOO?
EH? ARE YOU A DOC-TOR?

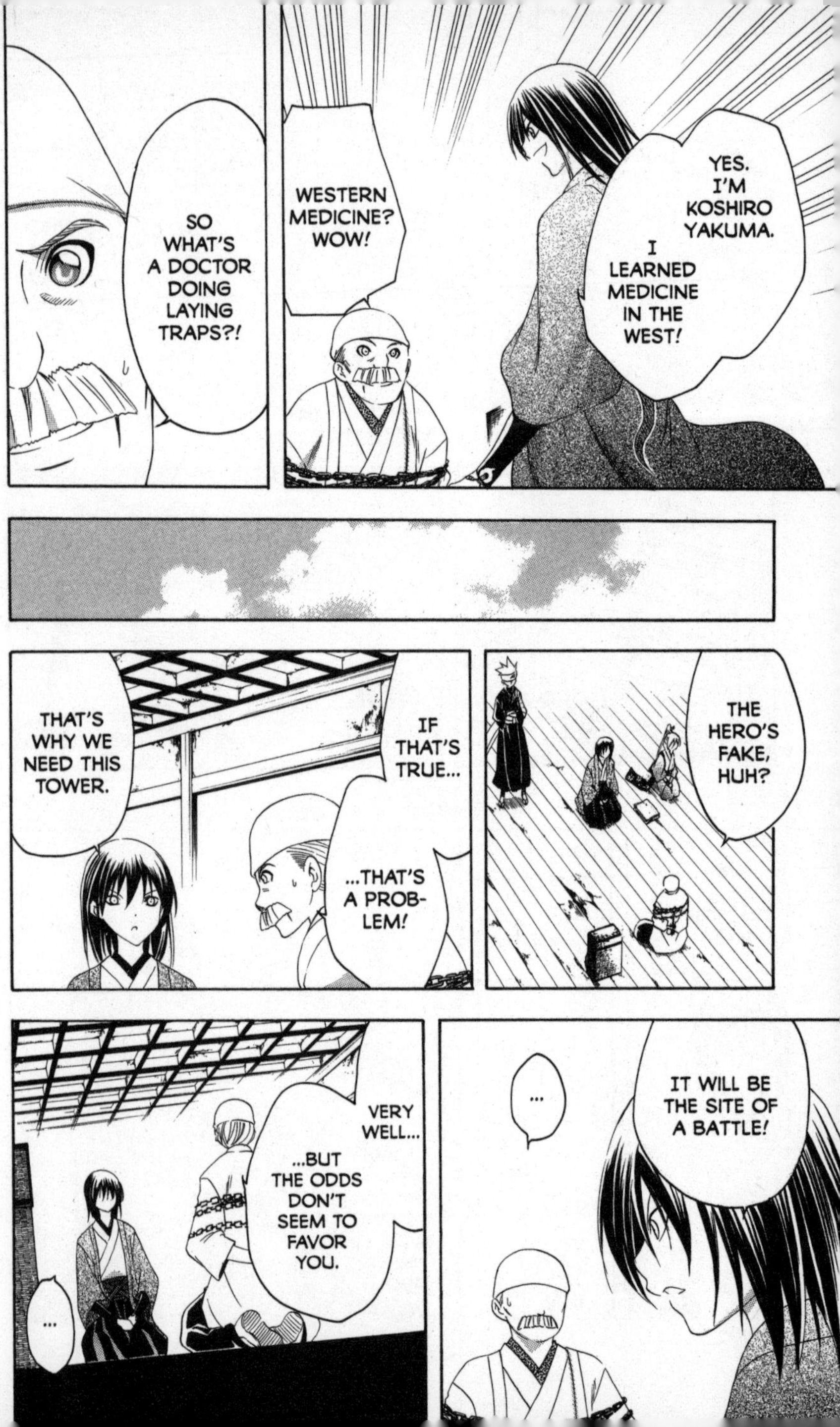
YES. I'M KOSHIRO YAKUMA.
I LEARNED MEDICINE IN THE WEST!
WESTERN MEDICINE? WOW!
SO WHAT'S A DOCTOR DOING LAYING TRAPS?!
THE HERO'S FAKE, HUH?
IF THAT'S TRUE...
...THAT'S A PROB-LEM!
THAT'S WHY WE NEED THIS TOWER.
IT WILL BE THE SITE OF A BATTLE!
...
VERY WELL...
...BUT THE ODDS DON'T SEEM TO FAVOR YOU.
...

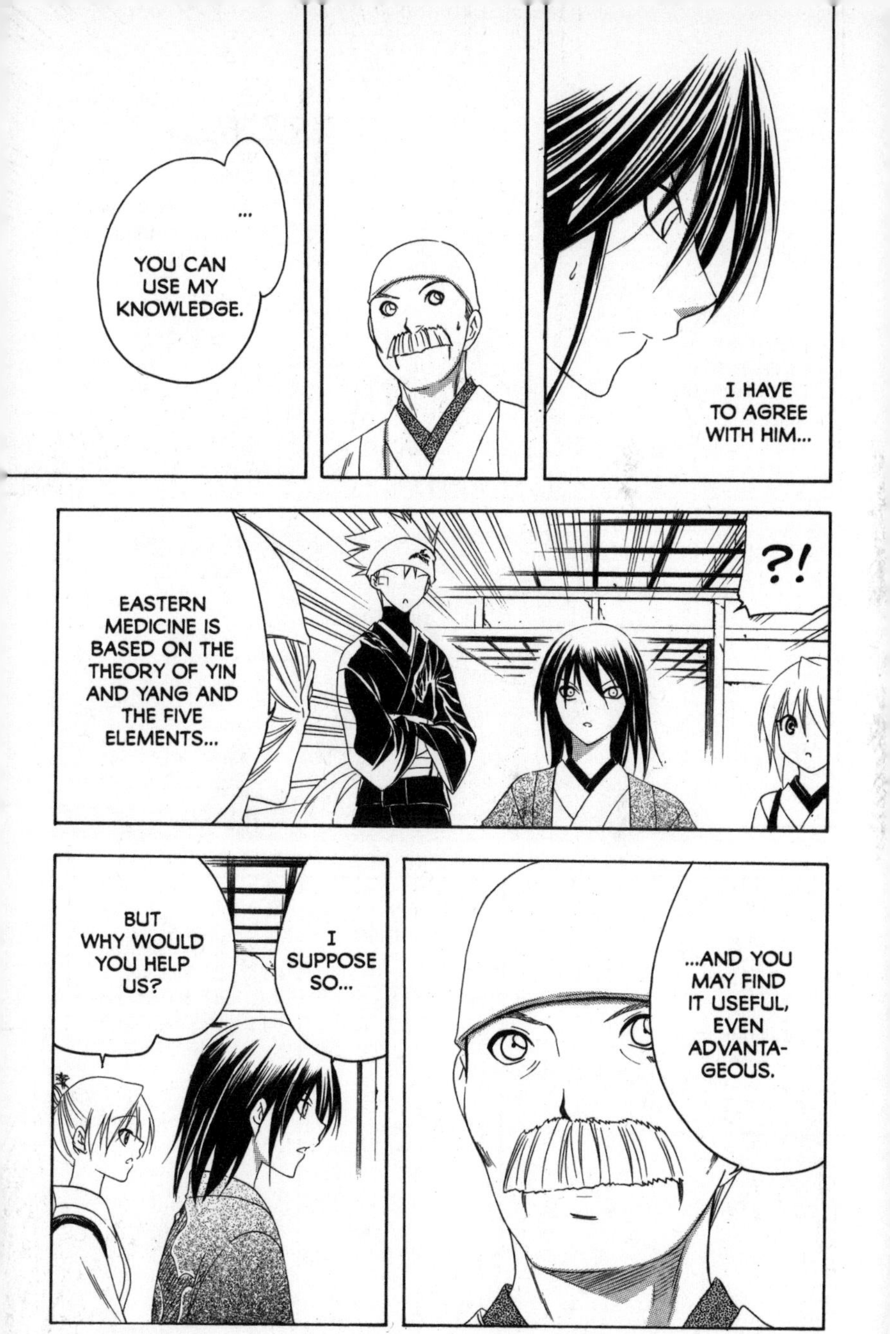

I HAVE TO AGREE WITH HIM...
...
YOU CAN USE MY KNOWLEDGE.
?!
EASTERN MEDICINE IS BASED ON THE THEORY OF YIN AND YANG AND THE FIVE ELEMENTS...
...AND YOU MAY FIND IT USEFUL, EVEN ADVANTAGEOUS.
I SUPPOSE SO...
BUT WHY WOULD YOU HELP US?

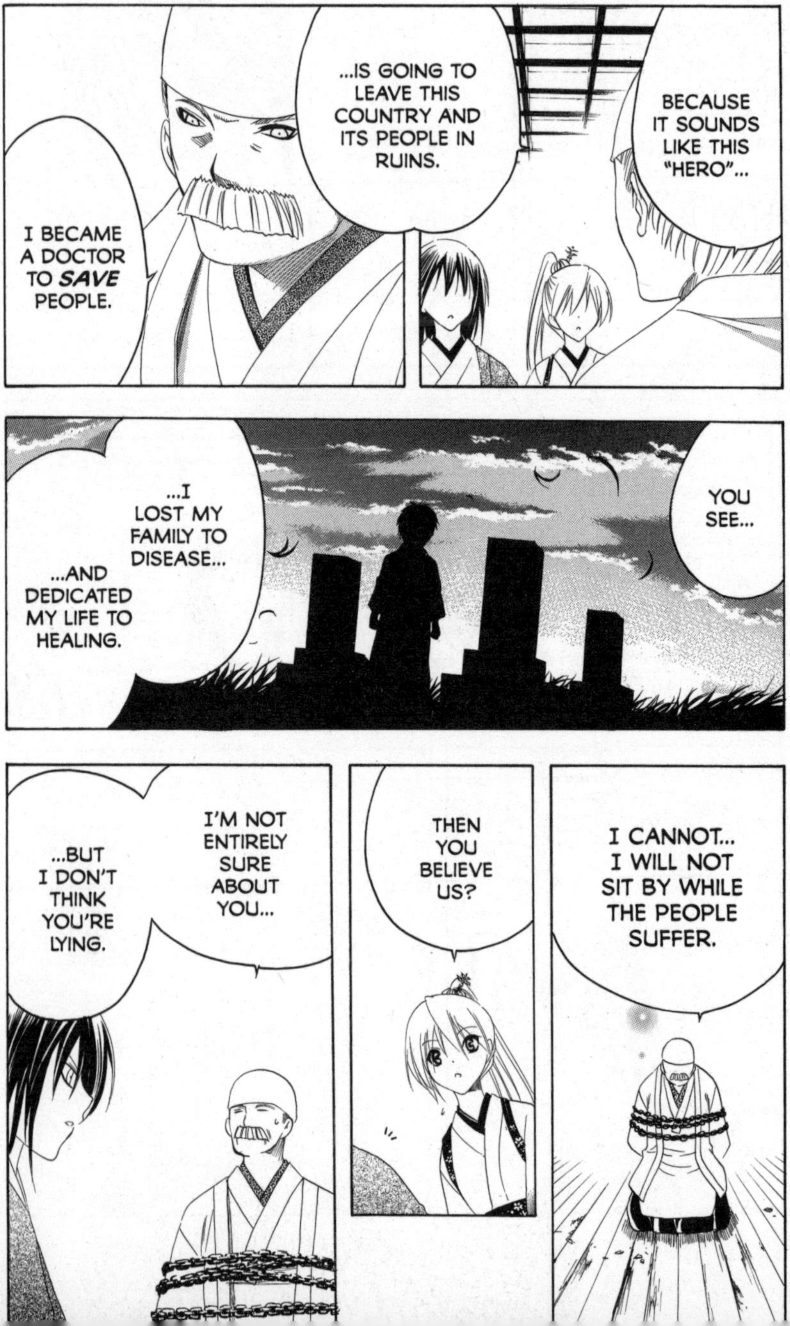
BECAUSE IT SOUNDS LIKE THIS "HERO"...
...IS GOING TO LEAVE THIS COUNTRY AND ITS PEOPLE IN RUINS.
I BECAME A DOCTOR TO *SAVE* PEOPLE.
YOU SEE...
...I LOST MY FAMILY TO DISEASE...
...AND DEDICATED MY LIFE TO HEALING.
I CANNOT... I WILL NOT SIT BY WHILE THE PEOPLE SUFFER.
THEN YOU BELIEVE US?
I'M NOT ENTIRELY SURE ABOUT YOU...
...BUT I DON'T THINK YOU'RE LYING.

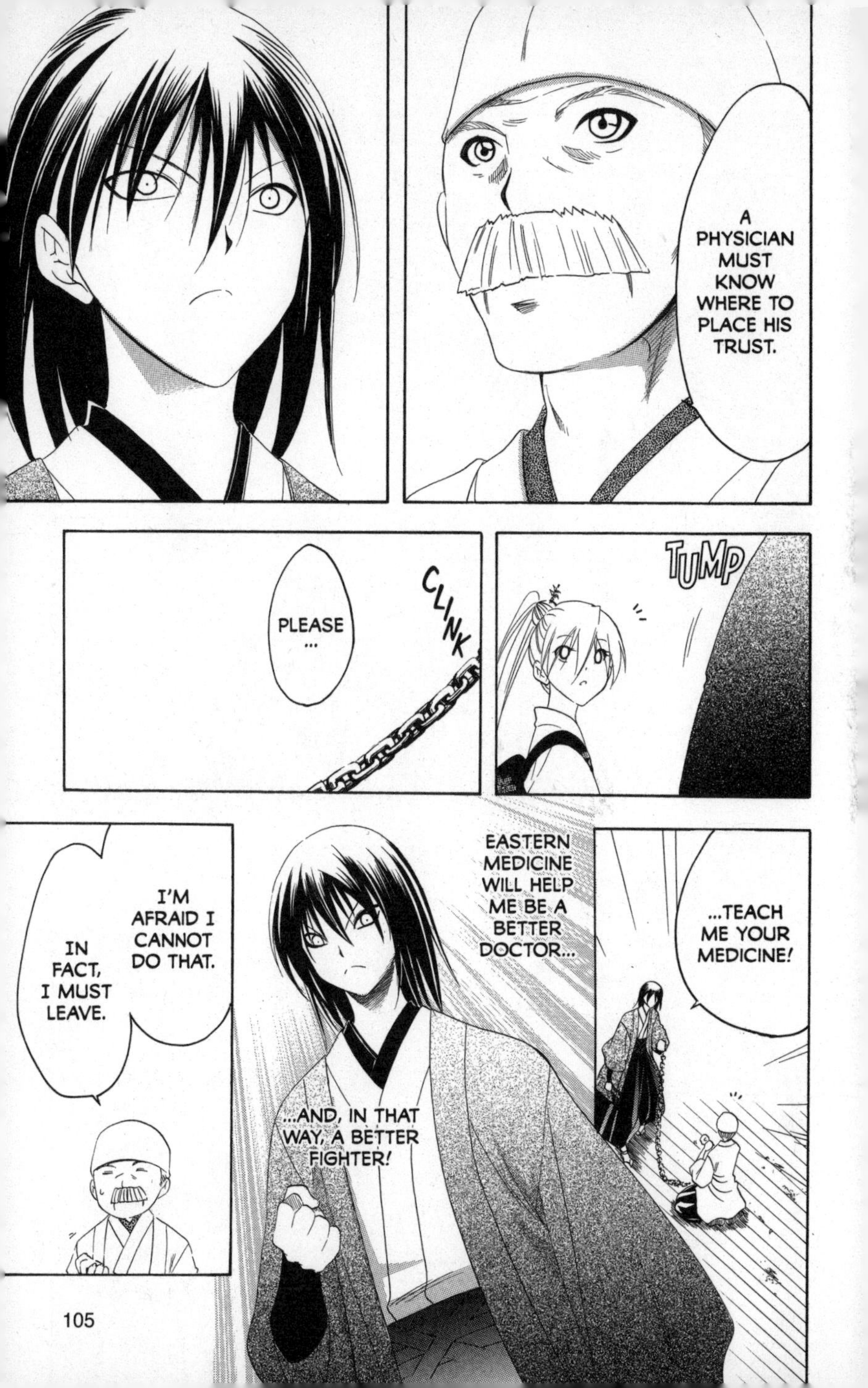
A PHYSICIAN MUST KNOW WHERE TO PLACE HIS TRUST.
TUMP
CLINK
PLEASE ...
...TEACH ME YOUR MEDICINE!
EASTERN MEDICINE WILL HELP ME BE A BETTER DOCTOR...
...AND, IN THAT WAY, A BETTER FIGHTER!
I'M AFRAID I CANNOT DO THAT.
IN FACT, I MUST LEAVE.

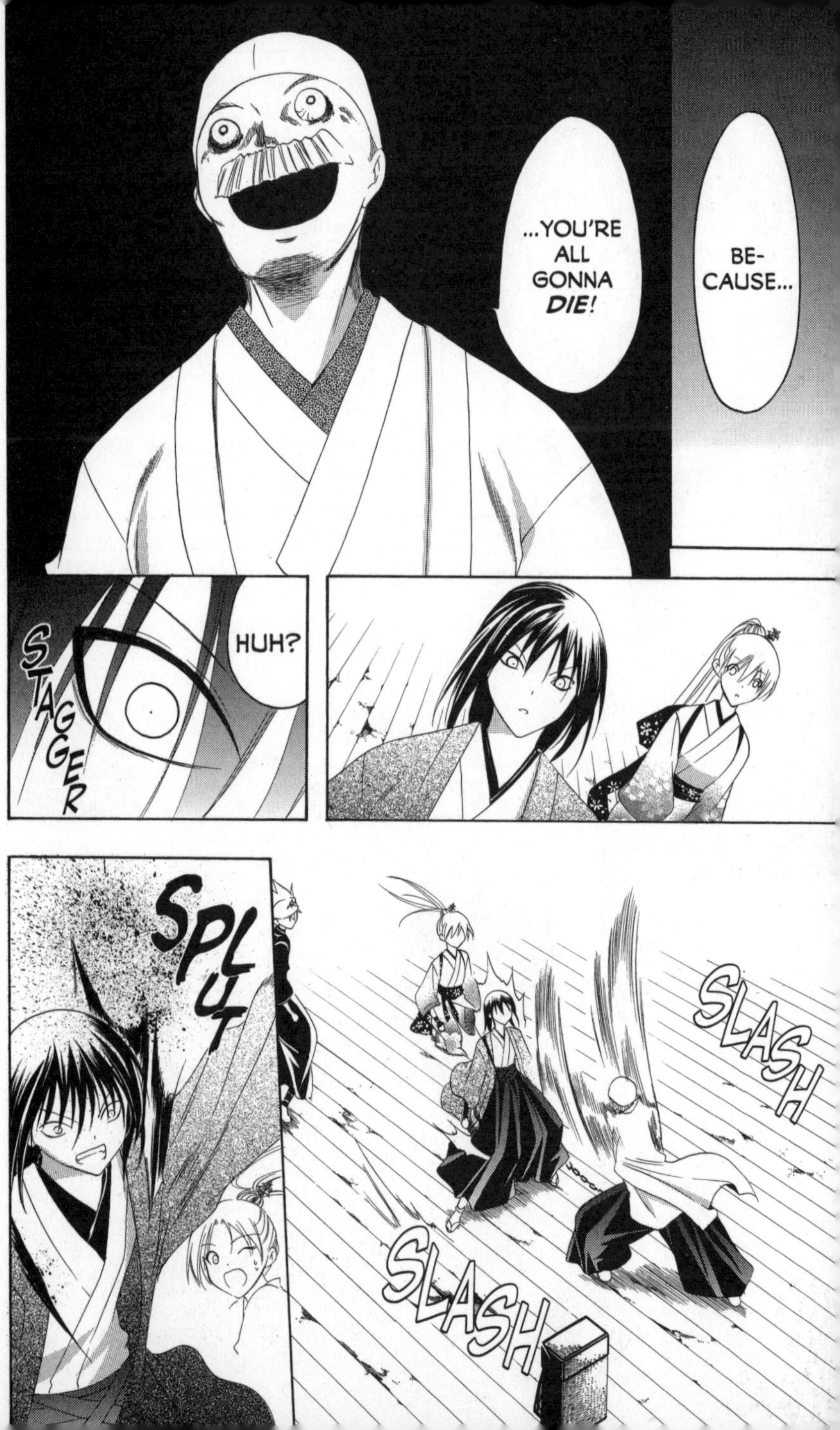
BE-
CAUSE...
...YOU'RE
ALL
GONNA
DIE!
STAGGER
HUH?
SLASH
SLASH
SPLUT

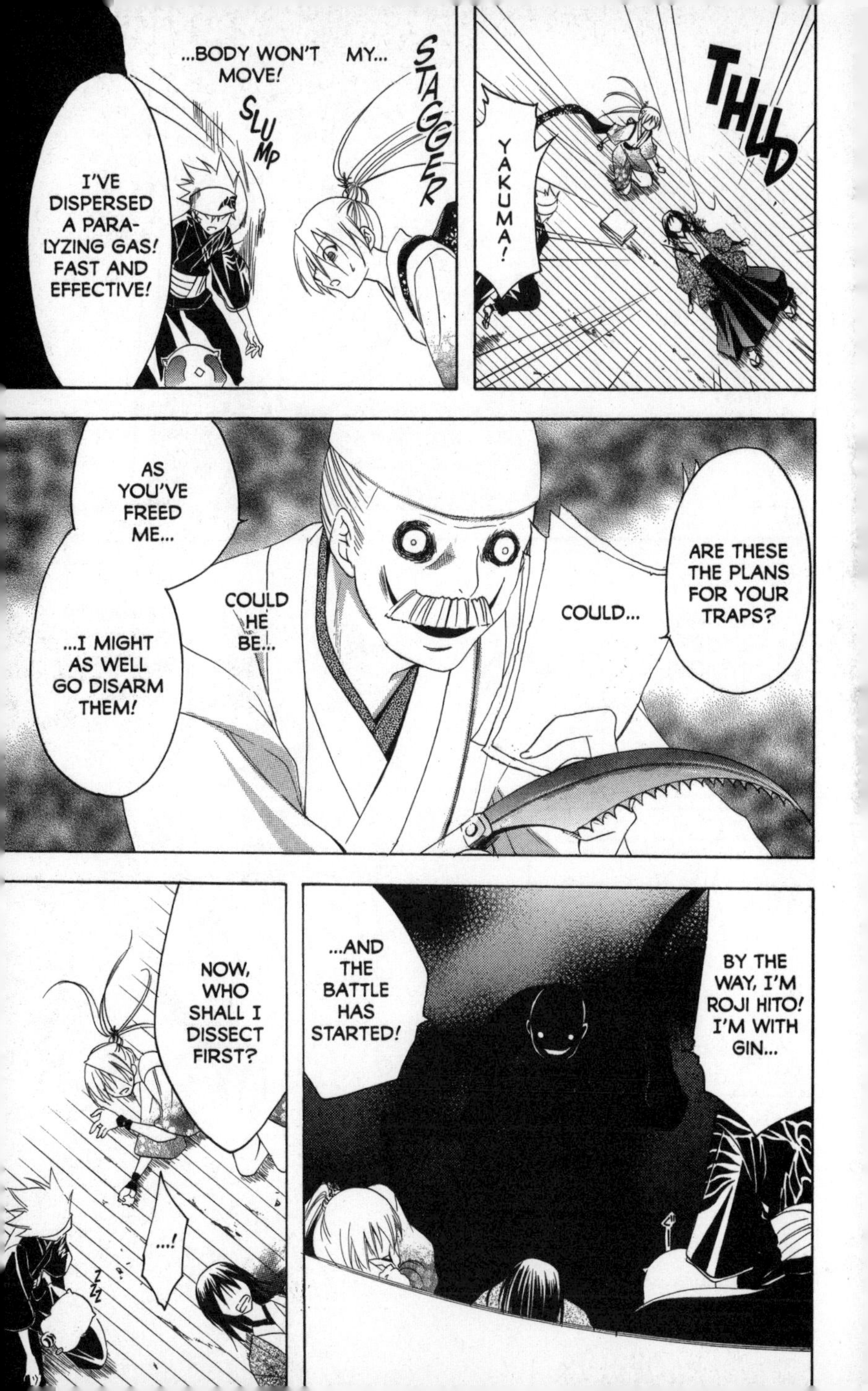
THUD
YAKUMA!
STAGGER
MY...
...BODY WON'T MOVE!
SLUMP
I'VE DISPERSED A PARALYZING GAS! FAST AND EFFECTIVE!
ARE THESE THE PLANS FOR YOUR TRAPS?
COULD...
COULD HE BE...
AS YOU'VE FREED ME...
...I MIGHT AS WELL GO DISARM THEM!
BY THE WAY, I'M ROJI HITO! I'M WITH GIN...
...AND THE BATTLE HAS STARTED!
NOW, WHO SHALL I DISSECT FIRST?
...!
ZZZ

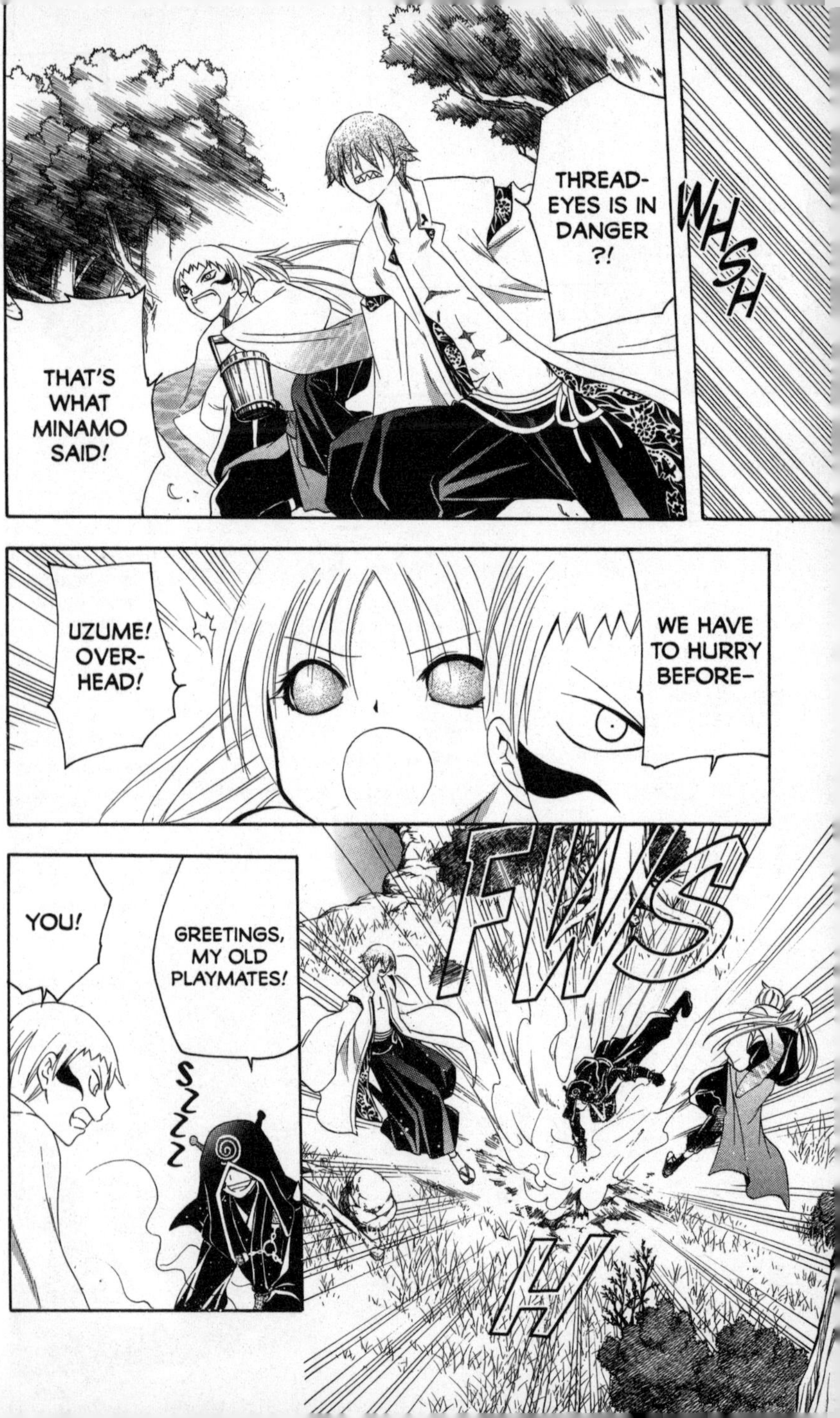
WHSH
THREAD-EYES IS IN DANGER?!
THAT'S WHAT MINAMO SAID!
WE HAVE TO HURRY BEFORE–
UZUME! OVERHEAD!
FWSH
GREETINGS, MY OLD PLAYMATES!
YOU!
SZZZ

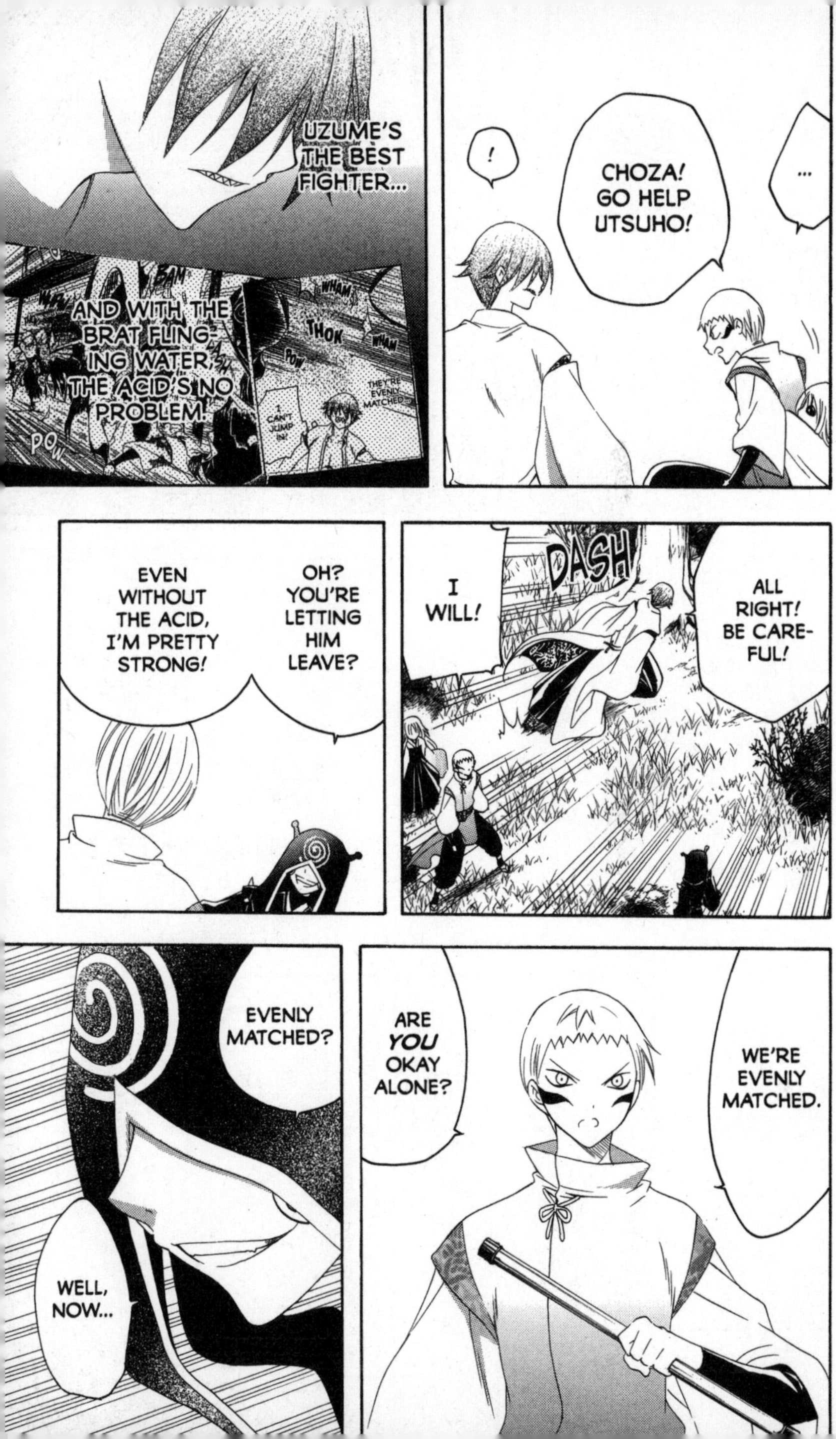
...
CHOZA! GO HELP UTSUHO!
!
UZUME'S THE BEST FIGHTER...
BAM
WHAM
THOK
WHAM
POW
THEY'RE EVENLY MATCHED
I CAN'T JUMP IN!
AND WITH THE BRAT FLING-ING WATER, THE ACID'S NO PROBLEM.
POW
ALL RIGHT! BE CARE-FUL!
DASH
I WILL!
OH? YOU'RE LETTING HIM LEAVE?
EVEN WITHOUT THE ACID, I'M PRETTY STRONG!
WE'RE EVENLY MATCHED.
ARE *YOU* OKAY ALONE?
EVENLY MATCHED?
WELL, NOW...

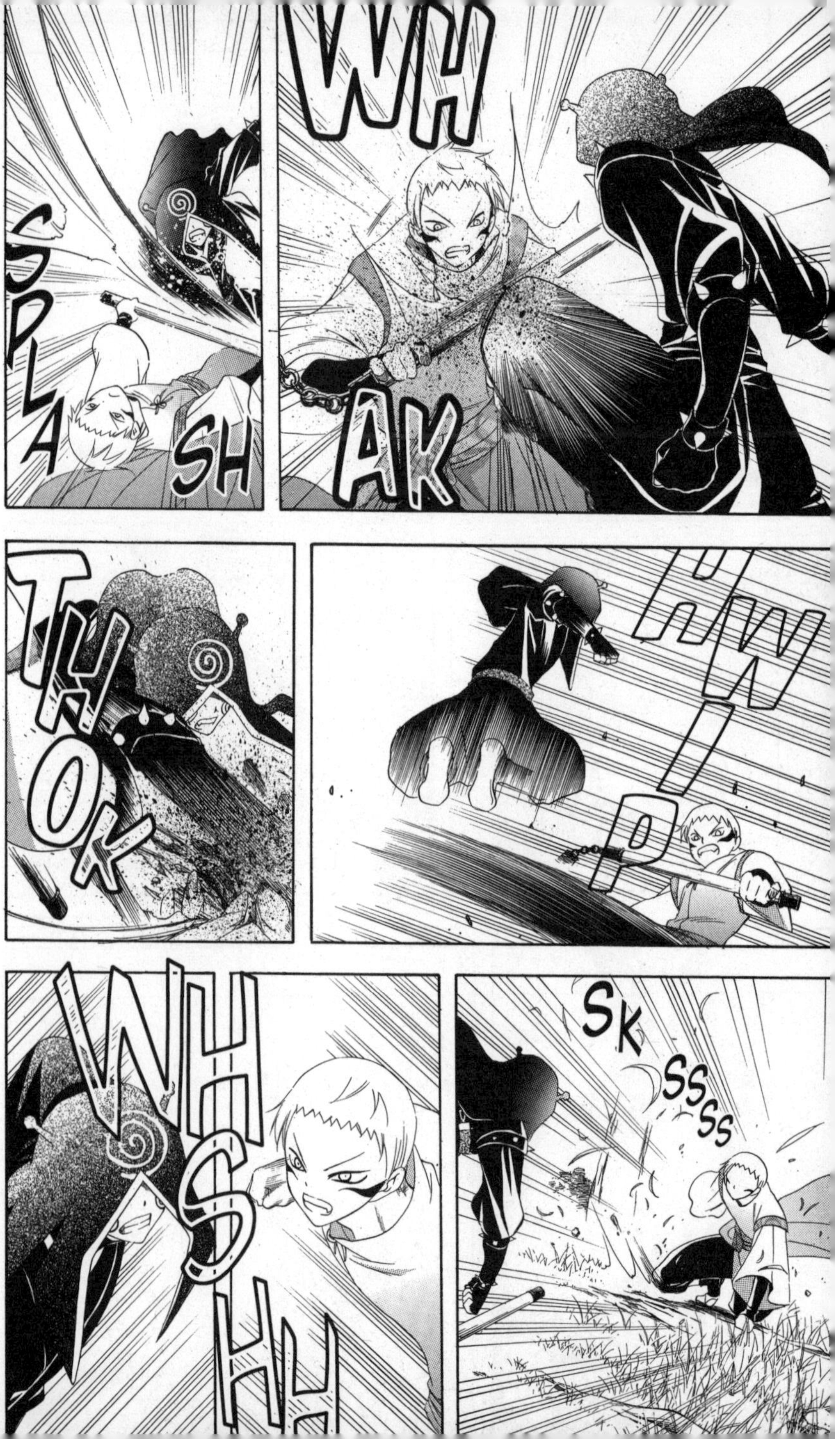
WHAK
SPLASH
WHIP
THOOK
SK
SSSSS
WHSHH

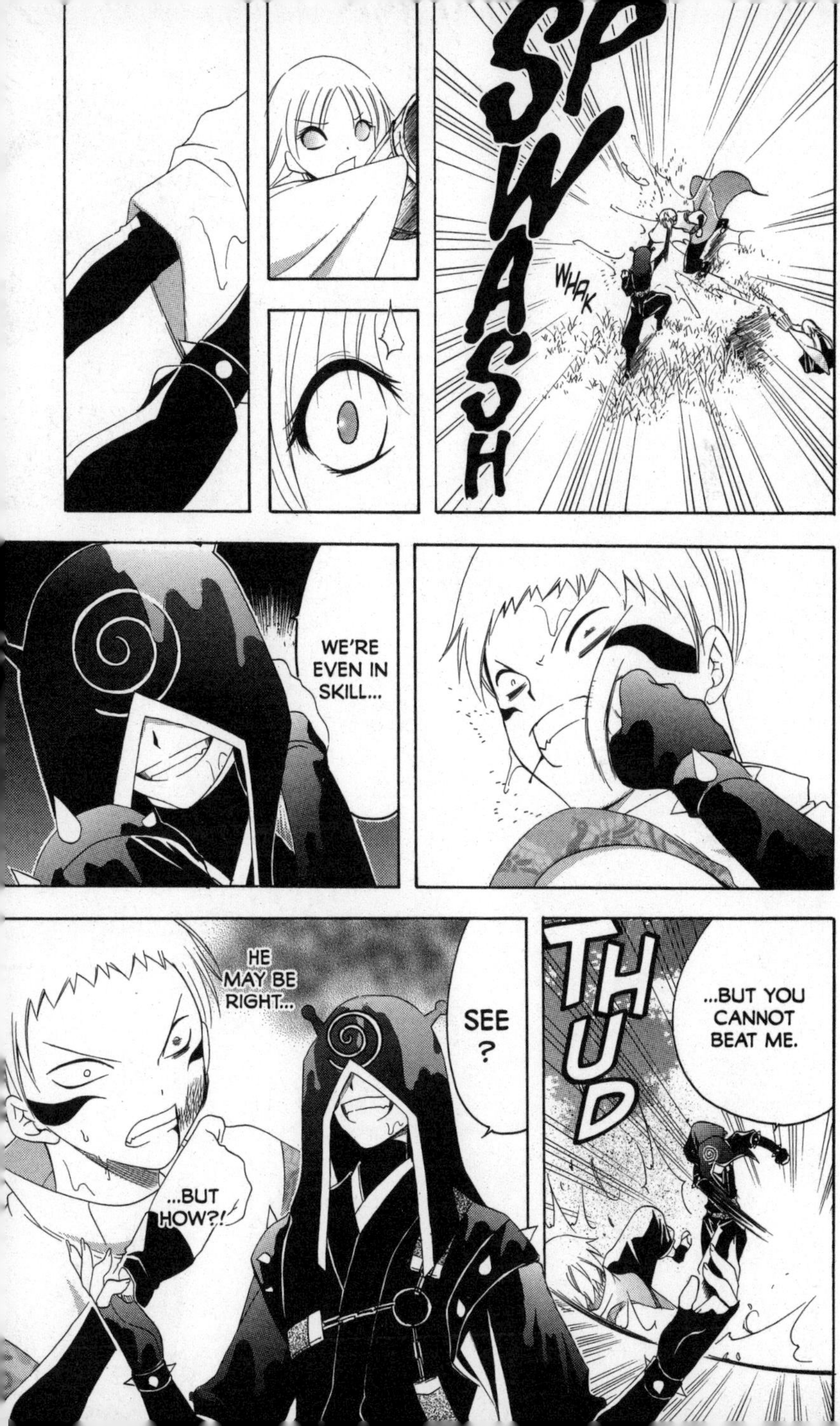
SPWASH
WHAK
WE'RE EVEN IN SKILL...
...BUT YOU CANNOT BEAT ME.
THUD
SEE?
HE MAY BE RIGHT...
...BUT HOW?!

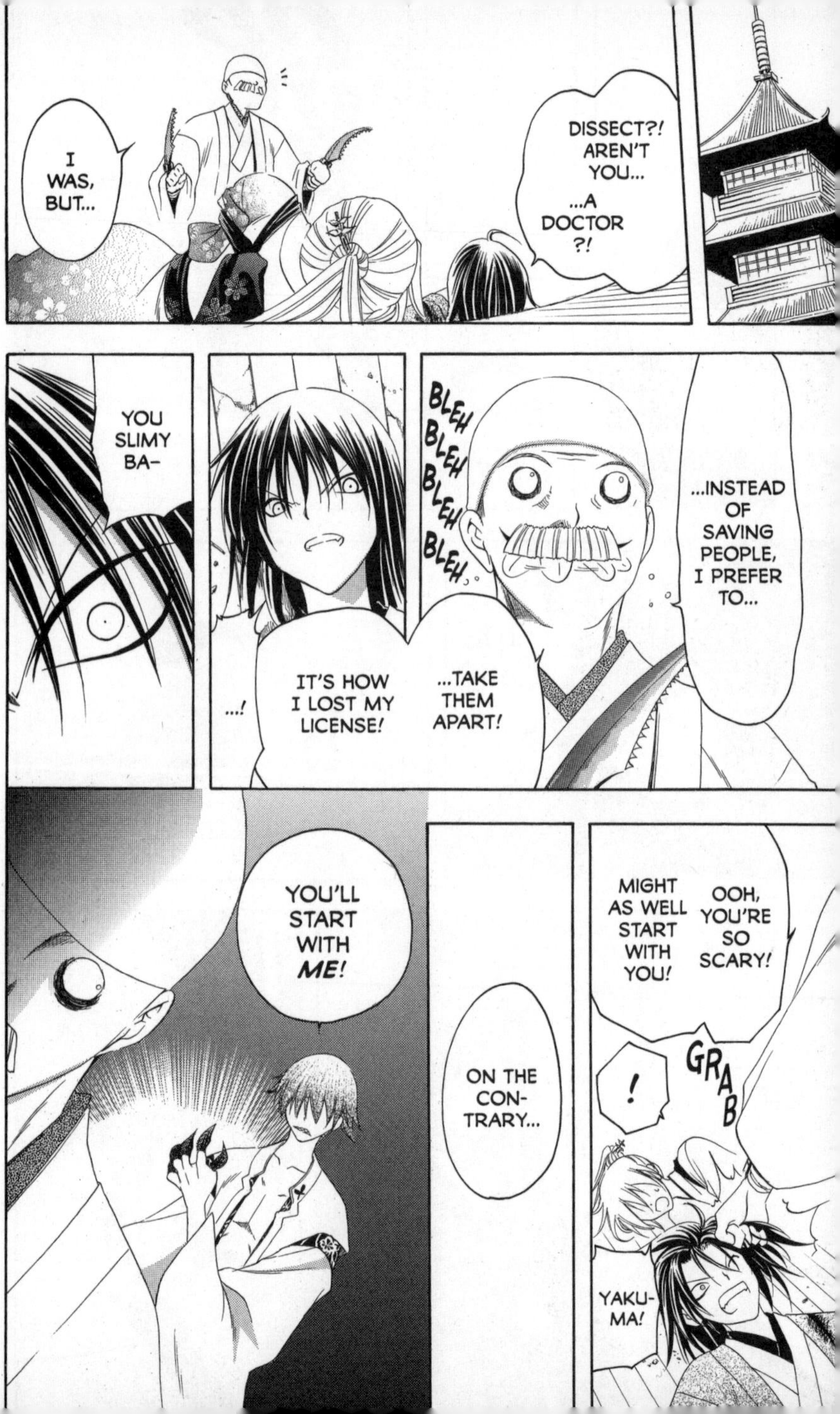
DISSECT?! AREN'T YOU... ...A DOCTOR ?!
I WAS, BUT...
...INSTEAD OF SAVING PEOPLE, I PREFER TO...
BLEH BLEH BLEH BLEH BLEH
...TAKE THEM APART!
IT'S HOW I LOST MY LICENSE!
...!
YOU SLIMY BA-
OOH, YOU'RE SO SCARY!
MIGHT AS WELL START WITH YOU!
GRAB
!
YAKUMA!
ON THE CON-TRARY...
YOU'LL START WITH *ME*!

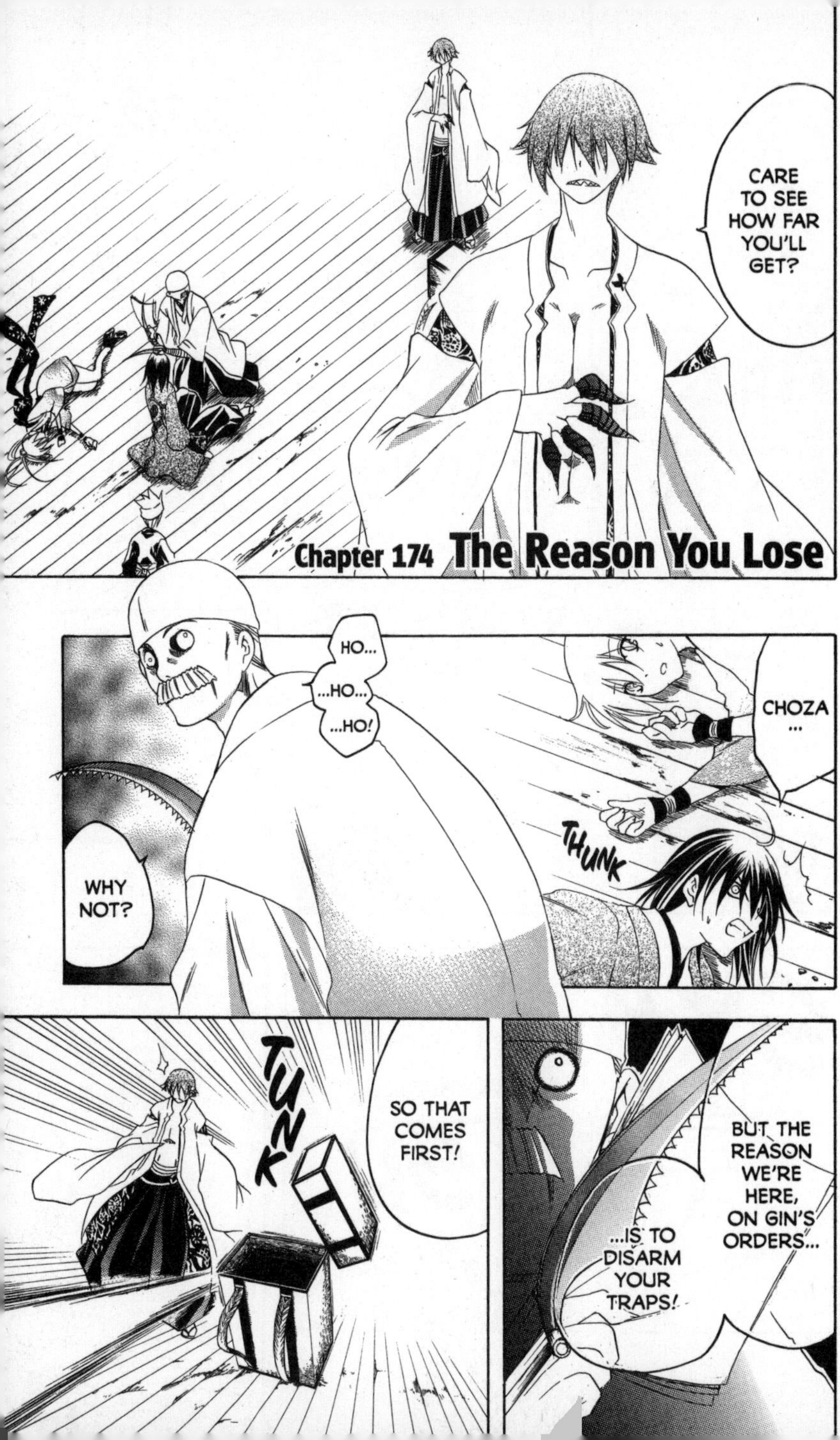
CARE TO SEE HOW FAR YOU'LL GET?
Chapter 174 The Reason You Lose
CHOZA ...
THUNK
HO...
...HO...
...HO!
WHY NOT?
BUT THE REASON WE'RE HERE, ON GIN'S ORDERS...
...IS TO DISARM YOUR TRAPS!
SO THAT COMES FIRST!
TUNK

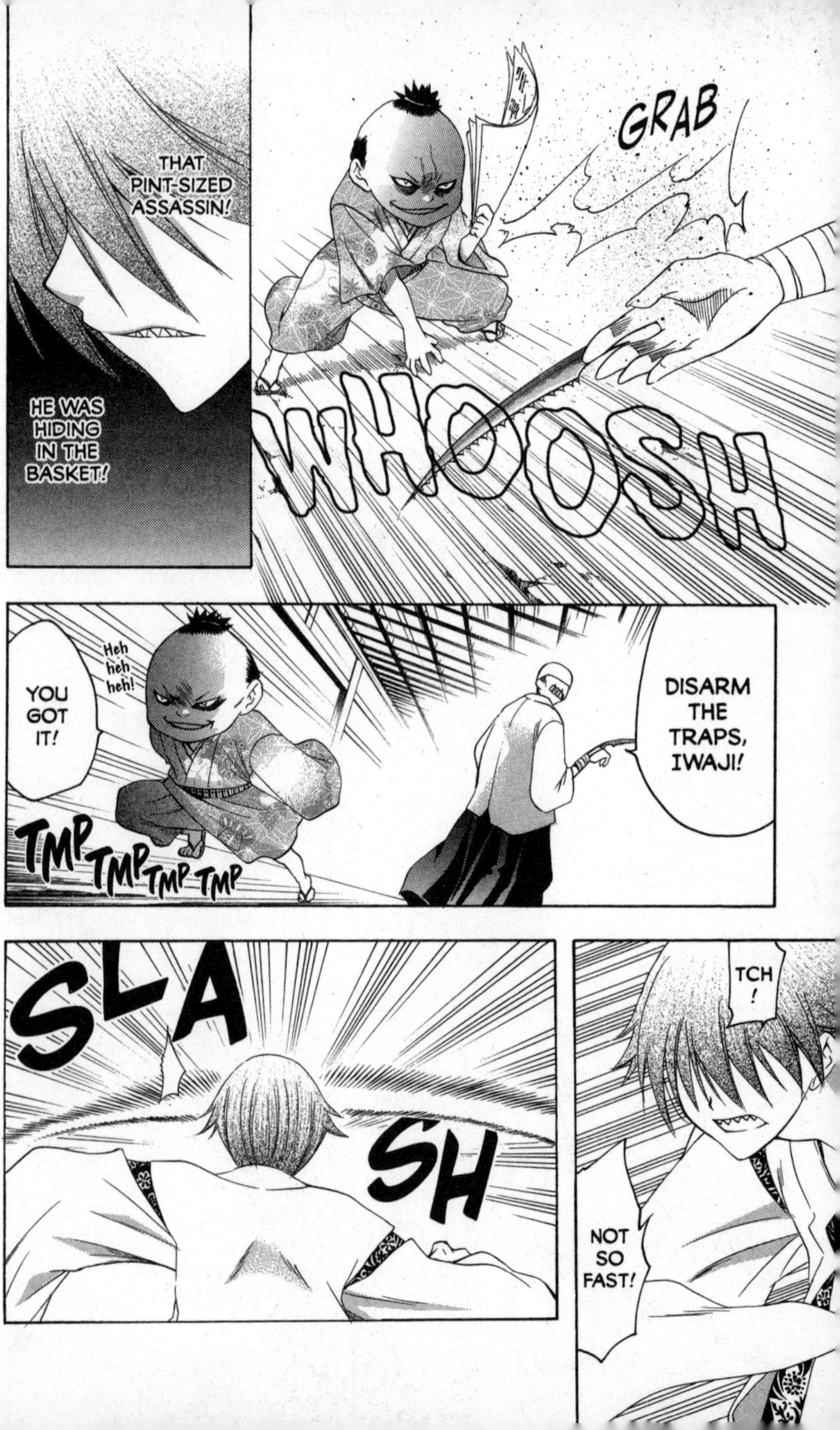
GRAB
WHOOSH
THAT PINT-SIZED ASSASSIN!
HE WAS HIDING IN THE BASKET!
DISARM THE TRAPS, IWAJI!
Heh heh heh!
YOU GOT IT!
TMP TMP TMP TMP
TCH!
NOT SO FAST!
SLASH

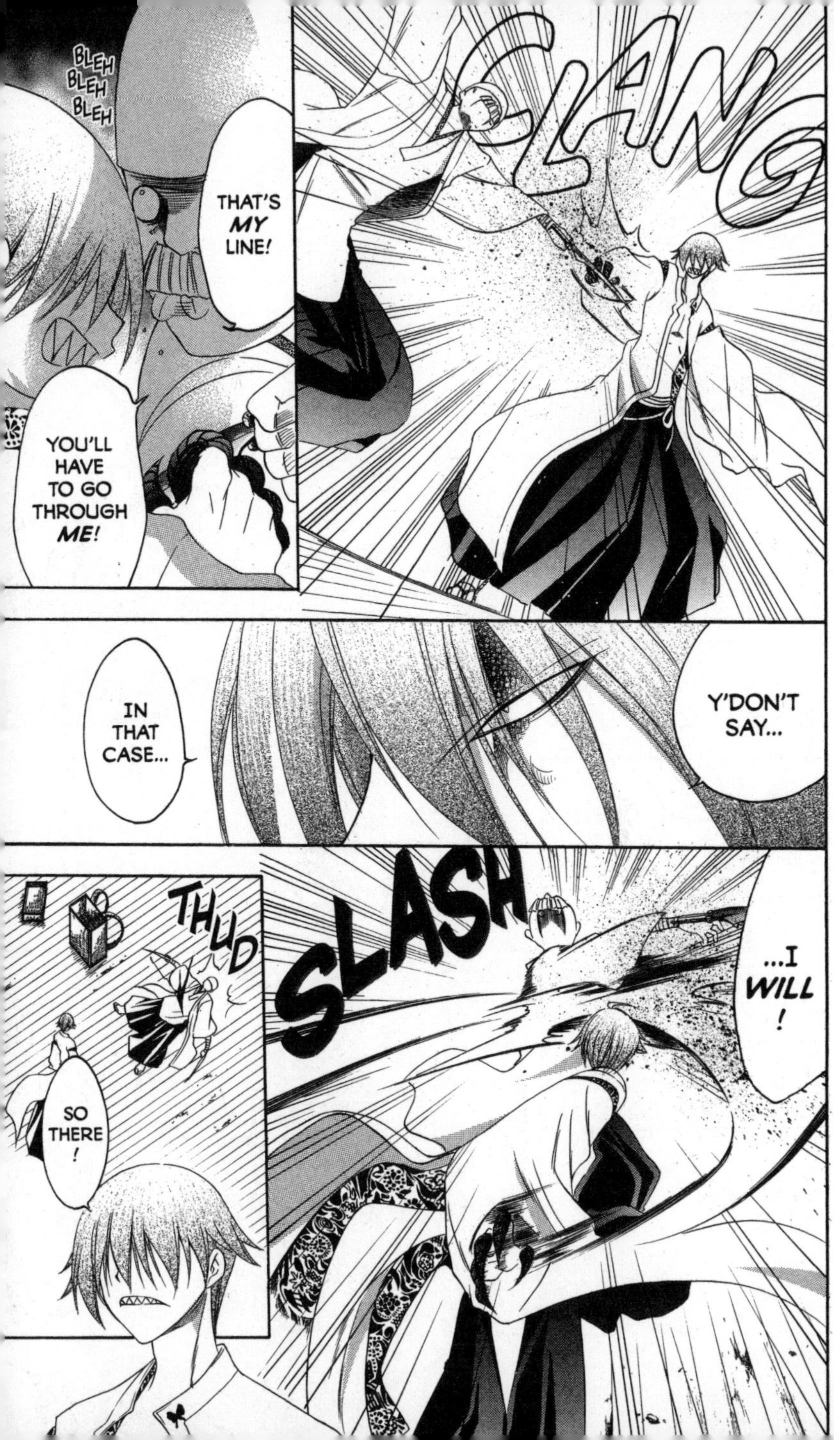
CLANG
BLEH BLEH BLEH
THAT'S *MY* LINE!
YOU'LL HAVE TO GO THROUGH *ME*!
Y'DON'T SAY...
IN THAT CASE...
...I *WILL*!
SLASH
THUD
SO THERE!

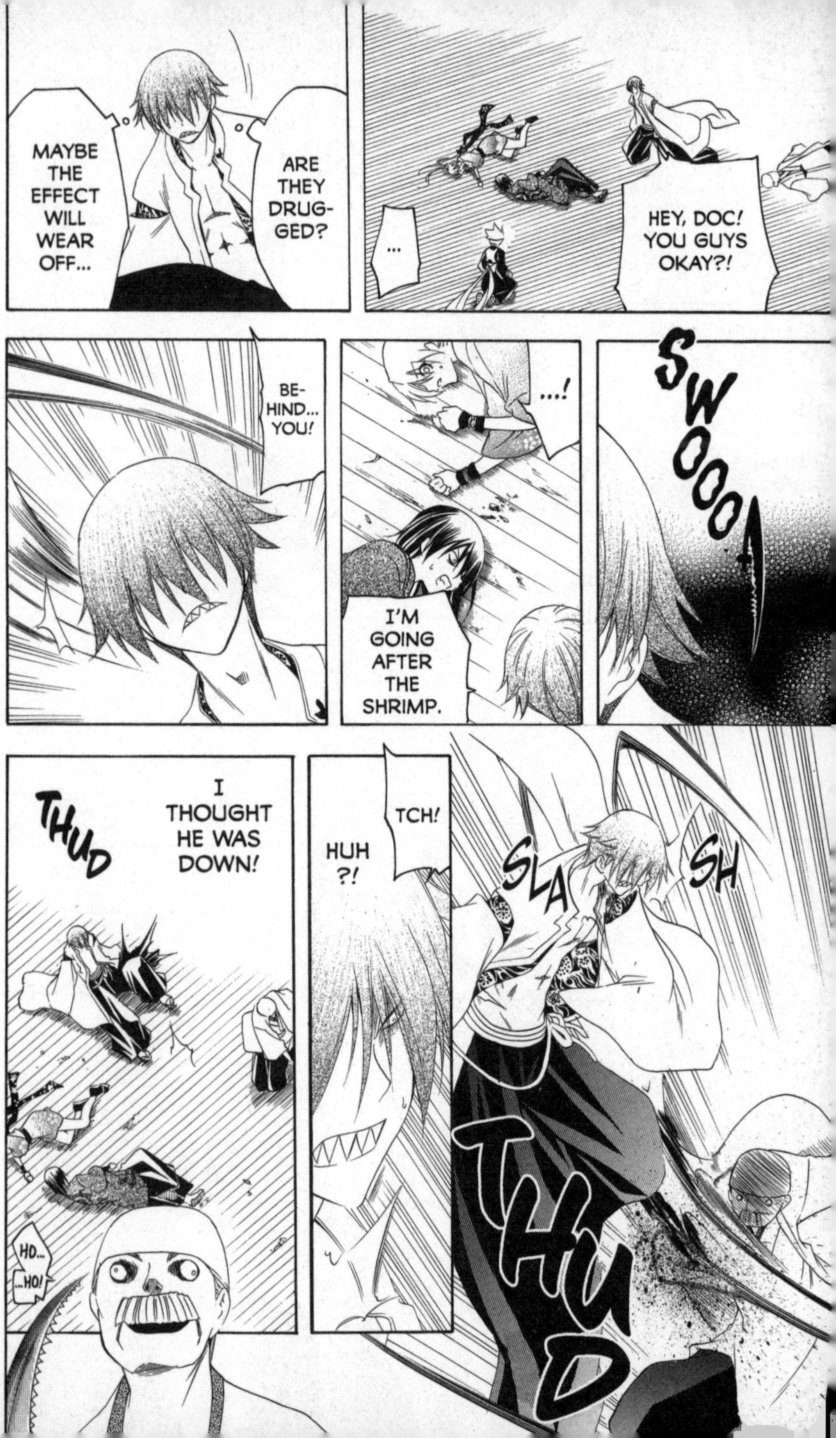
HEY, DOC! YOU GUYS OKAY?!
...
ARE THEY DRUG-GED?
MAYBE THE EFFECT WILL WEAR OFF...
SWOOO
...!
I'M GOING AFTER THE SHRIMP.
BE-HIND... YOU!
SLASH
THUD
TCH!
HUH?!
I THOUGHT HE WAS DOWN!
THUD
HO...
...HO!

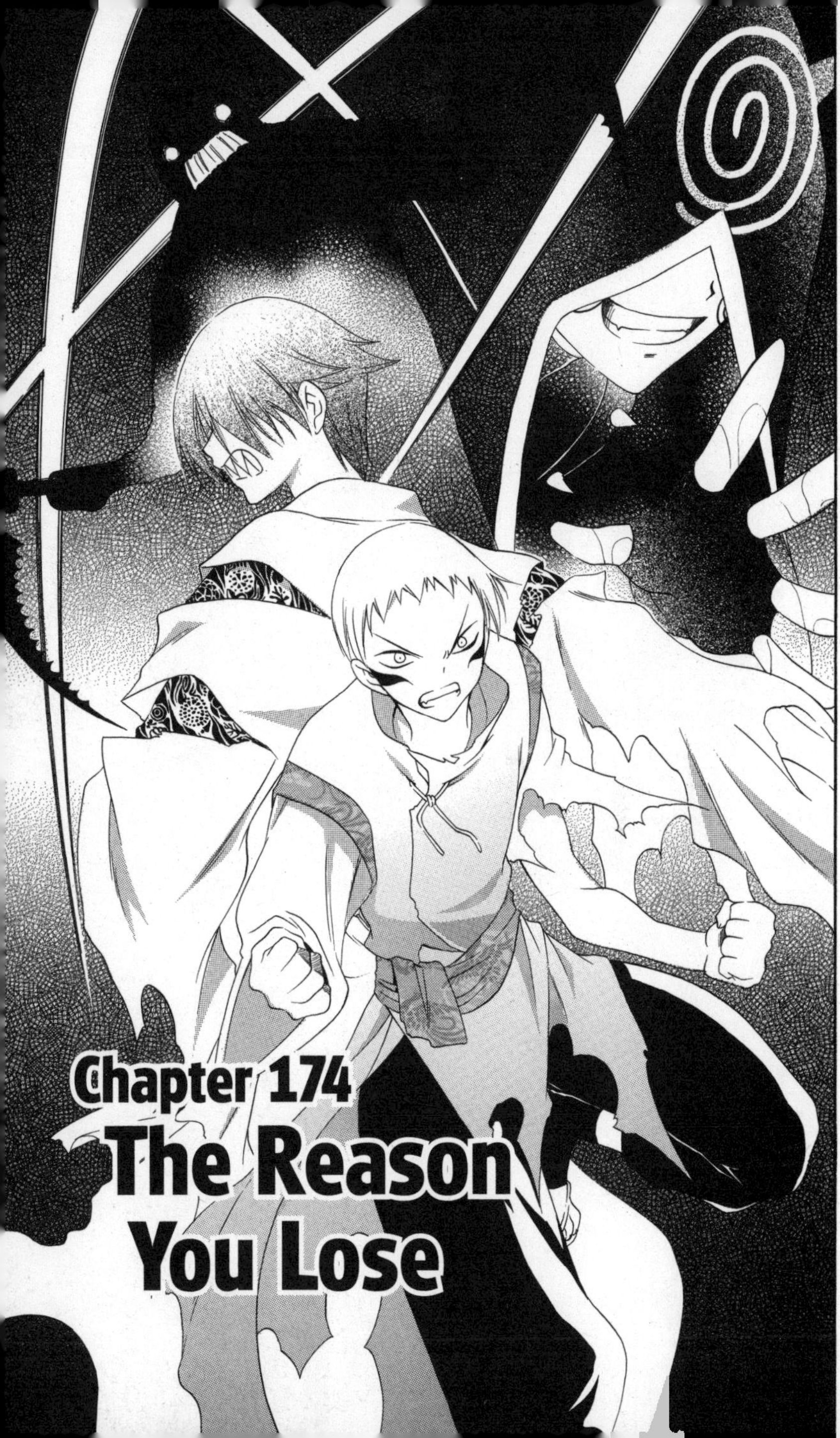
Chapter 174
The Reason You Lose

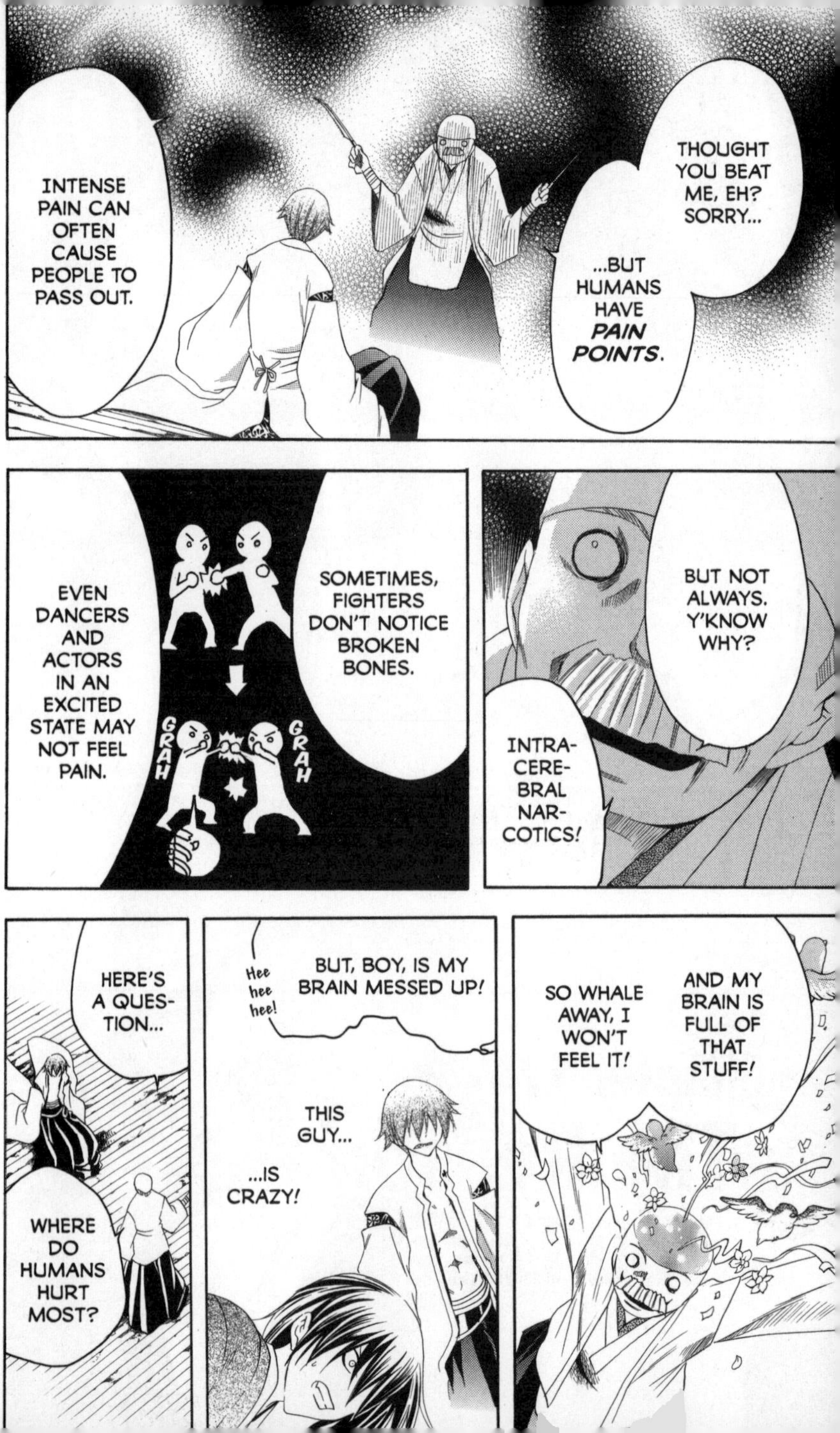
THOUGHT YOU BEAT ME, EH? SORRY...
...BUT HUMANS HAVE *PAIN POINTS*.
INTENSE PAIN CAN OFTEN CAUSE PEOPLE TO PASS OUT.
BUT NOT ALWAYS. Y'KNOW WHY?
INTRA-CEREBRAL NARCOTICS!
SOMETIMES, FIGHTERS DON'T NOTICE BROKEN BONES.
GRAH
GRAH
EVEN DANCERS AND ACTORS IN AN EXCITED STATE MAY NOT FEEL PAIN.
AND MY BRAIN IS FULL OF THAT STUFF!
SO WHALE AWAY, I WON'T FEEL IT!
BUT, BOY, IS MY BRAIN MESSED UP!
Hee hee hee!
THIS GUY...
...IS CRAZY!
HERE'S A QUESTION...
WHERE DO HUMANS HURT MOST?

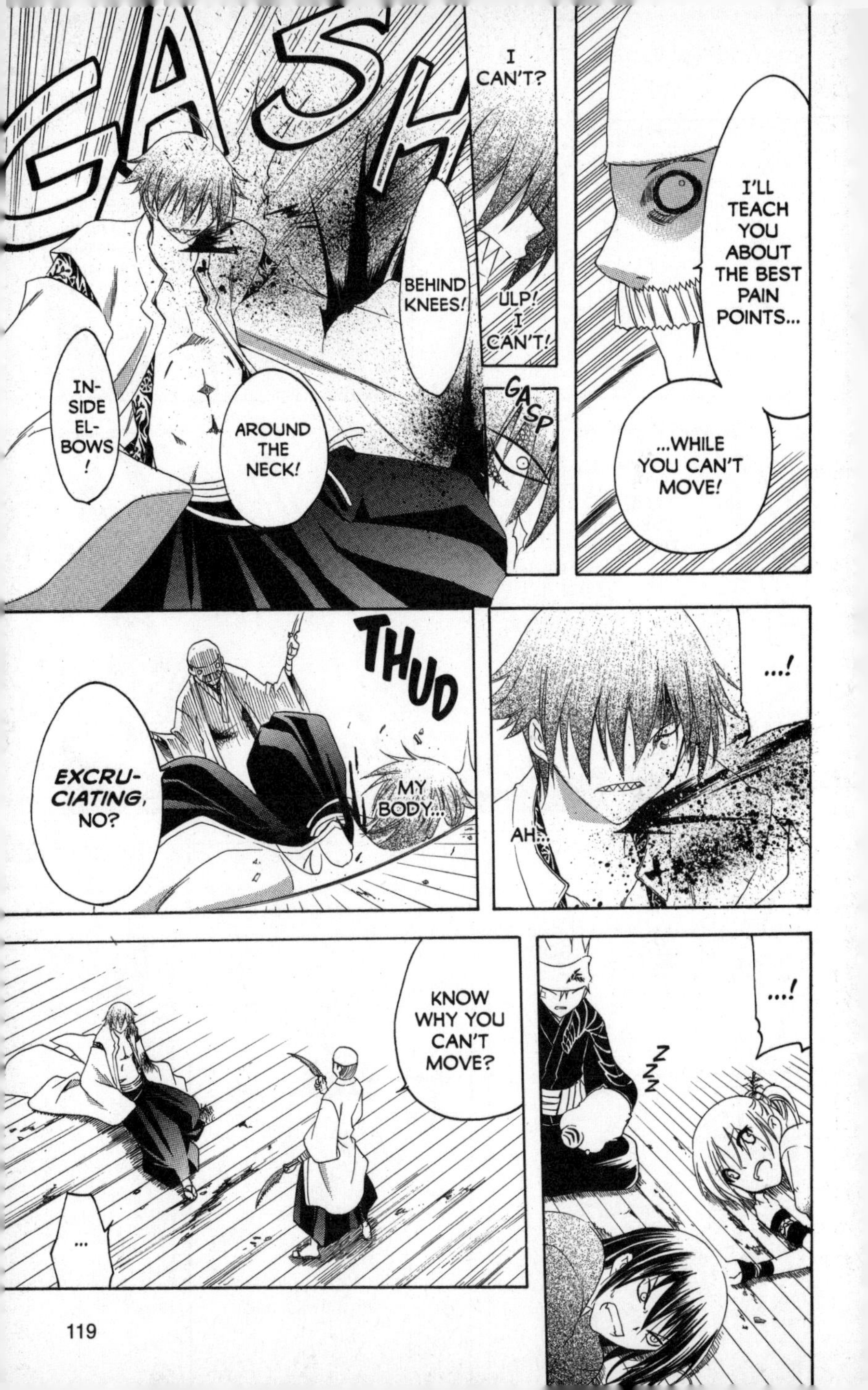
I'LL TEACH YOU ABOUT THE BEST PAIN POINTS...
...WHILE YOU CAN'T MOVE!
I CAN'T?
ULP! I CAN'T!
GASP
GASH
BEHIND KNEES!
AROUND THE NECK!
INSIDE EL-BOWS!
...!
AH...
THUD
MY BODY...
EXCRUCIATING, NO?
...!
ZZZ
KNOW WHY YOU CAN'T MOVE?
...

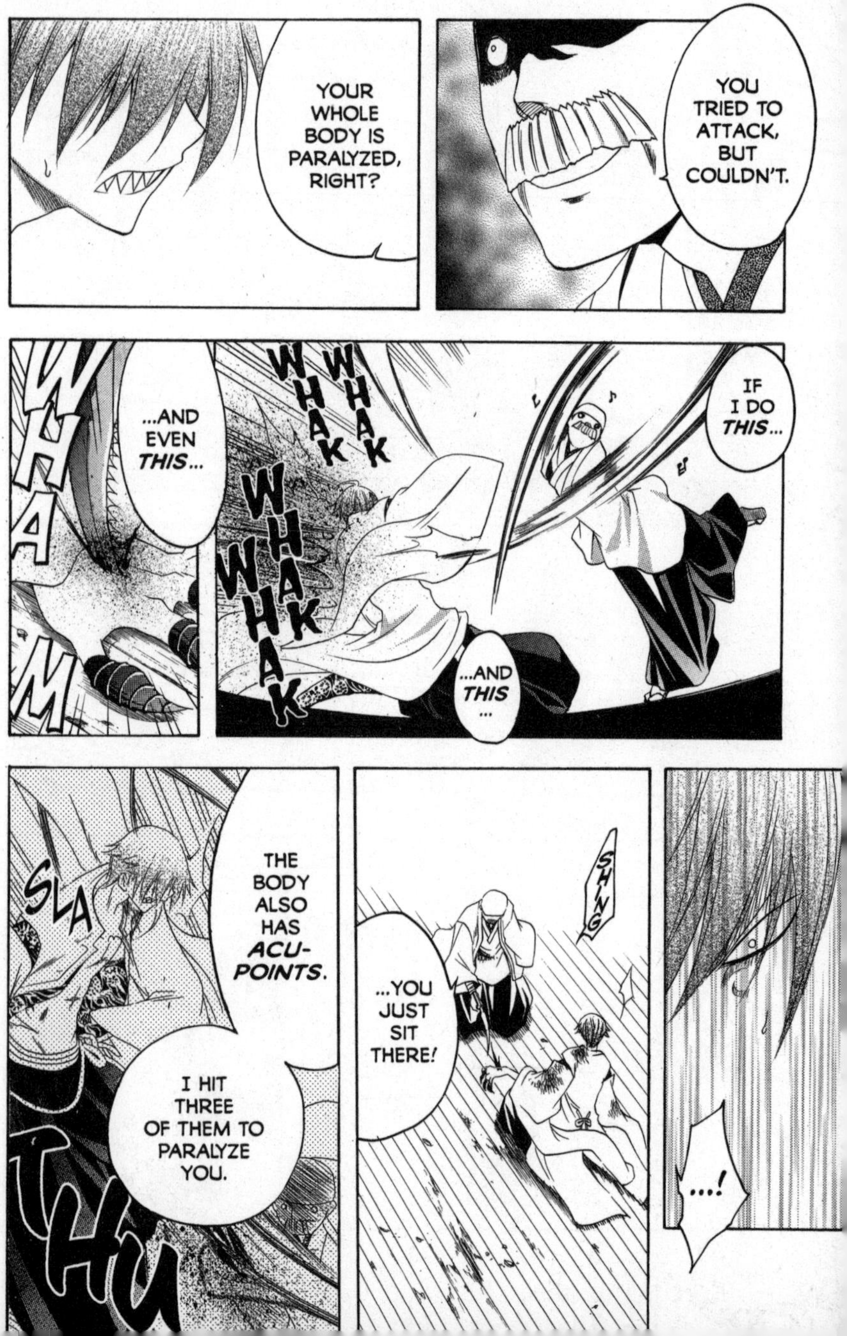

YOU TRIED TO ATTACK, BUT COULDN'T.
YOUR WHOLE BODY IS PARALYZED, RIGHT?
IF I DO *THIS*...
WHAK
WHAK
WHAK
WHAK
...AND *THIS*...
...AND EVEN *THIS*...
WHAM
...!
SHING
...YOU JUST SIT THERE!
THE BODY ALSO HAS *ACU-POINTS*.
I HIT THREE OF THEM TO PARALYZE YOU.
SLA
THU

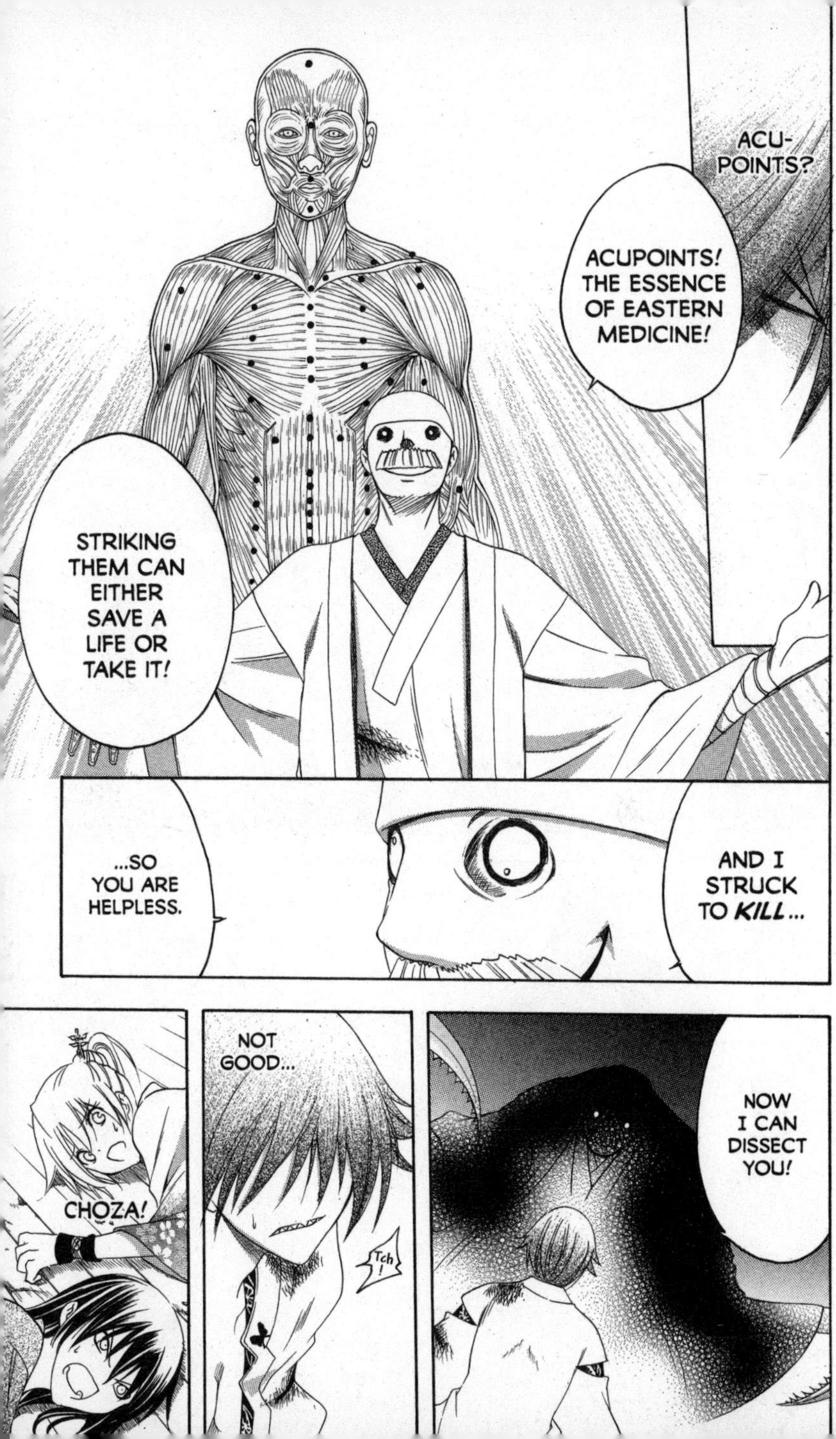
ACU-POINTS?
ACUPOINTS! THE ESSENCE OF EASTERN MEDICINE!
STRIKING THEM CAN EITHER SAVE A LIFE OR TAKE IT!
AND I STRUCK TO ***KILL***...
...SO YOU ARE HELPLESS.
NOW I CAN DISSECT YOU!
NOT GOOD...
Tch!
CHOZA!

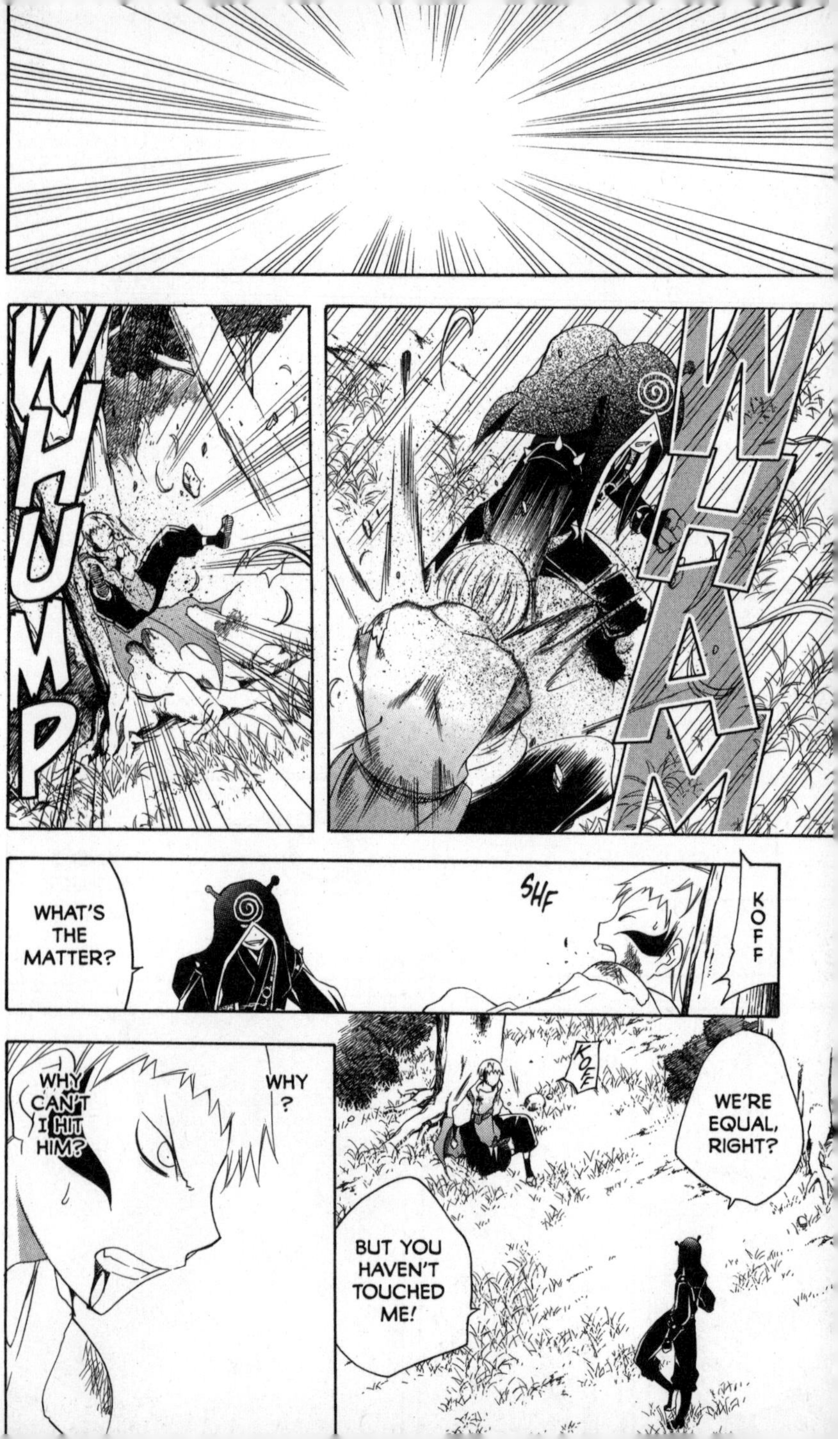
WHAM
WHUMP
KOFF
SHF
WHAT'S THE MATTER?
KOFF
WE'RE EQUAL, RIGHT?
BUT YOU HAVEN'T TOUCHED ME!
WHY?
WHY CAN'T I HIT HIM?

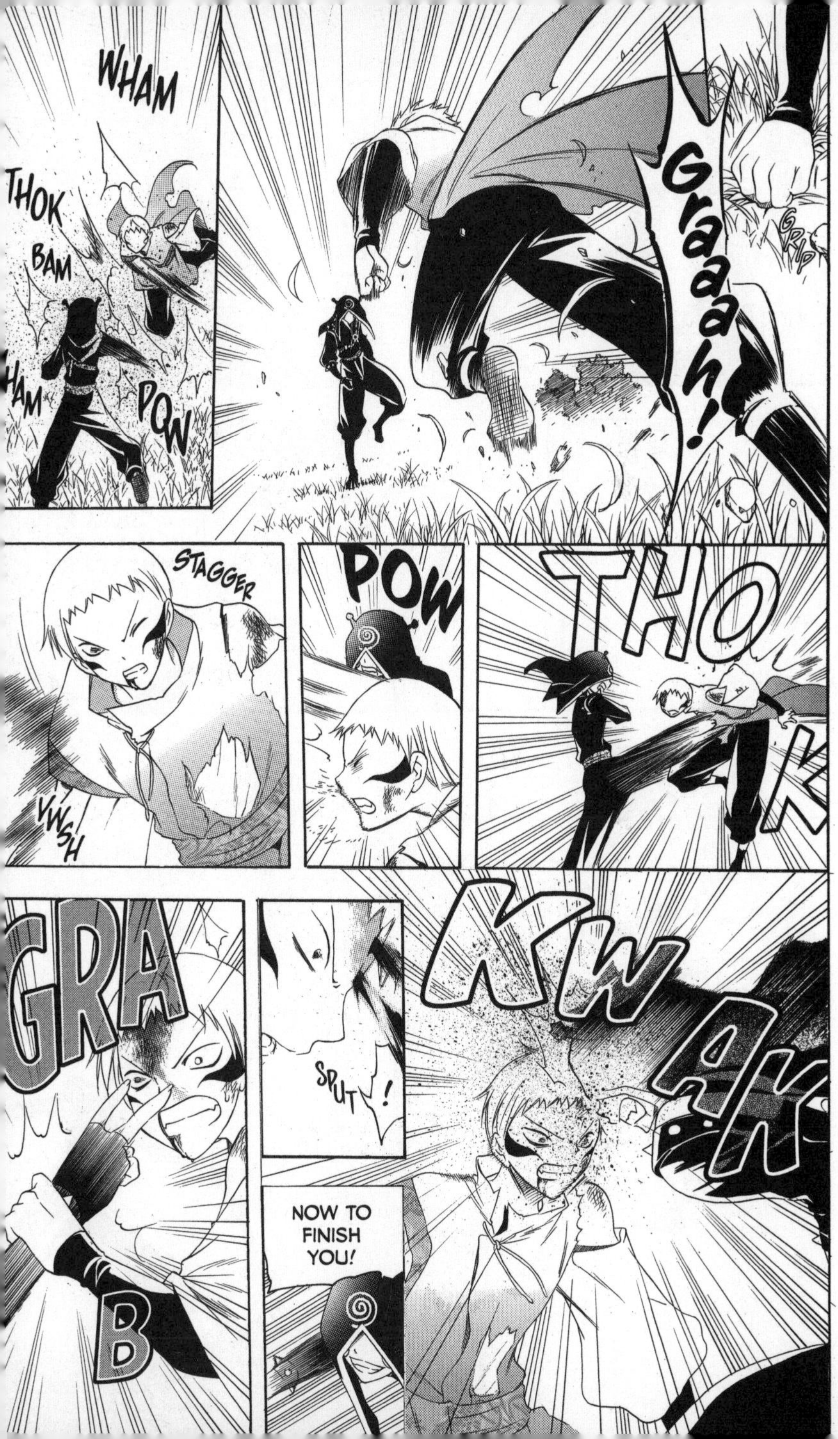
Graaah!
GRIP
WHAM
THOK
BAM
HAM
POW
THOK
POW
STAGGER
VWSH
KWAK
SPUT !
NOW TO FINISH YOU!
GRAB

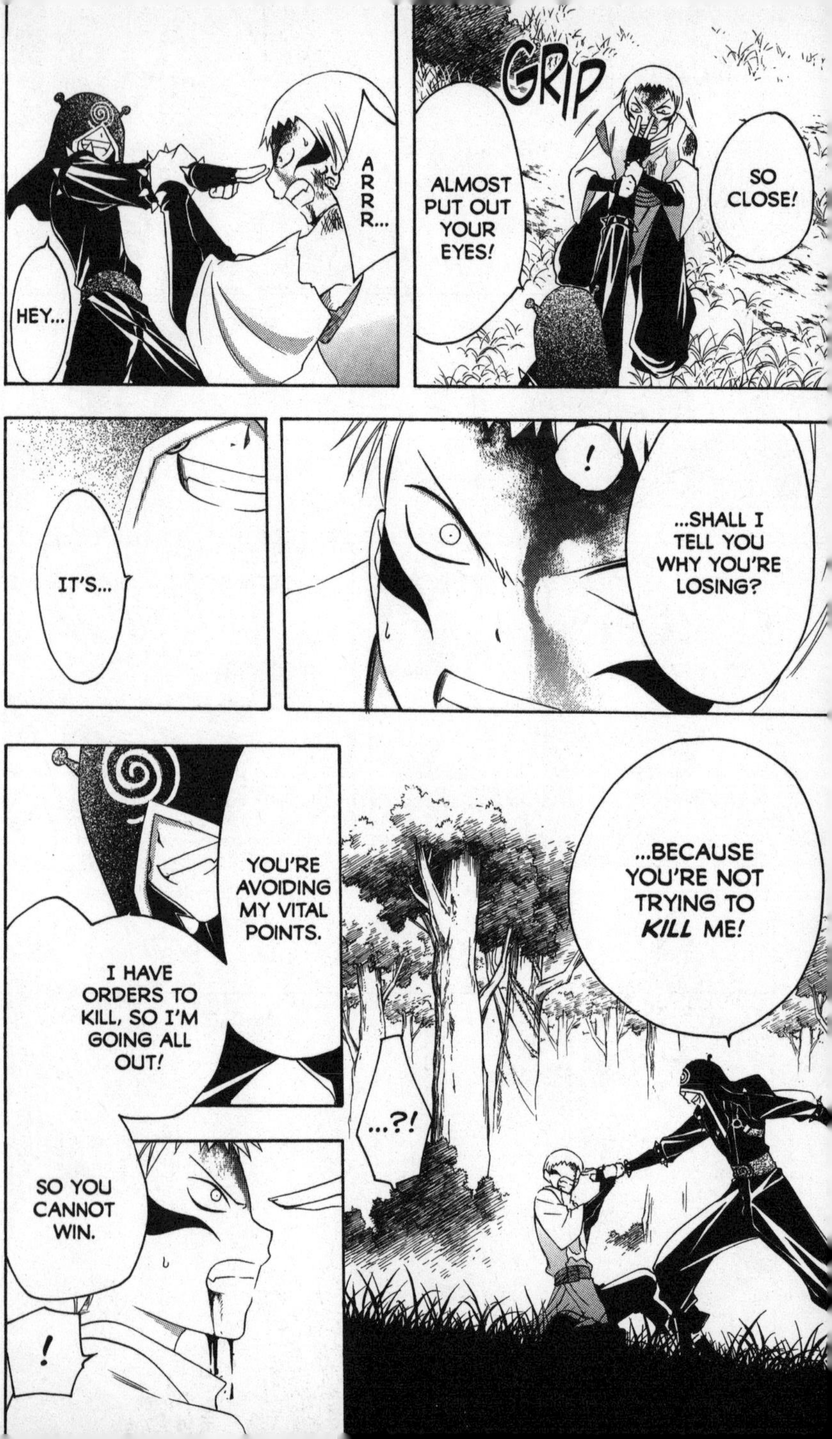
GRIP
SO CLOSE!
ALMOST PUT OUT YOUR EYES!
ARRR...
HEY...
!
...SHALL I TELL YOU WHY YOU'RE LOSING?
IT'S...
...BECAUSE YOU'RE NOT TRYING TO KILL ME!
...?!
YOU'RE AVOIDING MY VITAL POINTS.
I HAVE ORDERS TO KILL, SO I'M GOING ALL OUT!
SO YOU CANNOT WIN.
!

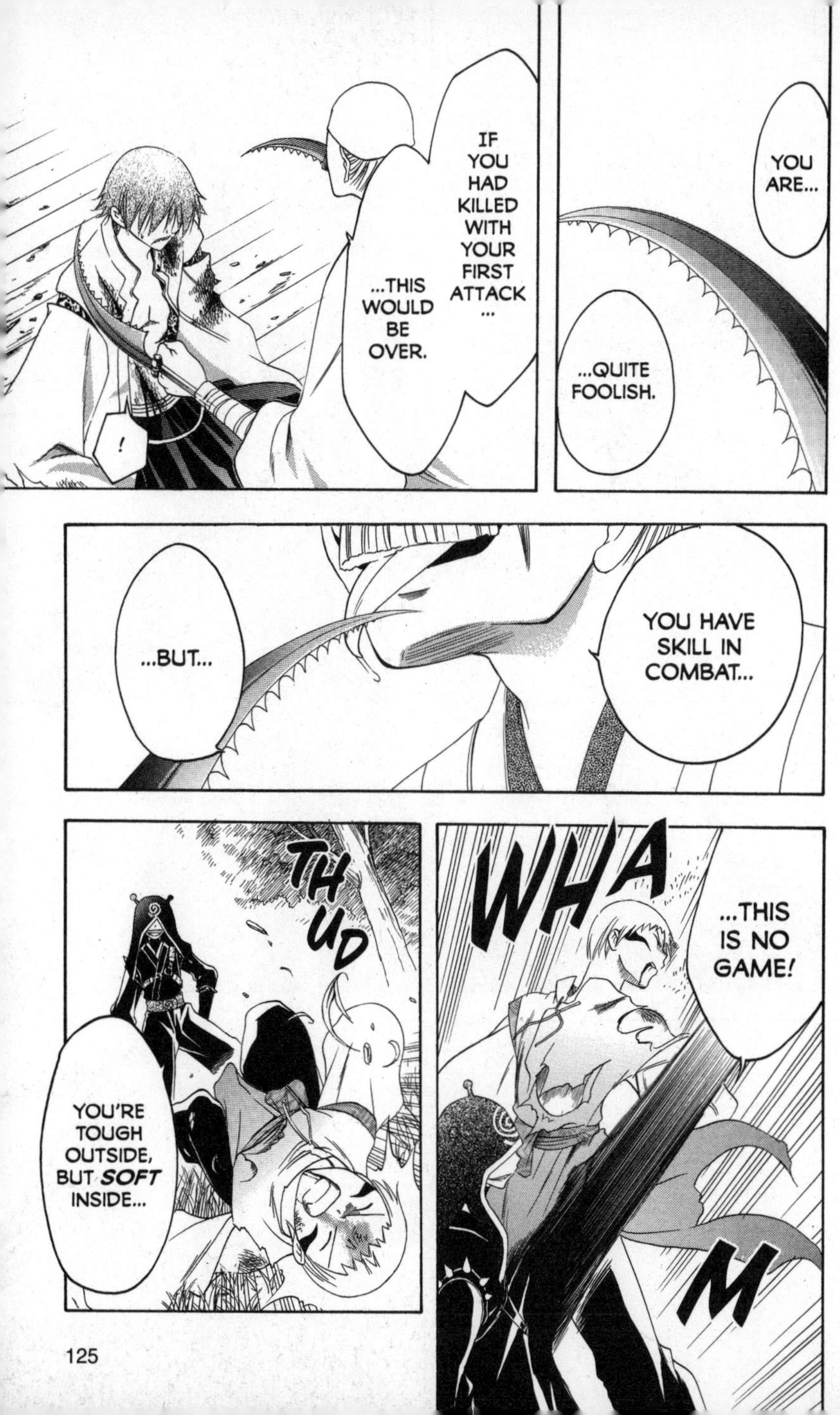
YOU ARE...
...QUITE FOOLISH.
IF YOU HAD KILLED WITH YOUR FIRST ATTACK...
...THIS WOULD BE OVER.
!
YOU HAVE SKILL IN COMBAT...
...BUT...
WHAM
...THIS IS NO GAME!
THUD
YOU'RE TOUGH OUTSIDE, BUT *SOFT* INSIDE...

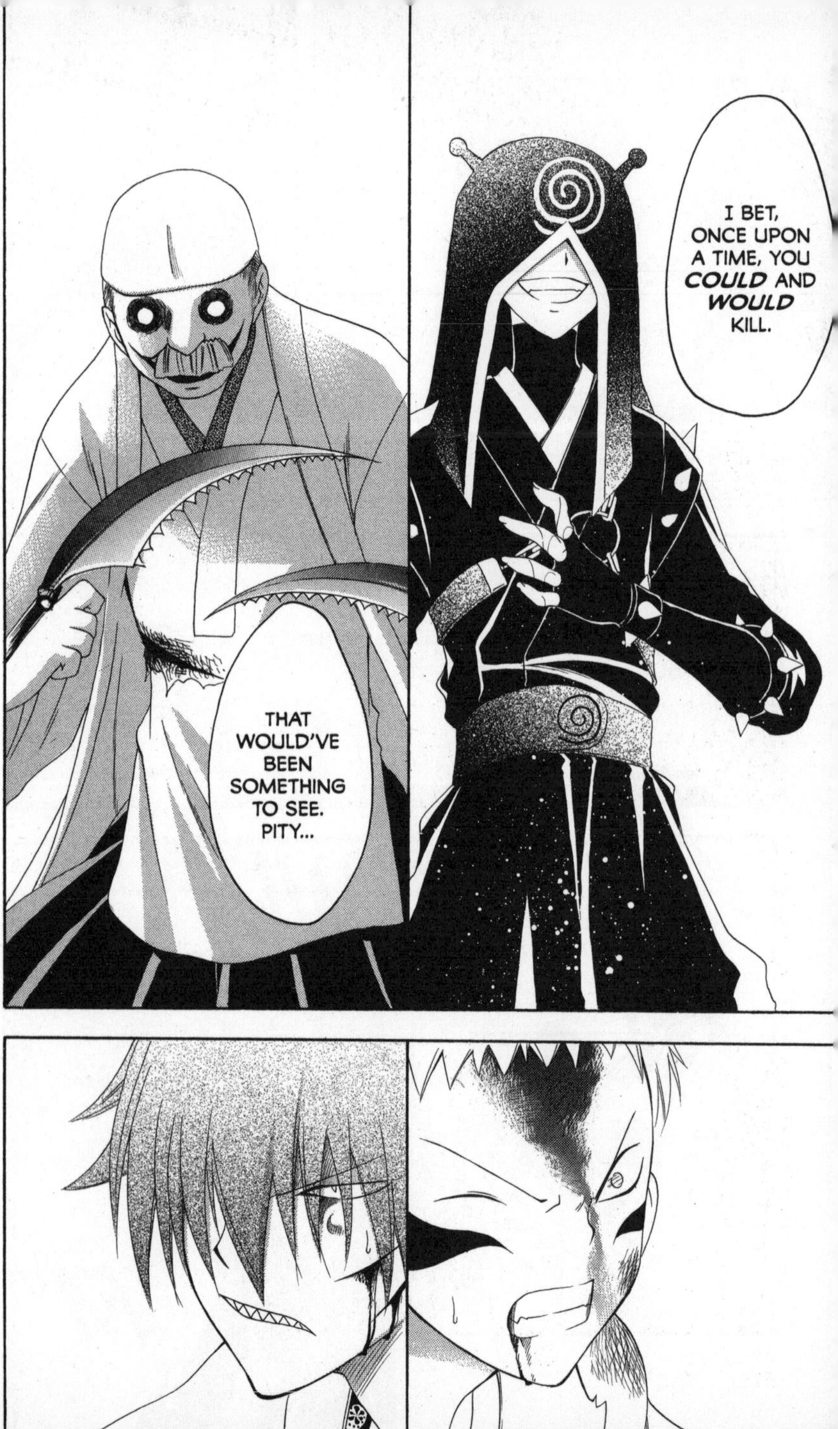
I BET, ONCE UPON A TIME, YOU *COULD* AND *WOULD* KILL.
THAT WOULD'VE BEEN SOMETHING TO SEE. PITY...

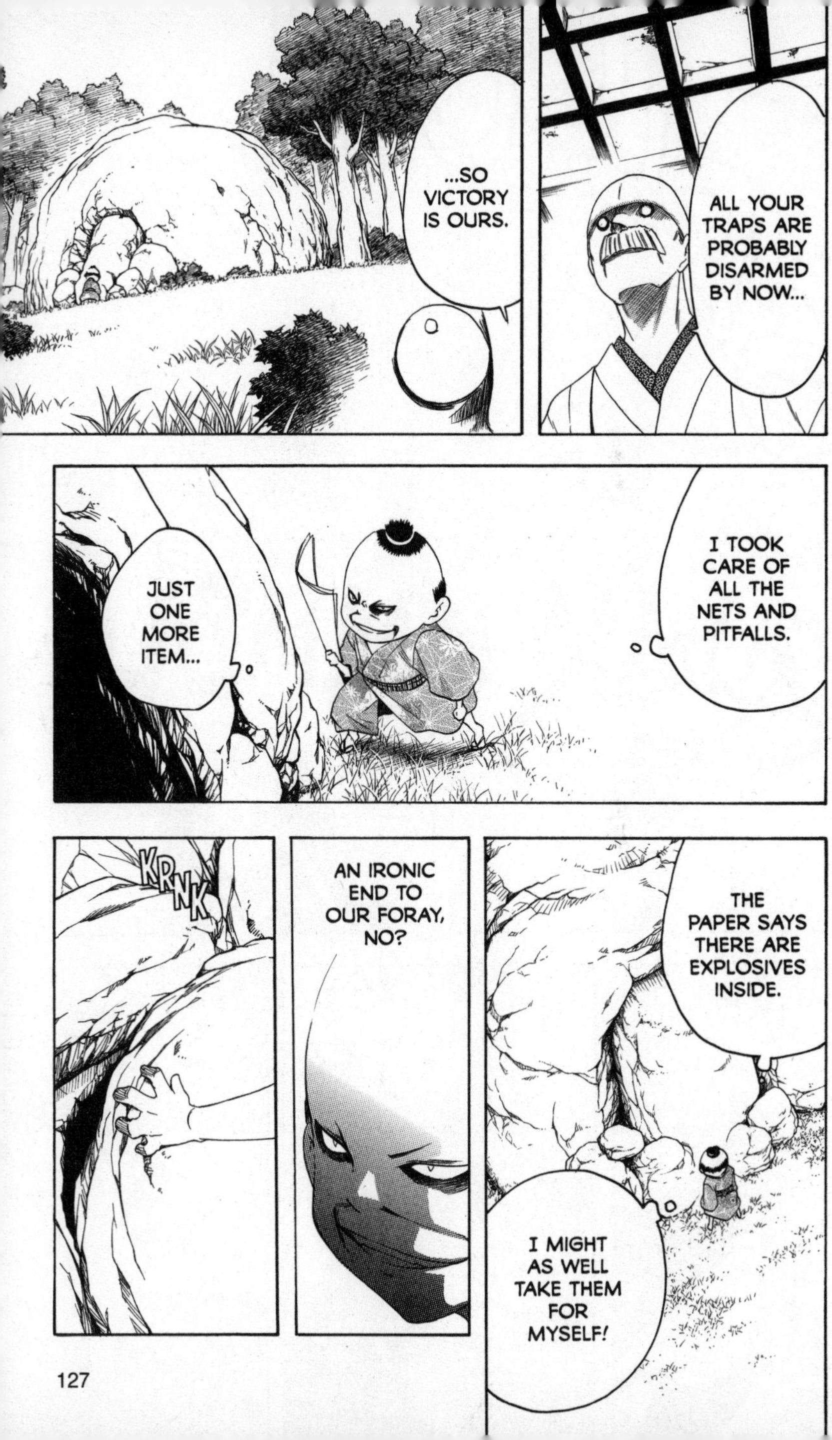
ALL YOUR TRAPS ARE PROBABLY DISARMED BY NOW...
...SO VICTORY IS OURS.
I TOOK CARE OF ALL THE NETS AND PITFALLS.
JUST ONE MORE ITEM...
THE PAPER SAYS THERE ARE EXPLOSIVES INSIDE.
I MIGHT AS WELL TAKE THEM FOR MYSELF!
AN IRONIC END TO OUR FORAY, NO?
KRNK

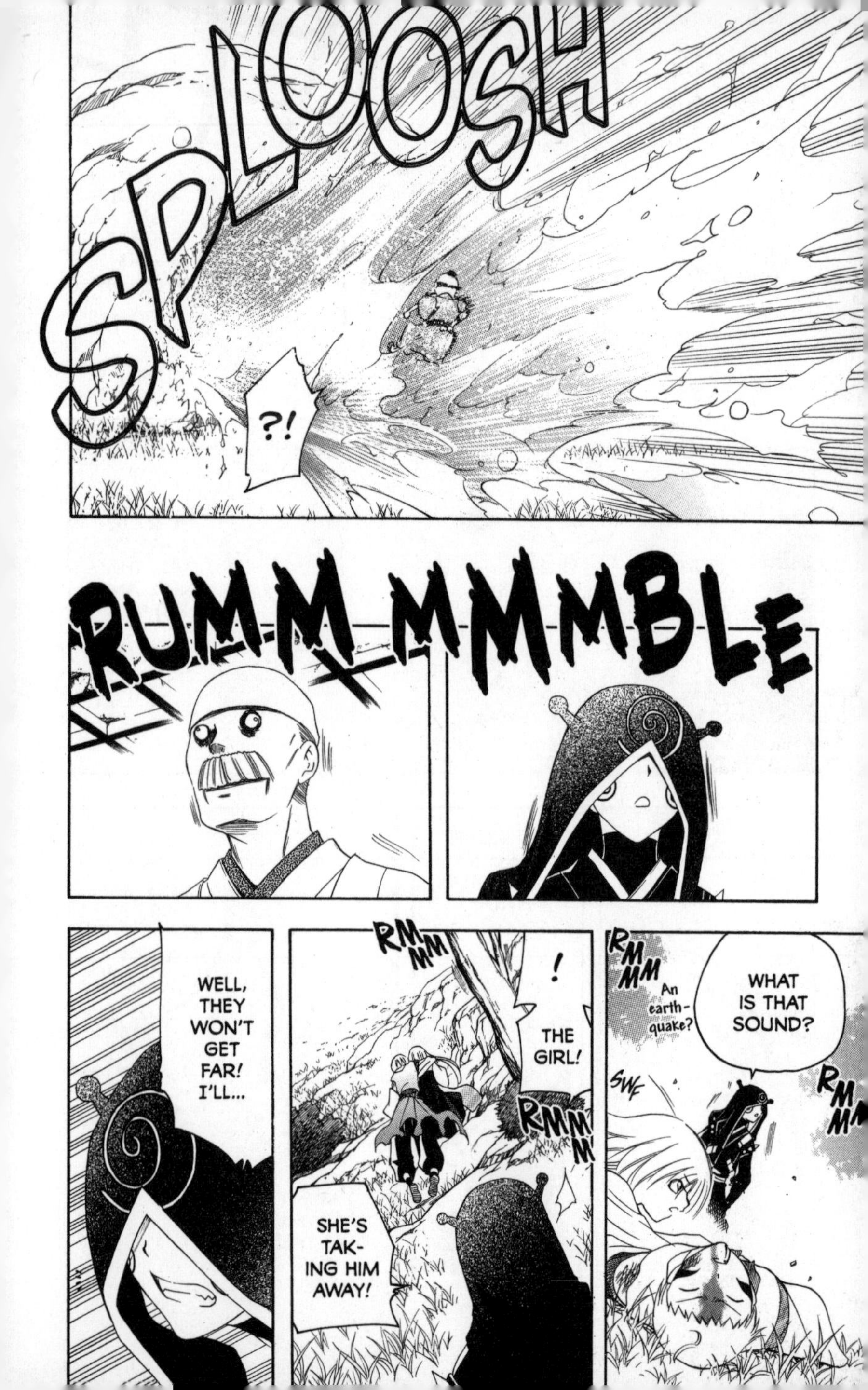
SPLOOSH
?!
RUMMMMMMBLE
WHAT IS THAT SOUND?
An earth-quake?
RMMM
SWF
RMMM
!
THE GIRL!
SHE'S TAK-ING HIM AWAY!
RMMM
RMMM
WELL, THEY WON'T GET FAR! I'LL...

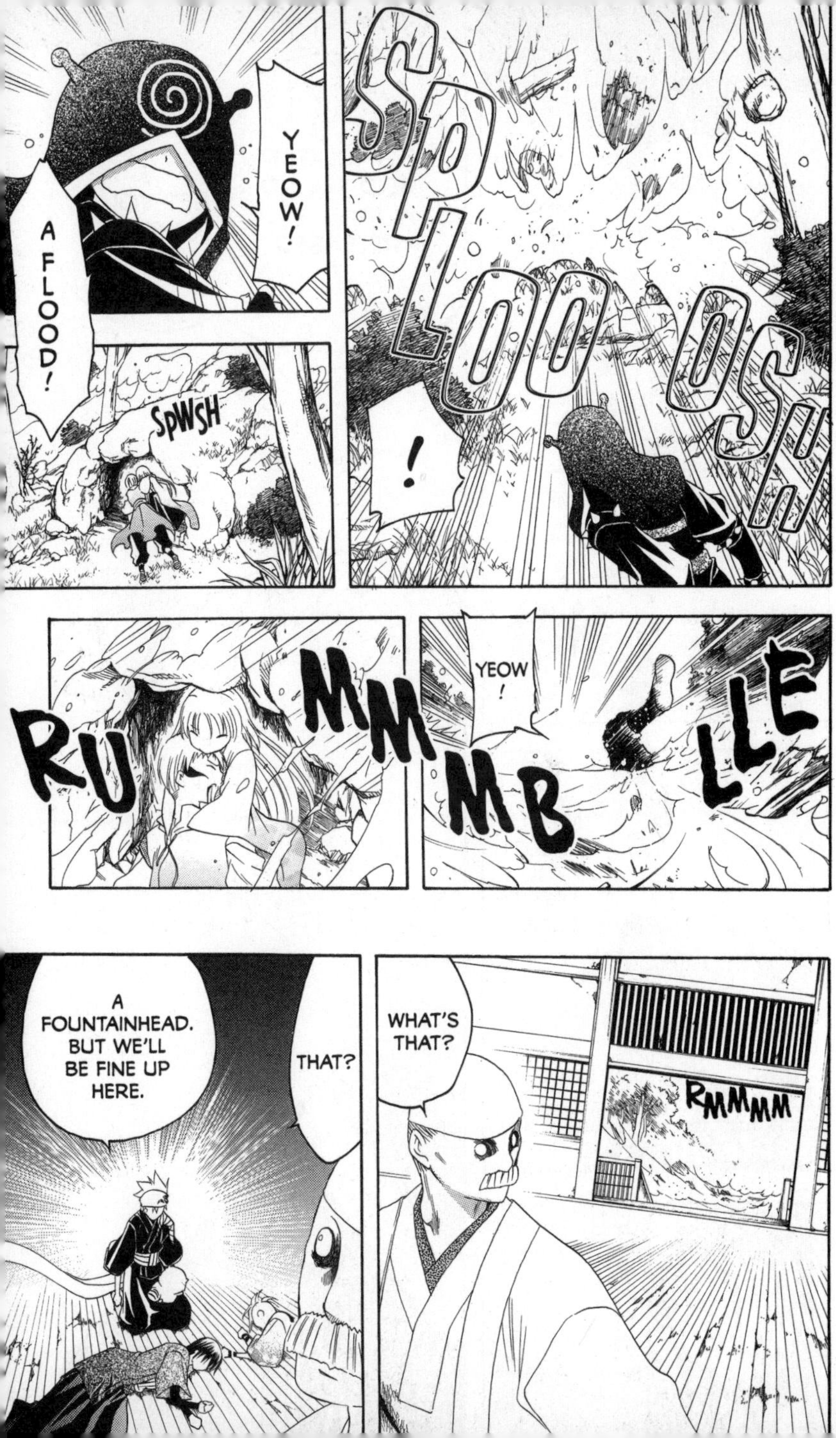
SPLOOOSH
!
YEOW!
A FLOOD!
SPWSH
YEOW!
RUMMMBLLE
WHAT'S THAT?
RMMMM
THAT?
A FOUNTAINHEAD. BUT WE'LL BE FINE UP HERE.

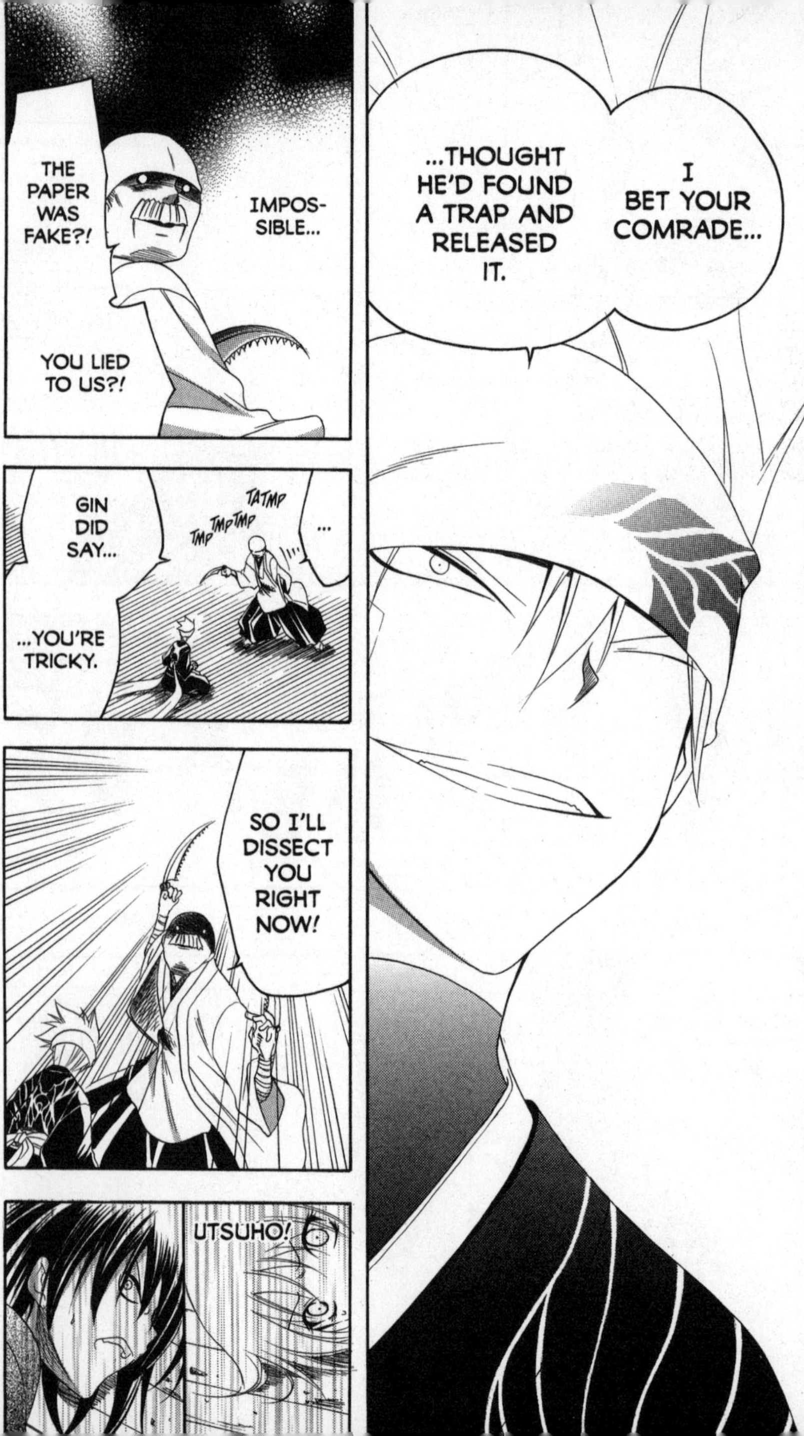
I BET YOUR COMRADE...
...THOUGHT HE'D FOUND A TRAP AND RELEASED IT.
IMPOSSIBLE...
THE PAPER WAS FAKE?!
YOU LIED TO US?!
...
TATMP TMP TMP TMP
GIN DID SAY...
...YOU'RE TRICKY.
SO I'LL DISSECT YOU RIGHT NOW!
UTSUHO!

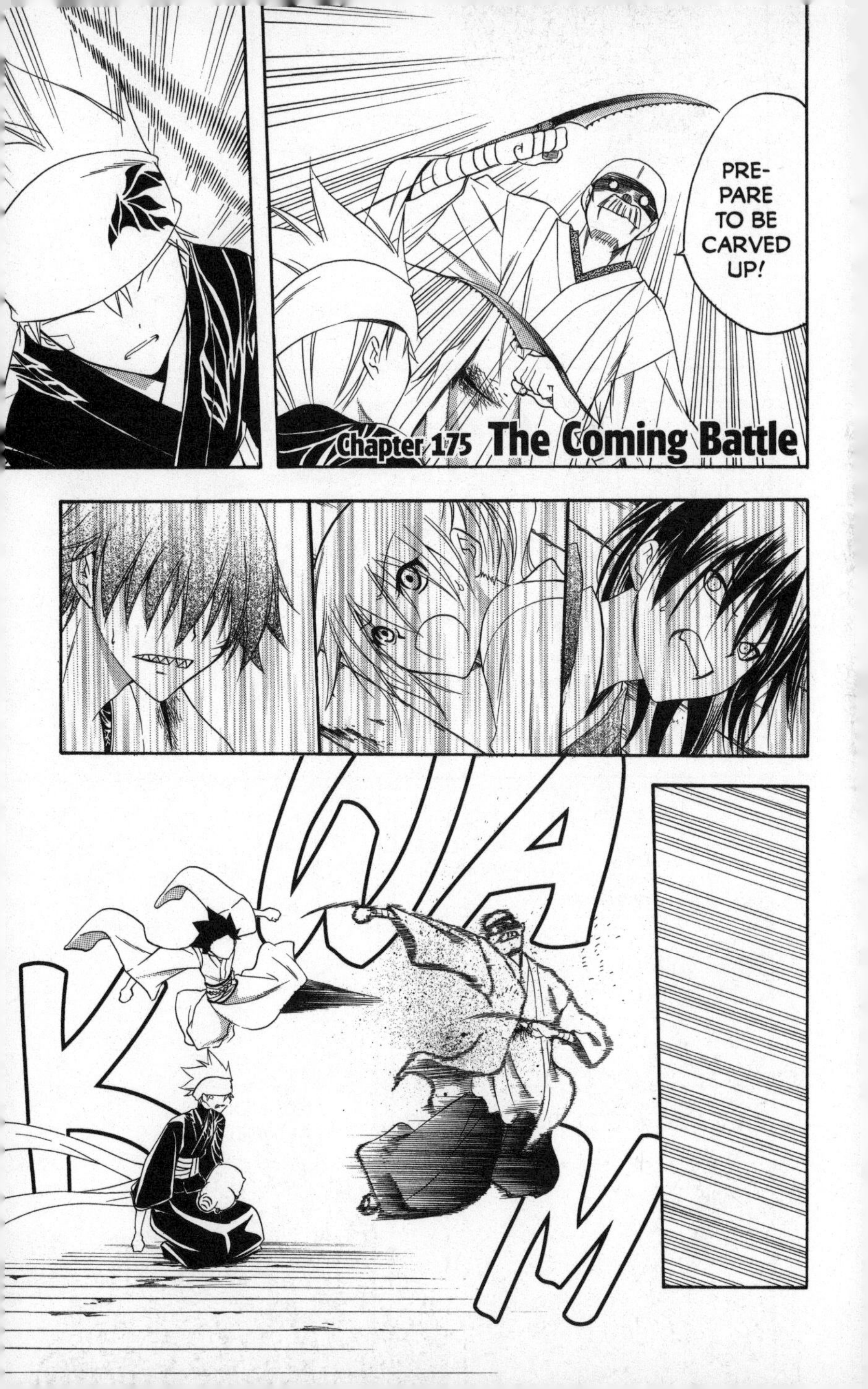
PRE-PARE TO BE CARVED UP!
Chapter 175 The Coming Battle
WHAM

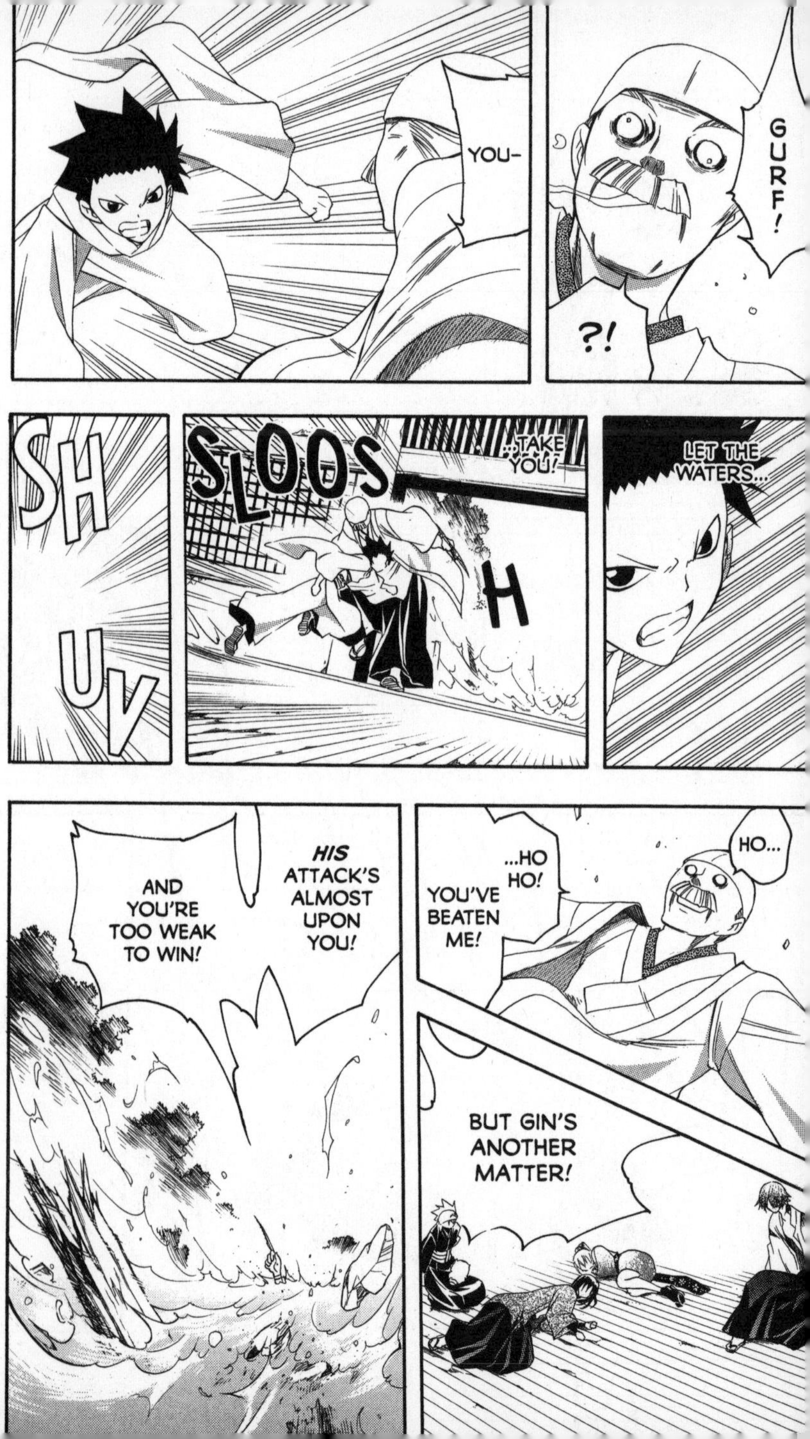
GURF!
?!
YOU-
LET THE WATERS...
...TAKE YOU!
SLOOSH
SHUV
HO...
...HO HO!
YOU'VE BEATEN ME!
BUT GIN'S ANOTHER MATTER!
HIS ATTACK'S ALMOST UPON YOU!
AND YOU'RE TOO WEAK TO WIN!

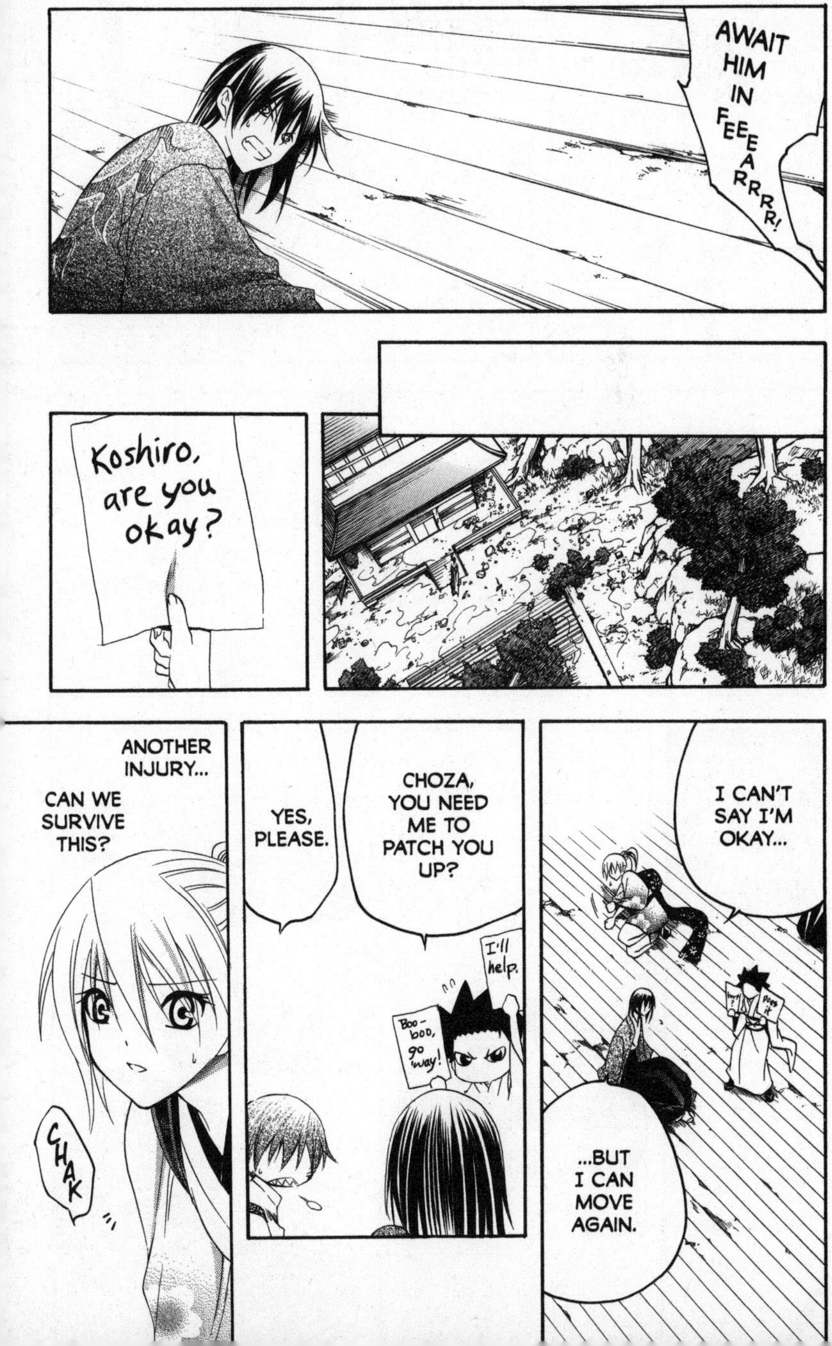
AWAIT HIM IN FEEEARRRRR!
Koshiro, are you okay?
I CAN'T SAY I'M OKAY...
...BUT I CAN MOVE AGAIN.
CHOZA, YOU NEED ME TO PATCH YOU UP?
YES, PLEASE.
I'll help.
Boo-boo, go 'way!
ANOTHER INJURY...
CAN WE SURVIVE THIS?
CHAK

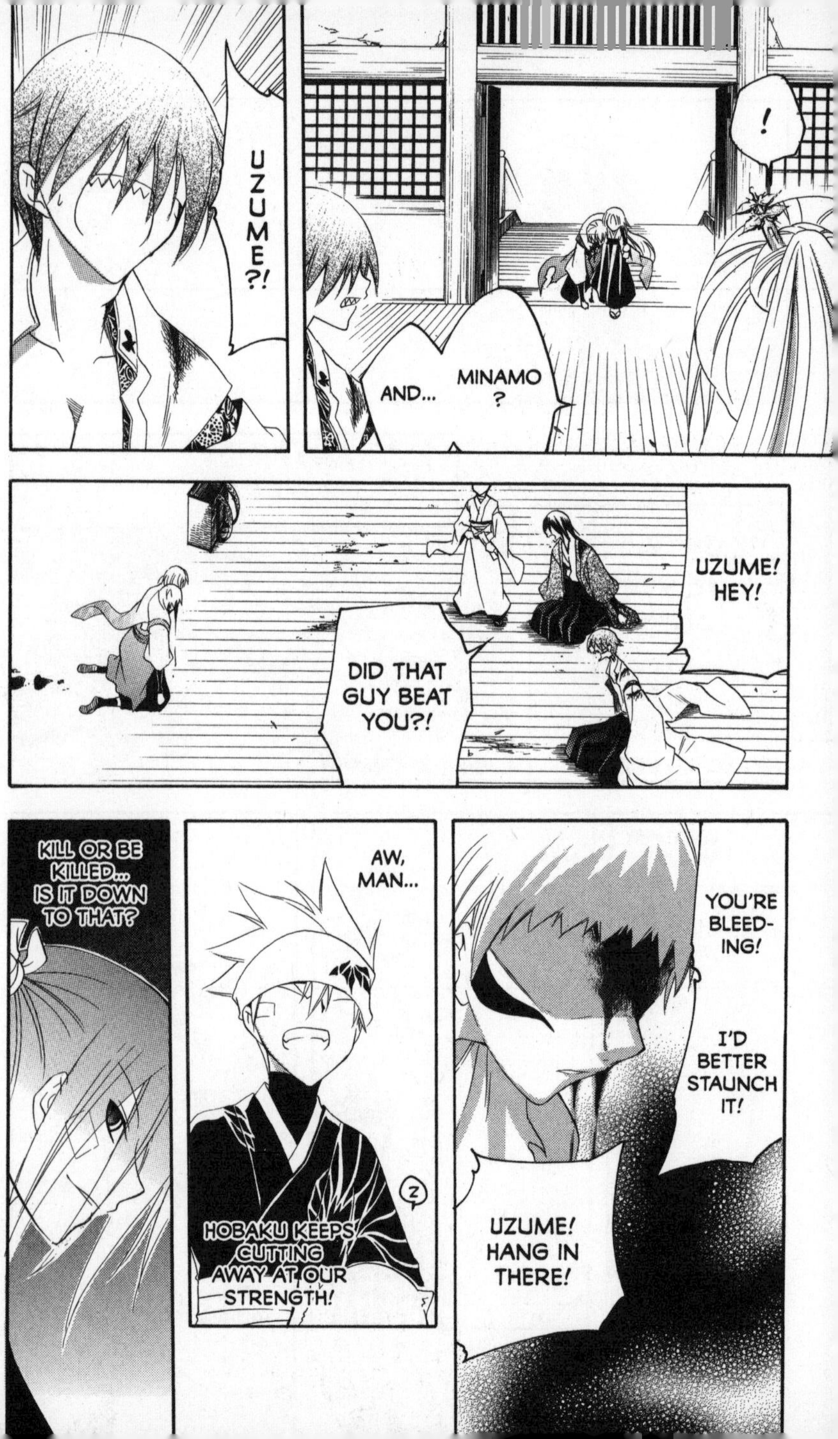
!
AND... MINAMO?
UZUME?!
UZUME! HEY!
DID THAT GUY BEAT YOU?!
YOU'RE BLEED-ING!
I'D BETTER STAUNCH IT!
UZUME! HANG IN THERE!
AW, MAN...
HOBAKU KEEPS CUTTING AWAY AT OUR STRENGTH!
Z
KILL OR BE KILLED... IS IT DOWN TO THAT?

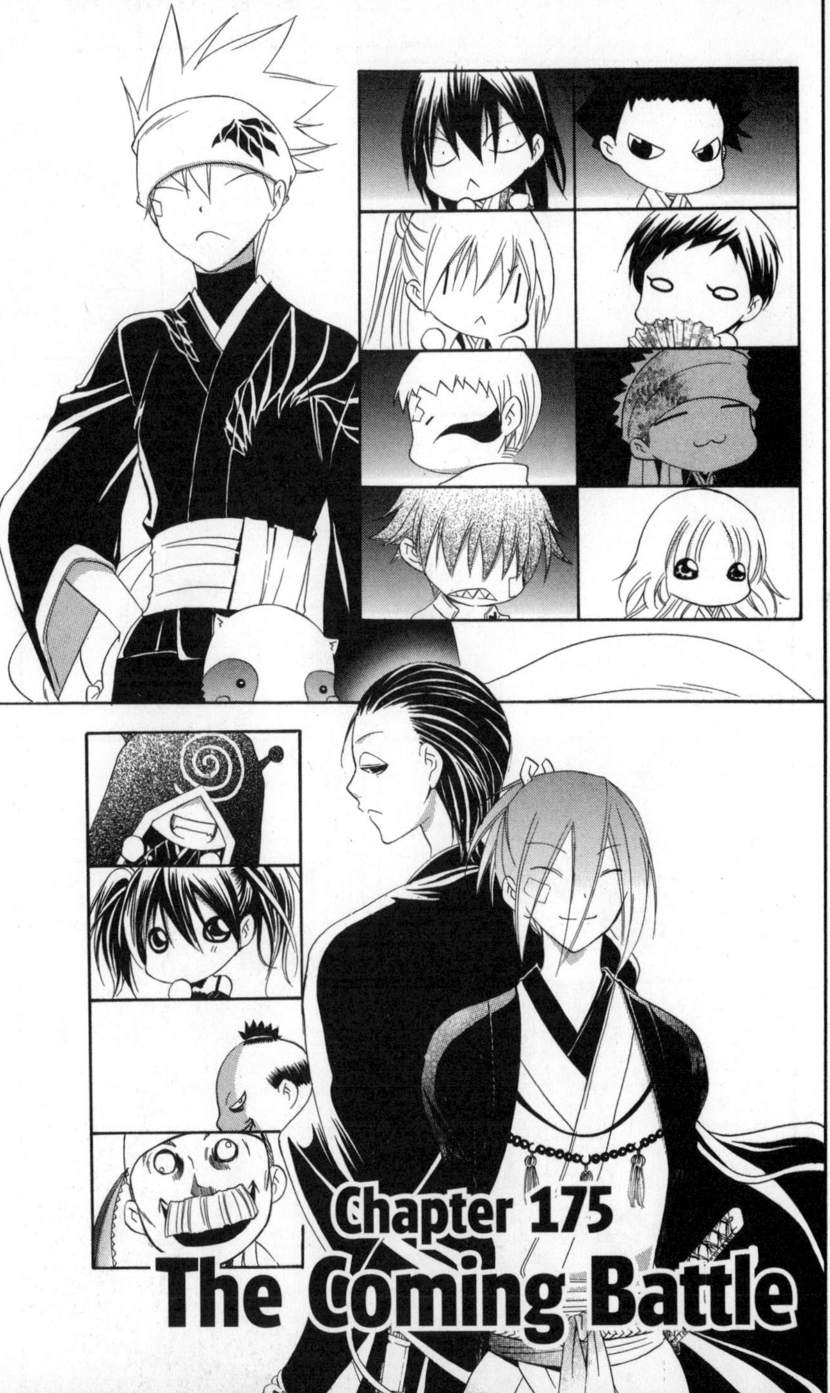
Chapter 175
The Coming Battle

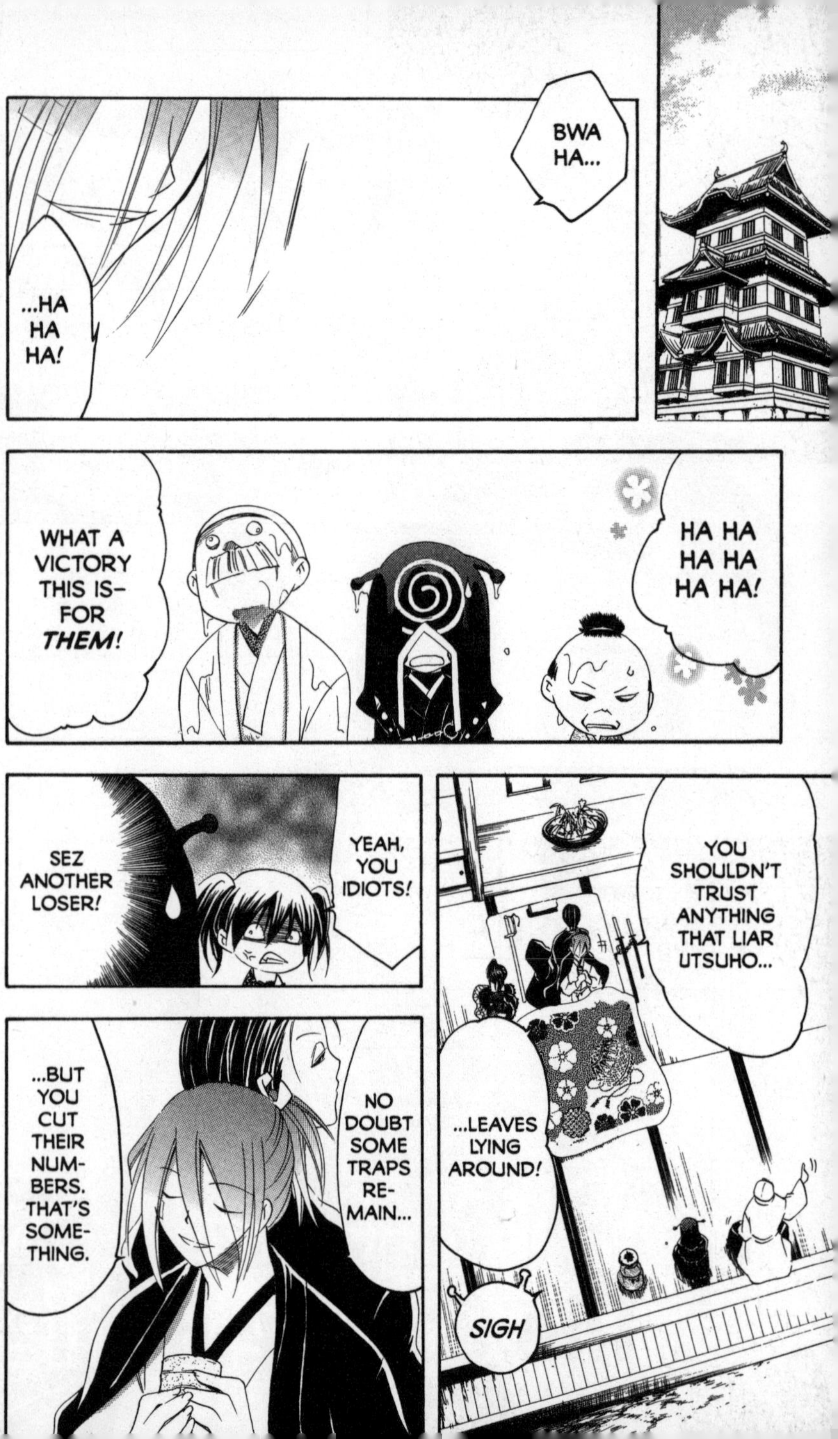
BWA HA...
...HA HA HA!
HA HA HA HA HA HA!
WHAT A VICTORY THIS IS—FOR *THEM*!
YOU SHOULDN'T TRUST ANYTHING THAT LIAR UTSUHO...
...LEAVES LYING AROUND!
SIGH
YEAH, YOU IDIOTS!
SEZ ANOTHER LOSER!
NO DOUBT SOME TRAPS RE-MAIN...
...BUT YOU CUT THEIR NUM-BERS. THAT'S SOME-THING.

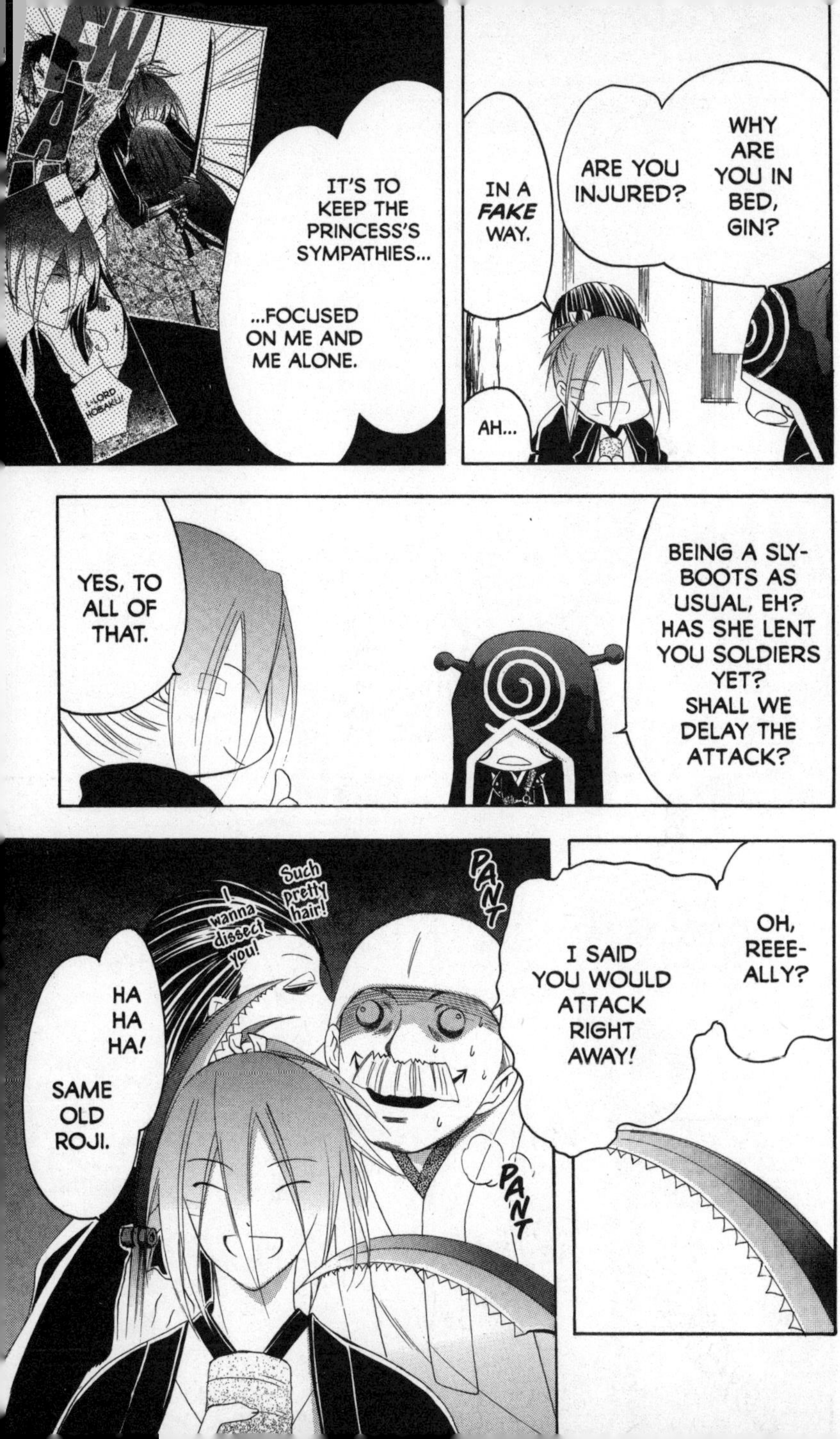
WHY ARE YOU IN BED, GIN?
ARE YOU INJURED?
IN A *FAKE* WAY.
AH...
IT'S TO KEEP THE PRINCESS'S SYMPATHIES...
...FOCUSED ON ME AND ME ALONE.
UNGH!
L-LORD HOBAKU!
BEING A SLY-BOOTS AS USUAL, EH? HAS SHE LENT YOU SOLDIERS YET? SHALL WE DELAY THE ATTACK?
YES, TO ALL OF THAT.
OH, REEE-ALLY?
I SAID YOU WOULD ATTACK RIGHT AWAY!
PANT
PANT
Such pretty hair!
I wanna dissect you!
HA HA HA!
SAME OLD ROJI.

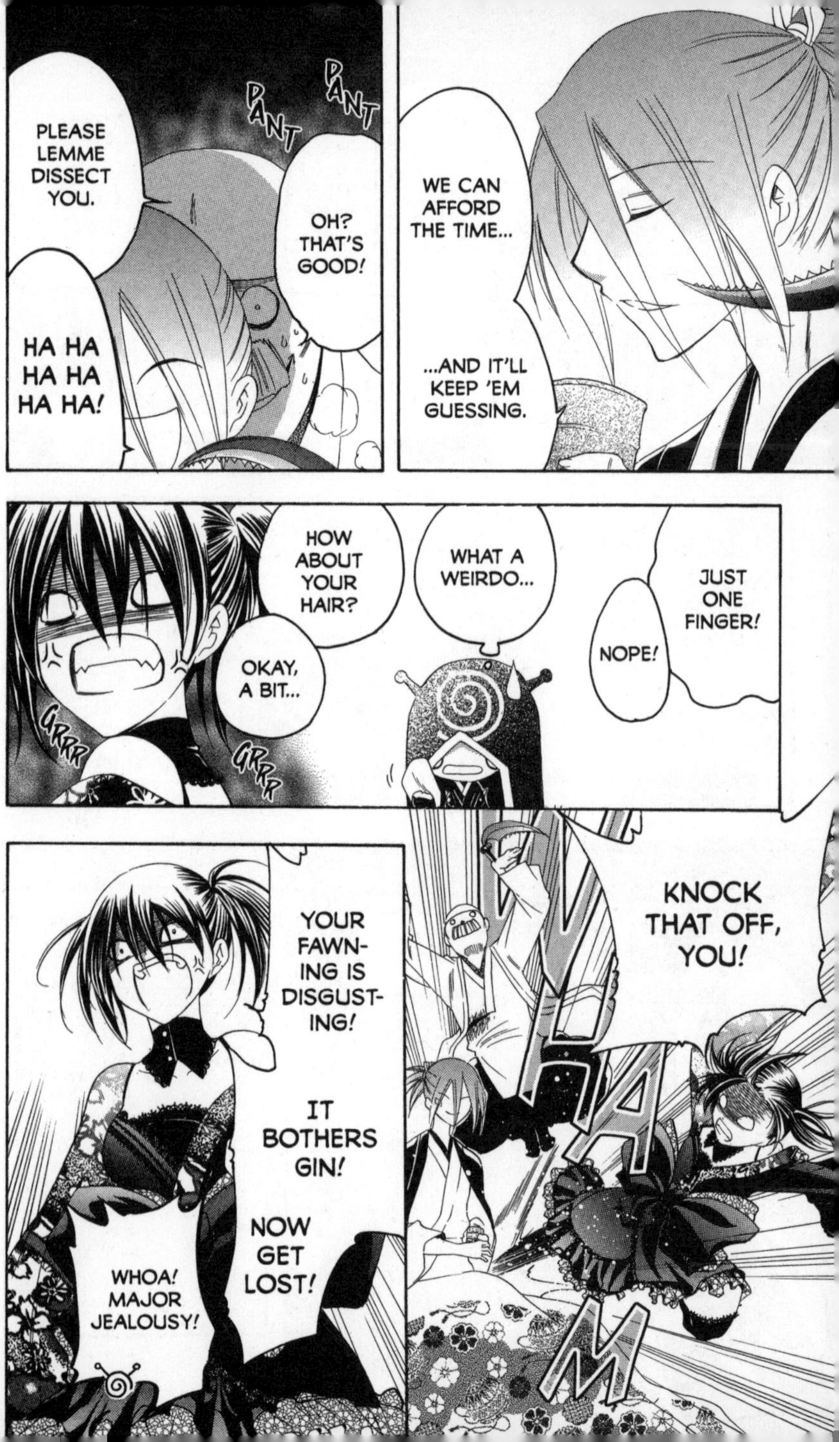
WE CAN AFFORD THE TIME...
...AND IT'LL KEEP 'EM GUESSING.
PANT PANT
OH? THAT'S GOOD!
PLEASE LEMME DISSECT YOU.
HA HA HA HA HA HA!
JUST ONE FINGER!
NOPE!
WHAT A WEIRDO...
HOW ABOUT YOUR HAIR?
OKAY, A BIT...
GRRR
GRRR
KNOCK THAT OFF, YOU!
WHAM
YOUR FAWNING IS DISGUSTING!
IT BOTHERS GIN!
NOW GET LOST!
WHOA! MAJOR JEALOUSY!

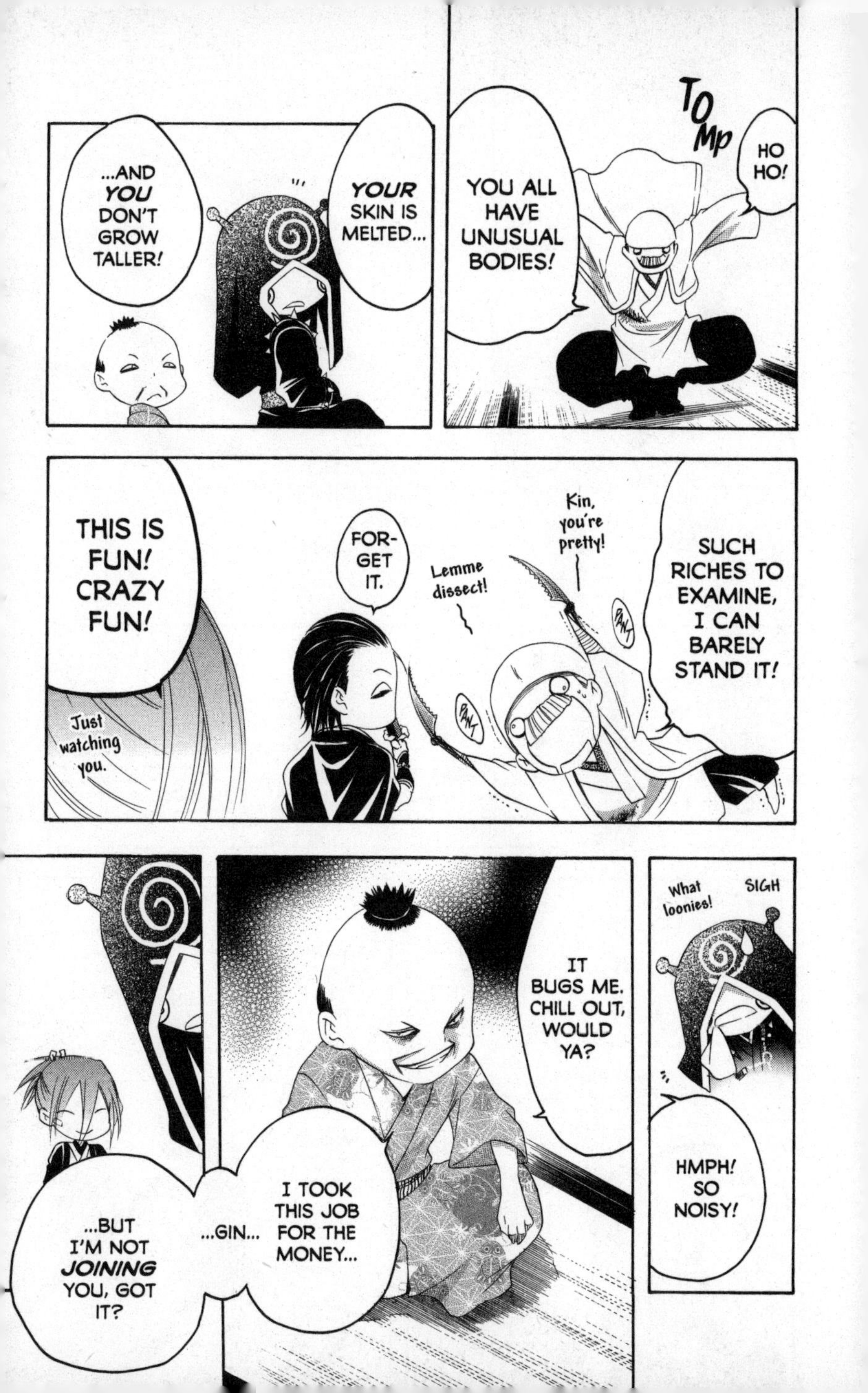
TOMP
HO HO!
YOU ALL HAVE UNUSUAL BODIES!
YOUR SKIN IS MELTED...
...AND YOU DON'T GROW TALLER!
SUCH RICHES TO EXAMINE, I CAN BARELY STAND IT!
Kin, you're pretty!
PANT
PANT
Lemme dissect!
FOR-GET IT.
THIS IS FUN! CRAZY FUN!
Just watching you.
What loonies!
SIGH
HMPH! SO NOISY!
IT BUGS ME. CHILL OUT, WOULD YA?
I TOOK THIS JOB FOR THE MONEY...
...GIN...
...BUT I'M NOT JOINING YOU, GOT IT?

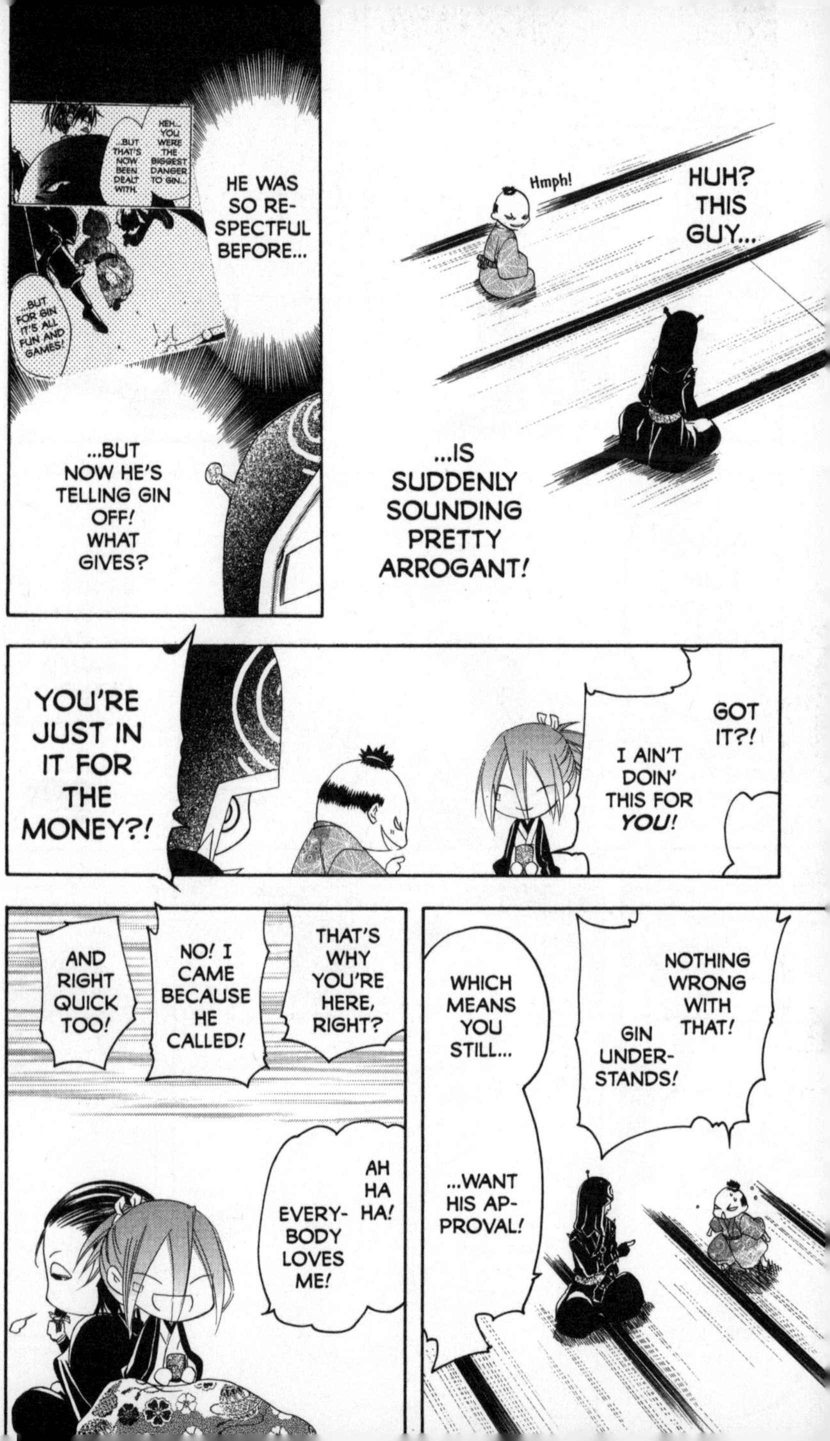
HUH? THIS GUY...
Hmph!
...IS SUDDENLY SOUNDING PRETTY ARROGANT!
HEH... YOU WERE THE BIGGEST DANGER TO GIN...
...BUT THAT'S NOW BEEN DEALT WITH.
...BUT FOR GIN IT'S ALL FUN AND GAMES!
HE WAS SO RE-SPECTFUL BEFORE...
...BUT NOW HE'S TELLING GIN OFF! WHAT GIVES?
GOT IT?!
I AIN'T DOIN' THIS FOR *YOU*!
YOU'RE JUST IN IT FOR THE MONEY?!
NOTHING WRONG WITH THAT!
GIN UNDER-STANDS!
WHICH MEANS YOU STILL...
...WANT HIS AP-PROVAL!
THAT'S WHY YOU'RE HERE, RIGHT?
NO! I CAME BECAUSE HE CALLED!
AND RIGHT QUICK TOO!
AH HA HA!
EVERY-BODY LOVES ME!

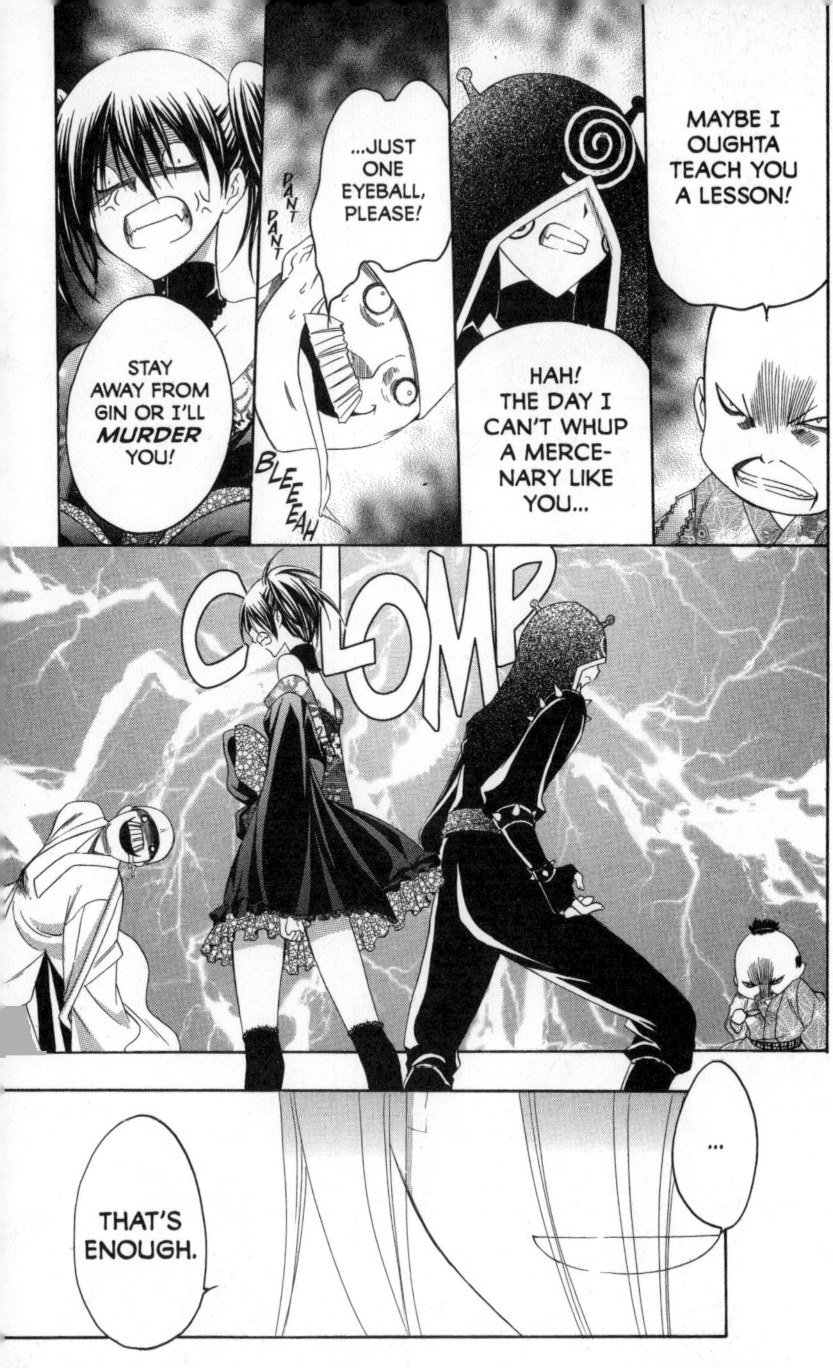
MAYBE I OUGHTA TEACH YOU A LESSON!
HAH! THE DAY I CAN'T WHUP A MERCENARY LIKE YOU...
...JUST ONE EYEBALL, PLEASE!
PANT PANT
BLEEEEAH
STAY AWAY FROM GIN OR I'LL *MURDER* YOU!
CLOMP
...
THAT'S ENOUGH.

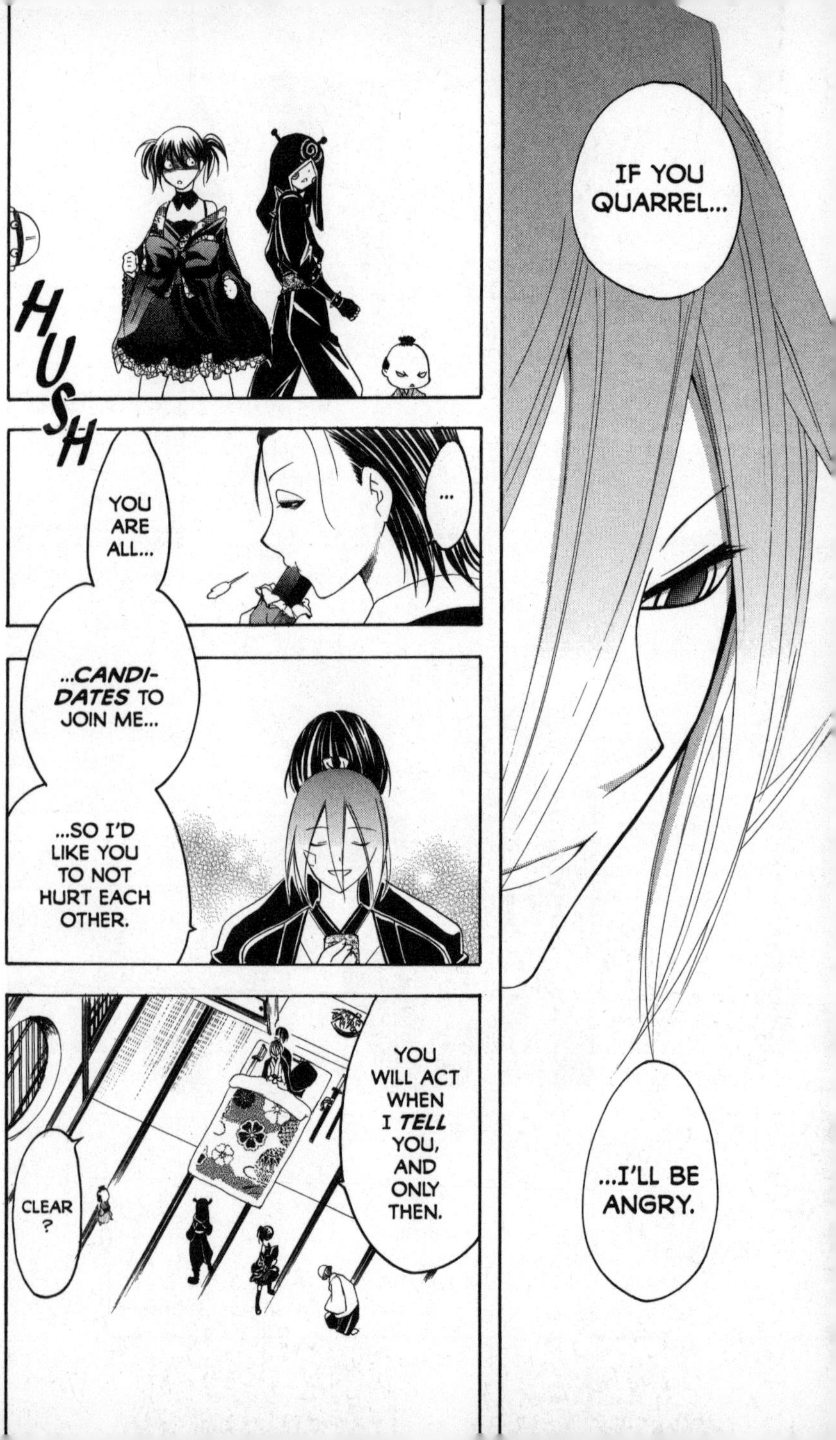
IF YOU QUARREL...
...I'LL BE ANGRY.
HUSH
YOU ARE ALL...
...
...*CANDIDATES* TO JOIN ME...
...SO I'D LIKE YOU TO NOT HURT EACH OTHER.
YOU WILL ACT WHEN I *TELL* YOU, AND ONLY THEN.
CLEAR?

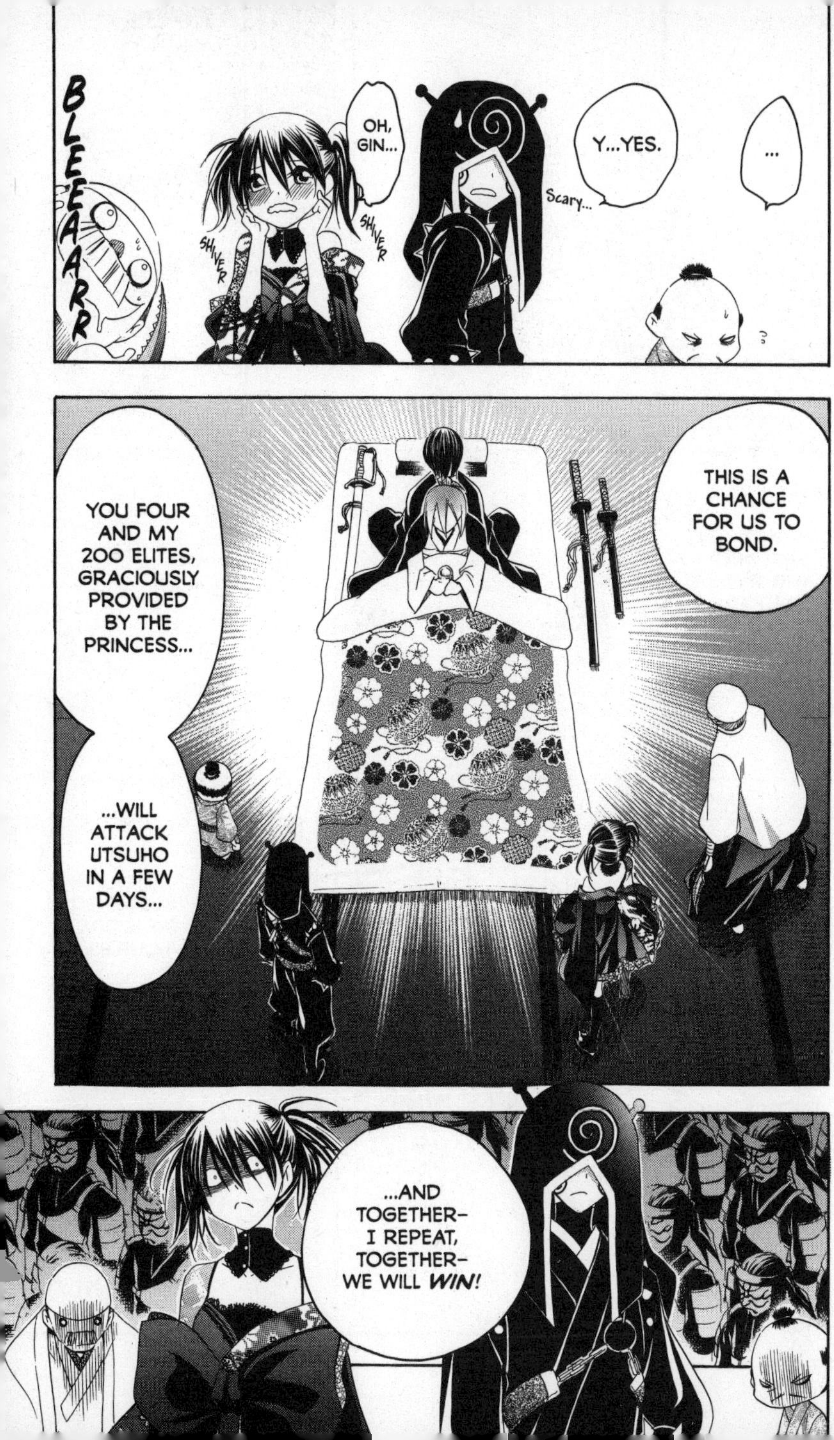
...
Y...YES.
Scary...
OH, GIN...
SHIVER
SHIVER
BLEEAARR
THIS IS A CHANCE FOR US TO BOND.
YOU FOUR AND MY 200 ELITES, GRACIOUSLY PROVIDED BY THE PRINCESS...
...WILL ATTACK UTSUHO IN A FEW DAYS...
...AND TOGETHER– I REPEAT, TOGETHER– WE WILL *WIN*!

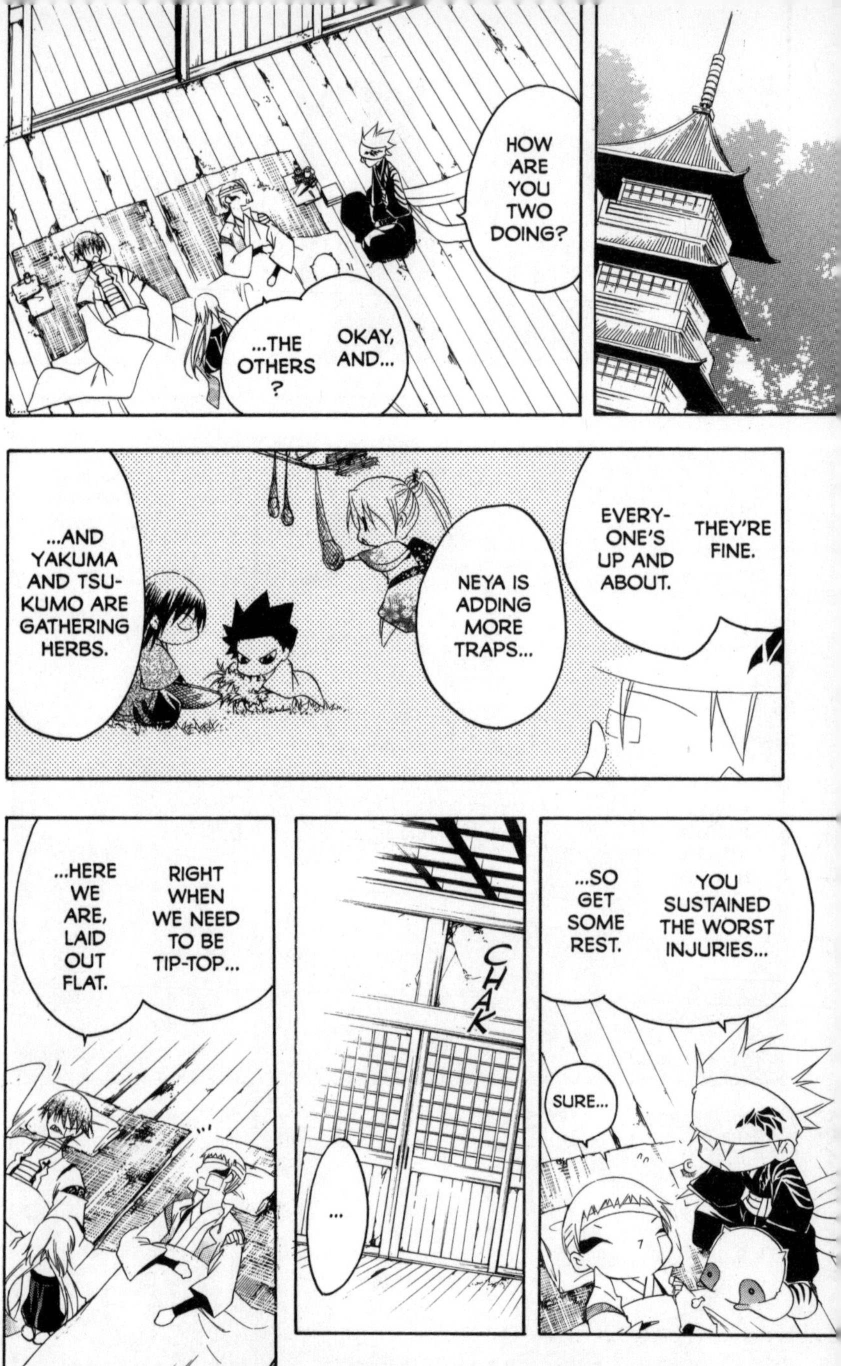
HOW ARE YOU TWO DOING?
OKAY, AND...
...THE OTHERS?
THEY'RE FINE.
EVERY-ONE'S UP AND ABOUT.
NEYA IS ADDING MORE TRAPS...
...AND YAKUMA AND TSU-KUMO ARE GATHERING HERBS.
YOU SUSTAINED THE WORST INJURIES...
...SO GET SOME REST.
SURE...
CHAK
...
RIGHT WHEN WE NEED TO BE TIP-TOP...
...HERE WE ARE, LAID OUT FLAT.

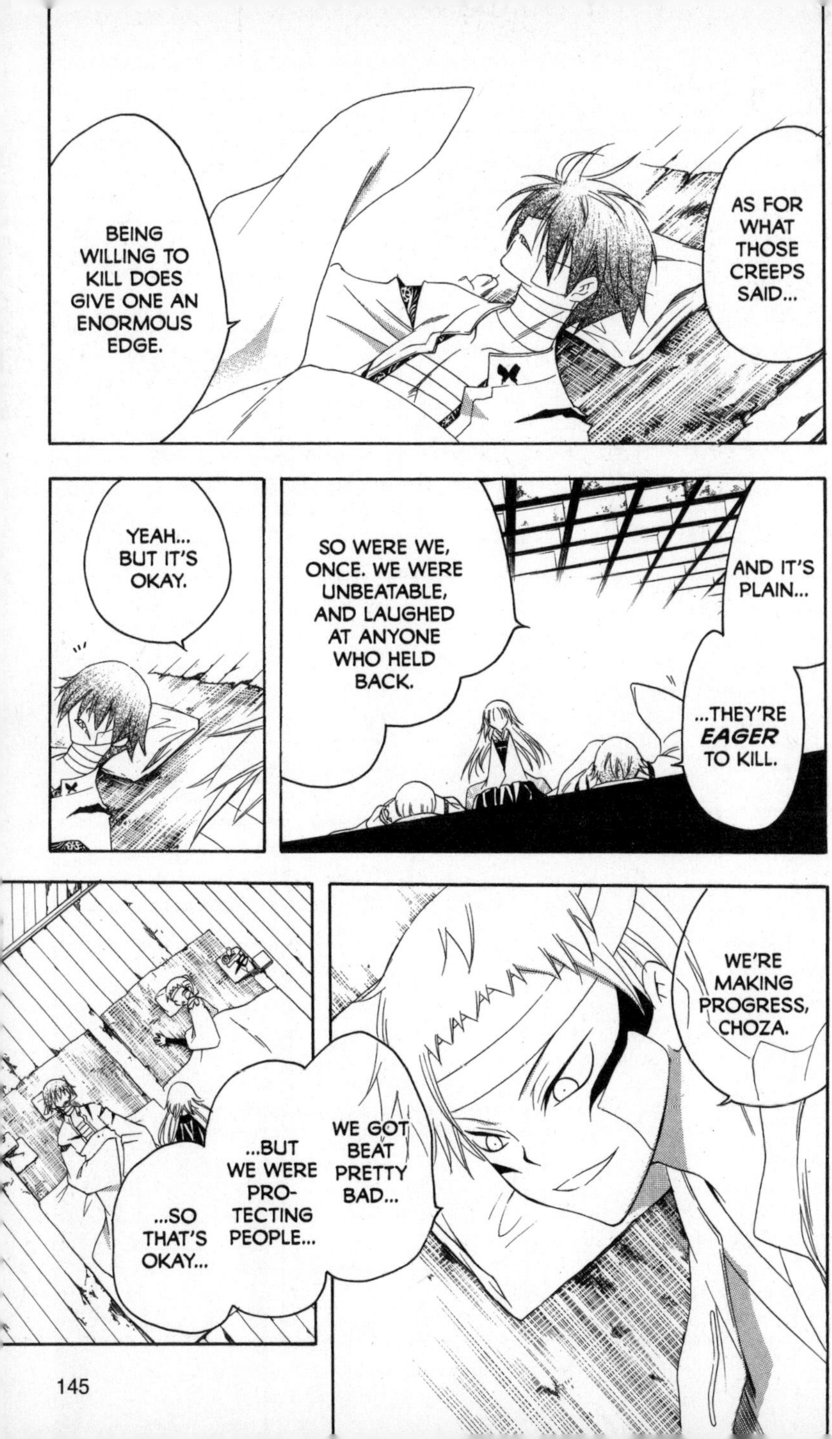
AS FOR WHAT THOSE CREEPS SAID...
BEING WILLING TO KILL DOES GIVE ONE AN ENORMOUS EDGE.
AND IT'S PLAIN...
...THEY'RE *EAGER* TO KILL.
SO WERE WE, ONCE. WE WERE UNBEATABLE, AND LAUGHED AT ANYONE WHO HELD BACK.
YEAH... BUT IT'S OKAY.
WE'RE MAKING PROGRESS, CHOZA.
WE GOT BEAT PRETTY BAD...
...BUT WE WERE PRO-TECTING PEOPLE...
...SO THAT'S OKAY...

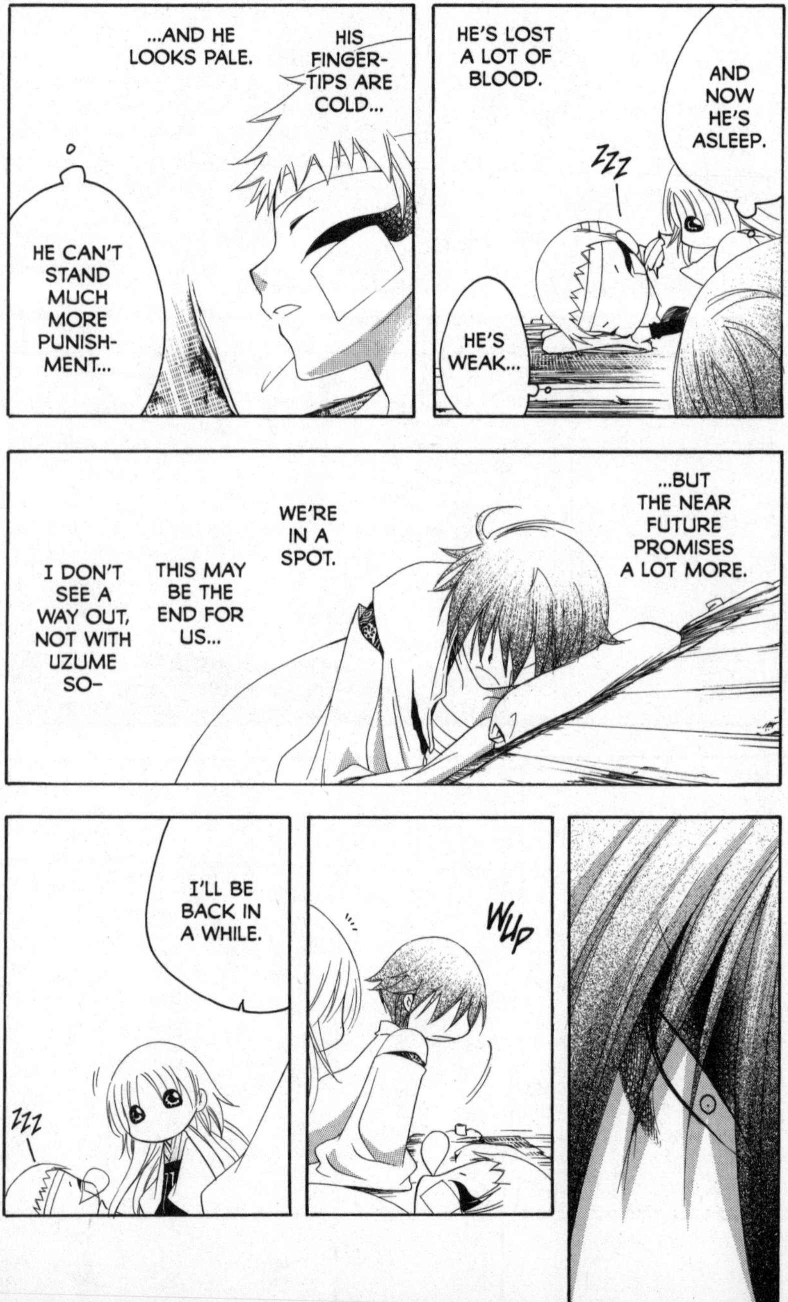
AND NOW HE'S ASLEEP.
HE'S LOST A LOT OF BLOOD.
ZZZ
HE'S WEAK...
HIS FINGER-TIPS ARE COLD...
...AND HE LOOKS PALE.
HE CAN'T STAND MUCH MORE PUNISH-MENT...
...BUT THE NEAR FUTURE PROMISES A LOT MORE.
WE'RE IN A SPOT.
THIS MAY BE THE END FOR US...
I DON'T SEE A WAY OUT, NOT WITH UZUME SO–
WUP
I'LL BE BACK IN A WHILE.
ZZZ

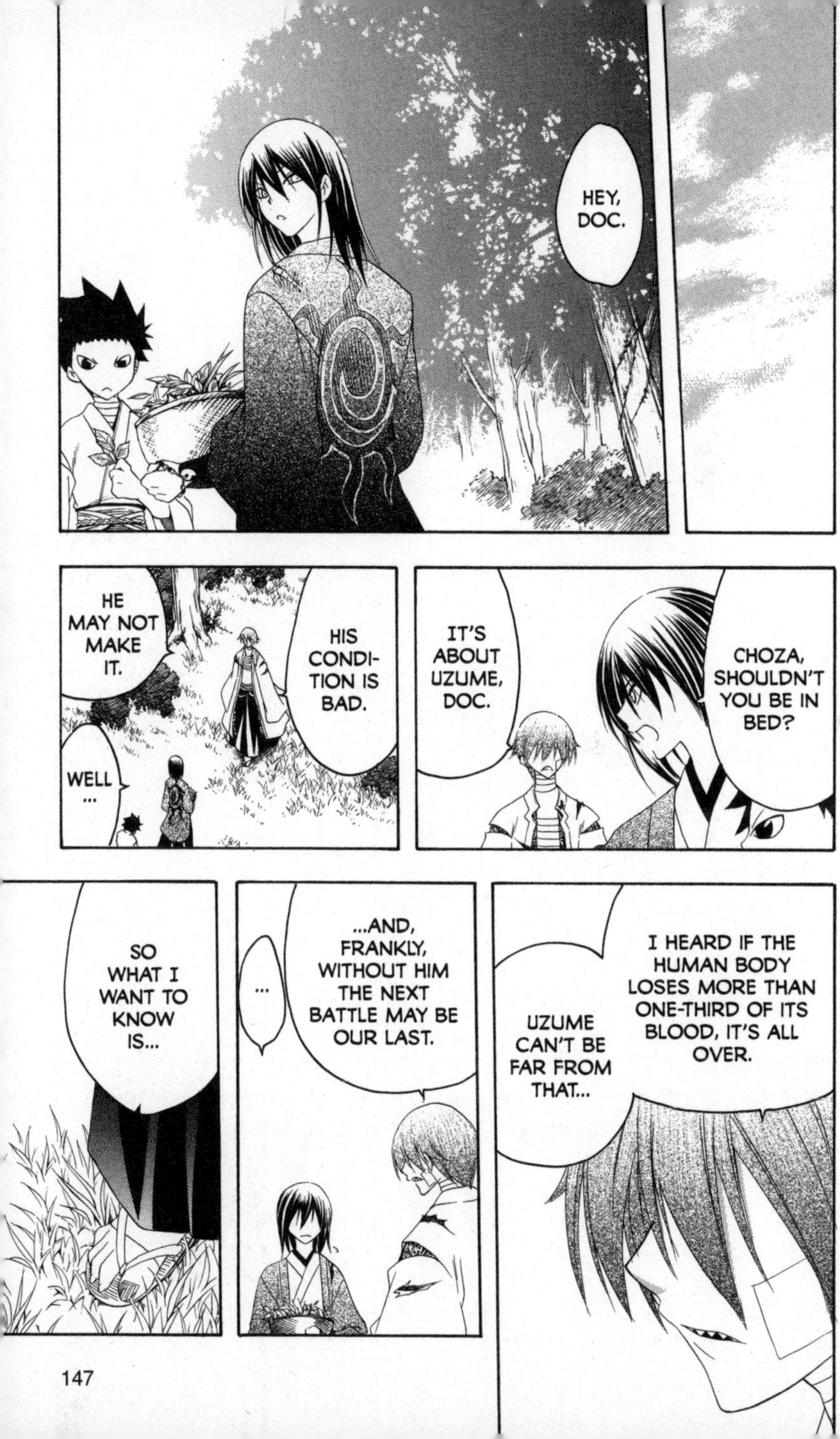
HEY, DOC.
CHOZA, SHOULDN'T YOU BE IN BED?
IT'S ABOUT UZUME, DOC.
HIS CONDITION IS BAD.
HE MAY NOT MAKE IT.
WELL ...
I HEARD IF THE HUMAN BODY LOSES MORE THAN ONE-THIRD OF ITS BLOOD, IT'S ALL OVER.
UZUME CAN'T BE FAR FROM THAT...
...AND, FRANKLY, WITHOUT HIM THE NEXT BATTLE MAY BE OUR LAST.
...
SO WHAT I WANT TO KNOW IS...

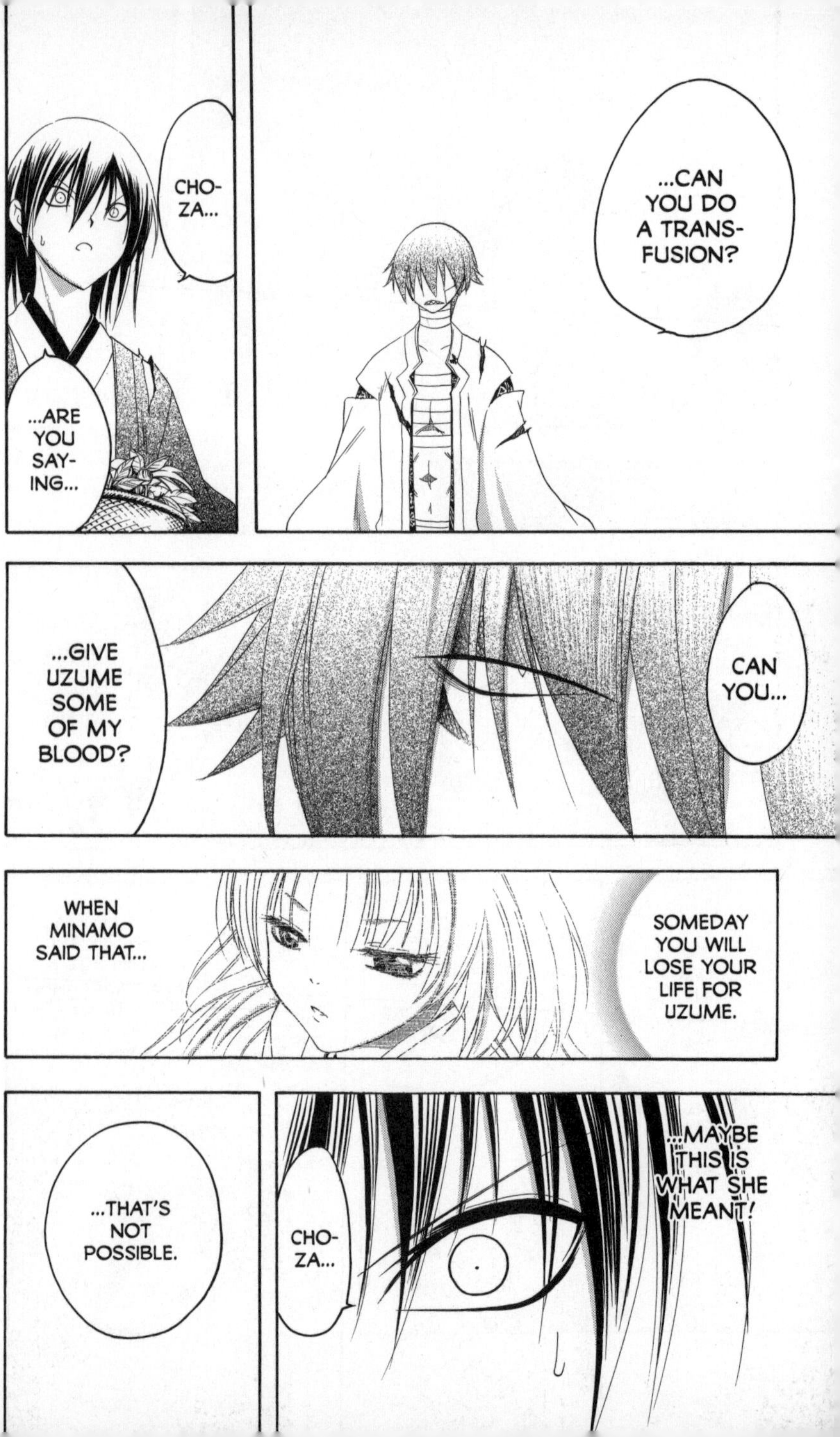
...CAN YOU DO A TRANS-FUSION?
CHO-ZA...
...ARE YOU SAY-ING...
CAN YOU...
...GIVE UZUME SOME OF MY BLOOD?
SOMEDAY YOU WILL LOSE YOUR LIFE FOR UZUME.
WHEN MINAMO SAID THAT...
...MAYBE THIS IS WHAT SHE MEANT!
CHO-ZA...
...THAT'S NOT POSSIBLE.

Chapter 176 Kin's Objective

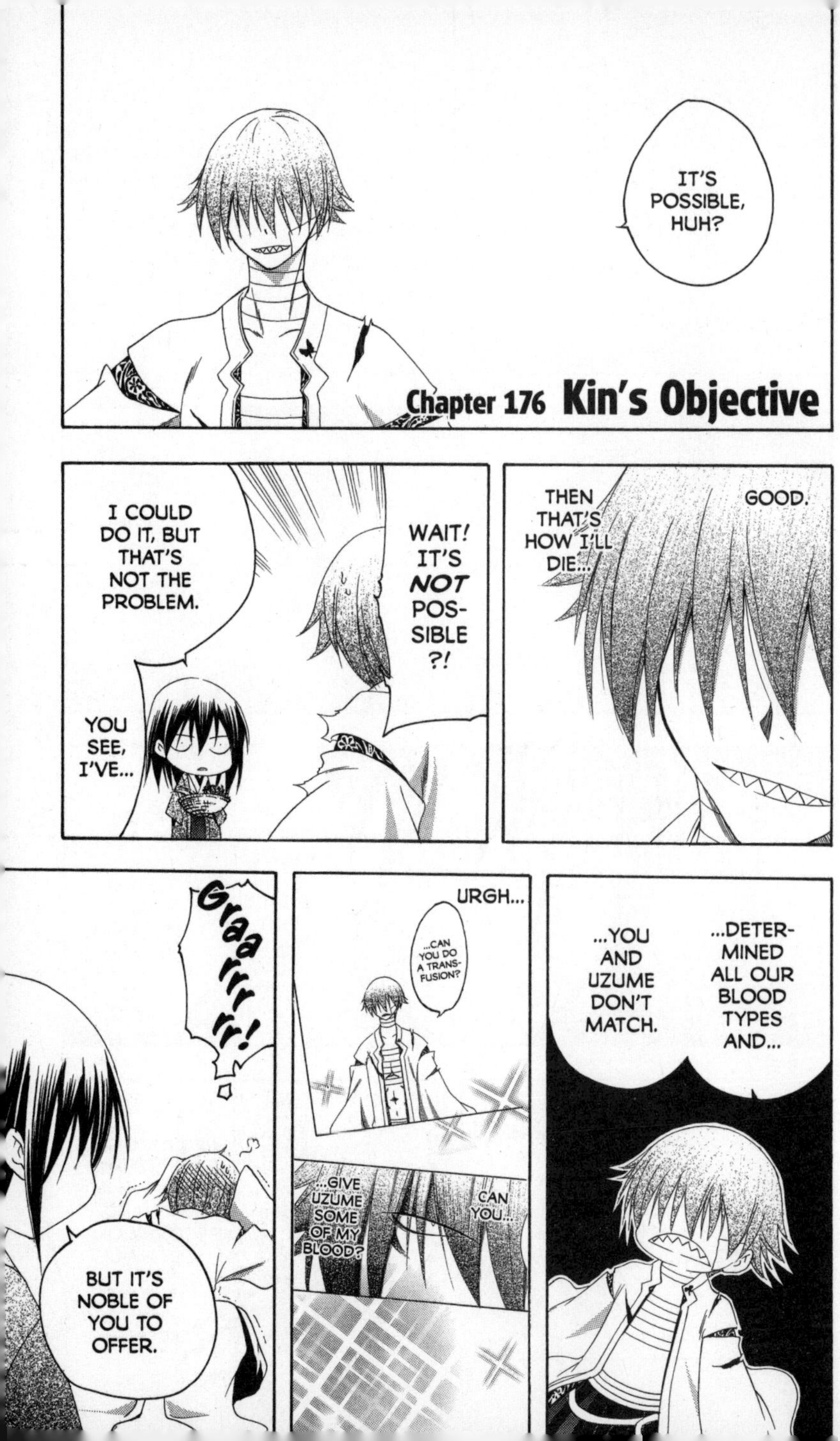
IT'S POSSIBLE, HUH?
GOOD.
THEN THAT'S HOW I'LL DIE...
WAIT! IT'S *NOT* POSSIBLE?!
I COULD DO IT, BUT THAT'S NOT THE PROBLEM.
YOU SEE, I'VE...
...DETERMINED ALL OUR BLOOD TYPES AND...
...YOU AND UZUME DON'T MATCH.
URGH...
...CAN YOU DO A TRANSFUSION?
CAN YOU...
...GIVE UZUME SOME OF MY BLOOD?
Graaarrrrr!
BUT IT'S NOBLE OF YOU TO OFFER.

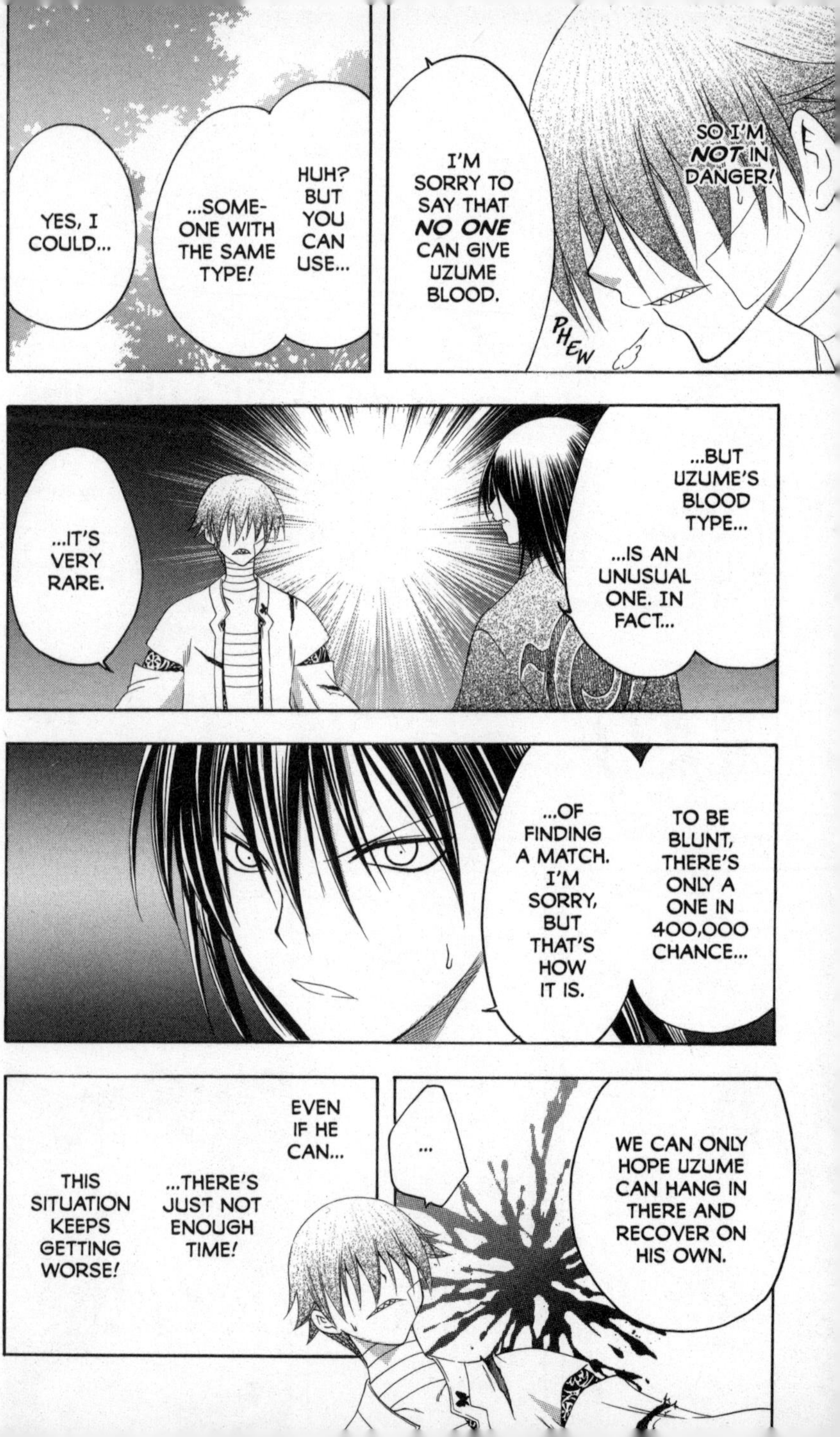
SO I'M NOT IN DANGER!
PHEW
I'M SORRY TO SAY THAT NO ONE CAN GIVE UZUME BLOOD.
HUH? BUT YOU CAN USE...
...SOMEONE WITH THE SAME TYPE!
YES, I COULD...
...BUT UZUME'S BLOOD TYPE...
...IS AN UNUSUAL ONE. IN FACT...
...IT'S VERY RARE.
TO BE BLUNT, THERE'S ONLY A ONE IN 400,000 CHANCE...
...OF FINDING A MATCH. I'M SORRY, BUT THAT'S HOW IT IS.
WE CAN ONLY HOPE UZUME CAN HANG IN THERE AND RECOVER ON HIS OWN.
...
EVEN IF HE CAN...
...THERE'S JUST NOT ENOUGH TIME!
THIS SITUATION KEEPS GETTING WORSE!

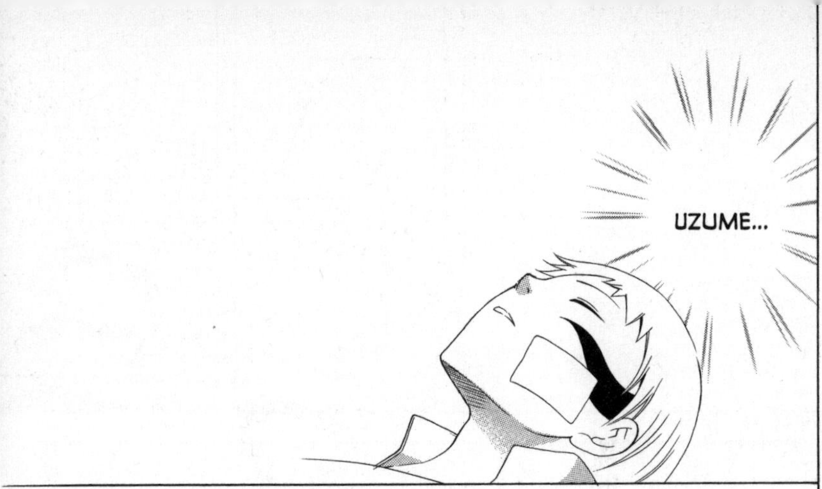
UZUME...

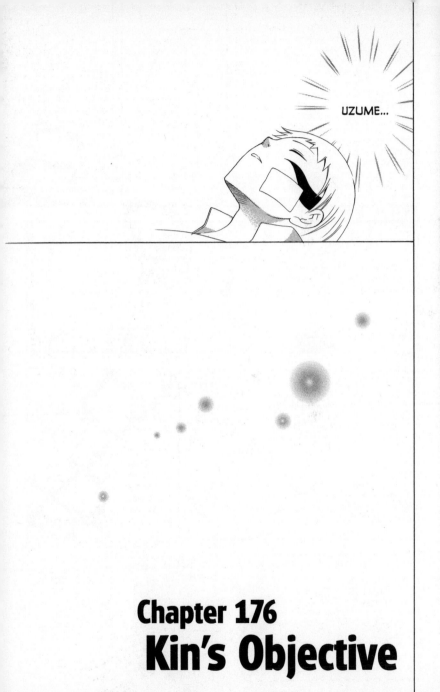

Chapter 176
Kin's Objective

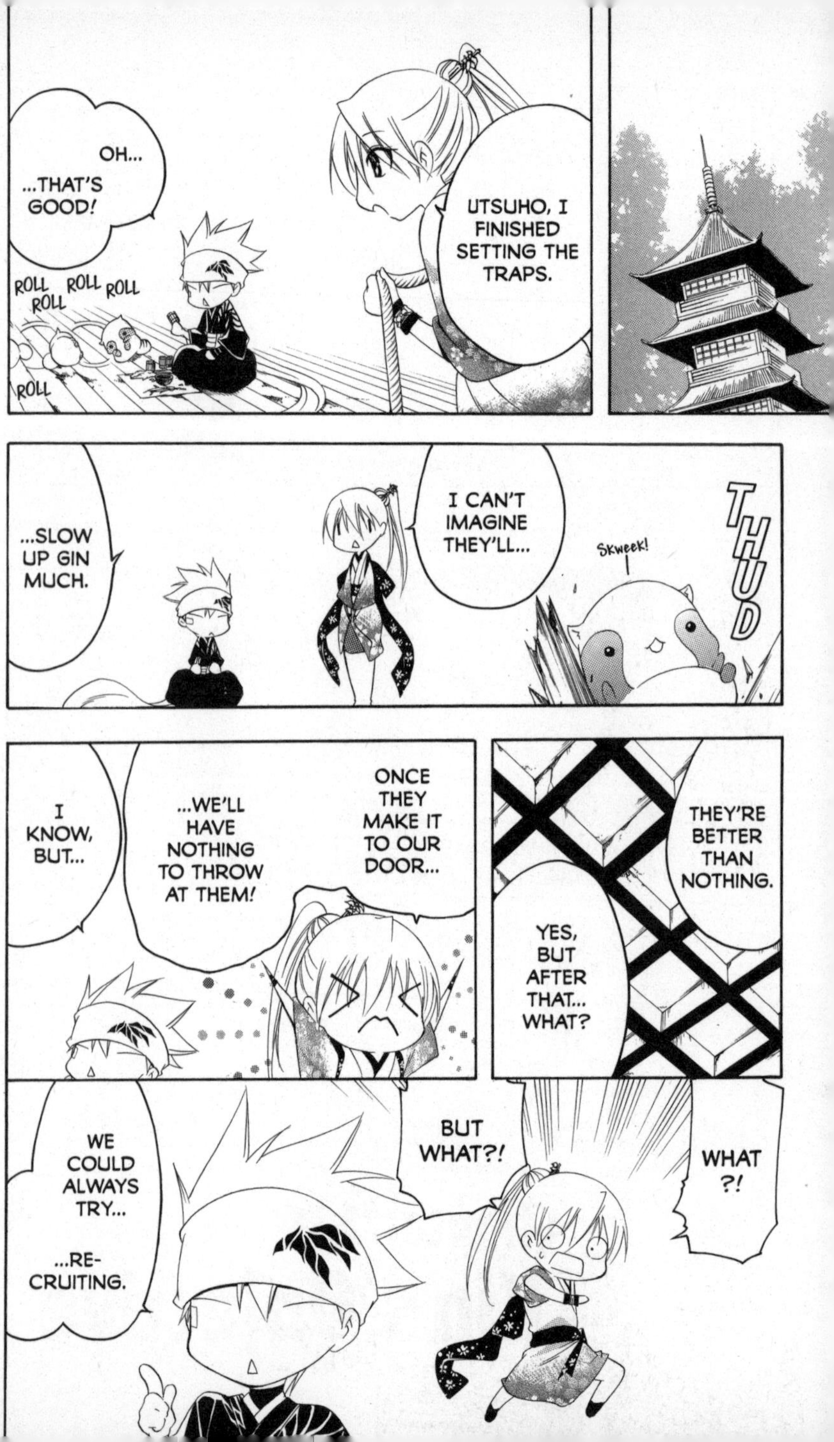
UTSUHO, I FINISHED SETTING THE TRAPS.
OH... ...THAT'S GOOD!
ROLL ROLL ROLL ROLL
ROLL
THUD
Skweek!
I CAN'T IMAGINE THEY'LL...
...SLOW UP GIN MUCH.
THEY'RE BETTER THAN NOTHING.
YES, BUT AFTER THAT... WHAT?
ONCE THEY MAKE IT TO OUR DOOR...
...WE'LL HAVE NOTHING TO THROW AT THEM!
I KNOW, BUT...
WHAT?!
BUT WHAT?!
WE COULD ALWAYS TRY...
...RE-CRUITING.

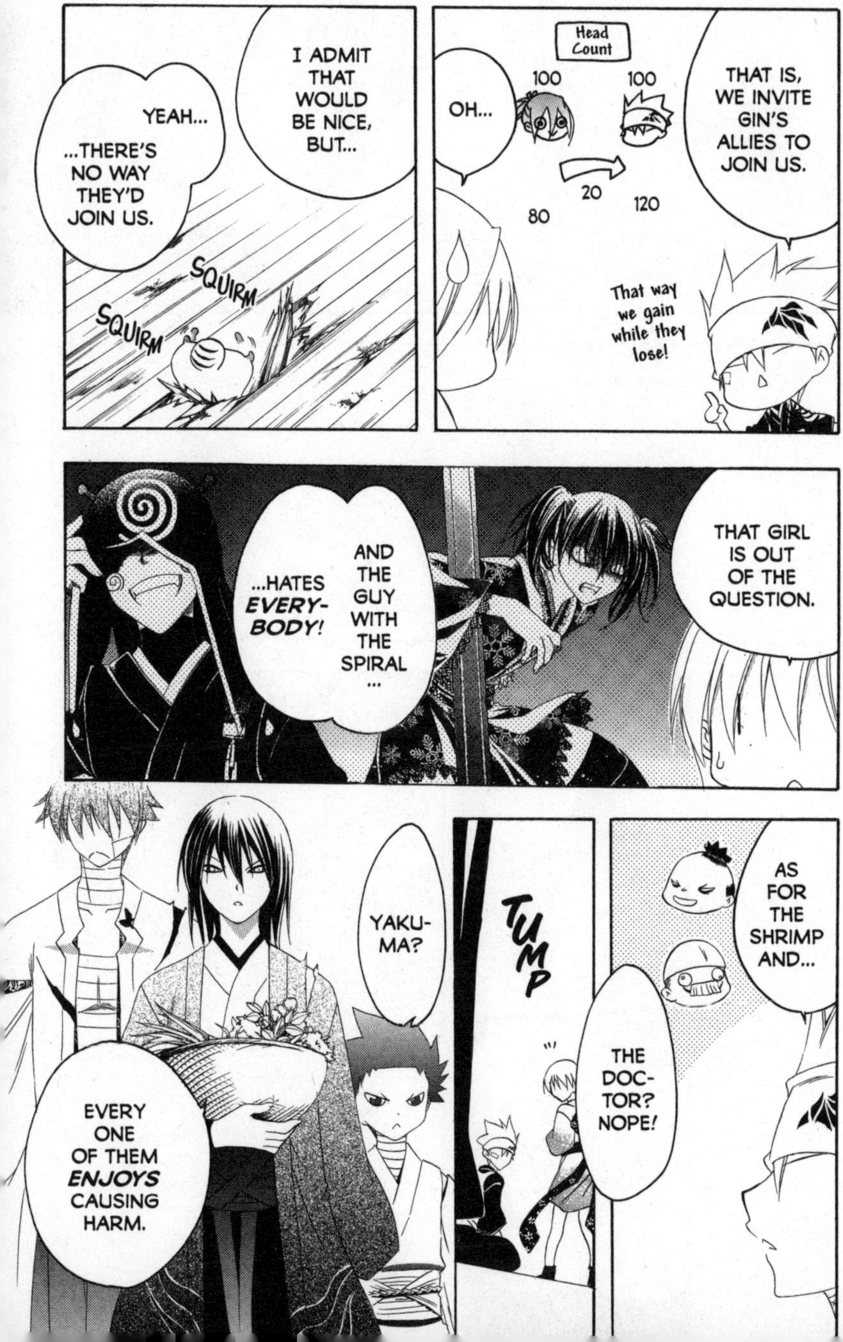
THAT IS, WE INVITE GIN'S ALLIES TO JOIN US.
Head Count
100
100
20
80
120
OH...
That way we gain while they lose!
I ADMIT THAT WOULD BE NICE, BUT...
YEAH...
...THERE'S NO WAY THEY'D JOIN US.
SQUIRM
SQUIRM
THAT GIRL IS OUT OF THE QUESTION.
AND THE GUY WITH THE SPIRAL...
...HATES *EVERYBODY*!
AS FOR THE SHRIMP AND...
THE DOCTOR? NOPE!
TUMP
YAKUMA?
EVERY ONE OF THEM *ENJOYS* CAUSING HARM.

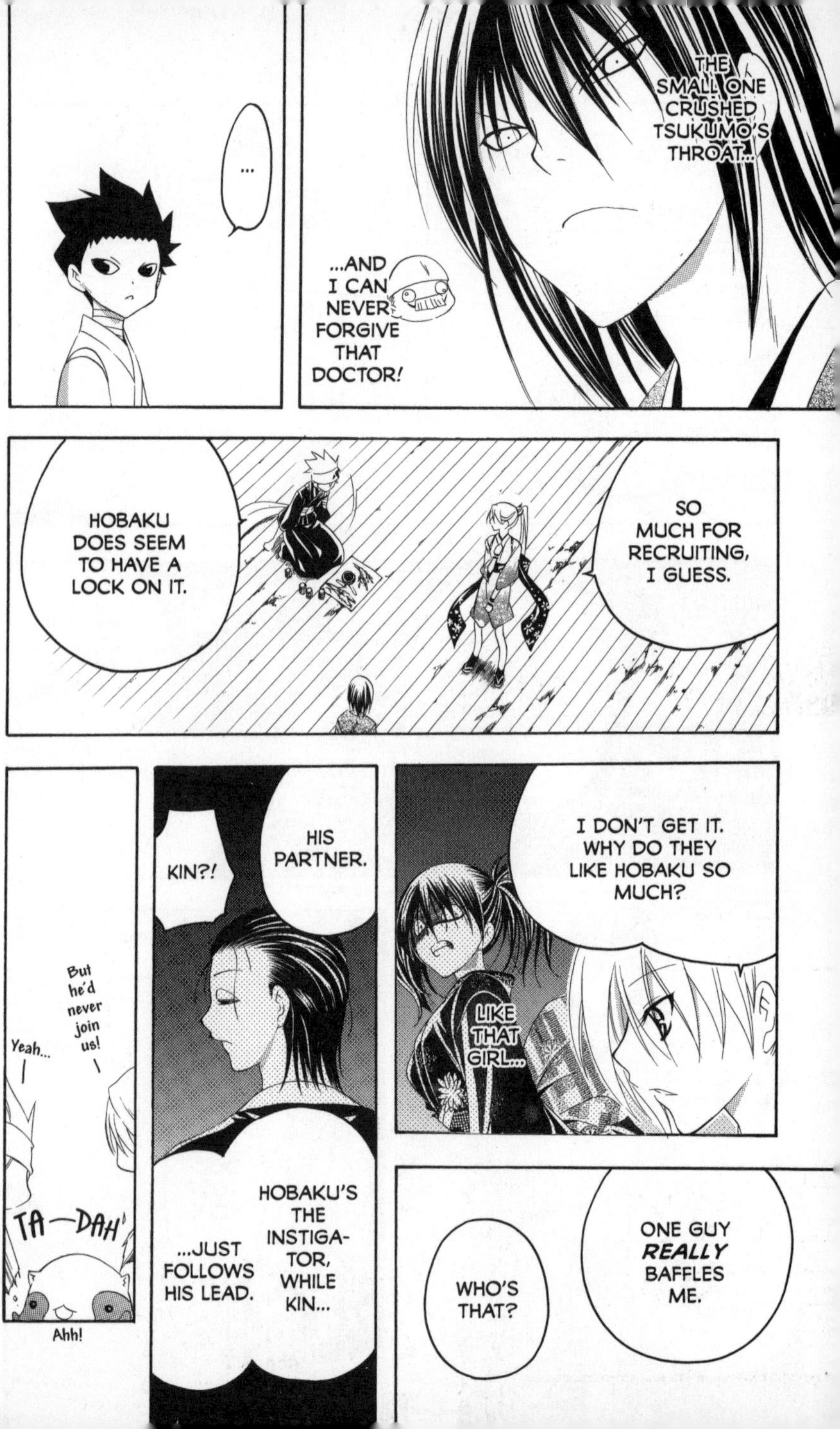
THE SMALL ONE CRUSHED TSUKUMO'S THROAT...
...AND I CAN NEVER FORGIVE THAT DOCTOR!
...
SO MUCH FOR RECRUITING, I GUESS.
HOBAKU DOES SEEM TO HAVE A LOCK ON IT.
I DON'T GET IT. WHY DO THEY LIKE HOBAKU SO MUCH?
LIKE THAT GIRL...
ONE GUY *REALLY* BAFFLES ME.
WHO'S THAT?
HIS PARTNER.
KIN?!
HOBAKU'S THE INSTIGA-TOR, WHILE KIN...
...JUST FOLLOWS HIS LEAD.
But he'd never join us!
Yeah...
TA-DAH
Ahh!

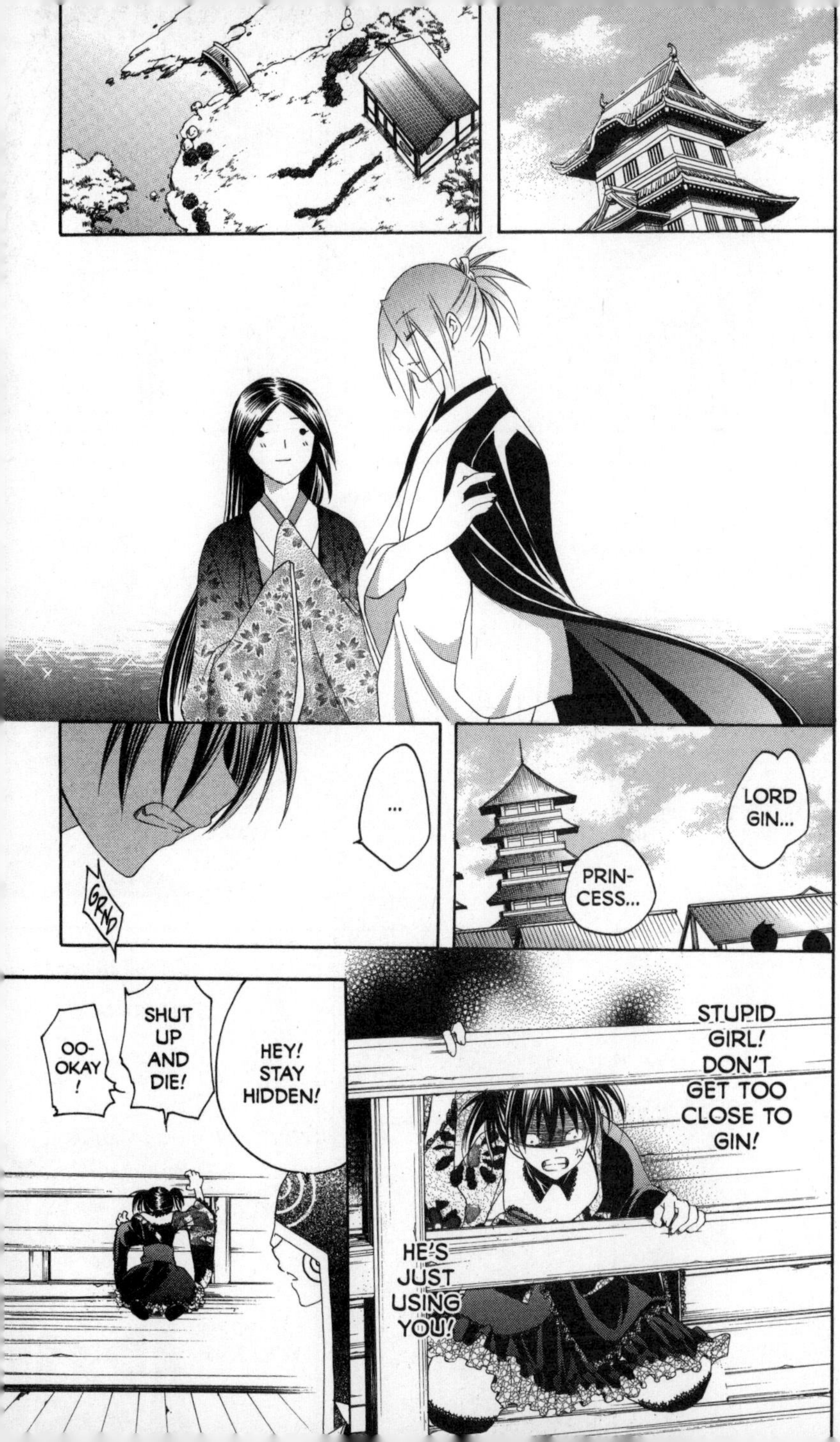
LORD GIN...
PRIN-CESS...
...
GRND
STUPID GIRL! DON'T GET TOO CLOSE TO GIN!
HE'S JUST USING YOU!
HEY! STAY HIDDEN!
SHUT UP AND DIE!
OO-OKAY!

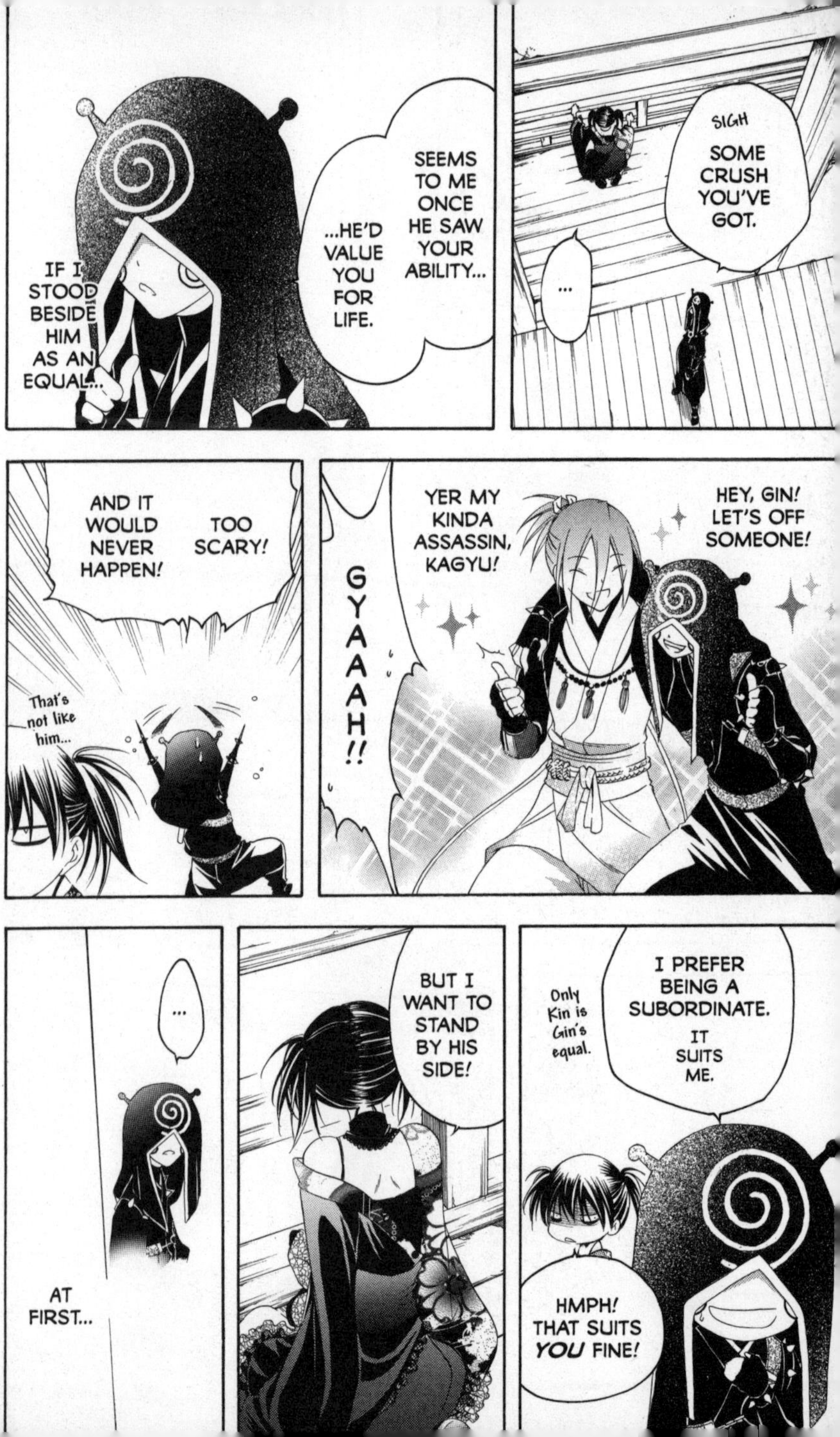
SIGH
SOME CRUSH YOU'VE GOT.
...
SEEMS TO ME ONCE HE SAW YOUR ABILITY...
...HE'D VALUE YOU FOR LIFE.
IF I STOOD BESIDE HIM AS AN EQUAL...
HEY, GIN! LET'S OFF SOMEONE!
YER MY KINDA ASSASSIN, KAGYU!
GYAAAAH!!
TOO SCARY!
AND IT WOULD NEVER HAPPEN!
That's not like him...
I PREFER BEING A SUBORDINATE.
IT SUITS ME.
Only Kin is Gin's equal.
HMPH! THAT SUITS *YOU* FINE!
BUT I WANT TO STAND BY HIS SIDE!
...
AT FIRST...

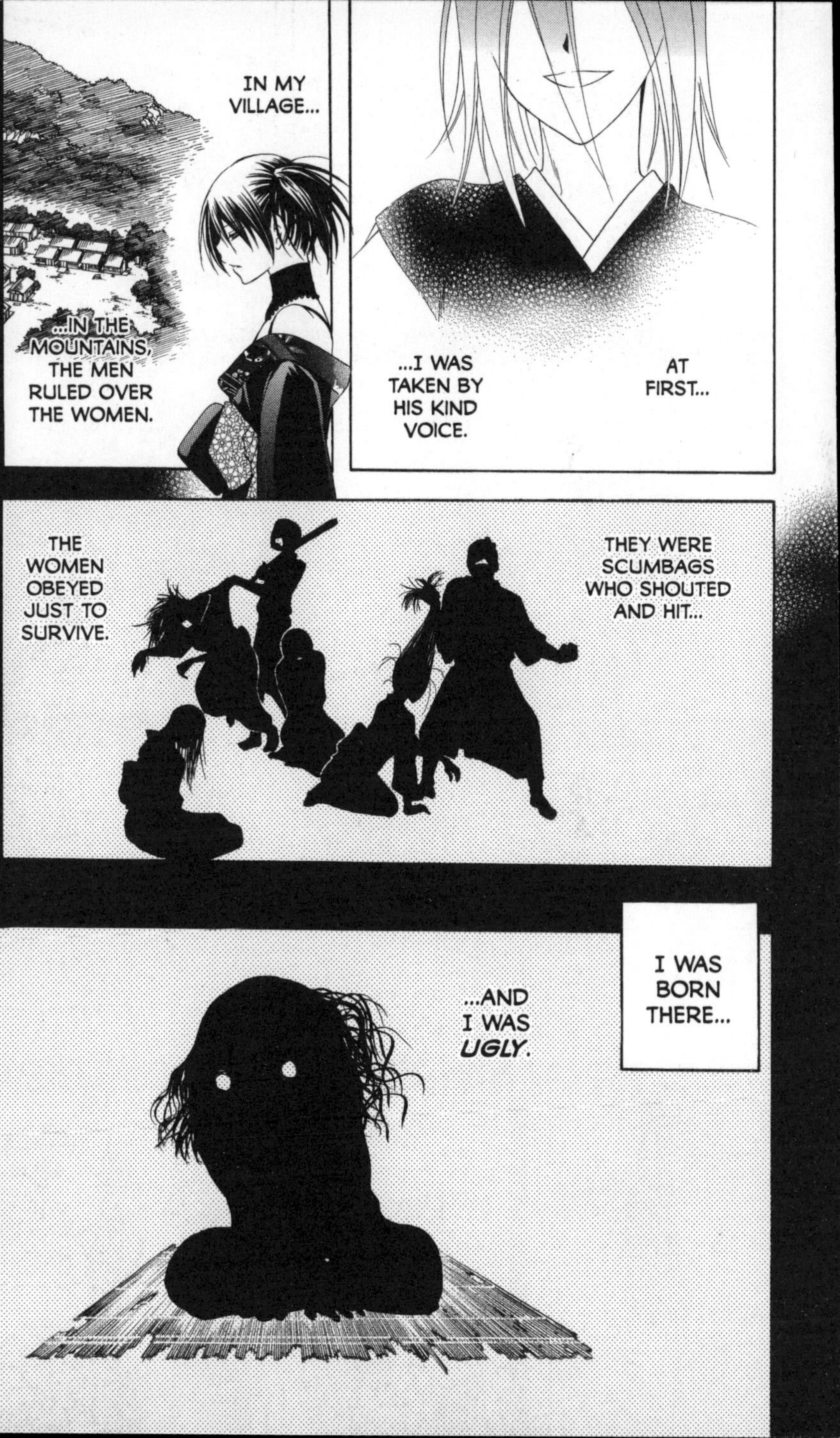
AT FIRST...
...I WAS TAKEN BY HIS KIND VOICE.
IN MY VILLAGE...
...IN THE MOUNTAINS, THE MEN RULED OVER THE WOMEN.
THEY WERE SCUMBAGS WHO SHOUTED AND HIT...
THE WOMEN OBEYED JUST TO SURVIVE.
I WAS BORN THERE...
...AND I WAS *UGLY*.

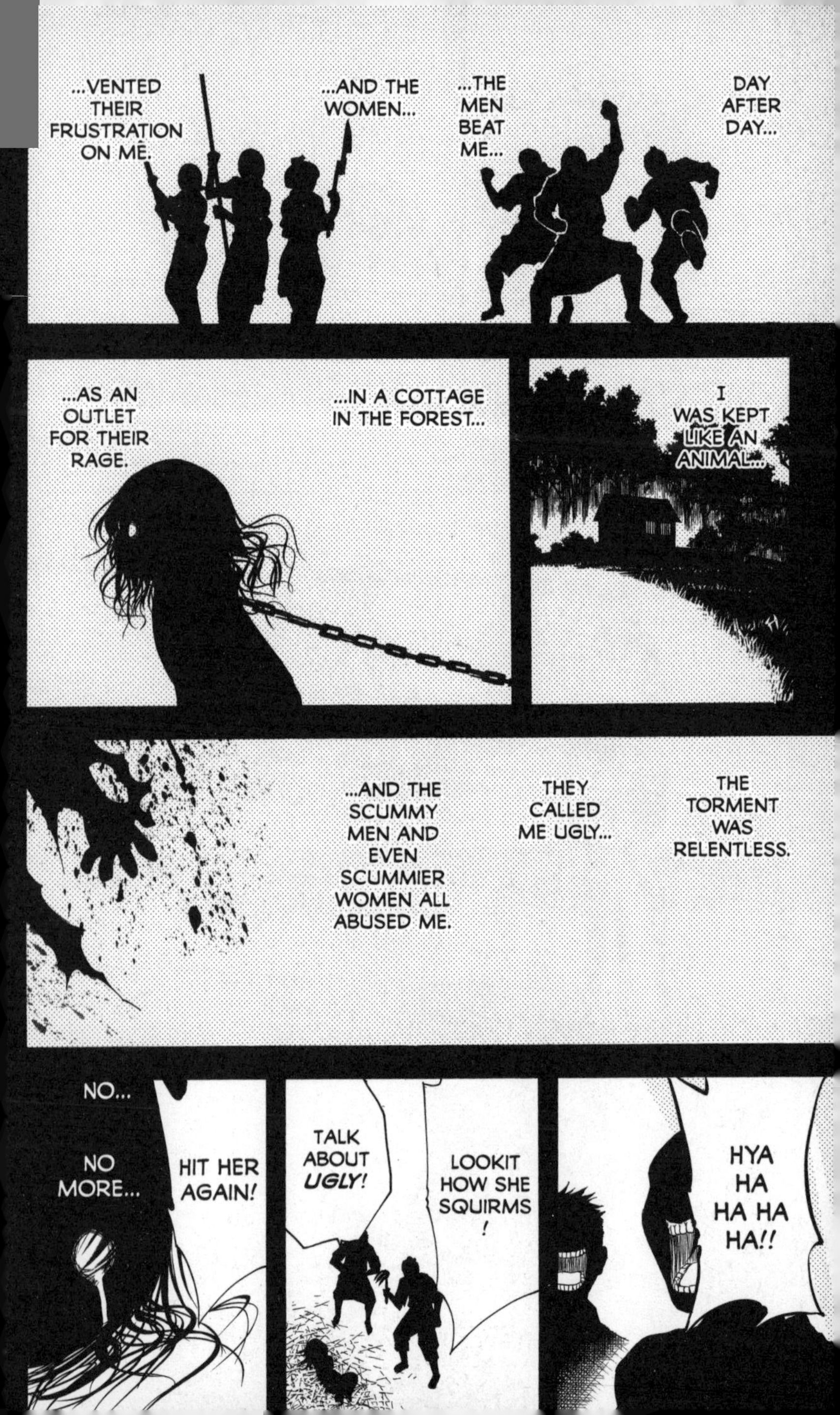
DAY AFTER DAY...
...THE MEN BEAT ME...
...AND THE WOMEN...
...VENTED THEIR FRUSTRATION ON ME.
I WAS KEPT LIKE AN ANIMAL...
...IN A COTTAGE IN THE FOREST...
...AS AN OUTLET FOR THEIR RAGE.
THE TORMENT WAS RELENTLESS.
THEY CALLED ME UGLY...
...AND THE SCUMMY MEN AND EVEN SCUMMIER WOMEN ALL ABUSED ME.
HYA HA HA HA HA!!
LOOKIT HOW SHE SQUIRMS!
TALK ABOUT *UGLY*!
HIT HER AGAIN!
NO...
NO MORE...

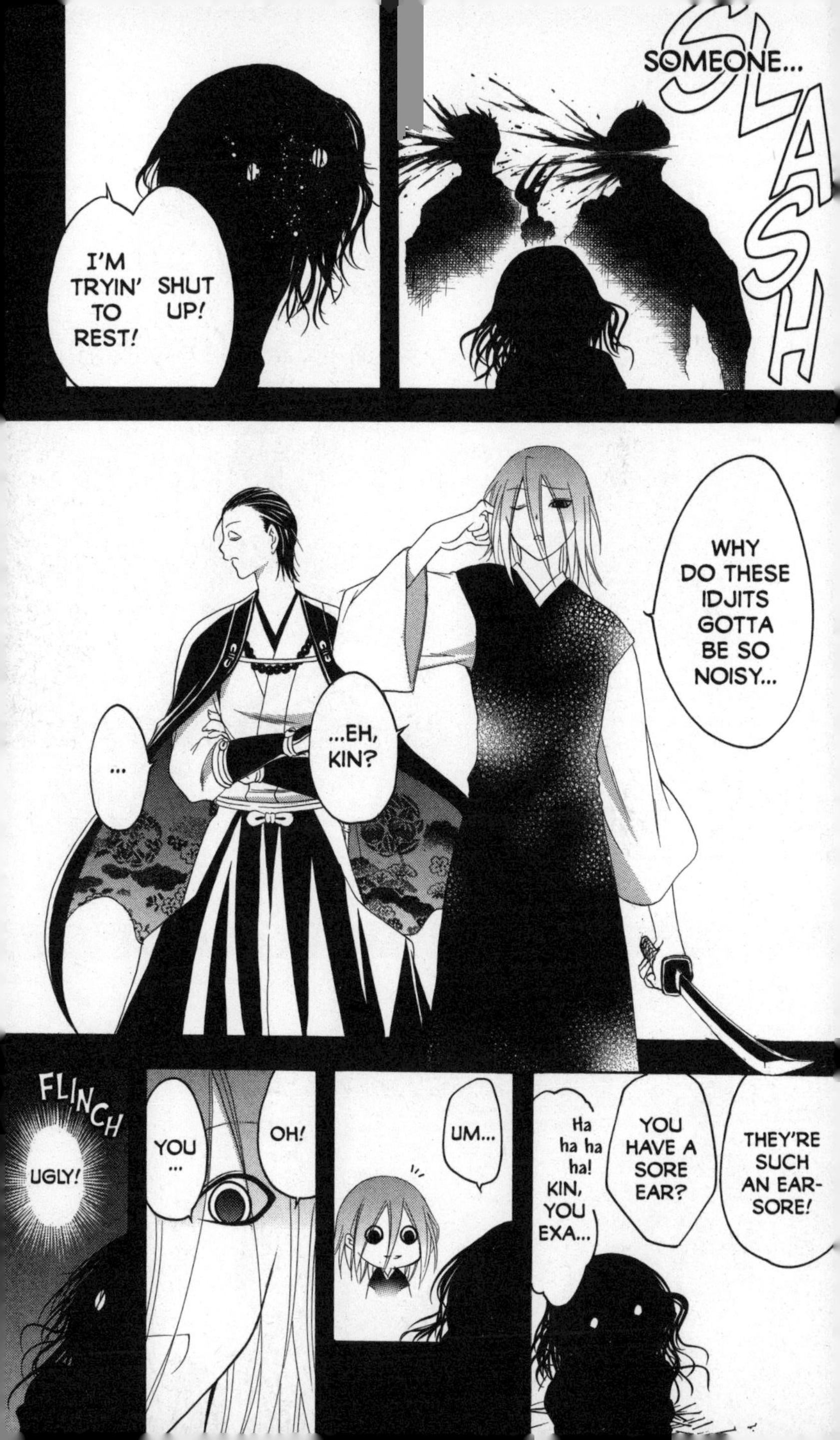
SOMEONE...
SLASH
SHUT UP!
I'M TRYIN' TO REST!
WHY DO THESE IDJITS GOTTA BE SO NOISY...
...EH, KIN?
...
THEY'RE SUCH AN EAR-SORE!
YOU HAVE A SORE EAR?
Ha ha ha ha! KIN, YOU EXA...
UM...
OH!
YOU ...
FLINCH
UGLY!

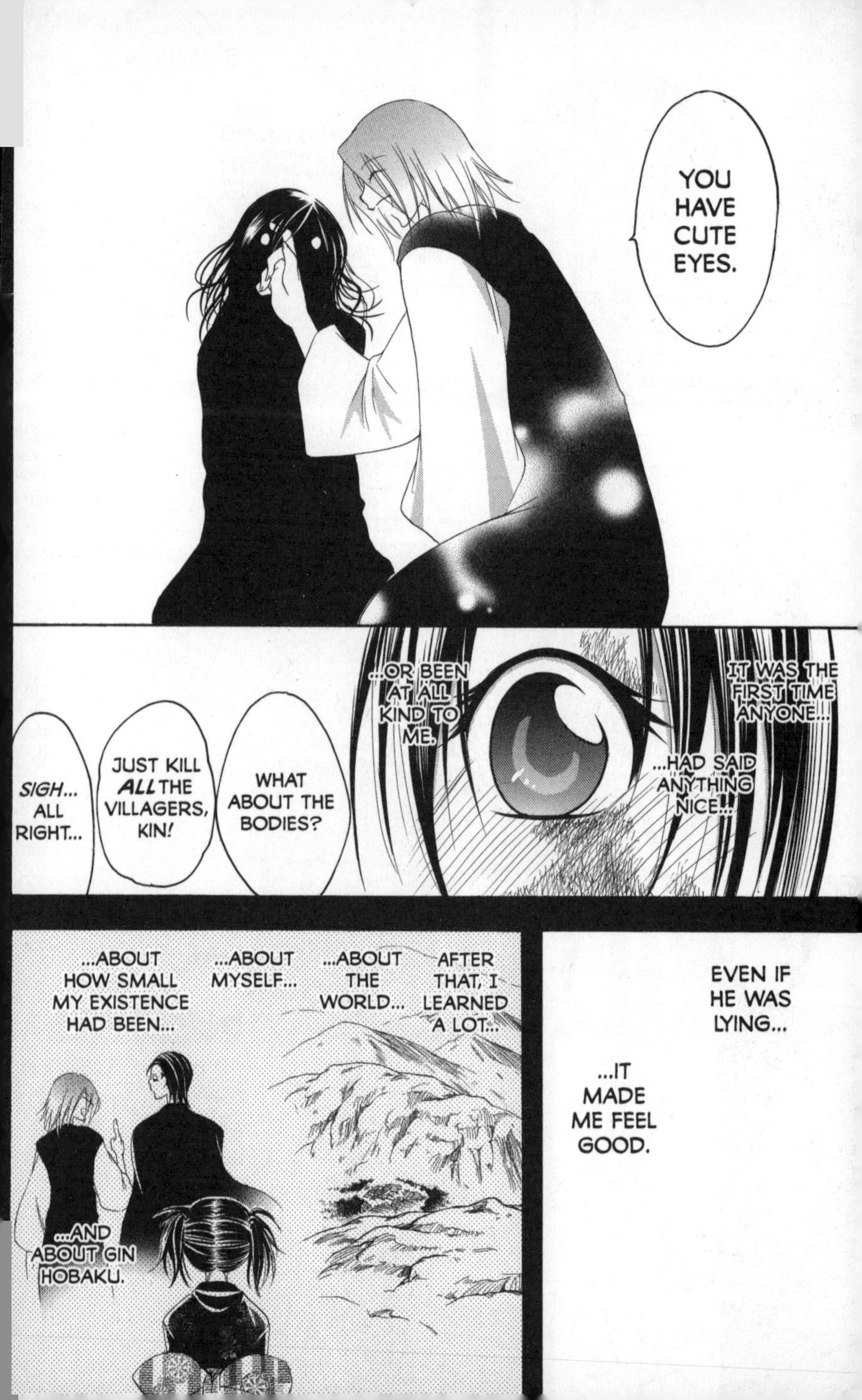
YOU HAVE CUTE EYES.
IT WAS THE FIRST TIME ANYONE...
...HAD SAID ANYTHING NICE...
...OR BEEN AT ALL KIND TO ME.
WHAT ABOUT THE BODIES?
JUST KILL *ALL* THE VILLAGERS, KIN!
SIGH... ALL RIGHT...
EVEN IF HE WAS LYING...
...IT MADE ME FEEL GOOD.
AFTER THAT, I LEARNED A LOT...
...ABOUT THE WORLD...
...ABOUT MYSELF...
...ABOUT HOW SMALL MY EXISTENCE HAD BEEN...
...AND ABOUT GIN HOBAKU.

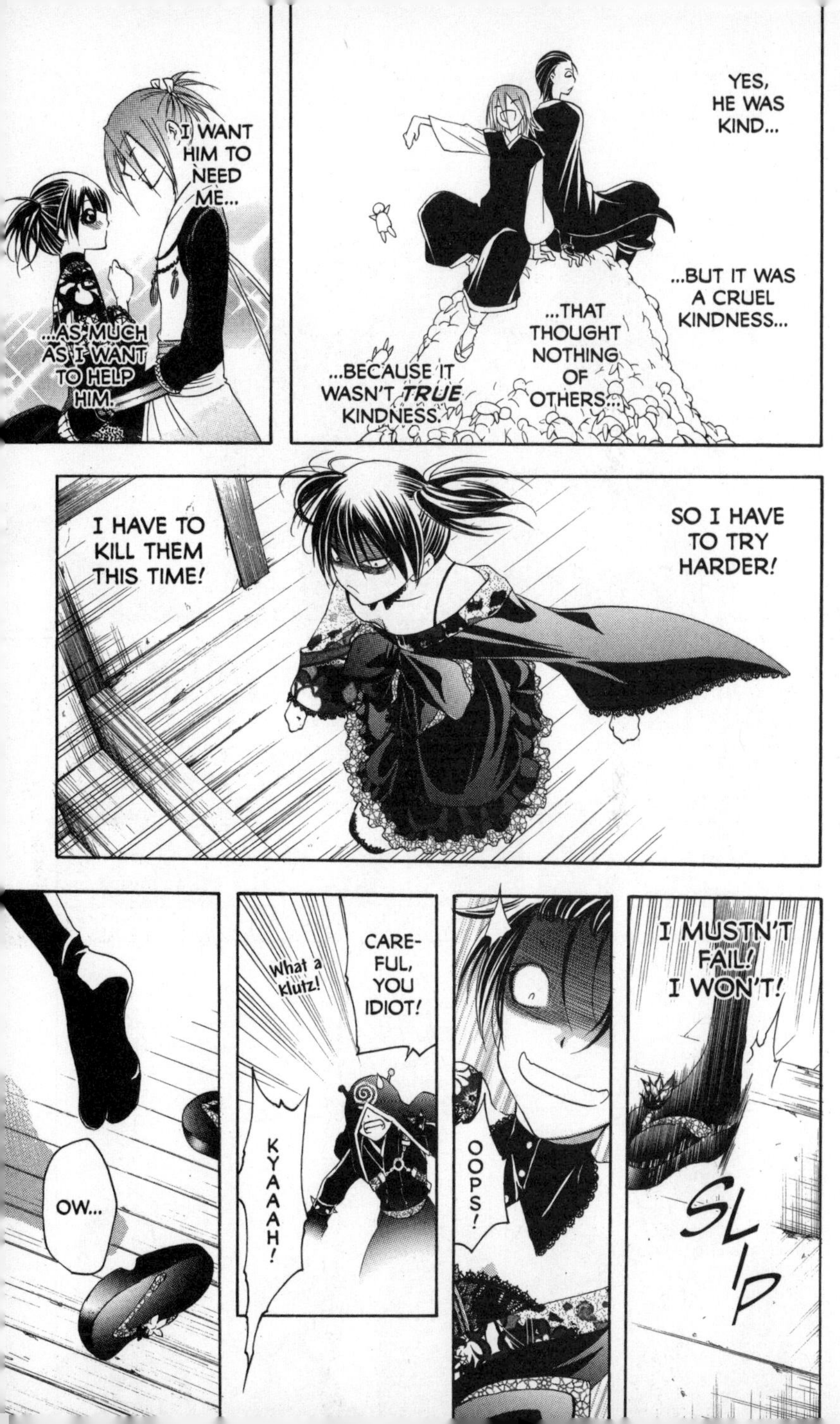
YES, HE WAS KIND...
...BUT IT WAS A CRUEL KINDNESS...
...THAT THOUGHT NOTHING OF OTHERS...
...BECAUSE IT WASN'T *TRUE* KINDNESS.
I WANT HIM TO NEED ME...
...AS MUCH AS I WANT TO HELP HIM.
SO I HAVE TO TRY HARDER!
I HAVE TO KILL THEM THIS TIME!
I MUSTN'T FAIL! I WON'T!
SLIP
OOPS!
CARE-FUL, YOU IDIOT!
What a klutz!
KYAAAH!
OW...

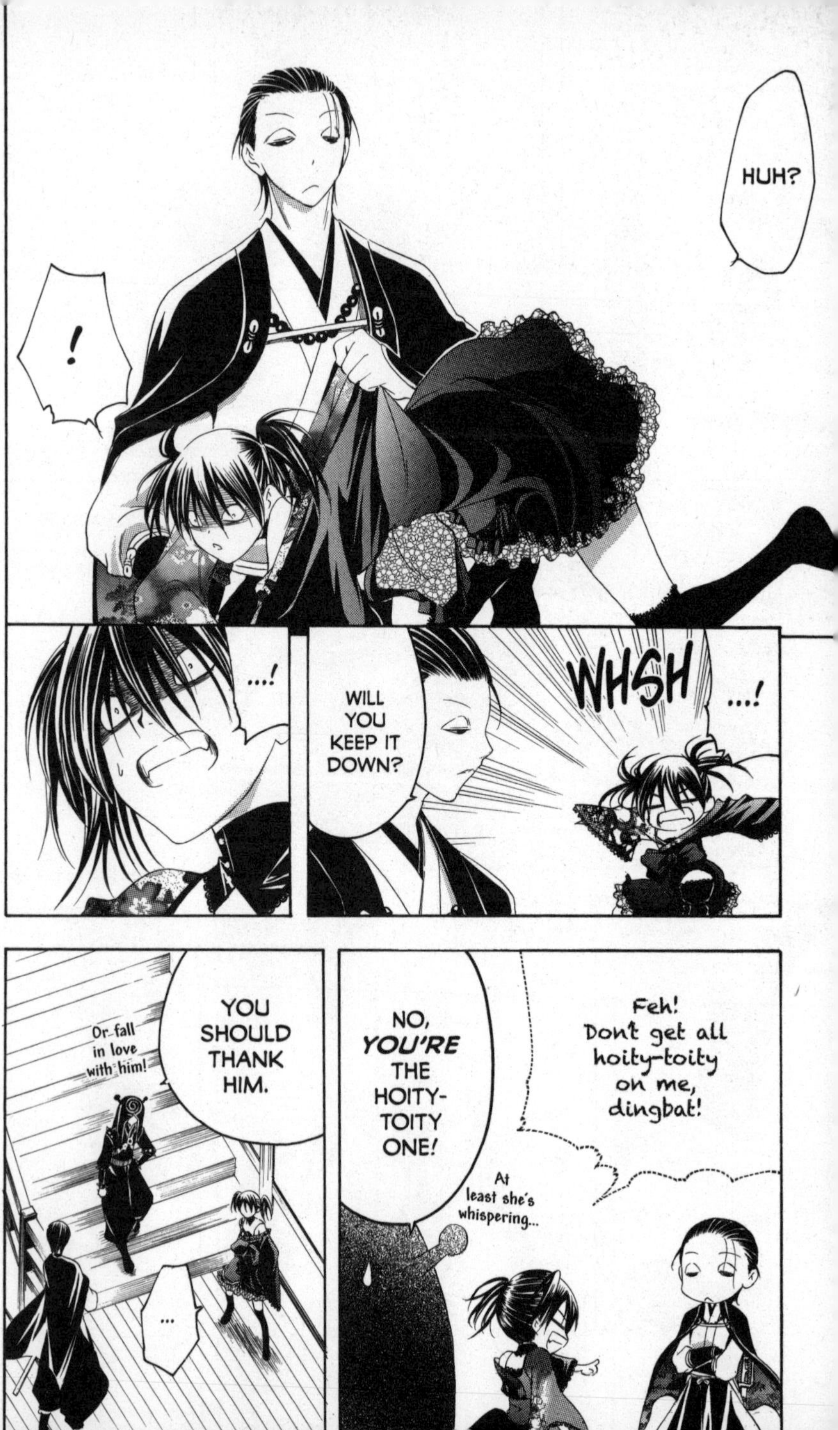
HUH?
!
WHSH
...!
WILL YOU KEEP IT DOWN?
...!
Feh! Don't get all hoity-toity on me, dingbat!
NO, *YOU'RE* THE HOITY-TOITY ONE!
At least she's whispering...
YOU SHOULD THANK HIM.
Or fall in love with him!
...

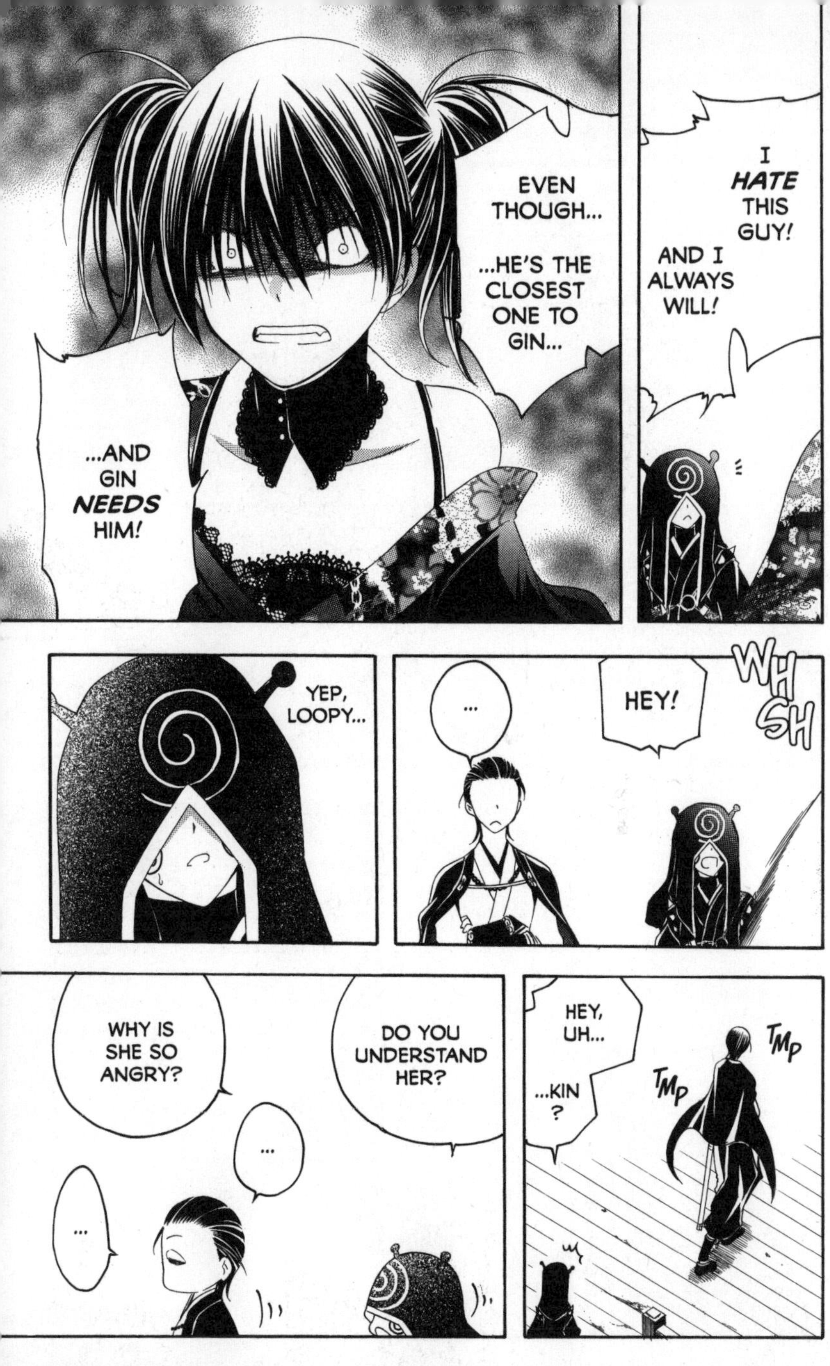

I HATE THIS GUY!
AND I ALWAYS WILL!
EVEN THOUGH...
...HE'S THE CLOSEST ONE TO GIN...
...AND GIN NEEDS HIM!
WHSH
HEY!
...
YEP, LOOPY...
TMP
HEY, UH...
...KIN?
TMP
DO YOU UNDERSTAND HER?
WHY IS SHE SO ANGRY?
...
...

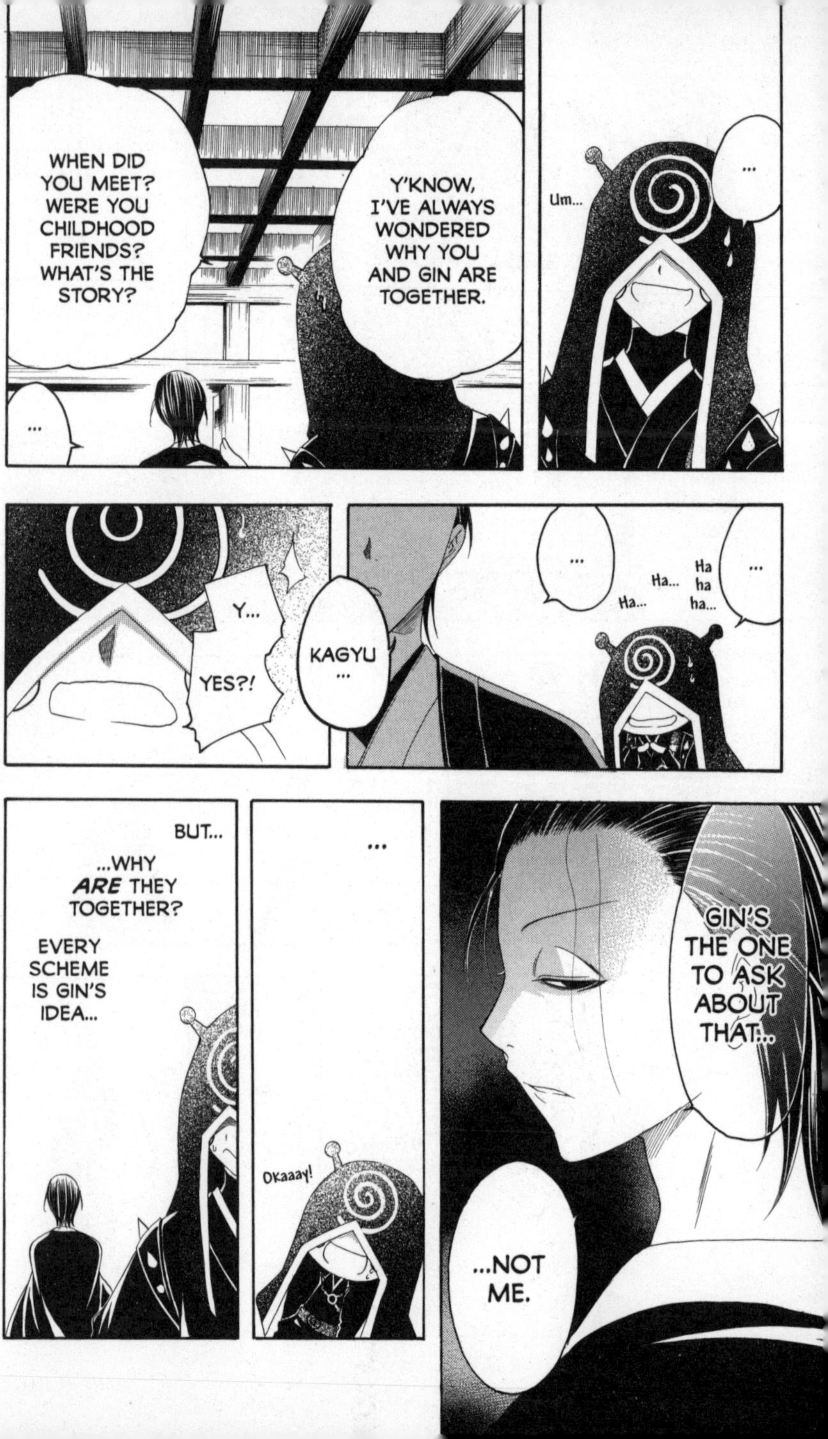
...
Um...
Y'KNOW, I'VE ALWAYS WONDERED WHY YOU AND GIN ARE TOGETHER.
WHEN DID YOU MEET? WERE YOU CHILDHOOD FRIENDS? WHAT'S THE STORY?
...
...
Ha ha ha...
...
Ha...
Ha...
KAGYU ...
Y...
YES?!
GIN'S THE ONE TO ASK ABOUT THAT...
...NOT ME.
...
Okaaay!
BUT...
...WHY *ARE* THEY TOGETHER?
EVERY SCHEME IS GIN'S IDEA...

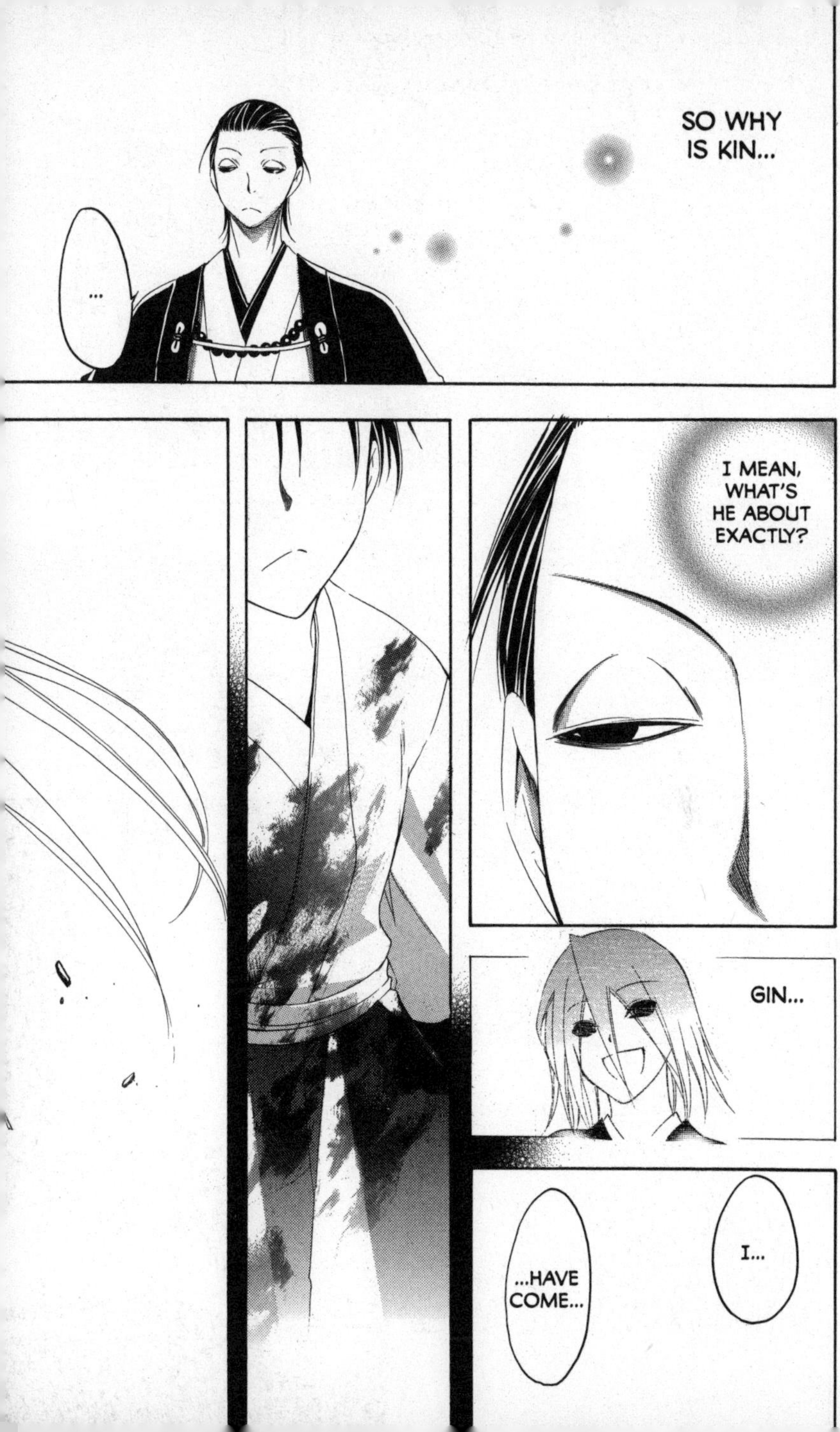
SO WHY IS KIN...
...
I MEAN, WHAT'S HE ABOUT EXACTLY?
GIN...
I...
...HAVE COME...

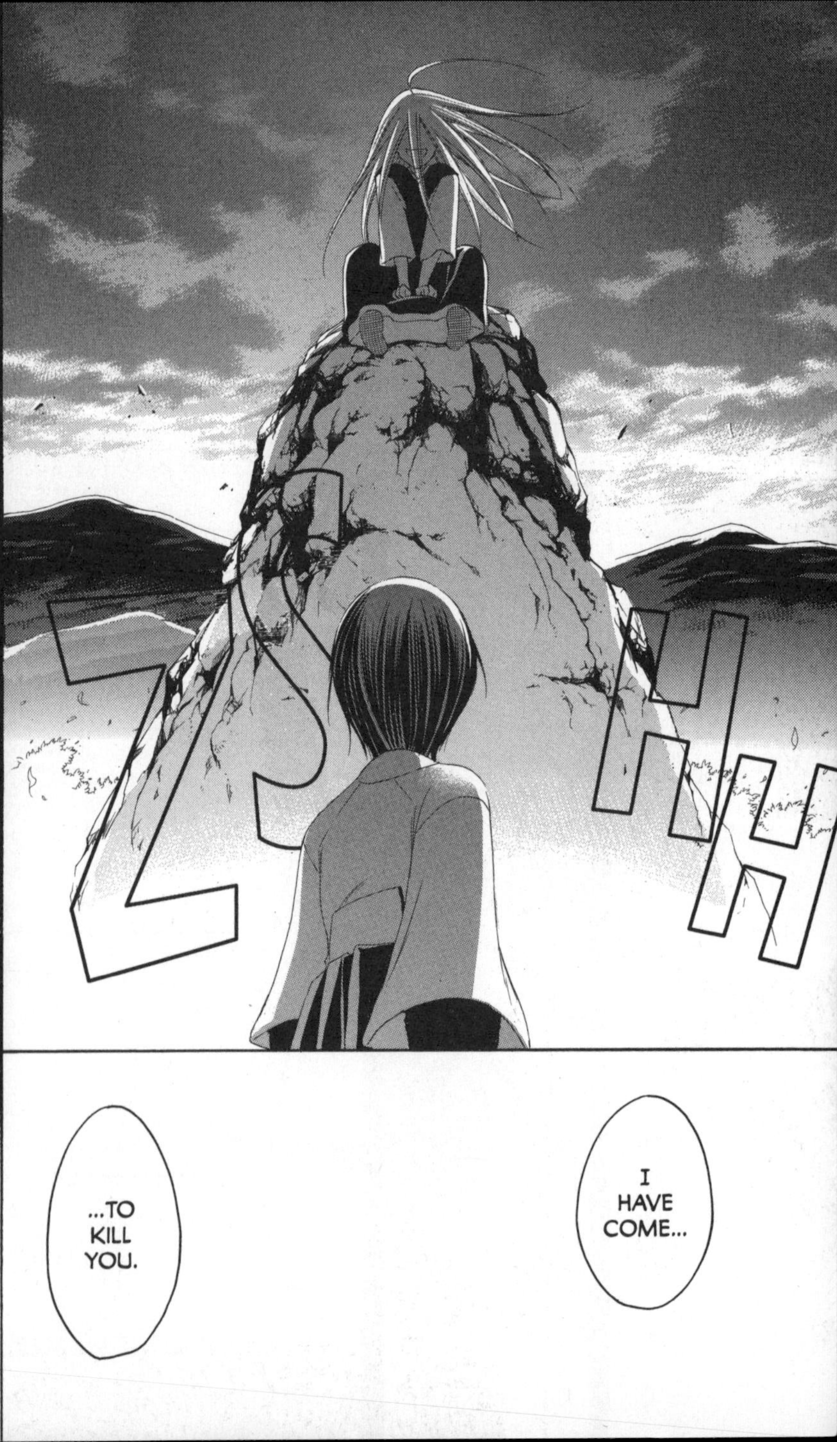
ZSHHH
I HAVE COME...
...TO KILL YOU.

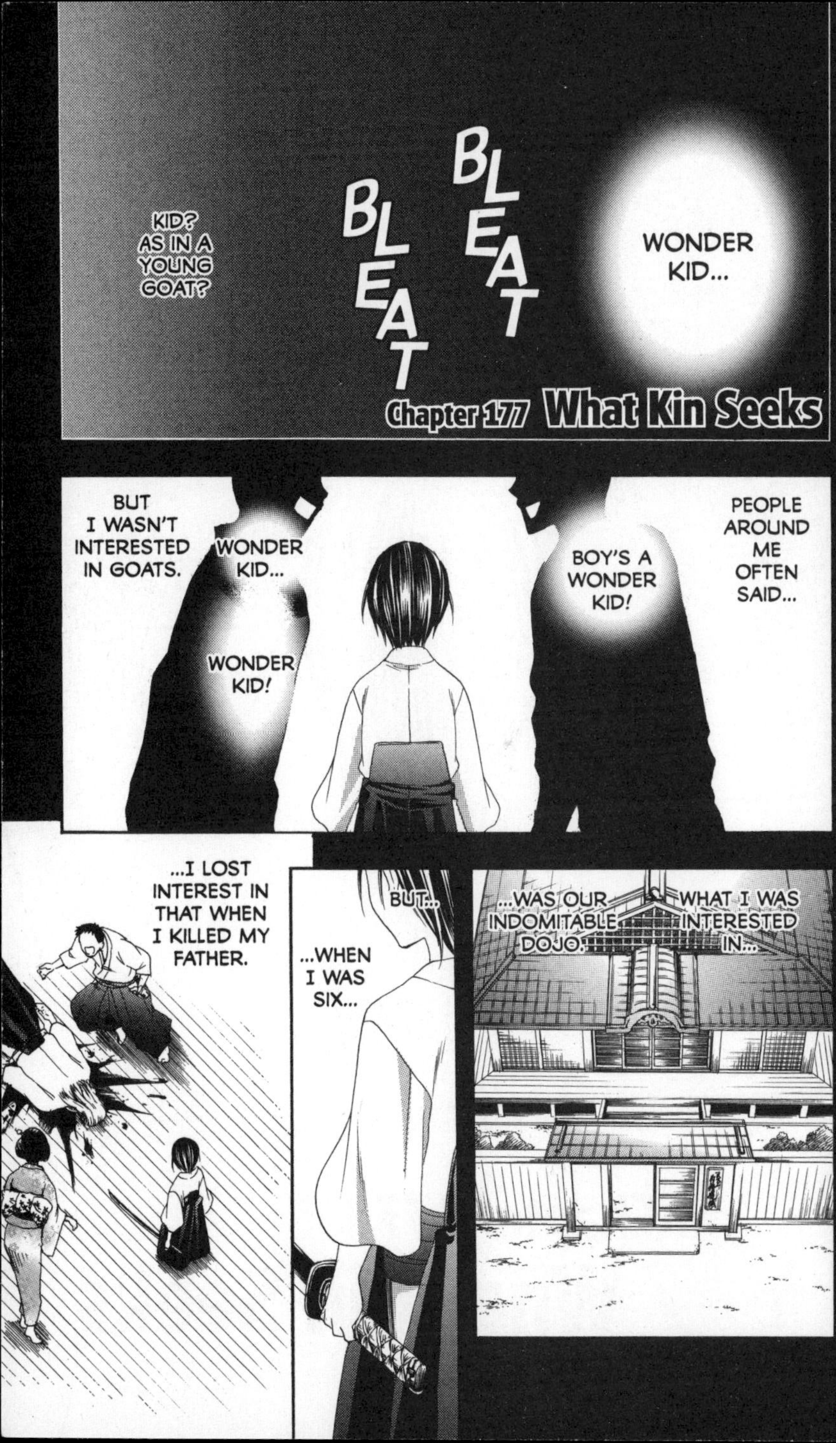
WONDER KID...
BLEAT BLEAT
KID? AS IN A YOUNG GOAT?
Chapter 177 What Kin Seeks
PEOPLE AROUND ME OFTEN SAID...
BOY'S A WONDER KID!
WONDER KID...
WONDER KID!
BUT I WASN'T INTERESTED IN GOATS.
WHAT I WAS INTERESTED IN...
...WAS OUR INDOMITABLE DOJO.
BUT...
...WHEN I WAS SIX...
...I LOST INTEREST IN THAT WHEN I KILLED MY FATHER.

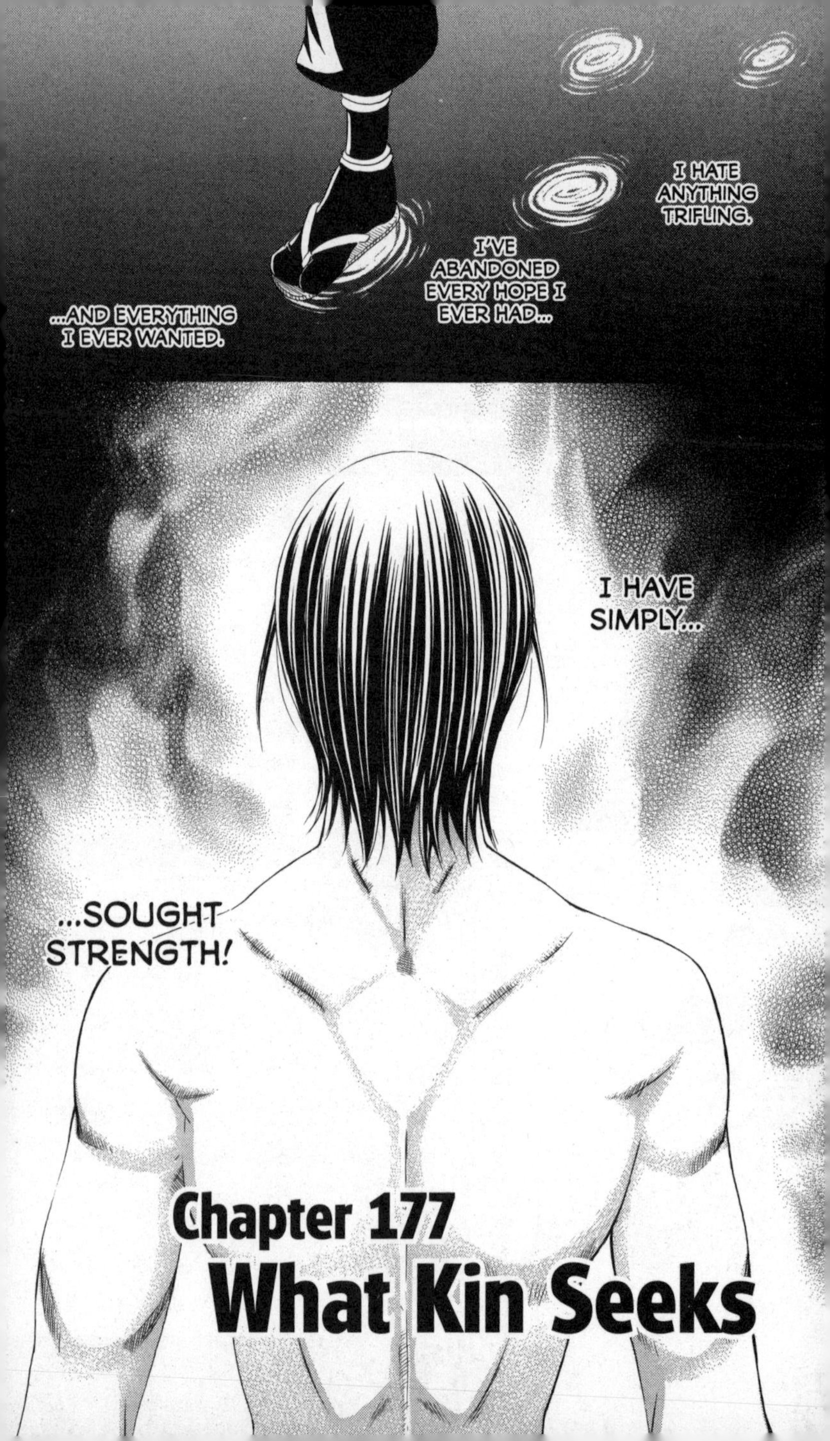
I HATE ANYTHING TRIFLING.
I'VE ABANDONED EVERY HOPE I EVER HAD...
...AND EVERYTHING I EVER WANTED.
I HAVE SIMPLY...
...SOUGHT STRENGTH!

Chapter 177
What Kin Seeks

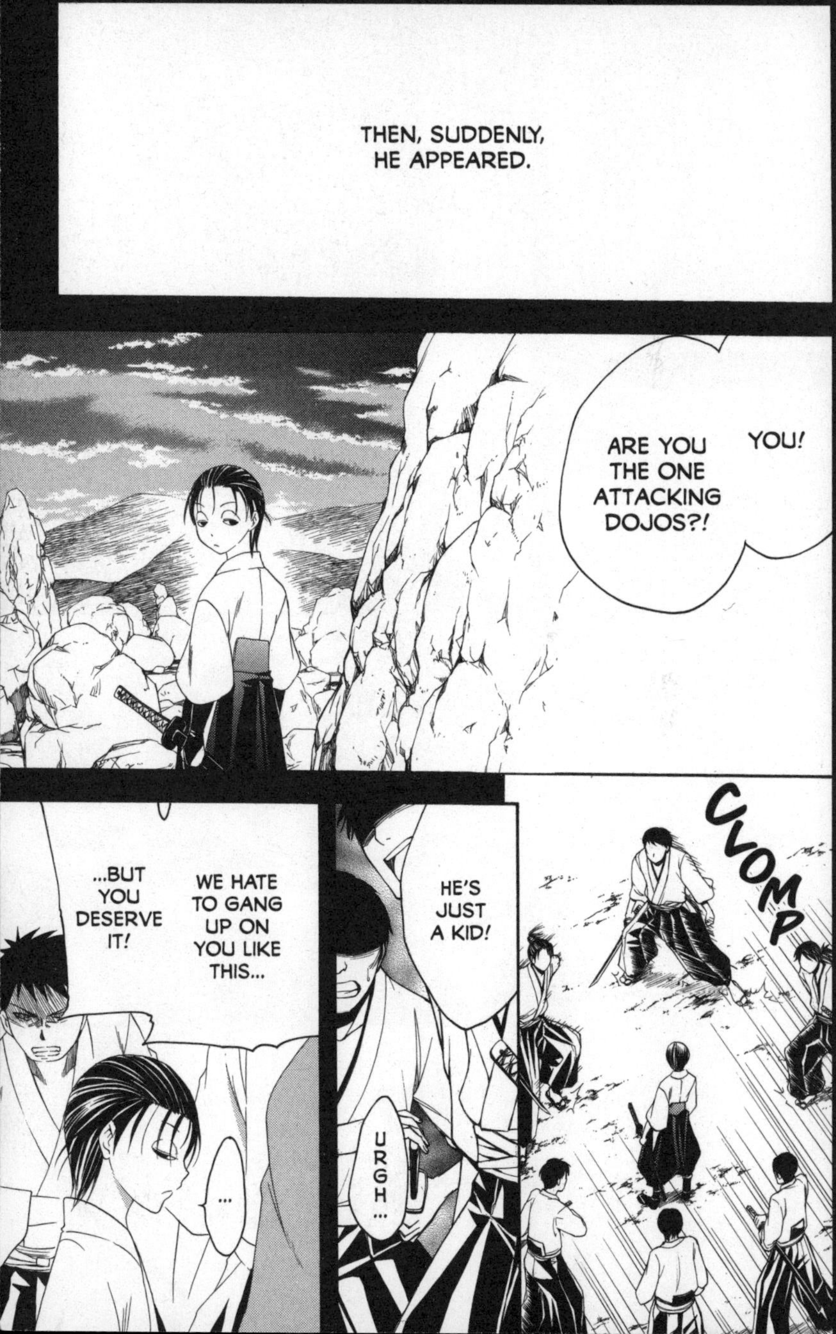
THEN, SUDDENLY, HE APPEARED.
YOU!
ARE YOU THE ONE ATTACKING DOJOS?!
CVOMP
HE'S JUST A KID!
URGH...
WE HATE TO GANG UP ON YOU LIKE THIS...
...BUT YOU DESERVE IT!
...

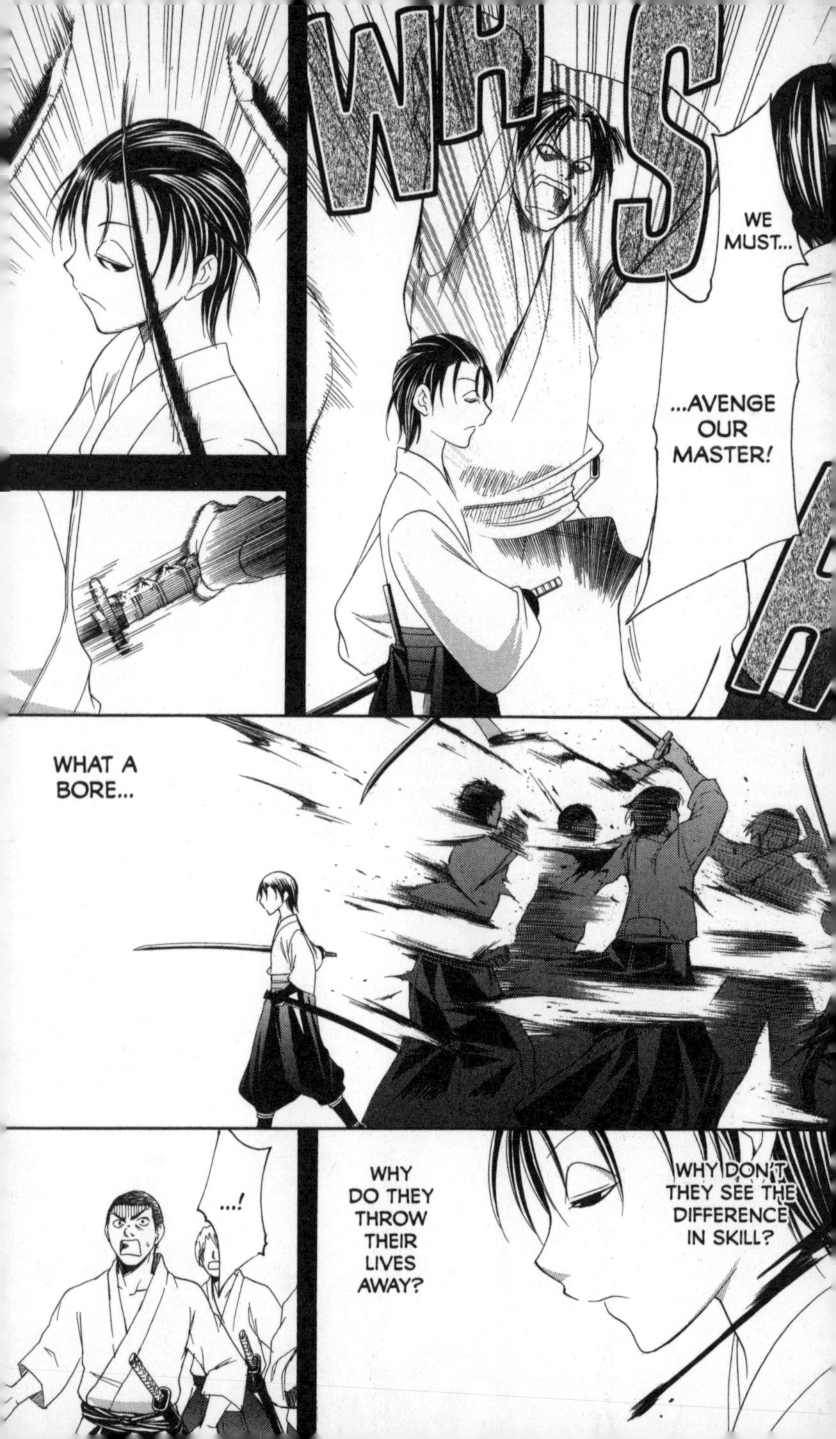
WE MUST...
...AVENGE OUR MASTER!
WHAT A BORE...
WHY DON'T THEY SEE THE DIFFERENCE IN SKILL?
WHY DO THEY THROW THEIR LIVES AWAY?
...!

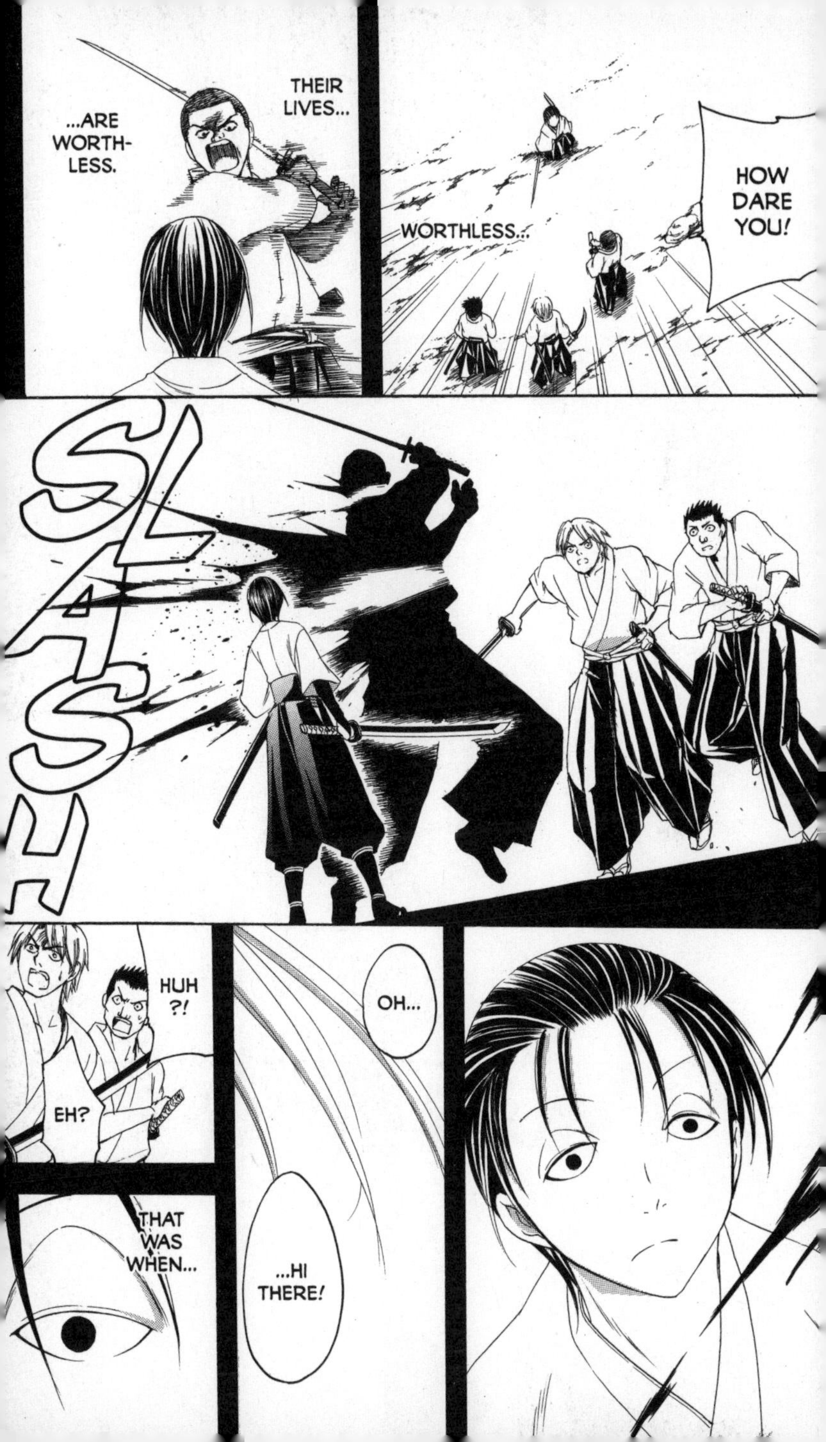
HOW DARE YOU!
WORTHLESS...
THEIR LIVES...
...ARE WORTHLESS.
SLASH
OH...
...HI THERE!
HUH ?!
EH?
THAT WAS WHEN...

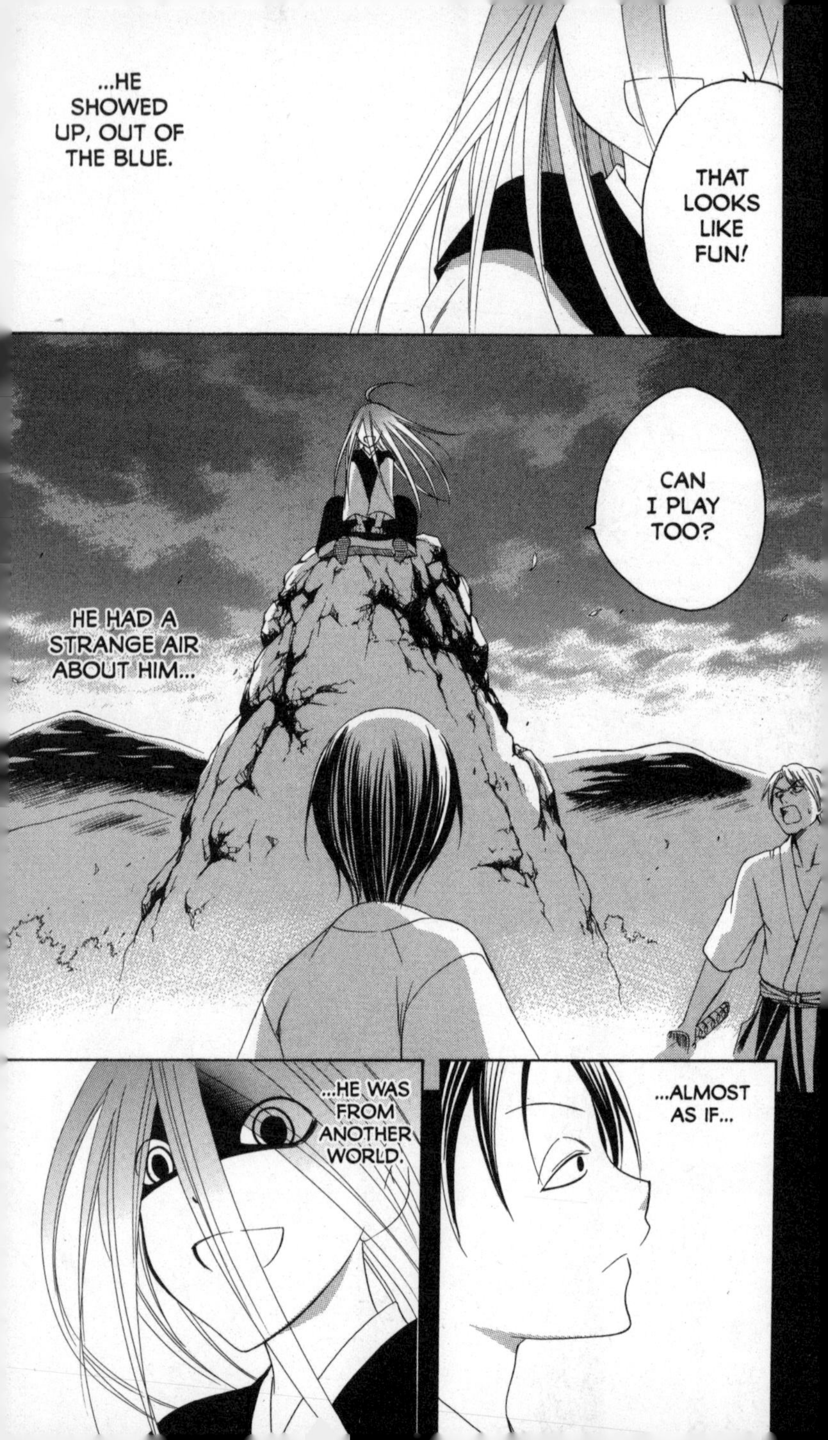
THAT LOOKS LIKE FUN!
...HE SHOWED UP, OUT OF THE BLUE.
CAN I PLAY TOO?
HE HAD A STRANGE AIR ABOUT HIM...
...ALMOST AS IF...
...HE WAS FROM ANOTHER WORLD.

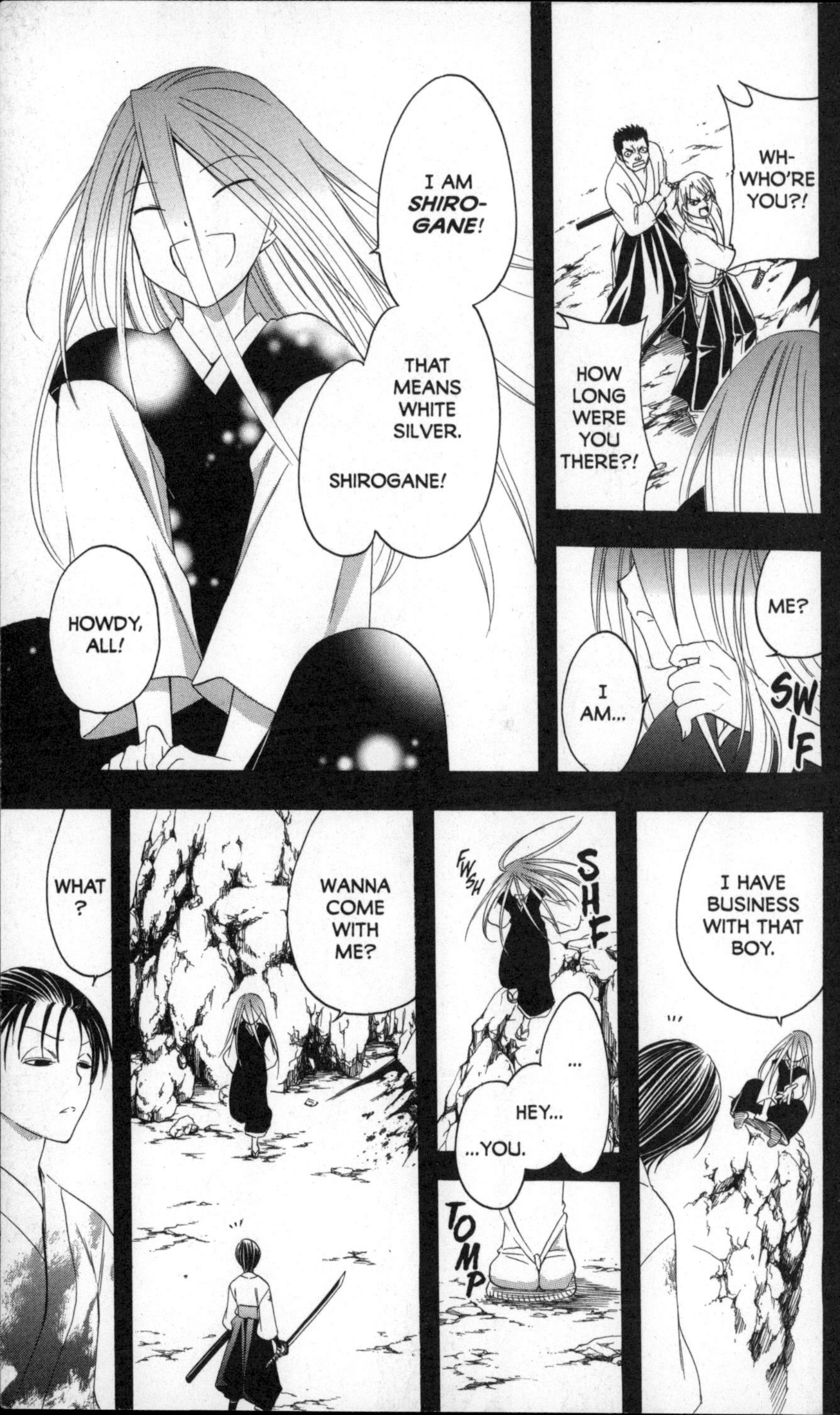
WH- WHO'RE YOU?!
HOW LONG WERE YOU THERE?!
ME?
I AM...
SWIF
I AM *SHIROGANE*!
THAT MEANS WHITE SILVER.
SHIROGANE!
HOWDY, ALL!
I HAVE BUSINESS WITH THAT BOY.
SHF
FWSH
...
HEY...
...YOU.
TOMP
WANNA COME WITH ME?
WHAT?

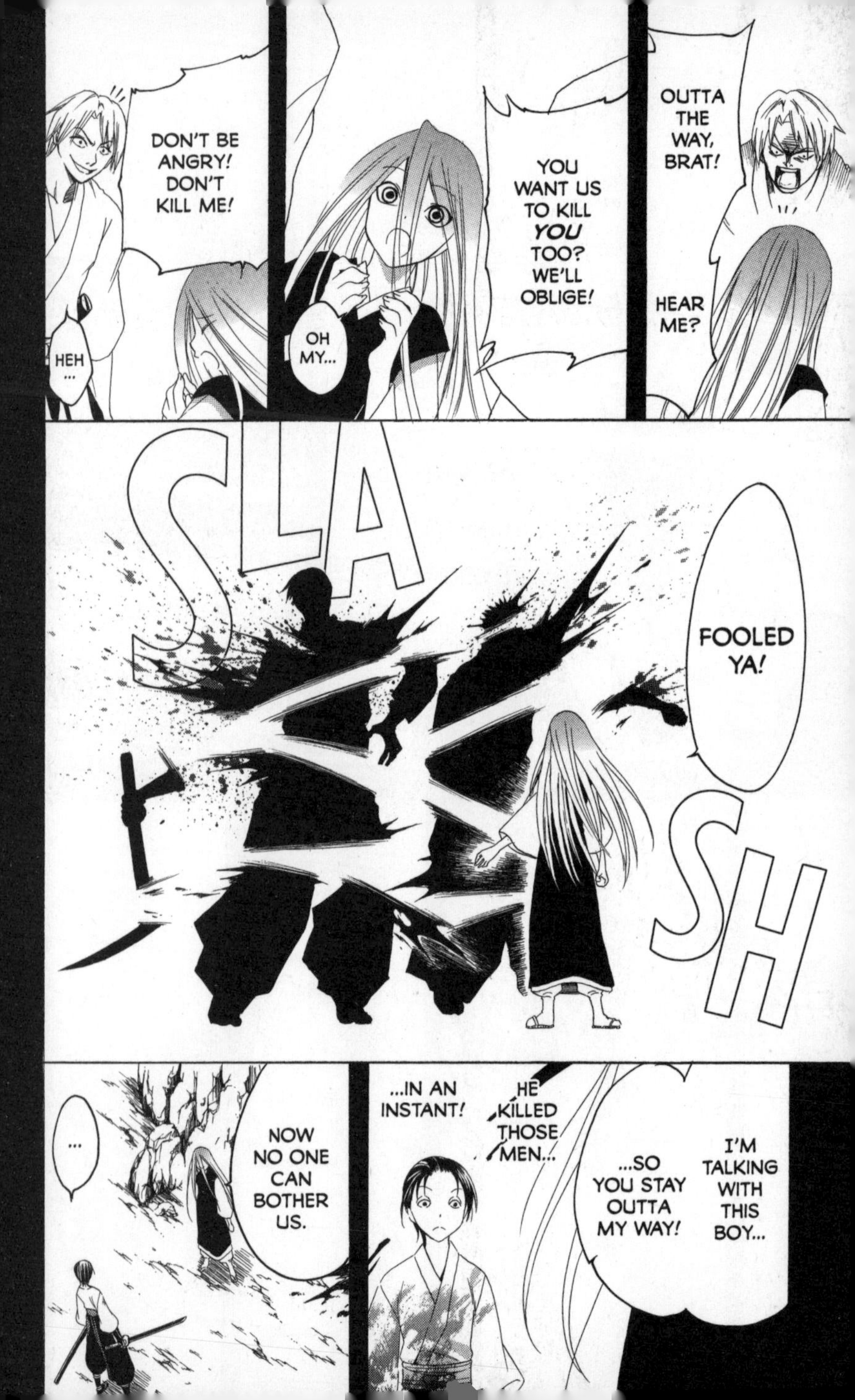
OUTTA THE WAY, BRAT!
HEAR ME?
YOU WANT US TO KILL *YOU* TOO? WE'LL OBLIGE!
OH MY...
DON'T BE ANGRY! DON'T KILL ME!
HEH...
FOOLED YA!
SLASH
I'M TALKING WITH THIS BOY...
...SO YOU STAY OUTTA MY WAY!
HE KILLED THOSE MEN...
...IN AN INSTANT!
NOW NO ONE CAN BOTHER US.
...

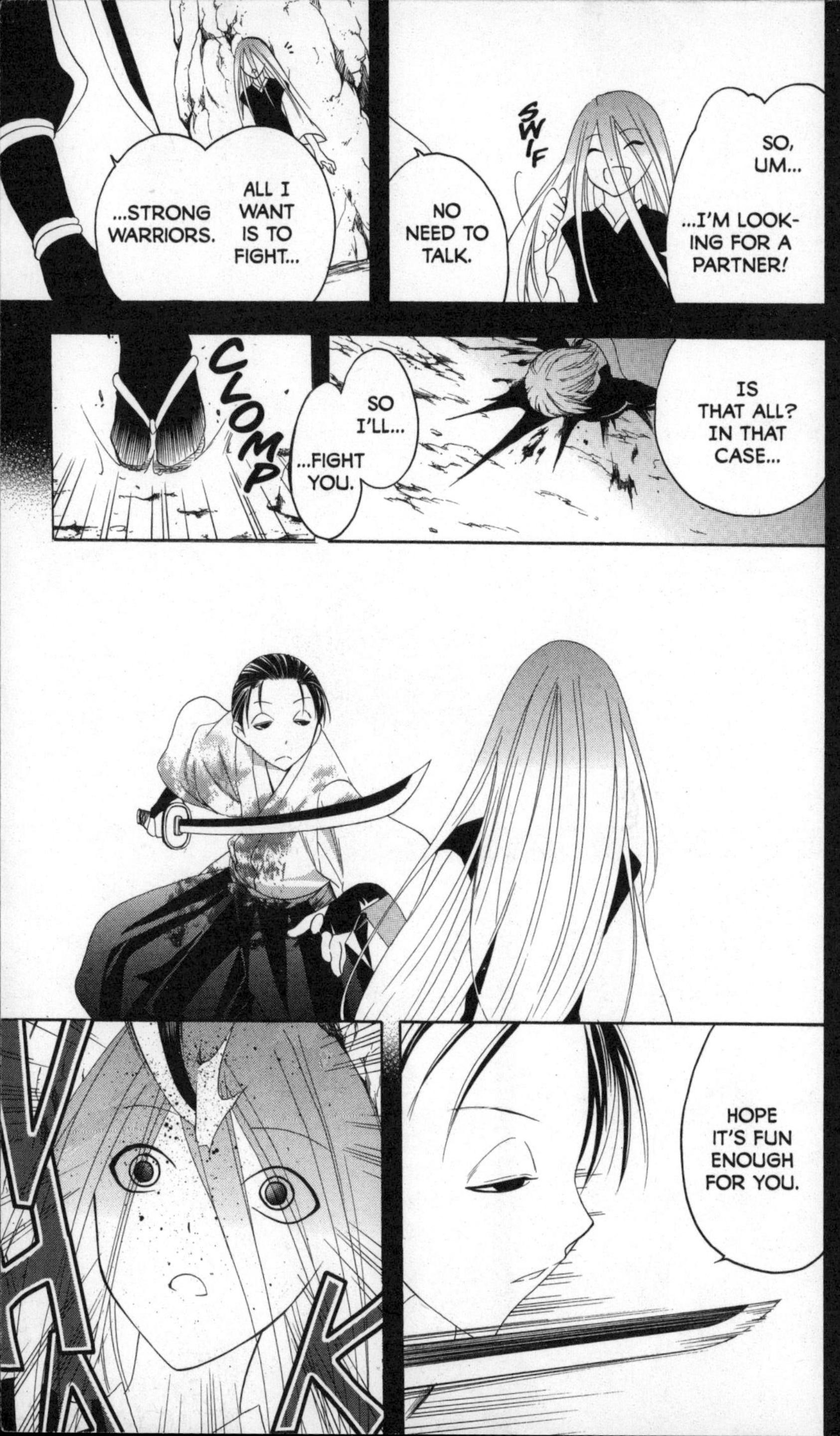
SO, UM...
...I'M LOOK-ING FOR A PARTNER!
SWIF
NO NEED TO TALK.
ALL I WANT IS TO FIGHT...
...STRONG WARRIORS.
IS THAT ALL? IN THAT CASE...
SO I'LL...
...FIGHT YOU.
CLOMP
HOPE IT'S FUN ENOUGH FOR YOU.

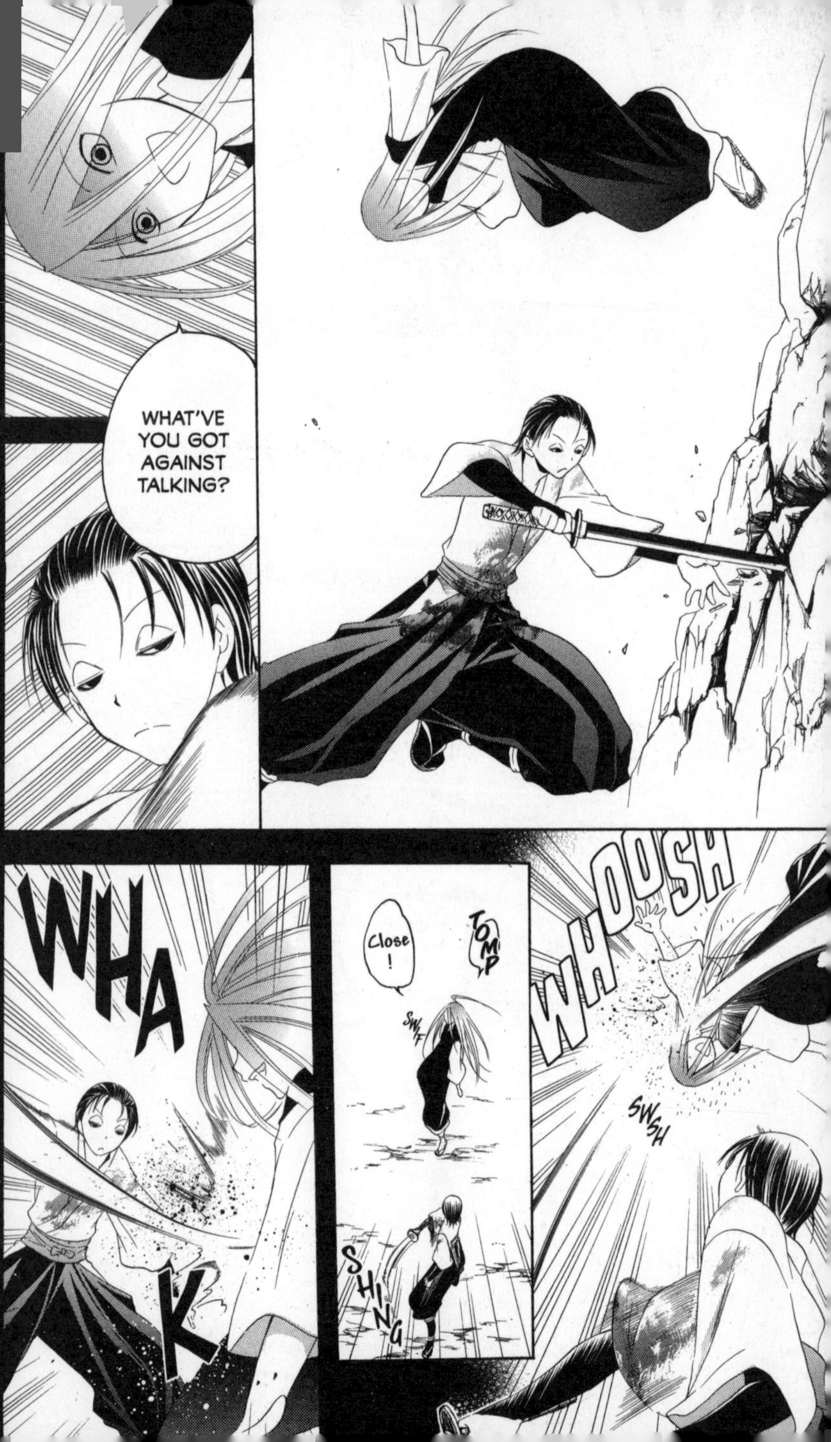
WHAT'VE YOU GOT AGAINST TALKING?
WHOOSH
SWSH
Close!
TOMP
SWIF
SHING
WHAK

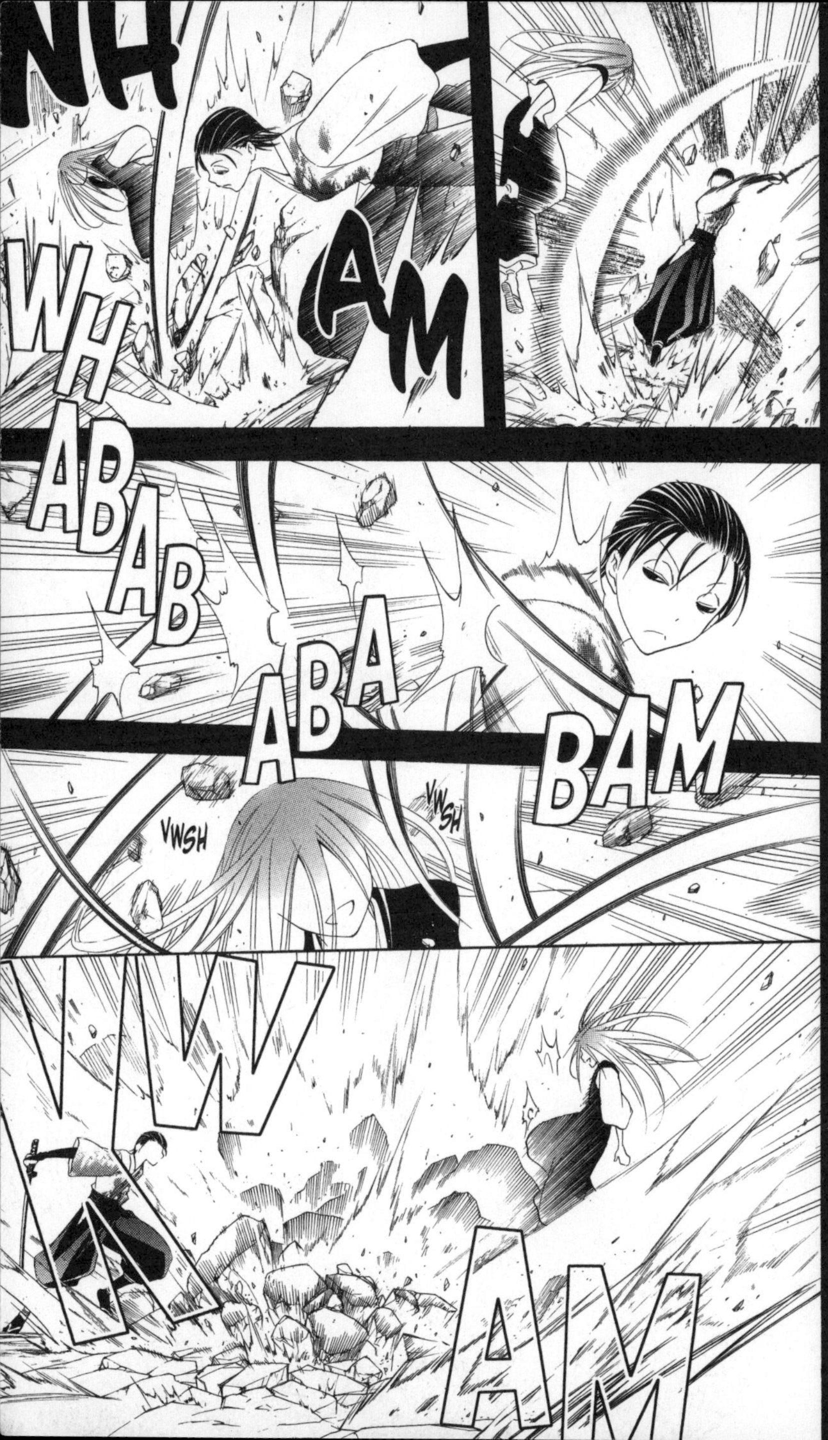

NH
AM
WHABABABABABAM
VWSH
VWSH
VWWAM

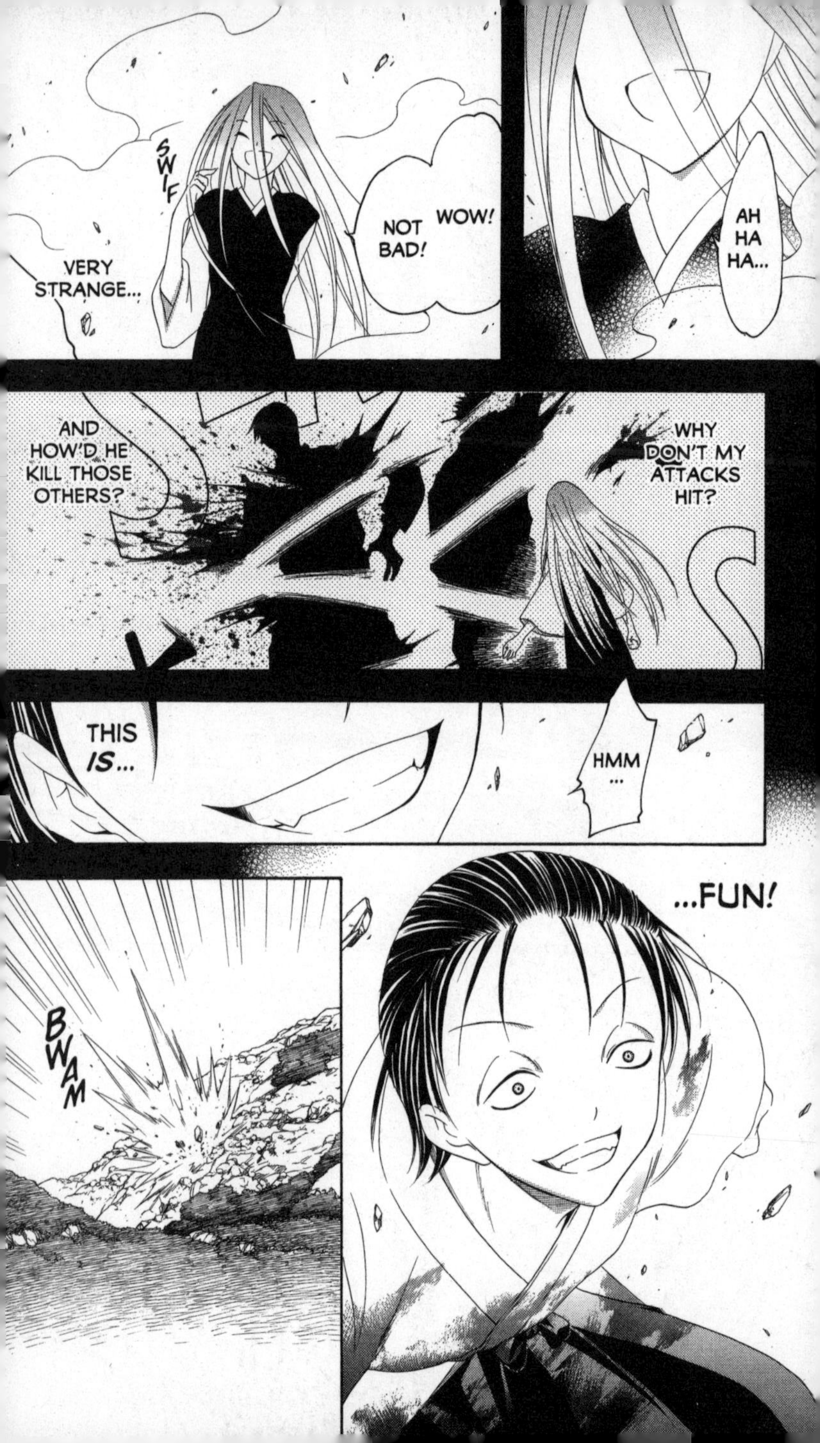
AH HA HA...
WOW!
NOT BAD!
SWIF
VERY STRANGE...
WHY DON'T MY ATTACKS HIT?
AND HOW'D HE KILL THOSE OTHERS?
HMM...
THIS *IS*...
...FUN!
BWAM

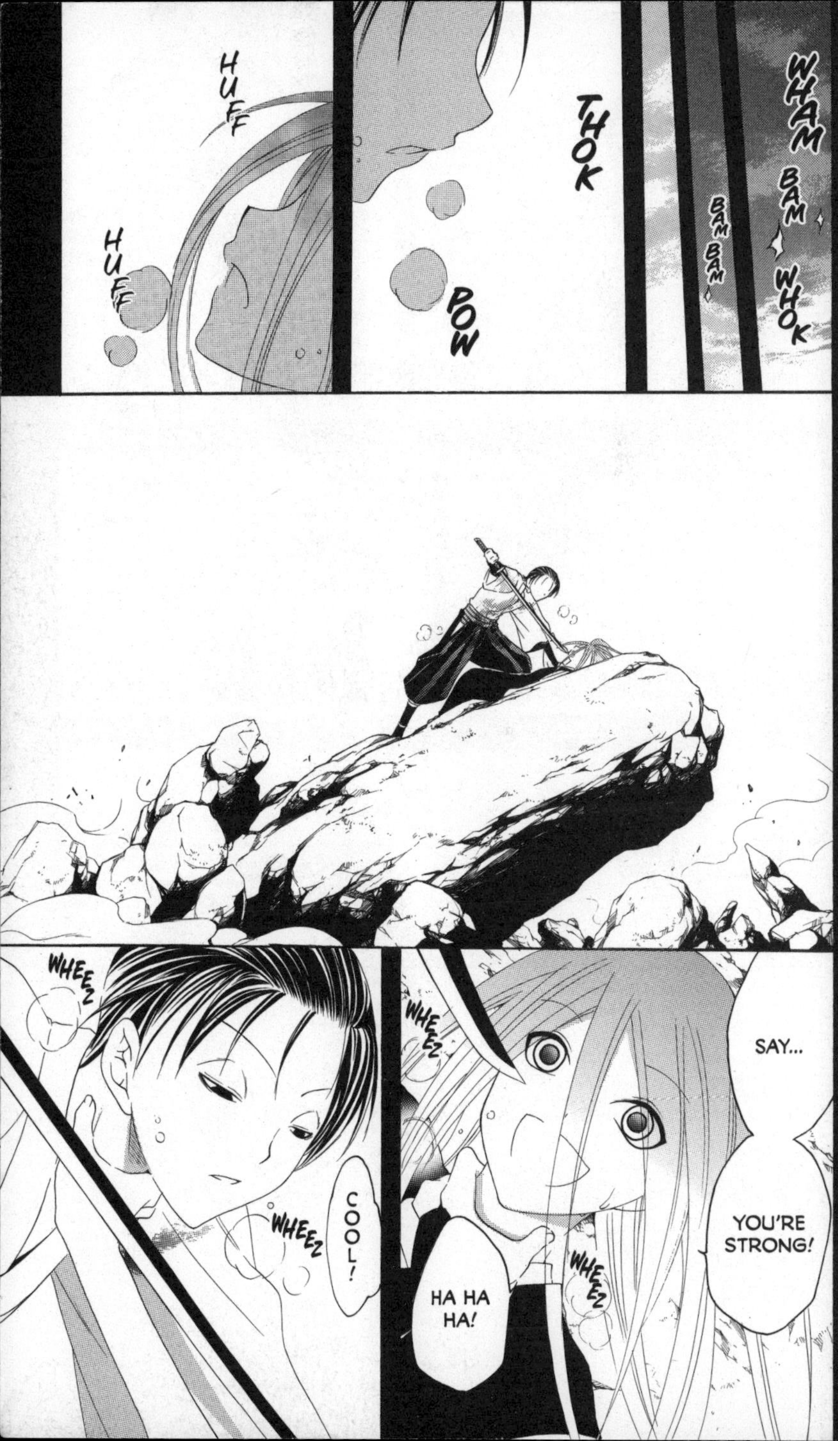
WHAM BAM WHOK
BAM BAM
THOK
POW
HUFF
HUFF
SAY...
WHEEZ
YOU'RE STRONG!
WHEEZ
HA HA HA!
WHEEZ
COOL!
WHEEZ

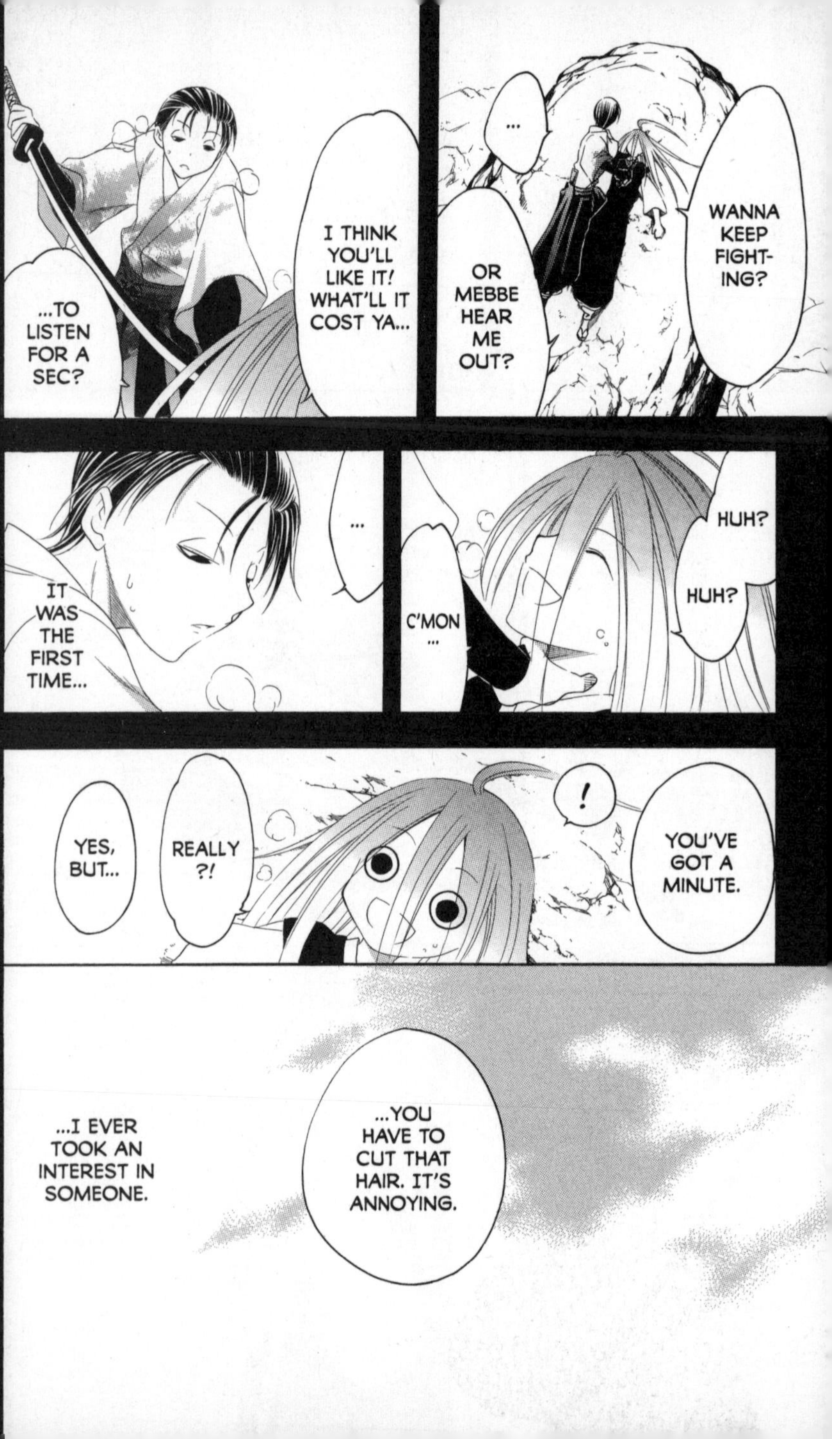
WANNA KEEP FIGHTING?
...
OR MEBBE HEAR ME OUT?
I THINK YOU'LL LIKE IT! WHAT'LL IT COST YA...
...TO LISTEN FOR A SEC?
HUH?
HUH?
C'MON ...
...
IT WAS THE FIRST TIME...
YOU'VE GOT A MINUTE.
!
REALLY ?!
YES, BUT...
...YOU HAVE TO CUT THAT HAIR. IT'S ANNOYING.
...I EVER TOOK AN INTEREST IN SOMEONE.

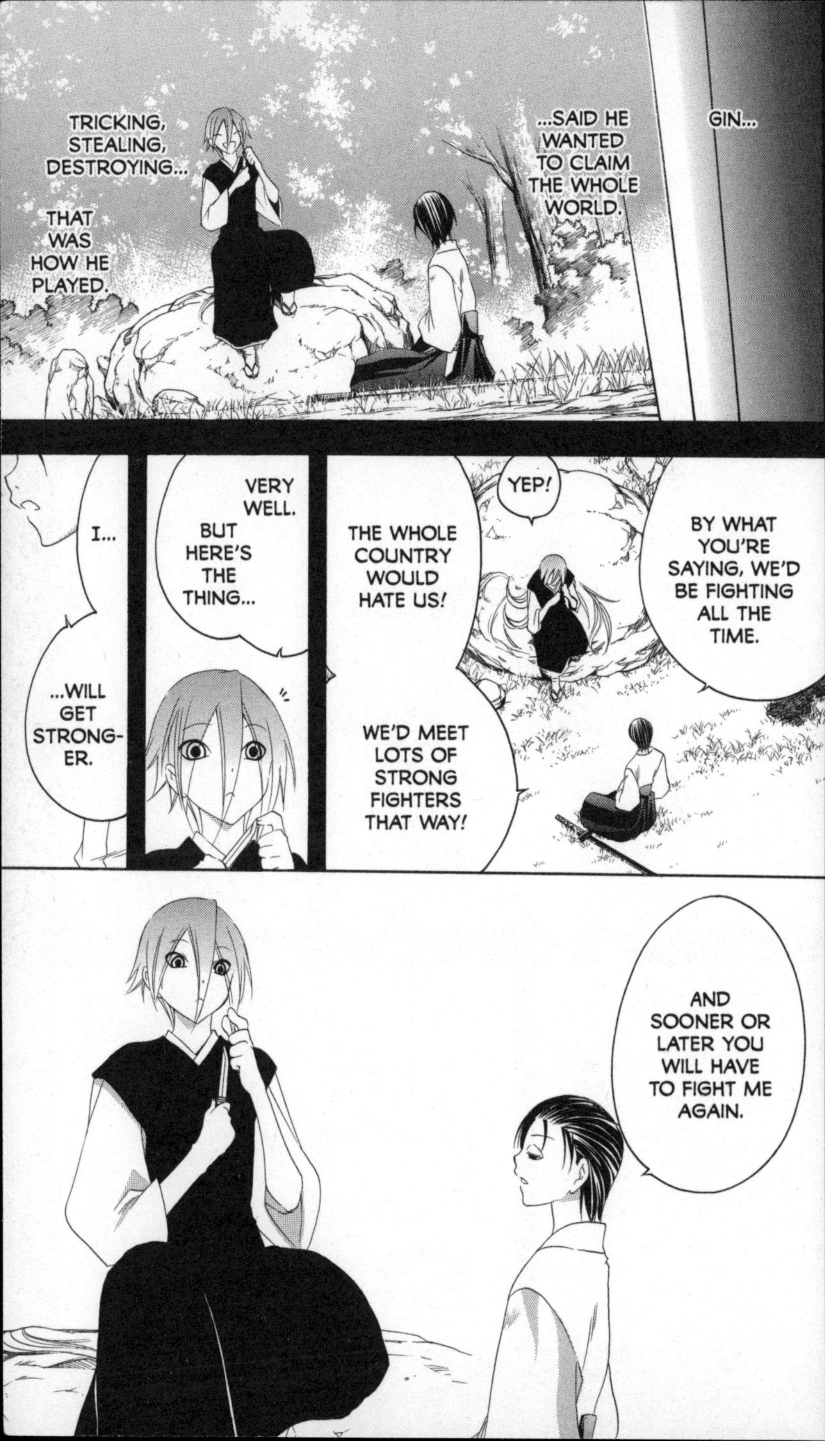
GIN...
...SAID HE WANTED TO CLAIM THE WHOLE WORLD.
TRICKING, STEALING, DESTROYING...
THAT WAS HOW HE PLAYED.
BY WHAT YOU'RE SAYING, WE'D BE FIGHTING ALL THE TIME.
YEP!
THE WHOLE COUNTRY WOULD HATE US!
WE'D MEET LOTS OF STRONG FIGHTERS THAT WAY!
VERY WELL.
BUT HERE'S THE THING...
I...
...WILL GET STRONG-ER.
AND SOONER OR LATER YOU WILL HAVE TO FIGHT ME AGAIN.

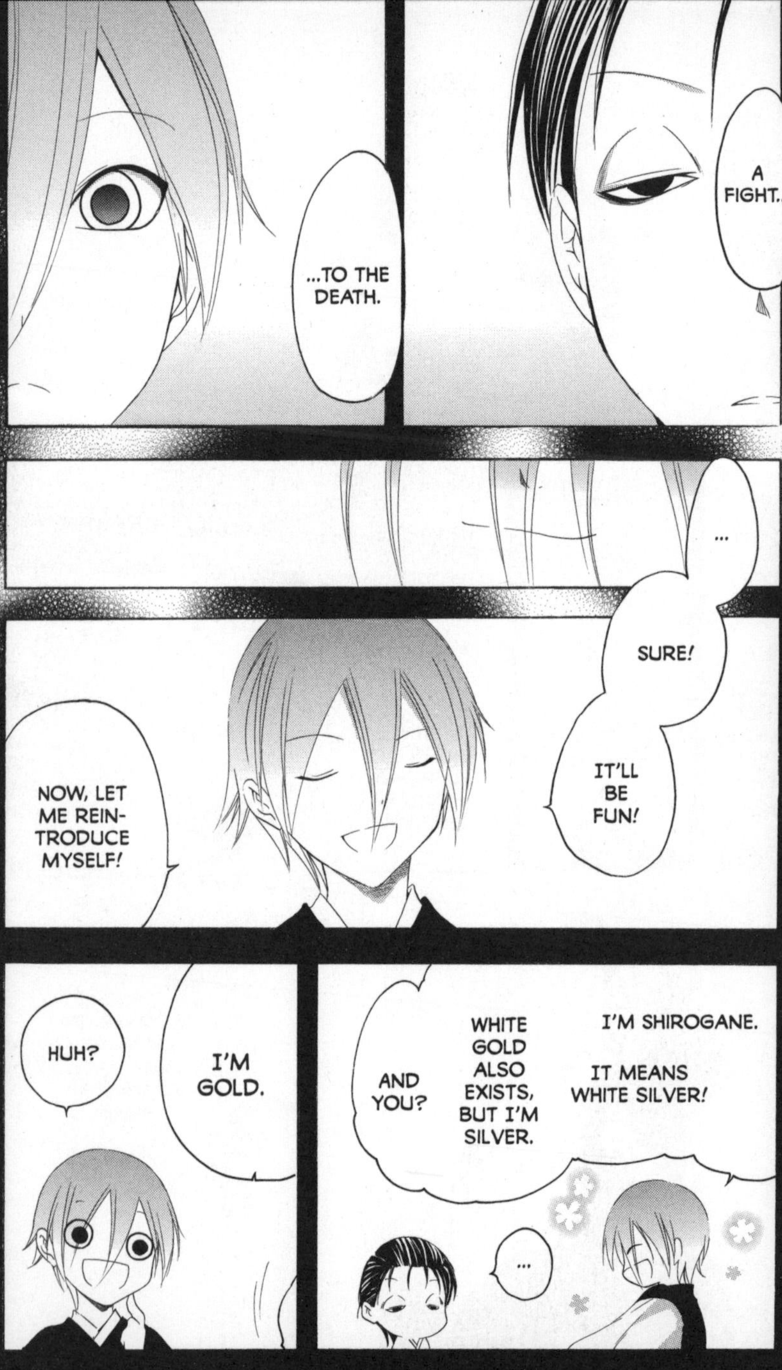
A FIGHT...
...TO THE DEATH.
...
SURE!
IT'LL BE FUN!
NOW, LET ME REIN-TRODUCE MYSELF!
I'M SHIROGANE.
IT MEANS WHITE SILVER!
WHITE GOLD ALSO EXISTS, BUT I'M SILVER.
AND YOU?
...
I'M GOLD.
HUH?

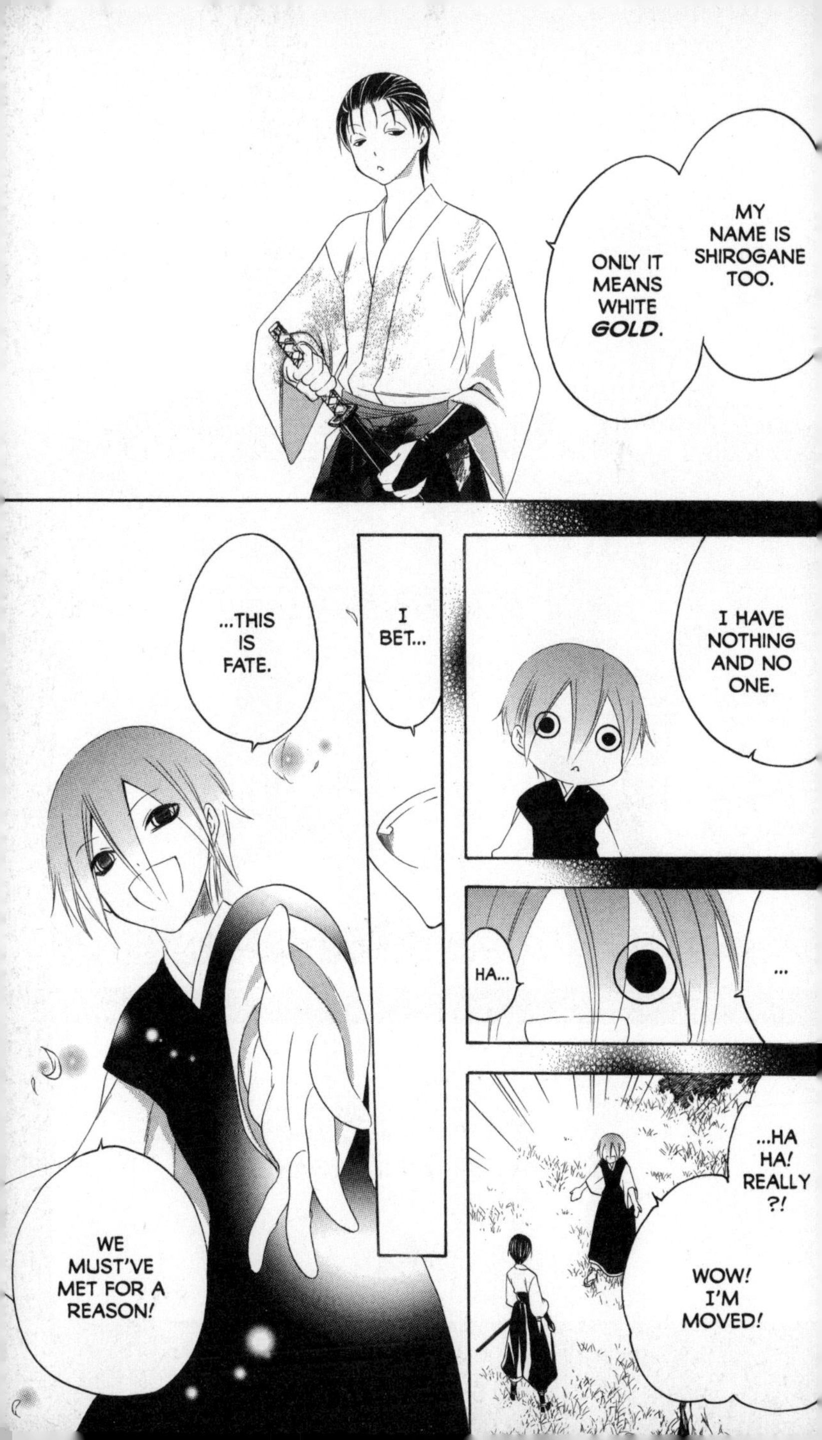
MY NAME IS SHIROGANE TOO.
ONLY IT MEANS WHITE *GOLD*.
I HAVE NOTHING AND NO ONE.
...
HA...
...HA HA! REALLY?!
WOW! I'M MOVED!
I BET...
...THIS IS FATE.
WE MUST'VE MET FOR A REASON!

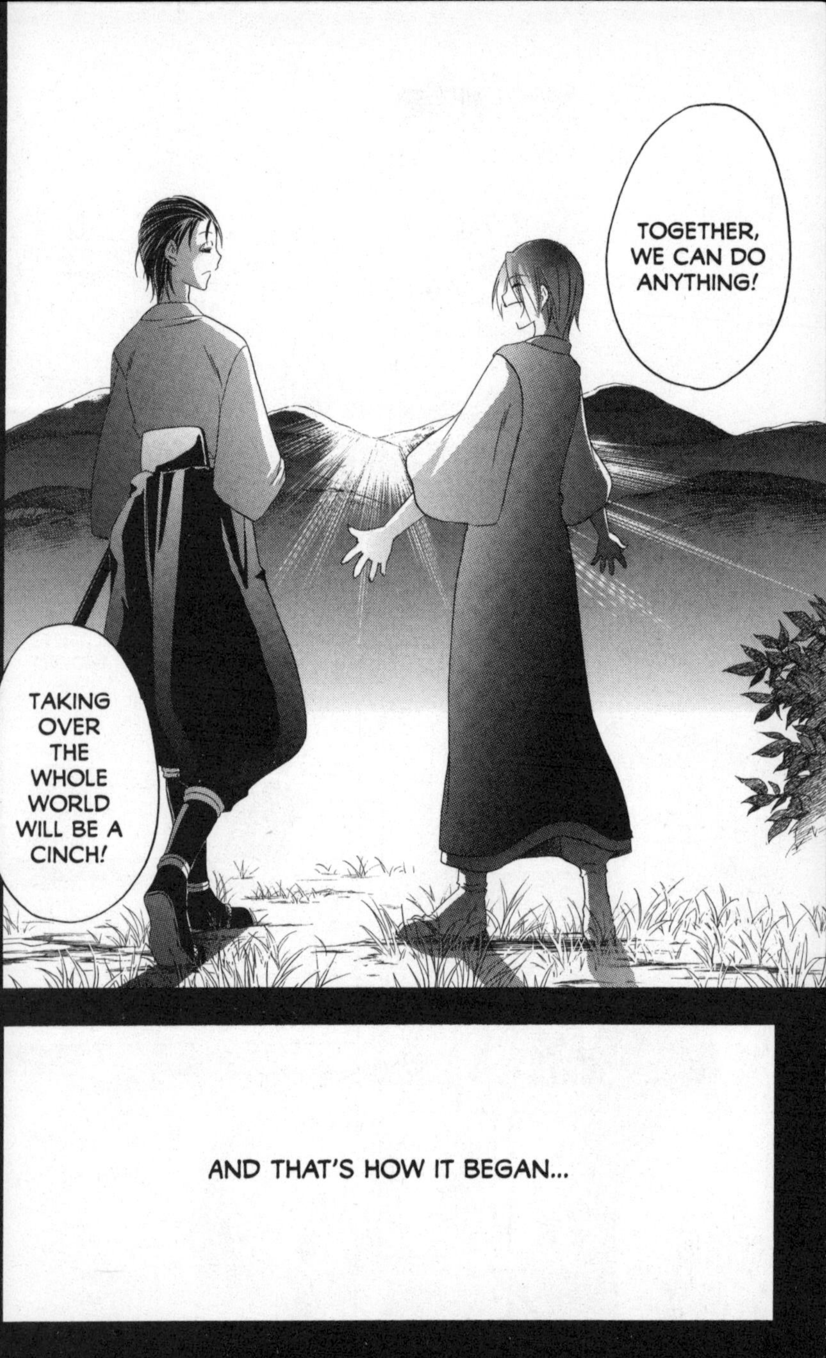
TOGETHER, WE CAN DO ANYTHING!
TAKING OVER THE WHOLE WORLD WILL BE A CINCH!
AND THAT'S HOW IT BEGAN...

Bonus Manga

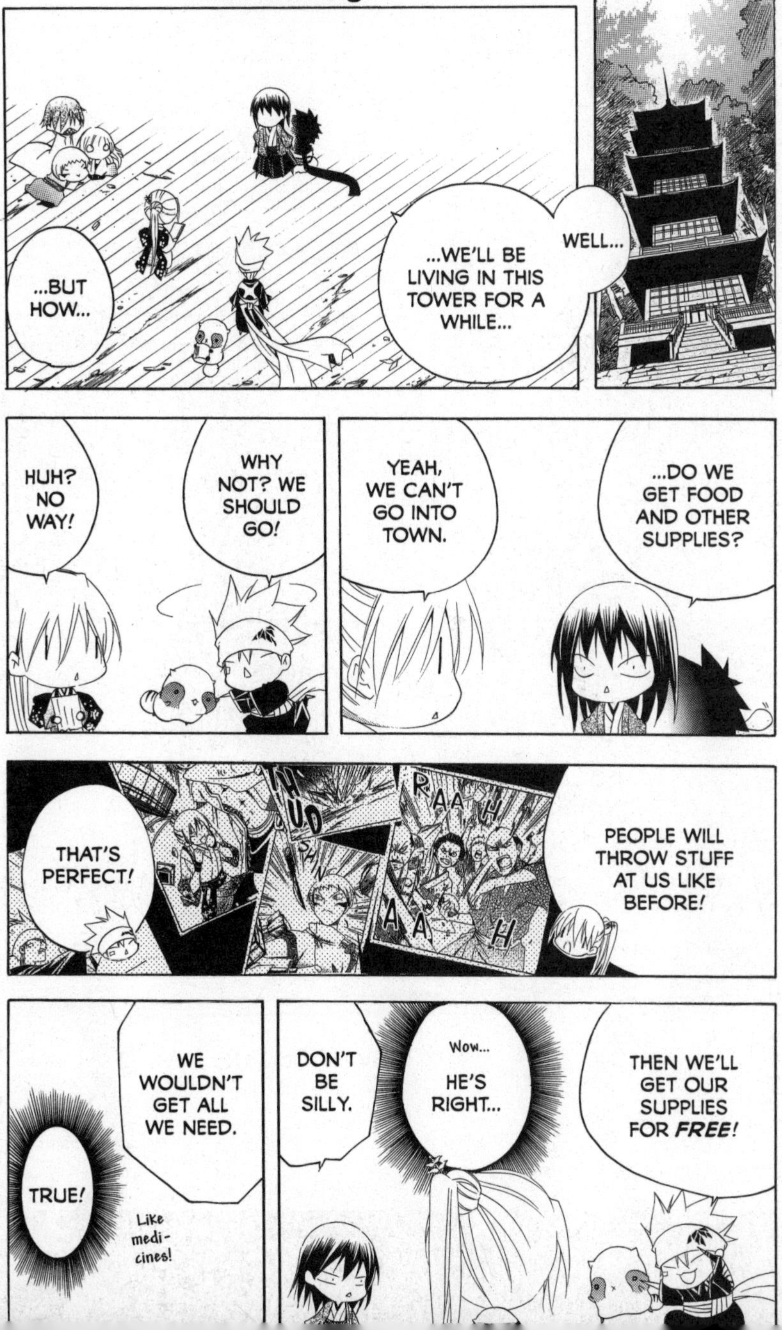
WELL...
...WE'LL BE LIVING IN THIS TOWER FOR A WHILE...
...BUT HOW...
...DO WE GET FOOD AND OTHER SUPPLIES?
YEAH, WE CAN'T GO INTO TOWN.
WHY NOT? WE SHOULD GO!
HUH? NO WAY!
PEOPLE WILL THROW STUFF AT US LIKE BEFORE!
THUD
THAT'S PERFECT!
THEN WE'LL GET OUR SUPPLIES FOR *FREE*!
Wow...
HE'S RIGHT...
DON'T BE SILLY.
WE WOULDN'T GET ALL WE NEED.
Like medicines!
TRUE!

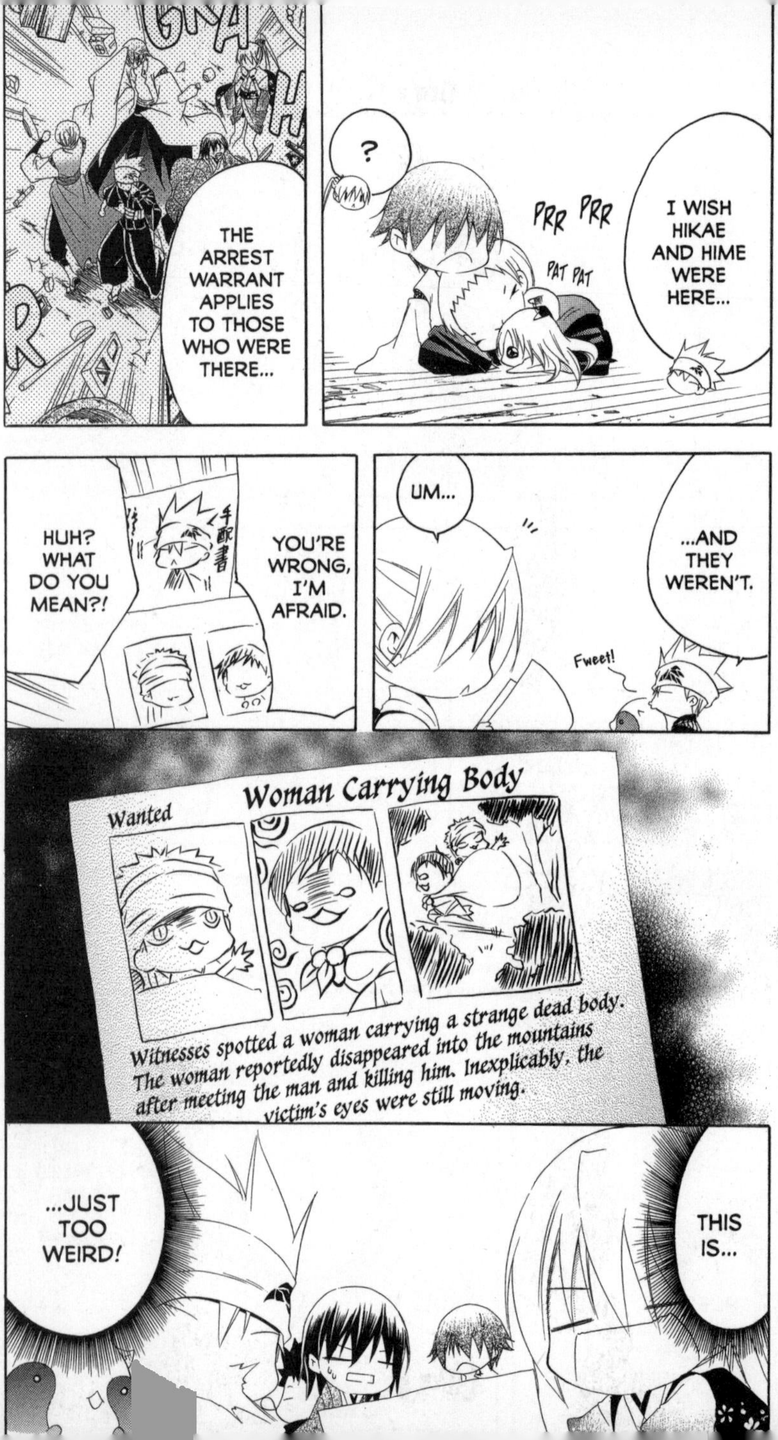
I WISH HIKAE AND HIME WERE HERE...
PRR PRR
PAT PAT
?
THE ARREST WARRANT APPLIES TO THOSE WHO WERE THERE...
GYA
HA
...AND THEY WEREN'T.
UM...
Fweet!
YOU'RE WRONG, I'M AFRAID.
手配書
HUH? WHAT DO YOU MEAN?!
Woman Carrying Body
Wanted
Witnesses spotted a woman carrying a strange dead body. The woman reportedly disappeared into the mountains after meeting the man and killing him. Inexplicably, the victim's eyes were still moving.
THIS IS...
...JUST TOO WEIRD!

Gin's Side

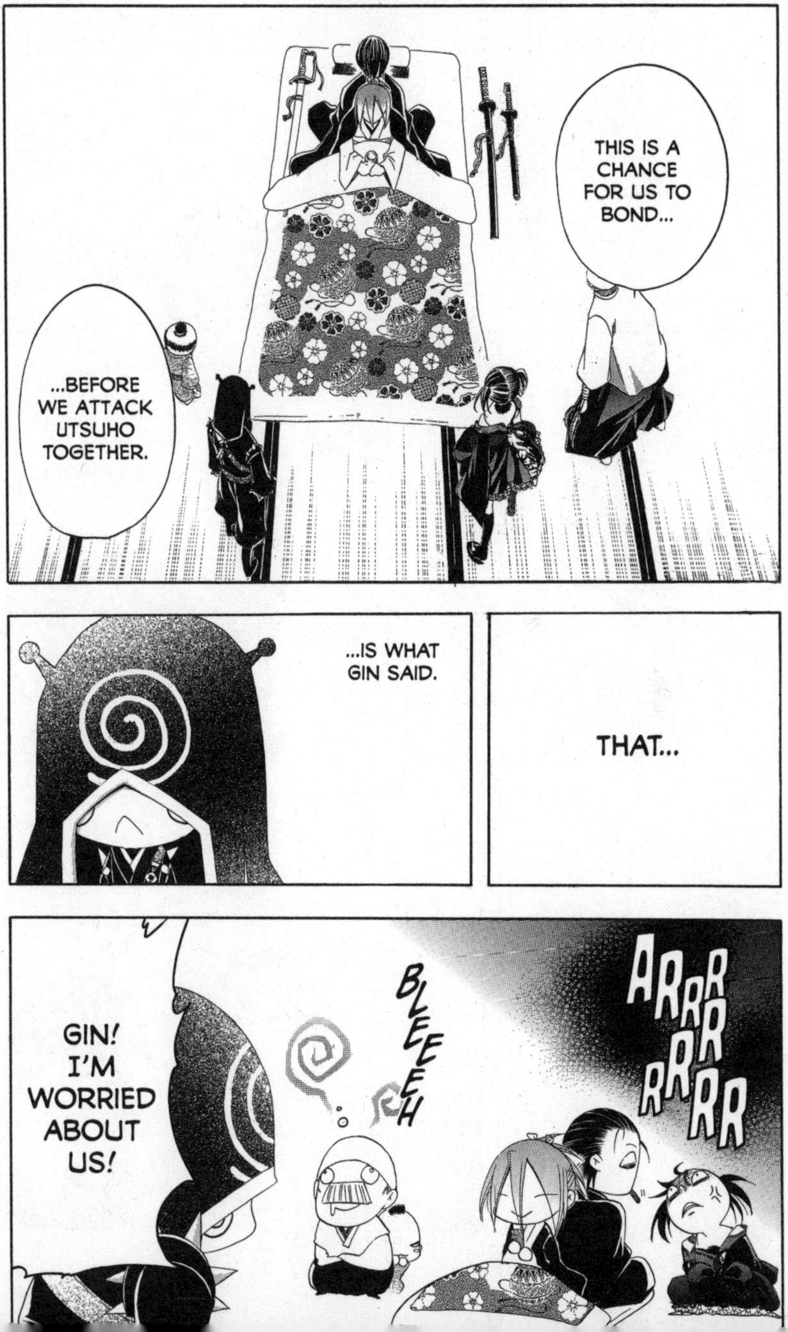
THIS IS A CHANCE FOR US TO BOND...
...BEFORE WE ATTACK UTSUHO TOGETHER.
THAT...
...IS WHAT GIN SAID.
ARRRRRRRRR
BLEEEEH
GIN! I'M WORRIED ABOUT US!

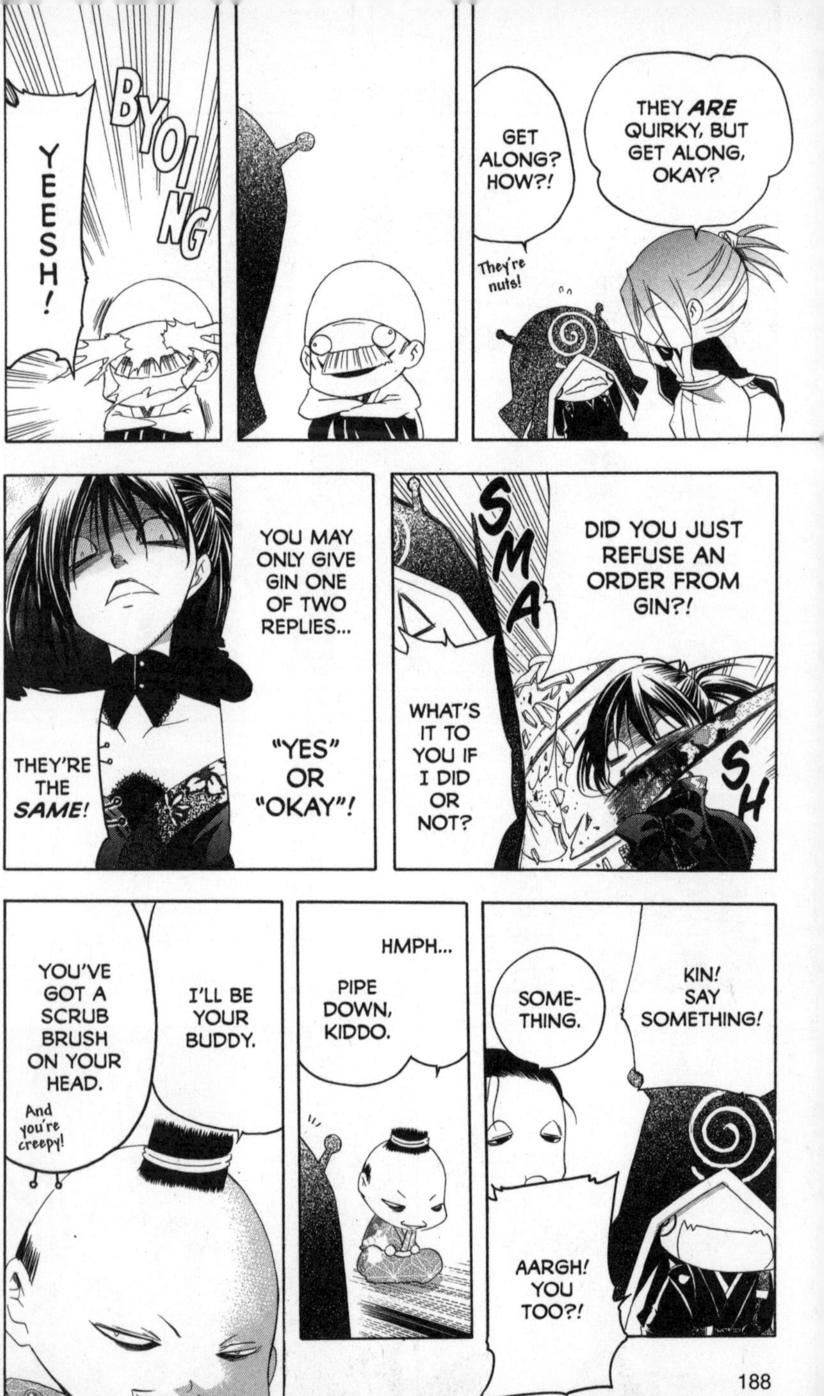
THEY *ARE* QUIRKY, BUT GET ALONG, OKAY?
GET ALONG? HOW?!
They're nuts!
BYOING
YEESH!
DID YOU JUST REFUSE AN ORDER FROM GIN?!
SMASH
WHAT'S IT TO YOU IF I DID OR NOT?
YOU MAY ONLY GIVE GIN ONE OF TWO REPLIES...
"YES" OR "OKAY"!
THEY'RE THE *SAME*!
KIN! SAY SOMETHING!
SOME-THING.
AARGH! YOU TOO?!
HMPH...
PIPE DOWN, KIDDO.
I'LL BE YOUR BUDDY.
YOU'VE GOT A SCRUB BRUSH ON YOUR HEAD.
And you're creepy!

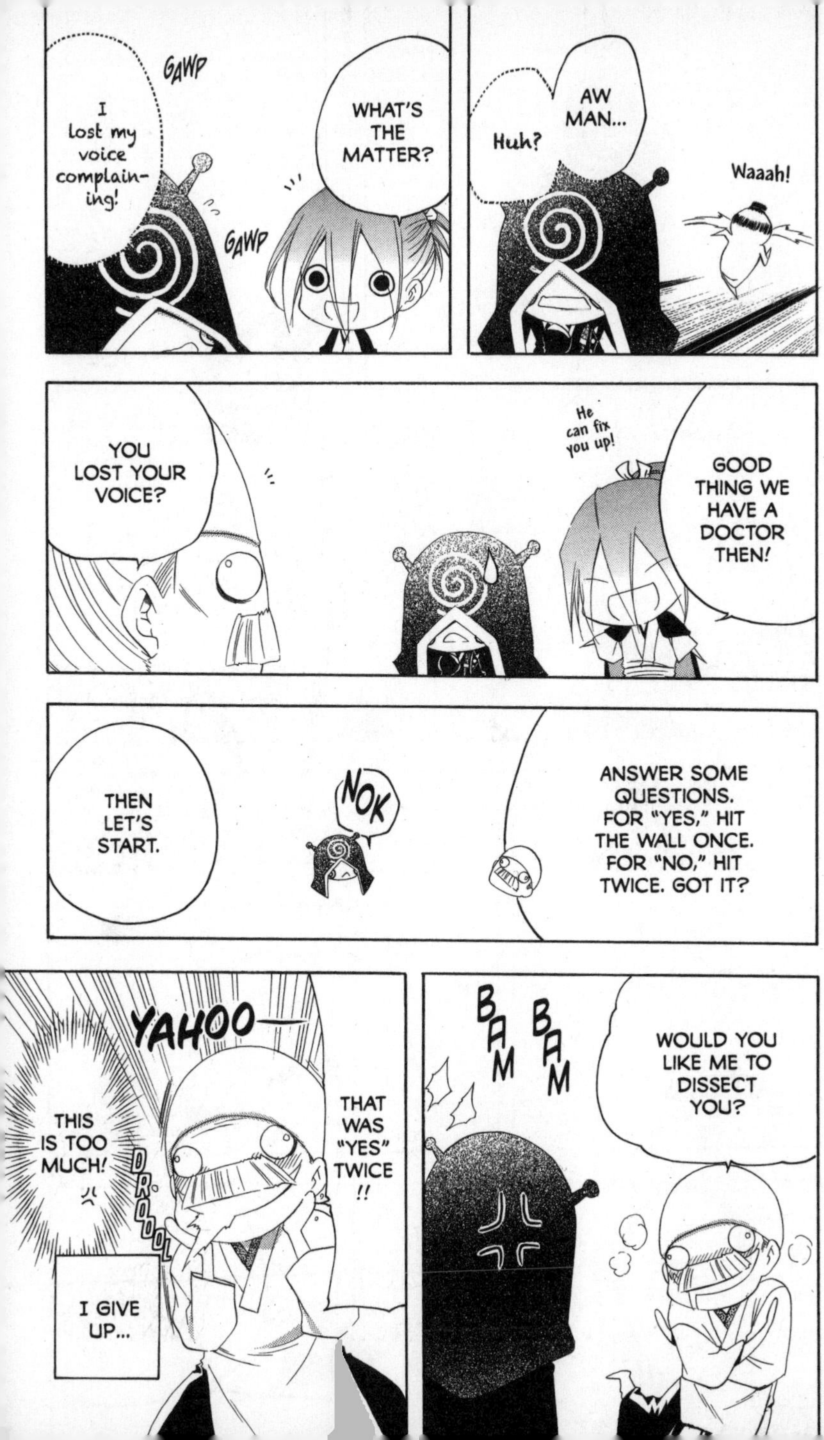
AW MAN...
Huh?
Waaah!
WHAT'S THE MATTER?
GAWP
I lost my voice complaining!
GAWP
GOOD THING WE HAVE A DOCTOR THEN!
He can fix you up!
YOU LOST YOUR VOICE?
ANSWER SOME QUESTIONS. FOR "YES," HIT THE WALL ONCE. FOR "NO," HIT TWICE. GOT IT?
NOK
THEN LET'S START.
WOULD YOU LIKE ME TO DISSECT YOU?
BAM BAM
THAT WAS "YES" TWICE!!
YAHOO—
THIS IS TOO MUCH!
DROOOL
I GIVE UP...

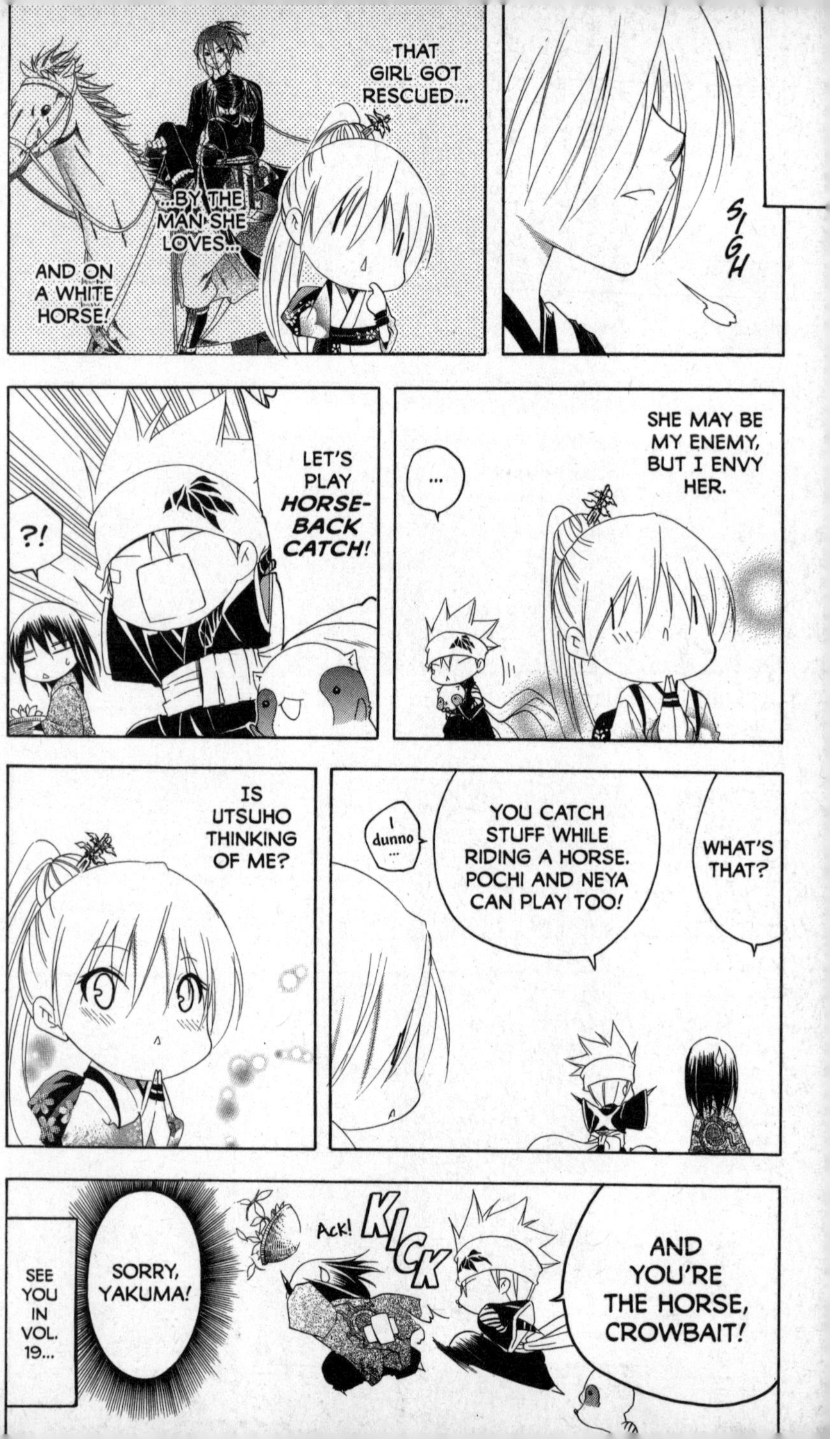
SIGH
THAT GIRL GOT RESCUED...
...BY THE MAN SHE LOVES...
AND ON A WHITE HORSE!
SHE MAY BE MY ENEMY, BUT I ENVY HER.
...
LET'S PLAY *HORSEBACK CATCH!*
?!
WHAT'S THAT?
YOU CATCH STUFF WHILE RIDING A HORSE. POCHI AND NEYA CAN PLAY TOO!
I dunno...
IS UTSUHO THINKING OF ME?
AND YOU'RE THE HORSE, CROWBAIT!
KICK
Ack!
SORRY, YAKUMA!
SEE YOU IN VOL. 19...